LETTERS FROM RUPERT'S LAND, 1826–1840

RUPERT'S LAND RECORD SOCIETY SERIES
Jennifer S.H. Brown, Editor

1 *The English River Book*
   A North West Company Journal and Account Book of 1786
   Edited by Harry W. Duckworth

2 *A Country So Interesting*
   The Hudson's Bay Company and Two Centuries of Mapping, 1670–1870
   Richard I. Ruggles

3 *Arctic Artist*
   The Journal and Paintings of George Back, Midshipman with Franklin, 1819–1822
   Edited by C. Stuart Houston
   Commentary by I.S. MacLaren

4 *Ellen Smallboy*
   Glimpses of a Cree Woman's Life
   Regina Flannery

5 *Voices from Hudson Bay*
   Cree Stories from York Factory
   Compiled and edited by Flora Beardy and Robert Coutts

6 *North of Athabasca*
   Slave Lake and Mackenzie River Documents of the North West Company, 1800–1821
   Edited with an Introduction by Lloyd Keith

7 *From Barrow to Boothia*
   The Arctic Journal of Chief Factor Peter Warren Dease, 1836–1839
   Edited and annotated by William Barr

8 *My First Years in the Fur Trade*
   The Journals of 1802–1804
   George Nelson
   Edited by Laura Peers and Theresa Schenck

9 *The Spirit Lives in the Mind:*
   Omushkego Stories, Lives, and Dreams
   Louis Bird
   Edited and compiled by Susan Elaine Gray

10 *Memories, Myths, and Dreams of an Ojibwe Leader*
   William Berens as told to A. Irving Hallowell
   Edited and with Introductions by Jennifer S.H. Brown and Susan Elaine Gray

11 *Letters from Rupert's Land, 1826–1840*
   James Hargrave of the Hudson's Bay Company
   Edited with an Introduction by Helen E. Ross

Letters from Rupert's Land, 1826–1840

JAMES HARGRAVE *of the* HUDSON'S BAY COMPANY

Edited with an Introduction by Helen E. Ross

MCGILL-QUEEN'S UNIVERSITY PRESS
MONTREAL & KINGSTON · LONDON · ITHACA

© McGill-Queen's University Press 2009
ISBN 978-0-7735-3573-2

Legal deposit fourth quarter 2009
Bibliothèque nationale du Québec

Printed in Canada on acid-free paper that is 100% ancient forest free (100% post-consumer recycled), processed chlorine free

This book has been published with the help of a grant from the Canadian Federation for the Humanities and Social Sciences, through the Aid to Scholarly Publications Programme, using funds provided by the Social Sciences and Humanities Research Council of Canada.

McGill-Queen's University Press acknowledges the support of the Canada Council for the Arts for our publishing program. We also acknowledge the financial support of the Government of Canada through the Book Publishing Industry Development Program (BPIDP) for our publishing activities.

LIBRARY AND ARCHIVES CANADA CATALOGUING IN PUBLICATION

Hargrave, James, 1798–1865
Letters from Rupert's Land, 1826–1840 : James Hargrave of the Hudson's Bay Company / edited by Helen E. Ross.

(Rupert's Land Record Society series ; 11)
Includes bibliographical references and index.
ISBN 978-0-7735-3573-2

1. Hargrave, James, 1798–1865 – Correspondence. 2. Hudson's Bay Company – History. 3. Fur trade – Canada, Western – History – 19th century. 4. York Factory (Man.) – History. 5. Frontier and pioneer life – Canada, Western. 6. Northwest, Canadian – History – To 1870. 7. Fur traders – Canada, Western – Correspondence. I. Ross, Helen E. II. Hudson's Bay Company III. Title. IV. Series: Rupert's Land Record Society series ; 11

FC3213.1.H375A4 2009   971.2'01   C2009-901968-X

Set in 11/14 Adobe Caslon with Voluta Script
Book design & typesetting by Garet Markvoort, zijn digital

To Martin, Francesca, and Federico

Contents

Preface and Acknowledgments
ix

Illustrations
xiii

Introduction
3

ENGAGEMENT CONTRACT WITH THE
NORTH WEST COMPANY, 1820
44

SELECTED LETTERS FROM THE LETTERBOOKS
OF JAMES HARGRAVE

ONE
3 January 1826 – 24 March 1827 · 51

TWO
24 March 1827 – 1 December 1827 · 87

THREE
2 December 1827 – 1 August 1828 · 110

FOUR
25 August 1828 – 11 July 1829 · 138

FIVE
13 July 1829 – 24 June 1830 · 155

SIX
25 June 1830 – 7 July 1831 · 182

SEVEN
8 July 1831 – 25 July 1832 · 198

EIGHT
25 July 1832 – 19 July 1833 · 230

NINE
20 July 1833 – 1 September 1834 · 249

TEN
2 September 1834 – 13 July 1835 · 269

ELEVEN
14 July 1835 – 31 May 1836 · 274

TWELVE
2 June 1836 – 13 March 1838 · 284

THIRTEEN
15 March 1838 – 15 September 1838 · 323

FOURTEEN
15 September 1838 – 25 July 1839 · 343

FIFTEEN
26 July 1839 – 18 May 1840 · 357

JOURNAL OF 1828–1829
373

Bibliography
385

Index
393

Preface and Acknowledgments

We are beguiled. It happens mostly in our old age, when our personal futures close down and we cannot imagine – sometimes cannot believe in – the future of our children's children. We can't resist this rifling around in the past, sifting the untrustworthy evidence, linking stray names and questionable dates and anecdotes together, hanging on to threads, insisting on being joined to dead people and therefore to life.

Alice Munro, *The View from Castle Rock*[1]

This book is an outcome of my rifling around in the lives of my great-great grandparents: James Ross was the first of my Scottish ancestors to cross the Atlantic and his wife, Mary, was a younger sister of the Hudson's Bay Company fur trader James Hargrave. In the early 1820s, James Ross chose a lot on a narrow point of land between the Châteauguay and Outarde rivers southwest of Montreal to settle his wife and growing family while he helped build the Lachine canal. I turned to his brother-in-law's letterbooks written more than a thousand miles away on Hudson Bay to try to uncover more of his story. I was beguiled by these letterbooks. I mean by this that they fascinated and captivated me, and not, I trust, that they particularly deceived or misled me about the lives of my great-great grandparents and their relations. Through the handwritten words of James Hargrave, I discovered far more than I expected about his life and the lives of his family and friends on both sides of the Atlantic and about what it meant to be an emigrant to British North America in the first half of the nineteenth century. To him, therefore, I owe my gratitude.

---

1 Munro, *View from Castle Rock*, 347.

A number of people have given generously of their time and knowledge in the course of the editing of Hargrave's letterbooks, and I would especially like to acknowledge the contributions of Jennifer S.H. Brown. Dr. Brown responded positively to my initial approach to the Rupert's Land Record Society (RLRS) about the possibility of publication of the letterbooks as part of the RLRS series in the McGill-Queen's University Press and has provided invaluable editorial advice on succeeding drafts of the manuscript since that time. Dr. Brown also generously offered bed and board and access to the library at her home during my three-day visit in May 2008 to the Hudson's Bay Company Archives, the Manitoba Archives, and the University of Manitoba Archives in Winnipeg. She introduced me to her administrative assistant, Anne Lindsay, at the Centre for Rupert's Land Studies, who worked efficiently and enthusiastically at finding obscure facts in the HBCA collection for some of the footnotes in the manuscript.

Copies of the microfilms of the letterbooks from which I transcribed the letters in this volume were provided to me by Library and Archives Canada in Ottawa. The copyright on these letterbooks has expired. Thanks are due to Marielle Lavertu at the Bibliothèque et Archives nationales du Québec for permission to include a transcription of James Hargrave's 1820 engagement contract with the North West Company. I also wish to thank Dr. Richard Virr of McLennan Library, McGill University, for permission to publish a transcription of Hargrave's 1828–29 Journal.

The artwork and maps included in the book were drawn from many sources and I wish to acknowledge the following individuals and institutions for their permission to publish these images: Debra Moore, Head, Acquisition and Special Media, at the Hudson's Bay Company Archives, Archives of Manitoba, for a map of Hudson's Bay Company Posts c. 1832 and an 1835 bill of lading; Sharon Foley at the Archives of Manitoba for a portrait of John George McTavish; Kelly-Ann Turkington at the Royal BC Museum for portraits of James Hargrave and Letitia Mactavish; Lucy Berkley, Rights and Reproductions Coordinator at the Oregon Historical Society, for a portrait of Sir George Simpson as a young man; Nicola Woods, Rights and Reproductions Coordinator at the Royal Ontario Museum, for a painting of Sir George Simpson by Henry James Warre; Veronica Denholm, Access Manager at the National Library of Scotland, for portraits of Robert Fyshe and Reverend Douglas from *The History of Galashiels* published in 1898; Jean-François Palomino at the Bibliothèque et Archives nationales du Québec for parts of an 1829 map and an 1831 map of Lower Canada; Malcolm Sissons, a descendant of James Hargrave's brother, John, for his photo of the Hargrave family home in Quebec; Lia Melemenis, Registrar and Photo Coordinator at the Glenbow Museum, for two Peter Rindisbacher drawings of Fort Garry and the 1826 flood; Tanja Hutter at Canada's National History Society for a reprint of a 1923 extract from *The Beaver*; Shelley Sweeney, Head, the University of Manitoba Archives and Special Collections, for a photo of Kilchrist House in Scotland; and the National Museums Scotland for a photo of snowshoes donated by James Hargrave in 1858. The two Peter Rindisbacher watercolours and the image of York Factory, c. 1853 housed at Library and Archives Canada and included in this book, are in the public domain. Brian Ally produced the map of Roxburghshire.

I wish to acknowledge the contributions of Hargrave family descendants, Kermit Murray, Malcolm Sissons, and Jim and Grace Hargrave, in helping me unravel the strands of our family tree. In 2007 Yvan Faille, the current owner, and his family invited me in to see the Joseph Hargrave family home at Ste Clotilde, Quebec and showed me documents and photos relating to the history of the house. Douglas Scott at the University of British Columbia provided valuable information on William Lockie and Hawick. Helen Elliot, secretary of the Old Gala Club in Galashiels, Scotland, volunteered her research on some of Hargrave's correspondents. Nicole St-Onge at the University of Ottawa looked for Hargrave's notarial contract with the North West Company in her extensive database and Pierre Beaulieu at the Bibliothèque et Archives nationales du Québec located it for me. I would like to thank the staff of the Hudson's Bay Company Archives who helped in my research on site as well as from afar, and the staff of the interlibrary loan department at the Toronto Reference Library. On the other side of the Atlantic, Helen Osmani, Chantal Knowles, Brenda McGoff, and Pam Kerr at the National Museums Scotland provided valuable information on artifacts deposited with the Industrial Museum of Scotland in Edinburgh by James Hargrave in 1858. Finally, thanks are due to Jessica Warner for her encouragement and advice in the writing of this book.

Illustrations

James Hargrave
2

Letitia Mactavish
7

Map of Roxburghshire, Scotland
9

Selective family tree of the Hargrave and Mactavish families
10–11

Robert Fyshe
14

Reverend Dr Robert Douglas
14

Part of an 1829 map of Lower Canada showing Williamstown
20

Part of an 1831 topographical map of the district of Montreal,
Lower Canada, showing "Beach Ridge" and the rest
of the township of Williamstown
21

George Simpson as a young man
24

York Factory, ca 1853
26

Departure of the second colonist transport from
York Fort to Rockfort, 1821
28

Difficult voyage up the Hill River to Rock Fort, 1821
29

Part of a map showing the location of York Factory and
some other Hudson's Bay Company posts, 1832
54

Only known sketch of the 1826 flood at Red River
59

Fort Garry, ca 1822
68

John George McTavish, 1821
70

A 1987 photo of the homestead that Joseph Hargrave built
in the late 1820s in Beechridge, Lower Canada
88

Part of a bill of lading for the *Prince Rupert* for
goods shipped by Hargrave in 1835
167

HBC Bill of Fare, York Factory, 1838
169

Kilchrist House, Campbelton, Argyllshire
308

"Voici le printemps"
329

Sir George Simpson passing the Chats Falls
in an HBC canoe, 1841
347

Snowshoes from York Factory
381

LETTERS FROM RUPERT'S LAND, 1826–1840

James Hargrave.
Courtesy of Royal BC Museum,
BC Archives, A-01789

Introduction

> I never should choose such a place as a permanent one of residence – a country to live and die in: no, indeed. My ruling object, and which is the object of every one who comes hither, is to provide a competency for old age, and then retire to enjoy it – either in Canada – or in Britain.
> James Hargrave to his parents, Fort Garry, 29 January 1827[1]

In 1819, twenty-year-old James Hargrave abandoned his native land to follow his family to Lower Canada in search of a better life than Scotland offered to most of her inhabitants at the end of the Napoleonic Wars. The young schoolmaster later left his parents and younger siblings on their farm at Beechridge, southwest of Montreal, and entered the service of the North West Company at Montreal in April 1820 as a wintering clerk. After the merger in 1821 of the North West Company with its competitor, the Hudson's Bay Company (HBC), Hargrave was retained as a clerk by the HBC. He served almost forty years in Rupert's Land,[2] rising before his retirement in 1859 to become chief trader and finally chief factor at York Factory on Hudson Bay, the gateway to the HBC's vast Northern Department. A prodigious letter writer and methodical record keeper,

---

1 James Hargrave to his parents, Fort Garry, 29 January 1827. James Hargrave and family fonds, Library and Archives Canada, Ottawa (LAC).
2 Rupert's Land was the name of the original territory ceded to the Hudson's Bay Company under its 1670 charter; the territory included the vast Hudson Bay watershed, equal to almost a million and a half square miles of today's western and northern Canada. With the union of the North West Company and the Hudson's Bay Company in 1821, the HBC monopoly was extended into Athabasca, across the Rocky and Coast mountains to the edge of the Pacific.

Hargrave began in 1826 a lifelong practice of drafting his voluminous business and personal correspondence in letterbooks which survive today in government archives;[3] he then copied in a copperplate hand the letters that he sent his correspondents. This volume presents the draft personal letters he wrote from Rupert's Land to family, friends, and acquaintances in Scotland, Lower Canada, and New York State from 1826 until the time of his marriage in 1840 to Letitia Mactavish, a member of a distinguished Scottish fur trading family. The letters he wrote to John George McTavish, the ex-Nor'Wester who saw early the promise in the young clerk and became his mentor in the amalgamated HBC and eventually his uncle-in-law, are also included. Together they account for about one-seventh of the drafts of over 1300 letters or memoranda in Hargrave's letterbooks of that period, the remainder being primarily business and private correspondence with HBC employees in Rupert's Land and elsewhere. Hargrave's is among the largest surviving outgoing correspondence of any fur trader in Rupert's Land.

These letters document in fine detail over many years how branches of the same Lowland Scottish family adapted to very different settings in North America and provide rich source material for readers interested in migration literature, social history, religious studies, women's studies, and fur trade history. They record his daily life at the North American hub of the HBC fur trade, his observations of fur trade social life and of farm life in Lower Canada, his views on religion, history, politics, and literature in Scotland and in his adopted land, his romantic attachments and attitudes toward women and their place in the world, as well as his views on the Native peoples who supplied the furs that allowed him to escape the hard manual labour of his family's farm. In them he appears as the dutiful and loving son to his aged parents, the advice-giving eldest brother, the loyal, deferential, and moderately ambitious HBC employee, the highly proper and rather strait-laced man upholding the codes of correct conduct in business,[4] the educated reader of books

3 LAC. In 1950, the Champlain Society, which had acquired the papers from a granddaughter of James Hargrave, Mary Letitia (Ogston) Grierson, donated private papers to LAC which now holds the James Hargrave and family fonds, R7784-0-9-E. The letterbooks of James Hargrave, 1826–58, vols. 21–6, available on reels C-80 to C-82, form part of the Hargrave family papers.

4 The subject matter of his letters to family and friends outside the HBC network was necessarily somewhat restricted by the need to keep his company's

of literature and history, the solitary "bluff bachelor, free of wife or other encumbrance,"[5] the fur trader who knew French and Italian but never learned any Aboriginal languages and had little interest in the lives of the Natives, the enthusiastic game hunter, and the man who once described himself as having been accustomed in all his steps in life "to take reason as my polar Star."[6] The letters importantly provide a record of the lives of his family in Beauharnois County, Lower Canada, for a period and place where there is little such contemporary documentary evidence.[7]

James emigrated from his home in the Borders region of Scotland at a time when Britain had become Europe's most powerful imperial state. For more than a century, Scots, as T.M. Devine notes, had been thoroughly and systematically colonizing all areas of the British Empire from commerce to administration, soldiering to medicine, colonial education to the expansion of emigrant settlements.[8] The Scottish presence in Canada, however, really became significant only after 1783 "with the mass

---

business secrets. See below his 1820 engagement contract with the North West Company. ANQ, Henry Griffin notarial records, 3114.

5 James Hargrave to Mary Ross from York Factory, 19 July 1828. James Hargrave and family fonds, LAC.

6 James Hargrave to George Simpson from Edinburgh, 27 January 1840. James Hargrave and family fonds, LAC.

7 Robert Sellar (1841–1919) was a newspaper editor and author from Glasgow who in 1863 founded the *Canadian Gleaner* in the backwoods community of Huntingdon in Lower Canada. To write the history of this area he was forced to rely on the recollections of long ago events by several hundred elderly first settlers because he found so few documentary sources available. "When I began to prepare for the work, I counted on finding much documentary material. My hopes were quenched in a very short time. Not a letter, diary, or memorandum could I obtain. Repeatedly have I gone with confidence to the families of clergymen and other educated men to ask to be permitted to examine the papers they had left, only to be disappointed. Documents which, to me, would have been of the last consequence I could not obtain. Speaking from my experience, I would say the idea entertained by Mr Brymner, the keeper of the archives at Ottawa, and others, that there is much documentary material lying hid in families similar to that of the muniment-chests of Great Britain, is a delusion. The destruction of the papers of the seigniory-office was an irreparable loss to me, which would have been avoided had I assumed the task ten years sooner." Sellar, *History of Huntingdon*, v.

8 Devine, *Scotland's Empire*, xxvi.

movement of American Loyalists to the St Lawrence valley and elsewhere, the increase in Highland emigration to Canada which then followed, and the dynamic development of trade from the Clyde to Quebec, Montreal and Toronto."[9] By 1815, there were an estimated 15,000 Scots in Canada, most of them Gaelic speakers from the Highlands.[10] James and his family, in contrast, were Lowlanders. Their migration was part of a growing exodus from the Lowlands that became ever more pronounced as the nineteenth century wore on. The letters in this volume provide insight into the experience and views of this particular Lowlander family. They provide a counterpoint to the correspondence of the great majority of James's fellow officers in the Hudson's Bay Company who were either Highland or Aberdeenshire Scots.

The letterbooks complement two related volumes produced by the Champlain Society more than fifty years ago. The first was a selection of the private letters addressed to James Hargrave between 1821 and 1843 by men who staffed the Hudson's Bay Company outposts in North America.[11] They were chosen in an attempt to "throw light on the conditions of the country, the conduct of the trade, and the life of the traders."[12] The second volume presented letters of James Hargrave's wife, Letitia Mactavish, written between 1838 and 1852, describing her life as a woman in the fur trade in Rupert's Land.[13] The current volume adds the missing voice of the fur trader himself to these other voices. The period selected extends from 1826 when James began his letterbooks to 1840 when he married. The bulk of the letters addressed to family and friends date from the period while he was still a bachelor. His handwriting in the letterbooks, perhaps as a result of rheumatism as well as his increasing workload, became ever smaller and more difficult to read as the years went by.[14] His growing responsibilities as he climbed the company's career ladder also meant that

9 Devine, *Scotland's Empire*, 101.
10 Bumsted, "Scottish Diaspora," quoted in Devine, *Scotland's Empire*, 101.
11 Glazebrook, *Hargrave Correspondence*.
12 Ibid., xv.
13 Macleod, *Letters of Letitia Hargrave*.
14 James Hargrave to Donald Ross from York Factory, 18 March 1851. James Hargrave and family fonds, LAC. "You rally me about my almost unintelligible hand writing a defect I have myself long been conscious of. The truth is that when I sit down to a formal page of accounts I can still contrive to make a passably fair one; but I have for many years been so borne down by pressure of business that when I set about any matter, easily committed to

Introduction · 7

Letitia Mactavish. James Hargrave married her in Scotland in 1840. Courtesy of Royal BC Museum, BC Archives, A-01790.

he had less time to write to family and friends and his draft letterbooks started to note simply "Wrote to Andrew Hargrave" on such and such a date. His letters constituted a once- or twice-a-year lifeline to those in the world he had left behind, and an effort to describe to them an exotic place they would never see. The private letters he received in return from his family and friends in Lower Canada and Scotland have not surfaced and the voice in this volume remains his alone, except where he reports excerpts from others' letters.

paper, my pen literally runs riot and such are its caprices that should more leisure not improve it, I may have to return to School & recommence pot hooks."

In these letters, Hargrave reveals some of the ambivalence many immigrants feel about their adopted home. He arrived in Lower Canada as the educated son of a devout Protestant Borders sheep farm manager with few connections and little position in the world. Having made his choice to emigrate and to enter the fur trade in hopes of bettering himself, he found that he had placed himself in thrall to a lifetime of labour in Rupert's Land, primarily in the remote and desolate environs of York Factory with its disagreeable climate and voracious mosquitoes.[15]

Governor George Simpson's determined efforts to run the vast HBC enterprise as cheaply and efficiently as possible meant that, without adequate manpower to provide a suitable replacement, James's services were usually deemed too essential to permit even short absences from York Factory. While his letters to family and friends spoke often of his contentment with the lot in life Providence had granted him in the distant and wild country, he also made clear to his parents that he would never choose such a place to live and die in.[16]

During the first six years he toiled in Rupert's Land he sent yearly journals back to his father's farm in Beechridge[17] chronicling his life in the wilds of North America. Unfortunately, these journals have not been found and have probably not survived. James had already spent six years in Rupert's Land before the start of these letterbooks so we do not have a record of his first impressions as an immigrant to North America. In 1828, for example, he told his brother-in-law that the ways of the Natives had become so familiar to him that he could no longer write on the subject with the least hope of interesting the reader.[18] The modern reader is similarly deprived of his other early observations of life in the fur trade in Rupert's Land.

---

15 James Hargrave to William Lockie from York Factory, 2 August 1827. James Hargrave and family fonds, LAC.
16 James Hargrave to his parents from Fort Garry, 29 January 1827. James Hargrave and family fonds, LAC.
17 Named after the beech trees on the ridge when this area was opened up, Beechridge was located in Williamstown Township, in the Beauharnois Seigneury. It would have provided a well-drained area of the Haut-Saint-Laurent region, much of which comprised wetlands of swamps and marshes. The morainic stony ridges scattered through the area were covered with fine hardwoods. Brisson and Bouchard, "Haut-Saint-Laurent."
18 James Hargrave to James Ross from York Factory, 21 July 1828. James Hargrave and family fonds, LAC.

Introduction · 9

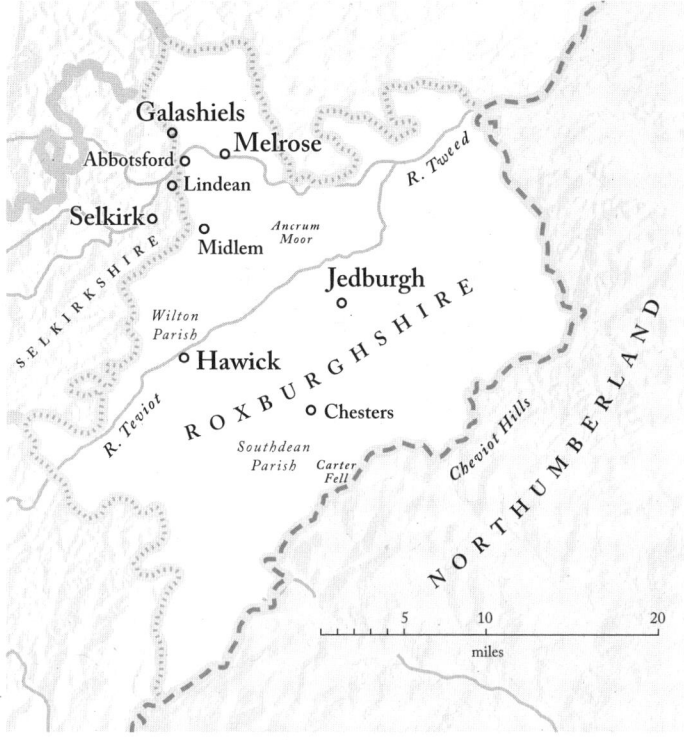

Map of Roxburghshire, Scotland, James Hargrave's childhood home, showing the parts of the county referred to in his correspondence. Map by Brian Ally.

By 1826 he had had considerable time to adapt to his new surroundings while still preserving some vivid memories of his Scottish childhood and youth. To better understand the letters in this volume it is useful first to explore his religious and educational upbringing in the Borders region of Scotland.

EARLY LIFE IN SCOTLAND

In a journal entry written on 19 November 1828 at York Factory, James tentatively announced, "This, according to my calculation is my Birth Day, which completes my 30th year."[19] His later efforts, in anticipation

---

19 See below for his Journal 1828–29.

A SELECTIVE FAMILY TREE OF THE HARGRAVE AND MACTAVISH FAMILIES

1. **Joseph Hargrave** (ca. 1755–1847) married
a) Janet Rutherford (d. 1797) →
  1. Janet Hargrave (b. 1784)
  2. Joseph Hargrave (1785–1873) married Nancy Dobson (1797–1873)
  3. Ruther Hargrave (1788–1879) married a) Agnes Goldie (1796–1831) b) Margaret Rutherford (1813–1885)

b) **Jane Melrose** (1767–1838) →
  1. *James Hargrave* (1798–1865) married a) **Letitia Mactavish** (1813–1854) →
    1. *Joseph James Hargrave* (1841–1894)
    2. William Hargrave (1842–1842)
    3. Letitia Lockhart Hargrave (1844–1880)
    4. Mary Jane Hargrave (1848–1873)
    5. Dugald John Hargrave (1850–1854)
  b) Margaret Alcock (d. 1899)
  2. Mary Hargrave (1800–1859) married James Ross (1793–1846) →
    1. William Ross (1824–1904)
    2. Jane Ross (1826–1916)
  3. Jane Hargrave (1805–1893)
  4. John Hargrave (1806–1874) married Jemima Moffat (1819–1869)
  5. Andrew Hargrave (1808–1882) married a) Margaret Lawson (d. 1845) b) Margaret McEwen (1824–1890)

2. James Hargrave (1756–1848) married Mary Jane Oliver →
  1. Walter Hargrave (1800–1873)
  2. Andrew Hargrave

This family tree describes the relationships between some members of the Hargrave and Mactavish families referred to in his correspondence. It also includes the five children of James and Letitia who were not yet born. Fur traders' names are italicized. Names in bold type signify that the person is identified more than once in the tree.

A SELECTIVE FAMILY TREE OF
THE HARGRAVE AND MACTAVISH FAMILIES / CONT'D

1. *John George McTavish* (1778–1847)
2. Dugald Mactavish (1782–1855) married Letitia Lockhart ⟶
   1. **Letitia Mactavish** (1813–1854) married *James Hargrave* (1798–1865)
   2. *Dugald Mactavish* (1815–1870)
   3. *William Mactavish* (1817–1871)
   4. *Hector Mactavish* (d. 1844)

1. **Jane Melrose** (1767–1838) married **Joseph Hargrave** (ca. 1755–1847)
2. Mary Melrose (ca. 1781–) married James Mitchell (ca. 1786–1850) ⟶
   1. Alexander Mitchell (ca. 1806–)
   2. Euphemia Mitchell (1811–)

of marriage, to confirm his calculation[20] came to grief on the imperfections and deficiencies of the parish register system in Scotland.[21] We will take him at his word that he was born in 1798 at Chesters, a hamlet in Southdean parish about ten miles east of Hawick, in Roxburghshire. The genealogical table (on pages 10–11) shows his family tree, including all the Hargrave relatives he wrote to from Rupert's Land and the members of his first wife Letitia's family who also became fur traders. He was the eldest son of Joseph Hargrave and his second wife, Jane Melrose, a native of Kelso, Roxburghshire. His younger siblings were Mary, Jane, John, and Andrew. He also had two older half-brothers, Joseph and Ruther, by his father's first marriage to Janet Rutherford. The elder Joseph Hargrave was a shepherd who, before his departure for Canada in 1819, worked as a grieve or overseer of a landed estate in Roxburghshire. Joseph's children were born in various locations in the county between 1784 and 1808.

20 James Hargrave to Rev. John Richmond and Rev. James Clark from Hawick Tower Inn, 10 January 1838, and to Rev. James Clark from Edinburgh Waterloo Hotel, 15 January 1838. James Hargrave and family fonds, LAC.
21 Tranter, "Demography," 108–12.

Education

James never forgot that, unlike his siblings and half-siblings, he received an education that allowed him as an adult to turn his back on the hardscrabble toil of farm life.[22] The reasons for this difference are unknown but may have been due to James's position as a first-born son (in his father's second family), his evident intellectual gifts, his family's relative poverty, and, perhaps, his mother's recognition of the importance of education. He first attended the local one-room parish school at Stouslie in Wilton Parish where his youngest brother, Andrew, was born in 1808. One of his teachers was William Lockie (1788–1853), a minor poet and the schoolmaster at Stouslie for thirty-seven years,[23] who was only ten years his senior. James wrote long and warm letters to Lockie for many years after he emigrated to North America. James then studied until the age of eighteen at Galashiels Academy, the parish school then known as Fyshe's Academy after its schoolmaster, Robert Fyshe.

Robert Hall, in his late nineteenth-century history of Galashiels, described the school and its schoolmaster at that time.[24] In 1810, advertisements were placed in the *Caledonian Mercury*, *Edinburgh Evening Courant*, and *Kelso Mail* requesting applications for the office of schoolmaster. The candidates were required to be qualified to teach English, writing, arithmetic, book-keeping, mensuration,[25] Latin, French, and church music. Three finalists were examined by the Presbytery, which handed a report to the heritors, the body of landowners responsible for the parish school, church, and manse at that time: "Mr Fyshe, from Linton, with less acquaintance with Latin and French [than another candidate], writes an admirable hand, is well acquainted with the common and higher branches of arithmetic, mensuration, and land surveying." The heritors considered that the qualifications of Mr Fyshe were the most suitable for the class of scholars attending the school and so he was elected. At his urging, the fees charged were raised to bring them in line with other schools in the district: two shillings and sixpence for reading per quar-

---

22 James Hargrave to Jane Hargrave from York Factory, 10 July 1833. James Hargrave and family fonds, LAC.
23 Scott, *A Hawick Word Book*, 723.
24 Hall, *The History of Galashiels*, 453–7.
25 The branch of mathematics dealing with the determination of length, area, or volume.

ter, and an additional sixpence each for writing and arithmetic. To cope with overcrowding an addition of fifteen feet was built onto the original twenty-seven-foot length (by eighteen-foot width) of the schoolhouse.

In 1819, a couple of years after James's departure, the following advertisement in a provincial newspaper described in glowing terms the school curriculum at the time:

> The school of Galashiels was this day examined by a committee of the Presbytery of Selkirk in presence of a great number of the heritors, clergy, ladies and gentlemen of the town and neighbourhood, and also from Edinburgh. The scholars, amounting to upwards of 137, were exercised in their knowledge of English, grammar, spelling, reciting, Latin, Greek, French, British history, antiquities, modern geography, mathematics with their application to mensuration, plain and spherical trigonometry, algebra, mechanics, etc., astronomy and use of the globes, arithmetic, book-keeping, and writing. In all these branches they showed such a proficiency as did great credit to Mr Fyshe, the teacher. The company were gratified by the whole performance, and were fully satisfied that Mr Fyshe is well entitled to the public favour which he has so long enjoyed.[26]

An attached note concluded, "This seminary is rapidly rising in usefulness and public favour. Many gentlemen in Edinburgh having children boarded and educated in it speak in terms of unqualified approbation of the zeal and ability of the teacher, as well as of his mild and fatherly system of discipline, and his attention to the health and morals of his pupils."[27]

Lindean, where James's family was living when he attended Fyshe's Academy, lay three miles south of Galashiels, which probably means that James attended as a day student rather than a boarder. Without financial assistance his parents could not have afforded to pay for boarding, which in 1819 cost thirty guineas per annum.[28] He may, however, have received such assistance from the Reverend Robert Douglas who served as minister at Galashiels from 1770 until his death in 1820. James later credited both Douglas and his parents with making possible the education

---

26 Hall, *The History of Galashiels*, 454.
27 Ibid.
28 Ibid.

left: Robert Fyshe. James Hargrave's teacher in Galashiels, Scotland, he taught for almost forty years at the parish school before retiring in 1849. From Hall, *The History of Galashiels*, 1898. Courtesy of the Trustees of the National Library of Scotland.

right: Reverend Dr Robert Douglas. A minister at Galashiels from 1770 until his death in 1820 whom James Hargrave felt had made possible his superior education. From Hall, *The History of Galashiels*, 1898. Courtesy of the Trustees of the National Library of Scotland

that allowed him to raise himself above "the life of toil and privation" to which he was born.[29]

The rural Scottish educational system from which James emerged was highly prized by the Scots themselves as a means of producing a more egalitarian society than England's. Parish schools provided the opportunity for the children of lairds to rub shoulders with the offspring of ploughmen.[30] The Kirk of John Knox had placed schooling and literacy at the heart of its program for religious revolution, as a means to instill the essential precepts of religious belief in the young, to provide direct access for all to the Word of God in the Bible, and to allow the laity to take a

29 James Hargrave to James Mitchell from York Factory, 10 September 1832. James Hargrave and family fonds, LAC.
30 See Devine, *The Scottish Nation*, 91–100, for the following description of the Scottish education system.

central part in church governance. The subsequent development of parish schools established by law and maintained through the taxation of local landowners provided low-cost elementary education to much of the rural population of Scotland by the end of the seventeenth century. By the second half of the eighteenth century, the Kirk-controlled parish schools were complemented by the prolific growth of private fee-paying "adventure" schools and those run by charitable societies in the Highlands such as the Scottish Society for the Propagation of Christian Knowledge. Despite wide availability of education, however, few students attended for more than four or five years. James stood out from the average both in the duration of his schooling and with respect to his writing ability. There is some evidence that many families mainly wanted their children to be able to read and regarded writing as a lower priority; writing as a subject was often charged separately from reading and was taught later.

Following graduation, Hargrave taught as a schoolmaster in the village of Midholm or Midlem, in Bowden parish, about seven miles from Selkirk. He appears to have taught his own brothers there as a "poor penniless Dominie."[31] Despite Scottish enthusiasm for education, salaries were low. The inflation of the 1780s had had a significant effect on the incomes of many parochial schoolmasters. Some ministers complained that because schoolteachers in poorer rural parishes were hardly able to earn more than field labourers, they suffered from low social and economic standing in their local communities.[32] Although the incomes of parochial schoolmasters by the 1820s had often doubled after 1803 when Parliament passed a new education act,[33] James still felt poorly paid before his departure for Lower Canada in 1819.

Religious Background

James was a descendant of a Covenanter minister from the north of England who fled to a cave in the Cheviot Hills in the Scottish Borders to escape persecution.[34] The Covenanters were post-Reformation Scottish

---

31 James Hargrave to John Hargrave from York Factory, 10 July 1831; James Hargrave to Alexander Mitchell from York Factory, 29 August 1835. James Hargrave and family fonds, LAC.
32 Withrington, "Education," 284.
33 Ibid., 285.
34 Schofield family fonds, British Columbia Archives (BCA), box 3, file 4, item 3.

Presbyterians who pledged themselves to covenants to maintain their chosen forms of church government and worship. A quarter century of severe persecution of Covenanters began in 1660 with the restoration of Charles II to the English throne after the interregnum of Cromwell. It ended with the ascent of the Dutch Protestant William III to the English throne in 1688. In 1690 Parliament passed an act re-establishing Presbyterian church government but did not renew the covenants, leading some of the more embittered and fanatical Covenanters to reject the settlement. According to a family manuscript,[35] James's ancestor set up his own ministry in Hawick, Roxburghshire and acquired an extensive collection of theology books.

James's father, Joseph Hargrave, was reputed to have studied these same books with zeal and attentiveness both at home and while he tended sheep on the high grassy plains of Carter Fell, a mountain ridge beside the Northumberland border. Born between 1749 and 1756 in Hawick, he was a deeply religious man and continued the family tradition of dissent. At the time of James's birth, he was attached to the Antiburgher Congregation in Jedburgh,[36] an offshoot of the Secession Church which itself had split from the established church before the middle of the eighteenth century over the divisive issue of patronage in the selection of ministers.[37] The split between Burghers and Antiburghers in the Secession Church had occurred in 1747 over the question of the Burgher Oath which required holders of public offices to affirm approval of the "true religion presently professed" in the kingdom. Burghers believed that this referred to the Protestant religion in general while Antiburghers understood the oath to refer to the established church and so refused to take it. Dissenters tended to be strict Calvinists who followed proper observance of the Sabbath.

By the nineteenth century, dissenters were drawn more and more from the ranks of the upwardly mobile, particularly in the towns and cities.

---

35 Schofield family fonds, BCA, box 3, file 4, item 2.
36 In 1838, contemplating marriage with Letitia Mactavish, Hargrave wrote to James Clark, the minister of this congregation, requesting a certificate of the registry of his baptism as a son of Joseph Hargrave and Jane Melrose; he was disappointed by the reply that no such record existed. James Hargrave to James Clark from Hawick, 10 January 1838. James Hargrave and family fonds, LAC.
37 Callum Brown, "Religion," 70–4.

According to Callum Brown, "membership of a dissenting congregation usually signalled a strong social and economic aspiration to 'get on' – to succeed in the new economic climate."[38] Joseph Hargrave fit this pattern. Before leaving for Lower Canada, he worked hard as a grieve[39] on a large estate, a position that entailed great responsibility for little reward. James dated his own decision to leave Scotland to improve the family's situation in the world to a talk with his father in one of the landowner's fields.[40]

James mentioned Providence many times in his letters home, usually in connection with how good it had been to him and his family. He expressed his belief in a world under the care and guardianship of a deity even as he refrained from displaying religious enthusiasm in front of potential doubters among his fur trading colleagues. The topic of religion permeated his letters to family and friends, most often those to his father, who provided parental advice on weighty religious tomes he thought James should be reading.[41] An avid reader, James still rebelled quietly at his father's "recommending The Marrow of M^n Divinity & the Four fold State to the study of a head so over jaded with Bills Ladings Invoices & all the intricacies of Tariffs that on an evening which stretched out on a Sopha in the silence & solitude of my bed room a chapter of the Evangelists is the deepest reading in Divinity which my mistified ideas can comprehend."[42] He also ridiculed the Red River colonists who in retirement, after years of chronic drinking or fathering large numbers of children with various sexual partners, became "born-again" converts

---

38 Callum Brown, "Religion," 74.
39 A grieve was responsible for a group of farm workers but did not have the rights of a tacksman who was a farm tenant who sub-let rents or tacks.
40 James Hargrave to Andrew Hargrave from York Factory, 18 July 1828. James Hargrave and family fonds, LAC.
41 Books with titles such as *The Gospel Mystery of Sanctification*, *The Marrow of Divinity*, *Human Nature in its Fourfold State*, *The Reign of Grace*, and *Truth's Victory over Error. Or, an Abridgement of the Chief Controversies in Religion, which since the Apostles days to this Time, have been, and are in Agitation, between those of the Orthodox Faith, and all Adversaries whatsoever*. Controversy over *The Marrow of Modern Divinity*, a seventeenth-century English work republished in Scotland in 1718, which argued for the doctrine of universal atonement against that of predestination, the basic tenet of conventional Calvinism, led eventually to the Secession Church.
42 James Hargrave to William Lockie from York Factory, 1 August 1828. James Hargrave and family fonds, LAC.

to psalm singing, abstinence, and continence. Toward the end of his fur trade career, Hargrave was so weighed down with the heavy demands of business that he implored a fellow officer in 1851 to try to keep the clergyman at Red River from coming to York Factory that autumn.[43]

Notwithstanding the many divisions and schisms in the history of the Scottish church, Hargrave himself argued for greater unity among the Scottish immigrants in North America in their religious practices. He wrote his father that the divisions in Scotland were based primarily on the question of lay patronage, an issue that did not exist in Canada. Having the choice of their clergy and acknowledging one system of doctrine, the Scottish immigrants had no reasonable grounds for worshipping separately in this country. Hargrave bemoaned the prejudice and ill temper with which members of the various sects in Scotland had looked upon and talked of each other. His early years with the HBC in Red River with its Anglican and Roman Catholic missionaries also predisposed him to a tolerant view of Roman Catholics. He greeted with pleasure the news of the passing of the Catholic Relief Act of 1829 in Britain. His former schoolmaster, Hargrave wrote, surely would not countenance a system that kept Catholics a band of servile helots to British Protestants, the staple of their ranks in war, and their hewers of wood and drawers of water in peacetime.[44]

Hargrave, on the other hand, in his letters was most condescending and patronizing in his attitudes toward the religious views of the Native peoples he came across in Rupert's Land. He described them as simple people sunk in the darkness of heathenism, with benighted notions of religion. Despite great efforts directed at their spiritual improvement, he

---

43 James Hargrave to Donald Ross from York Factory, 17 July 1851. James Hargrave and family fonds, LAC. "I cannot continue to support the doubling of labor & reduction of help that for some time has been brot to bear on my devoted head. Poor Colin Robertson's prophecy of 'York with Hargrave & a Cook' seems not yet to be lost sight of by those who rule our destinies ... 15 July. *Privately* – Try and keep your parson at home this autumn for we will have difficulties enough without the embarrassment of Preaching to clog our wheels. No man will have time to listen amid the stir of the crowds that will be with us of necessity and his admonitions 'saving eno' when in season will then only be 'cauld parritch' thrown down a stuffed throat. Keep this & him to yourself for my sake."

44 James Hargrave to William Lockie from York Factory, 10 June 1830. James Hargrave and family fonds, LAC.

wrote, both in North America and by the HBC directors in England, much time would need to elapse before their "darkened minds" could be illuminated by the truths of Christianity.[45] A modern reader is struck by the faith he placed in the benign effects of residential schools. He felt the best hope for the spiritual improvement of Natives lay longterm in the missionary school in Red River for Native children from all parts of the country where they would grow up to carry to their countrymen the arts of civilized man and the Christian message of salvation. Hargrave later designed the Church of St John of York Factory, known simply as the "Indian" or "Cree" church. It was constructed in 1858, the year before he retired.[46]

FUR TRADE CAREER

Hargrave set sail for America in 1819, following his family who had departed earlier that same year. They were trailing his father's younger brother, James Sr, who had left Scotland with his own family in 1812 and James's half-brothers, Ruther and Joseph, who emigrated in 1817. He joined his family in Beechridge, Beauharnois Seigneury, southwest of Montreal, before entering the North West Company (NWC) on 28 April 1820 in Montreal[47] for a four-year engagement as a means of obtaining

---

45 James Hargrave to Joseph Hargrave from York Factory, 2 November 1827. James Hargrave and family fonds, LAC.
46 Beardy and Coutts, eds., *Voices from Hudson Bay*, 137.
47 Montreal was described in 1821 by Nicholas Garry, a director of the Hudson's Bay Company who visited Canada to supervise the amalgamation of the HBC and NWC. "Montreal is very pleasantly situated on the St. Lawrence ... The Houses are built of Stone and with some exceptions are old fashioned and ill built – the stone has a gloomy dirty Appearance. This Town has been so often visited by Fires that the Inhabitants have hit upon an Expedient which renders the Town very uncomfortable – the Heat being almost insupportable. The Roofs of the Houses and Churches are covered with Tin Plates and the Shutters are of Iron. On my first Arrival we were dreadfully annoyed by an innumerable number of Flies which took possession of the town. They pay the Town an annual Visit and come with the Shad Fish. In walking it was necessary to keep the mouth shut. Montreal contains about 15,000 Inhabitants, three-fourths Canadian-French. The Island on which Montreal is built is about 30 miles in Length." Garry, *Diary*, 91.

Part of an 1829 map of Lower Canada showing Williamstown, the township south of Montreal close to the US border where James Hargrave's father and family lived. Courtesy of Bibliothèque et Archives nationales du Québec, 69579.

enough money to settle down as a farmer.[48] His starting salary was fifty pounds currency of Lower Canada. Hargrave served during his first winter in the fur trade as a wintering clerk at Sault Ste Marie, Upper Canada, a key post in the communication/transportation network of the NWC.[49] In the spring of 1821 he travelled to Fort William where he

48 James Hargrave to Joseph and Jane Hargrave from Fort Garry, 29 January 1827. James Hargrave and family fonds, LAC. His engagement contract with the North West Company stipulated that he was to have the privilege of spending one winter with his relations in Lower Canada, with his passage there and back to be paid by his employers. This contractual furlough was a casualty of the union of the HBC and NWC in 1821. ANQ, Henry Griffin notarial records, 3114.
49 See Van Kirk, "Hargrave, James," for the following biographical information.

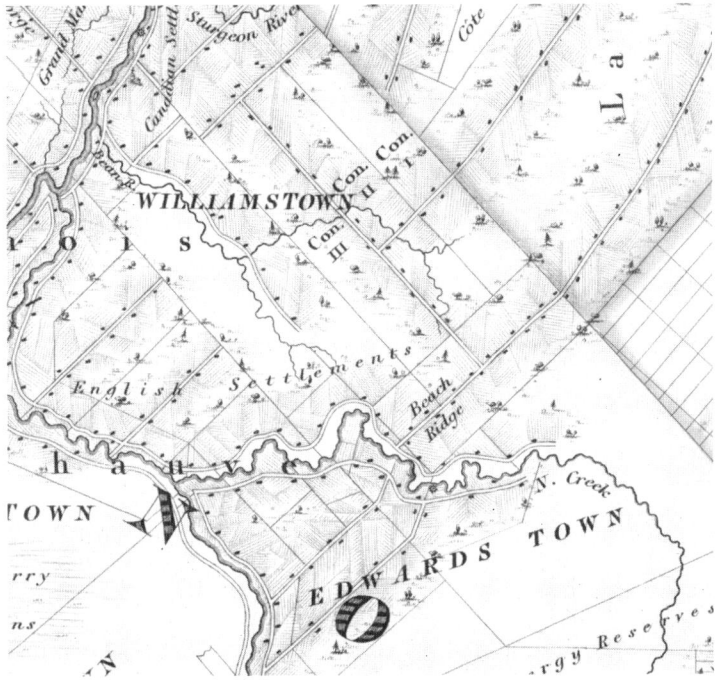

Part of an 1831 topographical map of the district of Montreal, Lower Canada, showing "Beach Ridge" and the rest of the township of Williamstown. Courtesy of Bibliothèque et Archives nationales du Québec, 90116_2.

attracted the notice of John George McTavish, the uncle of his future wife. After the union of the NWC and HBC in 1821 following years of fierce rivalry, he was retained as a clerk by the latter and spent the next season at York Factory under Chief Factor McTavish.[50] From 1823 to 1827 he wintered in the Lower Red River District but travelled with the fur

---

50 In the list of North West Clerks noted in an 1821 HBC List of Servants, James Hargrave is noted as one of twenty-nine apprentice clerks. The list included thirteen first-class and twelve second-class clerks, as well as ten "drunkards," seven "unfit" apprentices, and eighteen supernumeraries. The drunkards and unfit apprentices were not to have their "servitude" renewed. HBCA, B. 239/f/10. In another List of Servants of North West clerks in the Northern Department 1821/22, his annual salary was given as £50, and he was described as "A promising steady young man, excellent education & a good Clerk. Looks for promotion at the expiration of his apprenticeship."

brigades to York every summer. In 1827, after distinguishing himself as a "clerk, warehouse & shopkeeper," he was stationed permanently at York Factory.

Governor George Simpson, in his confidential Character Book of 1832, expressed his candid opinion of Hargrave the year before the latter was promoted to chief trader:

> A man of good Education and of highly correct conduct and character and very useful. Expresses himself well either verbally or on paper, is clear headed and possesses a better knowledge of general business than might be expected from the advantages he has had. Equal to the management of York Depôt and is better qualified for a Seat in Council than 9 out of 10 of our present Chief Factors. Has every reason to calculate on early promotion and may in due time reach the board of Green Cloth if he goes on as he promises: he has not however had any experience in the Indian Trade, can speak none of the Native Languages, his Health is not very good and his temper is rather Sour.[51]

It was to be another long eleven years before he was finally promoted to chief factor in 1844. He may have been held back in part for another reason not mentioned by Governor Simpson. In 1832, the Rev. William Cockran, an English-born Scot of humble origins who became a Church of England missionary in the Red River Settlement, told Hargrave that he suspected the latter's lack of Highland clan and kinship ties might have contributed to his failure to be promoted. "I begin to think that your name will have to be changed, into Mc-argrave. If you had a Mc- before it, I have little doubt, but that it would have done you real service."[52] Merit, according to fur trade historian Jennifer Brown, no more guaranteed success in the merged HBC than it had in the pre-merger HBC and NWC, "and its recognition was still assured by the cultivation of patron-

---

HBCA, B. 239/f/13. Yet another List of Servants for 1822–23 listed him as retained as a fourth-class clerk for a salary of £40. HBCA, B. 239/f/15. In the Engagement Register of the Northern Department, he is listed as No. 909, James Hargrave, appointed CTr. in 1833. HBCA, B. 239/u/1.

51 Williams, "'Character Book' of Governor George Simpson," 214.
52 William Cockran to James Hargrave, 9 August 1832, quoted in Jennifer Brown, *Strangers in Blood*, 41–2.

age, kinship, and friendship ties."[53] It was not until after his marriage to Letitia Mactavish, the niece of John George McTavish, a close friend of Governor Simpson,[54] that Hargrave was finally elevated to the position of chief factor. Hargrave himself had remarked in 1828 on the preference for North Westers in recruiting for the higher ranks, but he chose to explain it to a fellow clerk, George Barnston, as "a circumstance that speaks the superior enterprise and efficiency of the partners in the late concern."[55]

By happenstance, Hargrave's fur trade career, which stretched from 1820 to 1859, coincided almost exactly with that of George Simpson's. First hired in 1820, Simpson was made governor of the HBC's Northern Department in 1821 and in 1826 went on to govern all the company's affairs in North America until his death in 1860. Under his able and dedicated governorship, the HBC dominated the northern North American fur trade in the nineteenth century. His administrative and organizational abilities, immense energy, good educational background, social skills, Highland connections, and occasional ruthlessness and double-dealing all contributed to the success of the "Little Emperor," as he was described by the officers of the fur trade. With utter dedication to business affairs, he drove the company relentlessly down the paths of efficiency and economy.[56] Hargrave, recognizing the absolute necessity of pleasing his

53 Jennifer Brown, *Strangers in Blood*, 119.
54 John George McTavish was perhaps the closest friend of Simpson in the fur trade but he received a mixed review in the latter's Character Book of 1832: "Was the most finished man of business we had in the Country, well Educated, respectably connected and more of the Man of the World in his conversation and address than any of his colleagues. A good hearted Man and generous to extravagance, but unnecessarily dignified and high minded which leads to frequent difficulties with his associates by whom he is considered a 'Shylock,' and upon many of whom he looks down; rather strong in his prejudices against, and partialities for individuals, which frequently influences his judgement, so that his opinions on men and things must be listened to with caution; is about 54 Years of Age, has of late Years become very heavy, unwieldy and inactive; over fond of good living and I must fear is getting into habits of conviviality and intemperance." Williams, "Character Book," 171.
55 James Hargrave to George Barnston, 1 July 1828, quoted in Jennifer Brown, *Strangers in Blood*, 119.
56 At the time of the coalition in 1821 there were 1983 HBC employees. During the next four years this number was reduced to 827; wages of ordinary

George Simpson as a young man. Simpson's remarkable career as HBC's North American governor (1820–60), coincided with Hargrave's time with the HBC. Courtesy of the Oregon Historical Society, OrHi54480.

employer if he wished to avoid either dismissal or banishment to some remote and lonely outpost, was extremely deferential in his letters and his behaviour, both public and private, to Governor Simpson.[57]

After securing a chief tradership in 1833 he assumed the management of York Factory and was officially given charge of York Factory District in 1835. Suffering from ill health, he took a year's furlough in 1837 and while touring Scotland met and fell in love with Letitia Mactavish. Unexpectedly called back to York Factory early in 1838 he returned again to Scotland in the fall of 1839 and married Letitia in January 1840.

---

employees were slashed approximately 50 per cent. Hargrave himself had his salary reduced from 50 to 40 pounds per annum following the union of the two companies. Galbraith, *Little Emperor*, 60.
57 Venema, "As we are both deceived," 8–9.

They journeyed together to York Factory and started a family of five children, two of whom died in early childhood. The long-promised chief factorship finally came in January 1844. Two years later, he again went on furlough with his now ailing wife and placed his son, Joseph James, at school in Scotland. The family returned to York Factory in the summer of 1847 where Hargrave reluctantly remained another four years under the shadow of increasingly difficult job demands. In 1851 he gratefully relinquished that post to Letitia's brother, William, and took charge of Sault Ste Marie. After the sudden deaths of his wife and youngest child of cholera in 1854 he sailed for Scotland in 1855 before being forced to return once again to York Factory in 1856 to replace the ailing William Mactavish. He finally retired officially from the company's service on 1 June 1859 after another year's leave of absence in Scotland, with what he thought was the satisfactory amount of about £8700 as a competency for his old age.[58] Retirement had been much longer in coming than he had hoped in his early days in the fur trade.

Shortly after returning to Canada he married Margaret Alcock, and after a year in Toronto, they settled on a substantial property at Brockville where he died five years later in 1865 at the age of sixty-six. He was buried beside his first wife in the St James's Anglican cemetery in Toronto.

YORK FACTORY

Much the greatest part of Hargrave's working career with the HBC was spent at York Factory on the Hayes River near Hudson Bay. York Factory had been founded in 1682 and became the principal supply depot and transfer point between Britain and the North American western interior after the HBC began establishing inland trading posts in 1774 to counter competition for furs from the French. Its location was accessible by ocean-going vessels which would anchor at Five Fathom Hole where they could find safe harbour. Ships from England would arrive in late August or early September with new servants, provisions for the post employees, and goods for barter in the fur trade. They would pick up the furs that inland brigades had delivered to York Factory over the summer in smaller boats and depart from Hudson Bay for Britain in advance of the fall freeze-up with employees on furlough or retiring from the company. Navigation was an arduous undertaking requiring skilled masters and,

---

58 Bryce, *The Remarkable History*, 296.

York Factory, ca 1853. York Factory underwent significant rebuilding during the time that Hargrave served the HBC. Both the harsh climate and the demands of business were responsible for these changes. Courtesy of Library and Archives Canada (LAC), Peter Winkworth Collection of Canadiana, Acc. no. R9266-1615.

because the Hayes River was too shallow to accommodate larger ships, goods first had to be transferred to smaller boats to be taken ashore. After 1821 York Factory, with its immense warehouses, became the headquarters of the HBC's vast Northern Department. Hargrave spent most of his working career at its fiscal centre, where indents for all outfits and the annual financial statements for the whole department were prepared.[59]

Nicholas Garry, an HBC director sent out from London to supervise the amalgamation of the two fur trading companies, described York Factory in 1821 in his journal. This is what James Hargrave would have seen upon his own arrival as well.

> York Fort is situated on the West Side of Hayes River on a Point of alluvial Land formed by this River and the Nelson or N. River which is the Outlet of Lake Winnipic and of the vast Bodies of Waters which this Lake receives. The Soil is everywhere marshy –

---

59 For an account of the complex record system in use to requisition and distribute supplies for the Northern Department from 1834 to 1870, see May, "Cycle of commerce," 47-68.

the Country on every side flat covered with low stunted Pine, Willows (Poplar Willow called in England the Balsam Tree). The Fort is built on Piles – but though drained on every side is still sinking. The Buildings are surrounded by Stockades and are of an Octagon Form, which appear to have been so erected to form Bastions but are now converted into dwelling Rooms and Warehouses. It is two Storeys high. The Roof which forms a Sort of Walk or Look out is covered with Lead on which there is a Flag Staff, rigged as a Mast. In the Centre of the Building is the Hudson Bay Arms painted by Mr. Cooke.[60] Within the Stockade are several Buildings, a small Garden and the Powder Magazine which is a wooden Erection covered with Lead. It is in a most dangerous Situation and should be removed. The Fort may be about a hundred yards from the River. On landing there is a Warehouse to the right and one to the left. The former is called the Colony Warehouse. The Banks may be 60 or 70 Feet high and are of so loose and clayey a Nature that they are continually falling in. As a Fortification it is a Place of no Strength.[61]

The fort had been started in 1788 to a design by Joseph Colen, following the capture and burning of an earlier fort by the French in 1782.[62] It was built about a kilometre farther up the river to protect it from ice damage. Under the stewardship of Chief Factor John George McTavish the old fort began its refurbishment after 1821 with the addition of new stores, a powder magazine, and winter dwelling houses. The newly married wife of Governor George Simpson noted in 1830 that groceries, haberdashery, ironmongery, cutlery, medicines, and even perfumery could be bought in the York Factory stores more cheaply than in London shops.

By 1831, the octagon fort had to be replaced because its rigid stone and brick foundation and solid wood and brick walls were not flexible enough for the heaving and pressure of the permafrost. In a letter in December 1831 to McTavish, Hargrave reported that the old factory had become so leaky and unfit that a new substantial two and one-half storey storehouse,

60 William Hemmings Cook (1768–1846) who worked for the HBC from 1786 to 1819 before settling at Red River.
61 Garry, "Diary," 167–8.
62 Wilson, "Forts," 4–11. See this source for a fuller discussion of the development of York Factory over time.

Departure of the second colonist transport from York Fort to Rockfort, 1821. Watercolour by Peter Rindisbacher, one of the colonists who immigrated to Lord Selkirk's Red River settlement and documented the voyage with a series of drawings. Courtesy of LAC, Acc. no. 1988-250-17.

forty feet long and thirty wide, had been raised in its place.[63] It housed the packing and outfit rooms, as well as the apothecary and stationery rooms. Thirty-foot-long two-storey wings were added in 1832–33 to the great depot building to form a continuous 100-foot front, and included blanket and shop rooms among others.

The buildings at York Factory were laid out in an H shape with the depot building, a guest-house and a large summer mess house forming the centre bar. The wings of the H included fur stores, provison shop, trading room, and officers' and servants' quarters. The main gate in the encircling wooden palisade was centred on the depot entrance. Other structures, such as a boat shed, oil store, lumber house, ice house, powder magazine, cooper's shop, and smithy were scattered around the site and connected by a network of boardwalks.

63 James Hargrave to John George McTavish from York Factory, 1 December 1831. James Hargrave and family fonds, LAC.

Difficult voyage up the Hill River to Rock Fort, 1821. Watercolour by Peter Rindisbacher. Boatmen can be seen hauling their craft upstream. Courtesy of LAC, Acc. no. 1988-259-18.

By the time Hargrave arrived at York Factory the local Home Guard or Swampy Cree families no longer engaged in the fur trade themselves or as middlemen. The fur-bearing animals had been seriously depleted and the HBC now relied on its inland posts in the western interior to provide the furs required for the trade. Many Swampy Cree families consequently had gravitated from migrational life on the land to residence in permanent camps around the fort and relied on the company for many critical supplies. They trapped, hunted, and fished on a seasonal basis for the company and would barter this country food for trade goods. Adequate supplies of venison, moose, fish, ducks, ptarmigan, and berries could not be depended upon to arrive at the Factory and the post relied heavily on European food goods, particularly salted meats and agricultural produce.

York Factory's distribution system to the interior was served by a network of rivers and lakes. The main route ran southwest to Norway House at the north end of Lake Winnipeg and then south to Fort Garry at the forks of the Red and Assiniboine Rivers. From Lake Winnipeg the route westward lay along the Saskatchewan River to Edmonton and portages linked this avenue to the rivers that served the northern districts. During the early years of Hargrave's employment with the HBC when he was posted to Fort Garry he would return in the summers to York Factory along the 700-mile route. In a loaded boat, the back-breaking voyage downstream would usually take a couple of weeks while the return voyage back to Fort Garry could take from five to six weeks.

When Hargrave joined the HBC, York Factory was the gateway to North America for its employees and the Red River settlers. It served as the hub of the distribution system of the fur trade in the northern half of the continent. By the time he retired in 1859 an American river and Red River cart route had supplanted it because of the proximity of the Red River Settlement to St Paul and the competition of the American Fur Company. The establishment of a trading post at Pembina in 1843 and the use of Red River carts through the Red River valley to carry the cargoes of the fur trade meant that the American market was within a day's ride of the Red River Settlement. Because of the uncertainty of ships from England always being able to reach York Factory each year, the outfits had to be ordered two or three years in advance of delivery and reserves had to be kept on hand, filling valuable space in the company's warehouses. It was difficult to recruit men to work the heavy and perilous York boats in the interior. The York route was also unsuitable for an export trade from the Red River settlement as it could not be expanded to meet growing demands. Governor Simpson made a failed attempt to have a winter road built between Norway House and York Factory but in the event it was never needed as the River River settlement did not develop sufficient staples for export.

JAMES HARGRAVE AND "THE SEX"[64]

Hargrave spent twenty years with the Hudson's Bay Company as a "bluff bachelor, free of wife or other encumbrance, and ... in this land at least ... *determined* to keep ... so."[65] His friend, Thomas Simpson, in 1838 wrote to Donald Ross at Norway House inquiring about Hargrave: "And what has the latter been about that he still stands a guarded and solitary oak,

---

64 Hargrave referred to women from time to time in his letters as "the Sex."
65 James Hargrave to Mary Ross from York Factory, 19 July 1828. James Hargrave and family fonds, LAC.

ungraced by some fair twining ivy?"[66] Two years later, at the age of forty-one, Hargrave at last married a woman that his head and heart both approved of. Prior to the marriage, he wrote to his old schoolmaster and friend William Lockie describing his love who could not yet be named publicly.[67] He compared with pride her higher social status to that of his own as a Borders shepherd. Further, her unblemished conduct as a daughter and sister and her carefully finished education were qualities that were crowned by their mutual love. He saw her as a suitable partner for his household and a companion of taste in the wilds of Rupert's Land, whose talents for reading, conversation, and music would "raise a paradise" within his own home. Letitia may also have fit the physical description that Hargrave provided in a letter in 1827 to a fellow fur trader about his taste in women: "My dear fellow we are all clay, and I hold that a plump waist and well turned limb with a warm & yielding heart to animate them will soonest take the eye of that man whose breast beats warmest with love to his fellow creatures."[68] To top it all, she had two brothers and an uncle already in the service of the Hudson's Bay Company "so that in this land we will be surrounded with friends & allies."[69] Surrounded perhaps but still separated by thousands of miles from her brother Dugald on the west coast and her uncle John George at Lac des Chats on the Ottawa River in Lower Canada; only William was posted at York Factory.

Although Hargrave was willing to forgo the comforts of married life for many years, he had in fact been disappointed in love at least twice in his youth, once in Scotland and once in Lower Canada. A Miss A. Wilson refused to follow him as his wife across the ocean in 1820 and failed to reply to a subsequent proposal when his prospects seemed better. In 1828, Hargrave in turn refused, somewhat regretfully, an overture by Miss Wilson through his cousin Euphemia Mitchell in Galashiels to renew

---

66 Thomas Simpson to Donald Ross at Norway House, 28 September 1838. Quoted in Barr, *From Barrow to Boothia*, 210.
67 James Hargrave to William Lockie from York Factory, 8 September 1838. James Hargrave and family fonds, LAC.
68 James Hargrave to Cuthbert Cumming from Fort Garry, 24 March 1827. James Hargrave and family fonds, LAC.
69 James Hargrave to William Lockie from York Factory, 8 September 1838. James Hargrave and family fonds, LAC.

their correspondence. His views of life, he said, had changed so much that "it would be a weak *hankering* after what can never be accomplished" to write again to her.[70] In Lower Canada, another female acquaintance, Melinda Dewey, lived near his father's farm in Beechridge. Although he was apparently interested in the young woman before engaging as a clerk with the North West Company in 1820, her behaviour at that time and subsequently, in addition to her steadily declining number of childbearing years, later disqualified her in his view from being an eligible marriage partner.[71]

He attempted in 1827 to explain his continuing bachelor state to a former neighbour in Beechridge.[72] He disparaged Native women as unsuitable companions in the serious voyage of life and alluded to his unlucky and discouraging history with "fairer faces" and the probability that he would not tempt fortune again in such a search.

His sexual relationships with Native women in the North were hinted at in letters he wrote to friends and family but were more often referred to in his correspondence with fur traders. Despite some apparently sporadic sexual encounters he never set up house with or planned to marry a Native woman even in the face of a long tradition of "country marriages" between fur traders and Native women.[73] Nor is there any evidence that, unlike Governor Simpson, Hargrave ever fathered any illegitimate children in Rupert's Land. Given the lack of modern birth control techniques at that time, it may well be that he exercised some restraint in his sexual activities, particularly after the early years in Red River. By the 1820s nearly all HBC officers, and many of the lower ranks, had entered into marriage alliances with the "country-born" offspring of fur traders and Native women, a custom that proved valuable in securing trade ties and acculturating traders to Aboriginal languages and customs. Hargrave himself resisted this particular path through life.

70 James Hargrave to Euphemia Mitchell from York Factory, 25 August 1828. James Hargrave and family fonds, LAC.
71 James Hargrave to Jane Melrose from York Factory, 16 July 1835. James Hargrave and family fonds, LAC.
72 James Hargrave to Margaret Struthers from York Factory, 1 November 1827. James Hargrave and family fonds, LAC.
73 For a fuller discussion of marriage "à la façon du pays" see the following sources: Nelson, "A Strange Revolution," 23–62; Van Kirk, *Many Tender Ties*; Hyam, *Empire and Sexuality*.

In 1827 he wrote his parents regarding the regrettable consequences of "having formed connections in the country," by which he meant marriage according to the custom of the country. His goal in going to Rupert's Land was to give him the financial means to retire to Canada or Britain to enjoy the fruits of his labours. Other fur traders, despite the same desire, were forced to remain all their lives in the wilds of North America because they found themselves incapable of abandoning the families they had started in their youth. While no man of principle, Hargrave wrote, would ever attempt to leave his family, an equally painful prospect was bringing a Native wife back to the "civilized world." The usual result of these entanglements, he added, was that many fur traders buried themselves alive in the forests of the country, cut off from friends and almost everything they had considered in their youth as desirable in life.[74]

Hargrave's decision not to marry in Rupert's Land may have been in part due to his permanent station at York Factory, the headquarters of the vast Northern Department of the HBC. Unlike the fur traders in the outposts he was not directly involved in trading with the Native people and his job did not require that he learn their languages or even their customs. He also expressed the racist attitudes of many in Britain and Canada of that period in a letter to Letitia in 1838 regarding her mother's anxiety about Letitia's brother "taking a fancy to any of the Brown Faces."[75] A young gentleman from Britain, Hargrave opined, would as soon marry a contemporary of his grandmother as a "pure Squaw." While some might be tempted by money or kinder motives to wed the daughter of an officer in a mixed marriage, William, according to Hargrave, was too noble minded to marry for money and possessed too good taste to succumb to kinder feelings.

Hargrave's distinction between a "pure Squaw" and "the daughter of an Officer" reflected the reality from the early 1800s that fur traders in Rupert's Land had increasingly drawn their partners from the growing ranks of the offspring of fur traders and First Nations women. Many daughters of fur traders had acquired the skills, knowledge, and language of their mothers and were acculturated to the fur trade lifestyle but had

---

74 James Hargrave to Joseph and Jane Hargrave from Fort Garry, 29 January 1827. James Hargrave and family fonds, LAC.

75 James Hargrave to Letitia Mactavish from York Factory, 24 July 1838. James Hargrave and family fonds, LAC.

lighter skin and European features that made them more attractive as traders' wives.

According to Sylvia Van Kirk,[76] the arrival of white women further devalued Native wives in the eyes of status-conscious men. This was particularly true in settled areas, where a polished and graceful wife was supplanting Native skills and connections as a precondition for social mobility. Governor George Simpson, whose marriage in 1830 to his British cousin occurred after he abandoned a series of country-born partners, may have provided the role model for Hargrave in his own choice of wife ten years later. Hargrave, as a "gentleman" in the traditional HBC hierarchy of "gentlemen and servants," having some education and capacity for administration and in line for promotion, would also have been anxious to secure the approval of Governor Simpson,[77] on whose favour his career absolutely depended, for his choice of marriage partner.

Hargrave did admit in his correspondence to some sexual liaisons with women in Rupert's Land but seems to have been bothered by religious scruples about his conduct. In a letter to accountant Grant Forrest at the HBC post at Lake of Two Mountains about the flooding of the Red River Colony in May 1826, he wrote of "the loving present" (a baby presumably) Mrs Forrest had made to her husband since his arrival in Canada:

> Such Gifts make me look back with regret on the idle and dissipated life of We Bachelor Fur Traders "Our Vigour wasted in a thousand arms" – without any results but shame and self accusation. Fortunate fellows like you carry off without remorse every object of attraction that happens to stray to this remote & savage desert, so we are of necessity obliged to take shelter below the Embossed Blankets till age & want of better Society render the poor devil unfit to aspire to any thing better.[78]

Later that year Hargrave commented to fellow trader Richard Grant that the flooding of the Red River Colony with its 1500 inhabitants was adversely impacting his sex life among the women there at the time:[79]

76 Van Kirk, "The Custom of the Country," 83.
77 Venema, "As we are both deceived," 8.
78 James Hargrave to Grant Forrest from York Factory, 14 August 1826. James Hargrave and family fonds, LAC.
79 James Hargrave to Richard Grant from Fort Garry, 5 December 1826. James Hargrave and family fonds, LAC.

The upper end of the Settlement which was formerly inhabited by Canadians & Swiss, is now completely deserted, the whole having either left the country or gone to the plains. To reverse the proverb "'tis a good wind that blows nobody ill" – for though the peace of the Colony is secured by the absence of these hordes of beggars, yet entre nous among these my female acquaintance was entirely centred, and now since their desertion, a willing wench is scarcely to be found for love or money. No doubt industry might still pick up not a few from among the Psalm singing Scotch & Blues,[80] but these are completely monopolized by the Righteous who are so far liberal as to practise a community of such goods, but who punish with the unrelenting scourge of slander, every interloper from among the "Children of Darkness" who dares to poach in their sacred warrens.

After he had secured his chief tradership, Hargrave mentioned his own religious scruples in a letter of 1833 to John Siveright:

[Chief Factor Edward Smith] will also hand you a pair of Garnished Shoes & pair of Gloves from me which, if not the best the North can produce are as far as my taste serves me the work of the Sweetest Lassie I have met in it. Now draw none of your sinister conclusions from this, as I am still a Bachelor & she a married woman with 1000nds of miles between us so even were you not acquainted with my presbyterian scruples such facts would disarm suspicion.[81]

Hargrave showed a certain concern for the welfare of those women with whom he may have had sexual liaisons but he was always careful to preserve his own independence and reputation as well. In 1827, in a letter marked "Private & Confidential," he asked John McLeod at Norway House to help him in a delicate matter regarding Mary, the daughter of George Taylor, a former HBC schooner master and his Native wife, Jane Prince:

---

80 The "Blues" was a term frequently used at Red River to refer to retired fur trade officers and their families.
81 James Hargrave to John Siveright from York Factory, 20 July 1833. James Hargrave and family fonds, LAC.

From some silly report or other it appears Miss Taylor has got it into that pretty head of hers that I purposed last spring to take her into keeping, – and that she still has a notion she will be sent for hither this fall. My information adds that influenced by this expectation she has refused an opportunity of a favorable offer.[82] Will you oblige me by undeceiving her in the smoothest manner you may devise. With a view of returning again to my native land without burden or encumbrance I purpose if possible to keep clear from all matrimonial fetters in this country. Had I an eye towards picking up a play-mate, between ourselves, I have scarcely seen a young woman of her Caste I should have preferred before her; but looking at the consequences I have had resolution to forbear, and with your kind assistance this mistake will be quietly set to rights – I trust without affecting the poor girls future situation in life. Confiding implicitly on your honor that this will remain a profound secret between ourselves ... [83]

He wrote again a couple of months later thanking McLeod for settling the affair for him:

I am favored with your kind letter of Augt last, and feel sincerely obliged by your snug settlement of the little matter regarding which I wrote you in July. When an opportunity presents you shall find me not forgetful of your prompt & efficient assistance. I pity however the fate of the poor girl, for from what you say it would seem that interest can scarcely reconcile her to her present alliance.[84] But better so than if such a fate had been avoided at my expense.[85]

82 In 1827 Mary Taylor became the country wife of the Winnipeg District Chief Factor, John Stuart. She was also the sister of Governor George Simpson's country wife, Margaret. In 1837 Mary joined John Stuart in Scotland but after he reneged on his promise to marry her she returned to Rupert's Land in 1838. Macleod, *The Letters of Letitia Hargrave*, footnote, 20.
83 James Hargrave to John McLeod from York Factory, 12 July 1827. James Hargrave and family fonds, LAC.
84 Smith, "Stuart, John," *DCB*.
85 James Hargrave to John McLeod from York Factory, 8 September 1827. James Hargrave and family fonds, LAC.

Introduction · 37

In 1837 he confided in John Rendall, postmaster at York Factory:

> Private: *Secret & confidential.* By the way being inclined to do a little left hand charity just now I wish you would be my Almoner for the occasion. I have been *obliged* now & then/ any port in a Storm/ by the wife of the poor *indian* who died at the Factory 2 years ago & who this winter lives in the same tent with Outitawas family. This of course must be to you – *no great news,* so I shall not allude further to it than to say that I wish you would take out on my A/ a striped blanket of 2 ½ pts & give it to her from me, with strict injunctions to keep her mouth shut about the person who has been *so charitable*. About ship time next fall should she be then at the Factory, & in want, you can also give her 3 y^{ds} Blue List [cloth] on my a/ to help her to pass the winter. Now this last is really *right-handed charity* as it is given from pure humanity & is liable to no interpretation such as the former. Keep all this to yourself my good fellow – burn this letter – & believe me always Truly & faithfully Yours JH.[86]

Scandalous gossip was a staple of the lives of HBC employees in the isolated outposts of North America. Hargrave claimed, probably with justification, that he was the unfair target of some during his bachelor days. He wrote to Alexander Christie in 1837:

> Friend Ross[87] tells me that my name has got into the public mouth on the subject of women/ the Red River Simoom[88] par excellence/ & that some most disgraceful stories are attributed to me by a Girl whom McDermot[89] carried in to the Colony, in a very irregular manner by the way. All that I have heard are gross falsehoods/ as applicable to me, and as far as my knowledge went – equally so as

---

86 James Hargrave to Jn° Rendall from Norway House, 20 April 1837. James Hargrave and family fonds, LAC.
87 Donald Ross was chief trader at Norway House at the time.
88 Simoom is a strong, hot, sand-laden wind of the Sahara and Arabian deserts. The Arabic meaning is "poison wind" because it may cause heat stroke and has a suffocating effect.
89 Andrew McDermot, 1790–1881, an Irish free trader at Red River and member of the Council of Assiniboia at that time.

regards the Gentlemen who wintered with me.[90] I gratefully thank you for your friendly interference in discouraging this rumour otherwise likely to injure me by the publicity it would give so well suited as it is to the peculiar taste of this colony.[91]

A slanderous tale was again told about Hargrave in 1839 and he wrote concerned letters to two of his HBC colleagues about the matter:

I have lately been extremely annoyed by a matter connected with Red River[92] to adjust which I should feel deeply obliged by either your public Services or private aid. It has just come to my ears that the Fort Garry Cook "Angus"[93] has this spring spread a report that I had seduced Mrs Christies Maid[94] and that he had seen me coming out of her room early in the morning dressed only "in my Shirt & Trousers." This tale in all its parts is purely a *false and slanderous lie*, which as it regards myself I hold in the most supreme contempt, – but is affecting the character of, I firmly believe, a virtuous and modest young woman, I am compelled to notice by requesting that if possible such slander may be legally and [illegible] prevented or that if unhappily it may not be possible to make the case clear according to legal forms I sincerely trust you will agree with me that such a wretch is unworthy to be allowed to

---

90 This seems to suggest that the gossip relates to James's time in Red River in the 1820s before he was appointed to York Factory.
91 James Hargrave to Alexander Christie from Norway House, 8 March 1837. James Hargrave and family fonds, LAC. Hargrave may have wished to enlist Chief Factor Christie in quelling such a rumour before he set off to find himself a respectable wife in Scotland.
92 Hargrave had left York Factory in February 1839 to attend the Northern Department Council meeting in Red River in June. He had returned to York Factory by July of that year.
93 The only "Angus"es listed in the Northern Department Servants' Abstracts for 1838–39 are Angus McDonald and Angus McLeod. B.239/g/18. Angus McDonald (1816–99), from Dingwall, was listed as a general servant, no specific post in York District, with one year's service. He was sent as a general servant to Fort Colvile for 1839–40. Angus McLeod was a labourer with eight years' service at Red River who remained at Red River for 1839–40.
94 The serving maid of the governor of Assiniboia, Alexander Christie.

remain in any place where there are persons whose characters could be injured by his malicious fabrications.[95]

The black story "begotten" this spring at Fort Garry – is I solemnly assure you upon my honor as a gentleman in all its parts is a foul and slanderous lie – having no foundation but the malicious invention of a villain. I myself despise the wretchs story but as it may deeply affect the character of I sincerely and firmly believe, a most virtuous and modest young woman, I have been compelled to apply to our friend Mr Finlayson[96] for legal redress. Mr Christie now informs me that he had searched into the matter before I left and the poor girl felt so indignant at the charge that he could scarcely prevent her setting off forthwith to Mr Logan[97] [who] is a Magistrate to make affidavit as to the gross falsehood of the charge. It besides came out on this examination that the fellow himself (and he owned it) had made unequivocal gross and dishonest proposals which she (and he confessed it) had resisted and complained of to her mistress: in revenge for which it is my sincere opinion the wretch had invented this story in order to ruin her character. I trust however he will yet meet with his reward.[98]

His friend Duncan Finlayson cautioned Hargrave not to sue for slander because, despite her innocence, the publicity "would attach a stain to her character, let it be ever so spotless, that could not easily be washed off."[99] Hargrave took the advice. Within five months, he had married Letitia Hargrave, thus removing the possibility of further such embarrassing gossip.

95 James Hargrave to Duncan Finlayson from York Factory, 2 July 1839. James Hargrave and family fonds, LAC.
96 Duncan Finlayson (c. 1796–1862) was governor of Assiniboia at the time, supervising the Red River community and overseeing HBC interests.
97 Robert Logan (1773–1866) was a fur trader, merchant, and councillor of Assiniboia during his long life. He became a magistrate for the Middle District in 1837 but resigned in 1839 because of ill health.
98 James Hargrave to John Rowand from York Factory, 2 July 1839. James Hargrave and family fonds, LAC.
99 Duncan Finlayson to James Hargrave, 12 August 1839. James Hargrave and family fonds, LAC.

Hargrave's letters to his family also reveal his thoughts on the proper place of women in the home. He wrote to his mother asking her to intervene diplomatically with his father to dissuade him from having his sister Jane working in the fields on the farm.[100] Women's duties, he wrote to Jane, lay in the house rather than in the drudgery of outdoor labour, however poor "the Sex." He did allow that such "half-play" as reaping and making hay should be permitted. He added that "a respectable connection for life" was the important hinge on which the happiness, even use, of female existence depended.[101]

Hargrave was doubtless conditioned by what Jennifer Brown notes as the subordinate protected positions of British women of the period, subjected to rigorous moral standards and expected to be "frail" and properly domestic.[102] Brown argues that by the 1820s much improved communication channels allowed the influences of British culture in both Britain and Canada to reach the fur traders of Rupert's Land in many more ways. Instead of being cut off in the wilderness from their roots in Britain as earlier fur traders had been, they continued to be infused with what later were to be known as distinctively Victorian values and ideas, such as respectability and the importance of upward mobility.

OTHER VOICES

In this volume we hear the voice of one man. How was this man viewed by his contemporaries and others? We have no more than hints in published texts, starting with the Character Book of Governor Simpson quoted above. Author Ken McGoogan, in his book on John Rae, called Hargrave an "aloof, self-contained man." He reported the contemporary description provided by John Sebastian Helmcken, a young ship's surgeon on the *Prince Rupert* which arrived at York Factory. Helmcken wrote that Hargrave was friendly and affable while on board a sailing ship, but "no sooner did he set foot ashore than he became dignified, cold and distant! Like an admiral, who may be pleasant and urbane ashore, but the moment his foot touches the deck, he is the admiral – discipline

---

100 James Hargrave to his mother from York Factory, 1 July 1828. James Hargrave and family fonds, LAC.
101 James Hargrave to Jane Hargrave from York Factory, 1 July 1828. James Hargrave and family fonds, LAC.
102 Brown, *Strangers in Blood*, 151–2.

prevails, and he may or may not be a tyrant. Hargrave was nevertheless kind in his way, but ... he had to go into harness at once."[103] McGoogan also quoted John Rae's letter to Governor George Simpson: "Fortunately, I am under no personal obligation to Mr. Hargrave, he being one of the last persons of my acquaintance from whom I would like to ask a favour. Yet notwithstanding his disagreeable manner, he has a warm and kind heart when his selfishness will permit it." This, McGoogan speculated, may have been related to the handsome Rae's close friendship with Letitia Hargrave. Once Rae was safely away from York Factory, he and Hargrave developed a warm personal relationship.[104]

Another contemporary account by Robert Ballantyne, an HBC clerk from 1841–47, mentioned Hargrave's "benevolent, manly countenance." Ballantyne remembered with gratitude Hargrave's kindness to him at York Factory. Thomas Simpson in 1833 wrote of Hargrave: "a good, able, deep-thinking and deeply-read Scotchman from the banks of the Tweed – my most intimate friend in the country, and likely to become a very leading man."[105]

In 1938, G.P. de T. Glazebrook, the editor of the Hargrave Correspondence,[106] described him thus:

> Though he wrote frequent and affectionate letters to his parents, Hargrave was stationed too far off ever to see much of them again. They had endowed him with good health, intelligence, and a steady – if not overmastering – ambition. A sound education and favourable opportunities combined with this legacy to produce a happy and successful life. Hargrave's own letters are stilted, even for the style of the age; but they are well written and show a wide interest in reading and in politics. His friends – and they were many – addressed him in affectionate terms, and frequently referred to his scholarly tastes, his skill in business, and the certainty of his promotion. He seems to have been on the best of terms with his associates, and to have inspired admiration rather than jealousy, even on the part of those whose lack of education precluded them from the highest offices.

103 McGoogan, *Fatal Passage*, 53.
104 Ibid., 54.
105 Simpson, *Life and Travels*, 83.
106 Glazebrook, *The Hargrave Correspondence*, xvii.

The reader of this volume sees the man through the letters he wrote to his family, faraway friends, and to the fur traders who were to become part of his family upon his marriage in 1840 to Letitia Mactavish. By including all the correspondence to these particular people for the time period 1826–40, this documentary volume gives the reader the opportunity to see how Hargrave presented himself to them over time, what he chose to write about, and how he wrote about it. As Jennifer Brown and Elizabeth Vibert write in their introduction to *Reading Beyond Words*, language is not a neutral medium: the language of any cultural group or social group reflects and helps to constitute that group's view of the world.[107] The modern reader can discern the views of a nineteenth-century Scottish immigrant turned fur trader about his world and his position in it through a careful reading of these letters.

EDITORIAL PROCEDURES

The texts presented here consist of transcriptions of Hargrave's personal correspondence with family and friends in Scotland and Lower Canada as well as with the various Mactavish family members in his draft letterbooks of 1826–40. The originals of these are in Library and Archives Canada, James Hargrave and family fonds, R7784-0-9-E, Series I. These records were received in 1950 from the Champlain Society, which had acquired the papers from a descendant of James Hargrave, Lady Grierson.[108] The correspondence from letterbooks 1 through 15 was selected from copies of the originals on microfilm reels C-80 and C-81. The material is in the public domain. Hargrave's twenty-seven-page 1828–29 journal, located at McGill University, has been added at the end of the letterbooks. His 1820 contract with the North West Company is in the National Archives of Quebec.

Hargrave's handwriting, clear in his early years with the HBC, becomes increasingly difficult to read over time. In the letterbooks he crossed out and inserted words that clarify or alter the meaning of the sentences. I have presented the corrected drafts in this book, deleting the words he crossed out and including the revisions that he made to the original

---

107 Brown and Vibert, *Reading Beyond Words*, xv.
108 Mary Letitia Ogston, the widow of Sir Herbert John Clifford Grierson (1866–1960), a Scottish literary scholar, editor, and critic, was a granddaughter of James Hargrave.

drafts. Those words that are illegible are presented in square brackets as "illegible." Words repeated inadvertently by Hargrave in the draft letters have been deleted here. Dashes used by Hargrave that play no actual role in punctuation have also been deleted. Abbreviated words have been shown in full the first time, with square brackets identifying the missing letters. Individuals are usually identified at the first mention in brief footnotes. For clarity, the first names of individuals may be added in square brackets at the first mention of their surname in subsequent letters. The opening greeting and closing phrases of each letter have been standardized as flush left.

In annotating the text, I have attempted in the footnotes to identify the places, people, and objects referred to without placing an excessive burden on the reader. In order to map out the web of familial and fur trade relationships detailed in the letters of this volume, a family tree has been included. For completeness, it includes the children of James and Letitia, although they had not yet appeared on the scene in the period covered by this book. Their eldest son, Joseph James, followed his father into the fur trade and became a writer who contributed to the history of Rupert's Land.[109]

---

109 The author of *Red River*, published in 1871.

ENGAGEMENT CONTRACT
with the
NORTH WEST COMPANY, 1820

3114. 28th April 1820
Engagement
James Hargrave
    As Clerk
        To
The North West Compy

Before the Undersigned Public Notaries for the province of Lower Canada residing in the City of Montreal.

    Personally appeared James Hargrave, late from Scotland now of Montreal aforesaid Gentleman who declared to have engaged and by these presents doth engage himself in the Capacity of a Wintering Clerk unto Messrs William McGillivray, Simon McGillivray, Archibald Norman McLeod Thomas Thain and Henry McKenzie all of Montreal aforesaid Merchants and Copartners trading together under the name and firm of McTavish McGillivray and Company and the said Thomas Thain and Pierre DeRocheblave Esqrs agents for the North West Company hereto present and accepting to depart from this City at the first requisition of his said Employers & go to the Lake Superior and there winter for and during the term of four years at any post that his said Employers shall or may from time to time during the said term think fit, the said James Hargrave having the priviledge however of coming down to Lower Canada and spending one winter with his relations and again return in the spring following to complete the remainder of the present Engagement which passages shall be furnished by his said Employers free of expense, and the said James Hargrave his said Employers faithfully shall save their Secrets shall keep their lawful Commands at all times willingly do obey and perform to the Utmost of his knowledge skill and abilities, he shall not trade on his own account But shall do every thing to forward and advance the Interest of his said Employers in every respect as far as he may be able, hurt to them he shall not do, nor knowingly suffer to be done by others, from the said Service, he shall not at any time depart or absent himself, but in all things shall and will demean and behave himself faithfully and honorably during the term of these presents.

 The present Engagement is thus made for and in consideration of the Salary of Fifty pounds Currency of the province of Lower Canada per annum which the said McTavish McGillivray and Company and the said North West Company stipulated for as aforesaid do hereby promise to pay or cause to be paid to the said James Hargrave during the said term, also to find and provide him with an equipment yearly such as is generally furnished

to the Gentleman Clerks in the Interior
of the North West for thus &c.

Election of domicile
at the Counting house of the said
McTavish McGillivray & Company
in Montreal Where &c.

Done and passed at
Montreal aforesaid in the office of
Henry Griffin one of the said Notaries the
Twenty eighth day of April in the year of
our Lord one thousand eight hundred
and Twenty in the fore noon and signed
by the said parties with us Notaries after
being duly read

  [Signed]

    Ja^s Hargrave
    Thomas Thain

Thos Barron
 N.P.   H. Griffin
      N.P.

EDITOR'S NOTE[1]

When James Hargrave signed on as a clerk with the North West Company in Montreal at the end of April 1820 he faced a 700-mile journey by canoe to Sault Ste Marie just east of Lake Superior. He would have prepared for the departure that May of a brigade of canoes from Lachine, nine miles from Montreal above the Lachine Rapids. The Montreal canoe or *canot du maître* he would travel in was thirty-five or forty feet long and was used on large rivers like the St Lawrence and on the Great Lakes. The birchbark canoes weighed less than 300 pounds but could carry 1000 pounds of crew and freight. The fourteen-man crew of voyageurs, usually French Canadians but sometimes Iroquois, would include a steersman

---

1 I am indebted to Grace Nute's authoritative account of the French-Canadian voyageurs who guided and paddled the canoes of the fur traders for my reconstruction of Hargrave's journey into fur trade country; see Nute, *Voyageur*, 1955.

who stood in the stern and a bowsman as a guide who used a large paddle when running rapids or leaping small falls.

The canoes had wooden tent poles placed along the bottom to protect the fragile hull. Heavier items were placed on the poles while lighter and regularly used items would be placed on top, the whole being covered by canvas tarps. Hargrave and other passengers would have been offered "seats" in the middle of the canoe, boards suspended on wattup (split spruce root) from the gunwales or thwarts. Because of the fragility of the canoes voyageurs and passengers had to sit for hours in one position without moving their feet, so as not to break the gum which waterproofed the seams of birchbark.

The loaded canoes proceeded up the St Lawrence River to Ste Anne's church, a chapel on the westernmost point of Montreal Island. The voyageurs, clerks, and *bourgeois* all would put coins in the box as offerings to Ste Anne for her protection on the tedious and perilous journey. The route lay along the St Lawrence and up the Ottawa to the Mattawa River, a distance involving eighteen portages and as many *décharges*, where the canoes would be partially unloaded and towed over the falls and rapids. The portages were measured in *posés*, about a third of a mile, the distance the canoes and cargo were carried each leg of the portage. Soon after leaving Ste Anne's, Hargrave as a new clerk would have been "baptized" in the chilly waters unless he offered the men some brandy to help them forget the sorrows of leaving home. The voyageurs sang while paddling and the rhythm of these tunes allowed the paddlers to keep time to the music. They often made a stroke a second and canoes could be propelled at four to six miles an hour in calm water. Headwinds or untoward weather usually put the voyageurs ashore in order to preserve the frail bark of their canoes. Tall wooden crosses on the banks of rivers near dangerous *saults* and rapids were memorials to those who had died.

After ascending the Mattawa River the canoes would have entered Lake Nipissing and exited this by the French River where the current would at last be with the voyageurs rather than against them. On water, the *pipe* was the standard of measurement of distance, being the distance covered between respites when the luxury of resting and smoking was indulged by the voyageurs. The route led to Georgian Bay and Lake Huron to Michillimackinac where a long halt would be made before Hargrave's brigade would continue on to Sault Ste Marie. The canoes that left him there would then continue on over the portage toward Lake Superior and the interior of the North American continent. The following spring of 1821, James departed for Fort William, the hub of the NWC fur trade, on the western end of Lake Superior, a 400-mile canoe trip over the treacherous Great Lake. There he met John George McTavish, the influential Nor'Wester who saw the potential in the raw young clerk. He was retained as clerk following the amalgamation that same year of the NWC and HBC.

Selected Letters from the Letterbooks of James Hargrave

[*Letterbook*]
N[o]. 1
Rough Copies Letters
by JHargrave
From 3rd Jany 1826 @ 24th March 1827

Red R[r] Jany 3rd 1826

My dear Lockie[2]

    I find that should I delay writing you till the receipt of your letter of the ensuing summer I shall run the risk of being obliged to write you in haste or possibly lose the opportunity of addressing you at all this season, I have therefore as last year sat down to file you a sheet at this early date, and shall reply to yours of Feby 1825 – The news it contains of the decease of my early friend D[r] Cavers[3] affects me much. That is one of the first Trials I have yet experienced which serves to wear the heart of man for this state of terrestrial being and invites him to look forward to that portion of time called Eternity "when friends shall be reunited, – and where all tears shall be wiped away from all eyes."[4] Your solicitude after my welfare and your anxious enquiries into the nature of this countrys climate together with the course of life we lead in it is too flattering to me and is made in too friendly a manner to allow me to pass over it. This country is neither blest with the riches or scourged with the diseases incident to a tropical climate. I cannot flatter myself that the splendid career your friendship foretells will ever be realised by me, but should my exertions secure nothing more for declining years than a comfortable competency

---

1 Red River.
2 William Lockie, the former schoolmaster of James Hargrave at Stouslie in Scotland. Stouslie – a farm and cottages – housed a school administered by Wilton Parish in one of the cottages. Scott, *Hawick Word Book*, 723, 1166.
3 According to James Hargrave's Journal of 1828–29 (see below), this was Walter Cavers, of Leehead, who had studied medicine and left Scotland for the West Indies as a surgeon about the same time as James departed for Canada. He prospered in Jamaica but died less than three years after settling there.
4 "And God shall wipe away all tears from their eyes; and there shall be no more death, neither sorrow, nor crying, neither shall there be any more pain: for the former things are passed away." *King James Bible*, Revelation 21:4.

yet I trust the course of life I lead in procuring it will secure to me a hale old-age to allow me to enjoy the fruits of my present occupations. My residence for six years since I entered the Indian Country has been about Latitude 45°30' north and west Longitude [blank].[5] This you will perceive by consulting any large map of this portion of the continent and when you point your finger to Lake Winipeg[6] upon it & pick out at its southern end the mouth of Red River you will then be able to trace for yourself my annual motions much better than I can describe them. Our habits of life are in general of the most healthy description. Gentle exercises at a Trading Estab[lishmen]*t* during the winter & traveling in Boats or Canoes during the summer[7] form the principal varieties in our Year and our simple style of living combined with the few temptations to Excesses of any description is a pretty sure guarantee to my "Corporal Permanency." Not but that we sometimes stick a little longer to our Wine than what the strict rules of Sobriety will allow and to confess the *whole* truth, on such occasions of *St. Andrews* Day, Christmas, New-Year &*c* our Port or Madeira stand a regular siege and it generally requires wiser heads than our own on such evenings to find out the way from our dining room – to our beds. These scenes however occur so seldom (not more than twice or thrice a year) that even in point of health they do us I am apt to believe more good than harm, as a tempest serves to purify the atmosphere. I am inclined to look upon such scenes with the more indulgence as Spirituous Liquors are never tasted by us. Whisky is out of the question none being ever imported, and rum is entirely left to the men – for a Gentleman in the Service to get drunk on Spirits is considered actual degradation and would affix a Stigma on his name which all subsequent efforts could never thoroughly efface. This feeling which is inoculated into all who enter the country arises from liquor forming an article of Traffic and as this Goods

---

5 Present day Winnipeg, located at 49°53'N and 97°09'W, lies at the confluence of the Red and Assiniboine Rivers on the site of Fort Garry, a Hudson's Bay Company trading post which was established in 1822 to serve as the centre of the fur trade within the Red River Settlement. Hargrave would seem to be rather uncertain about his location.

6 Charles Bell notes various spellings for Lake Winnipeg in printed works up until 1833 when the current spelling became fixed. Bell, *Historical Names and Places*.

7 Hargrave speaks with some nonchalance about the challenges of his yearly 700-mile trips to and from York Factory.

for the Trade comes completely under the control of the different Officers in the country, should they not be restrained by some other principle more strong than merely a dislike to liquor many would in the lonely lives they lead be induced to divert the tedium with a glass which insensibly would lead to habits of dissipation and consequently to much serious loss & neglect in the co[mpan]ys affairs. Our provisions in general are what you would consider delicacies – Fresh Buffalo, Deer,[8] and Fowl also plenty of excellent fish with a more sparing proportion of European Luxuries such as Sugar, Tea, Fruit, Wines, Flour &^{c} – This simple & nourishing diet combined with the excellence of the climate (than which I have never experienced a more salubrious, my native one not excepted) renders our lives unusually healthy, and I scarcely can say that I have ever had an hours sickness for these Six Years bygone – Our clothing differs little from the European Fashion on the main though Strangers find many points in it which attract observation. Our formal dress is the Coys Uniform differing little from that of an Officer in the British Navy, but on the voyage and at the wintering Establishments we dress in general according to our own Tastes, but always plainly & warmly. We in general wear Arms more especially on the Voyage when a brace of Pistols and a Short, broad Straight hanger or "Couteau de Chase"[9] form our constant companions both for defence & amusement.

To your inquiries after the system of our trade I can scarcely return you an explicit answer without devoting an entire sheet to it. The following are a few of its outlines. The European Goods required for it are annually sent out from London to the different Factories on the Coast of Hudsons Bay[10] and consist chiefly of Coarse Cloths, Blankets, Clothing, Guns, Ammunition, Iron works, Kettles, Trinkets, Tobacco & Liquor which are every summer shared at the Factories among the Districts into which the whole Country is divided, and is sent inland in the Craft which come to the coast with the Furs Traded during the bygone Winter. Every District is under the superintendance of a Factor, the highest rank to be attained in this country, and on him devolves all the responsibility of the business transacted in it. The Districts are again subdivided into smaller portions called Outposts for the convenience under the charge of Clerks who every

8 HBC men called Lowland Caribou deer.
9 "Couteau de chasse" means a hunting knife.
10 Hudson's Bay was named after its discoverer, Henry Hudson. Modern usage drops the "'s" to give "Hudson Bay."

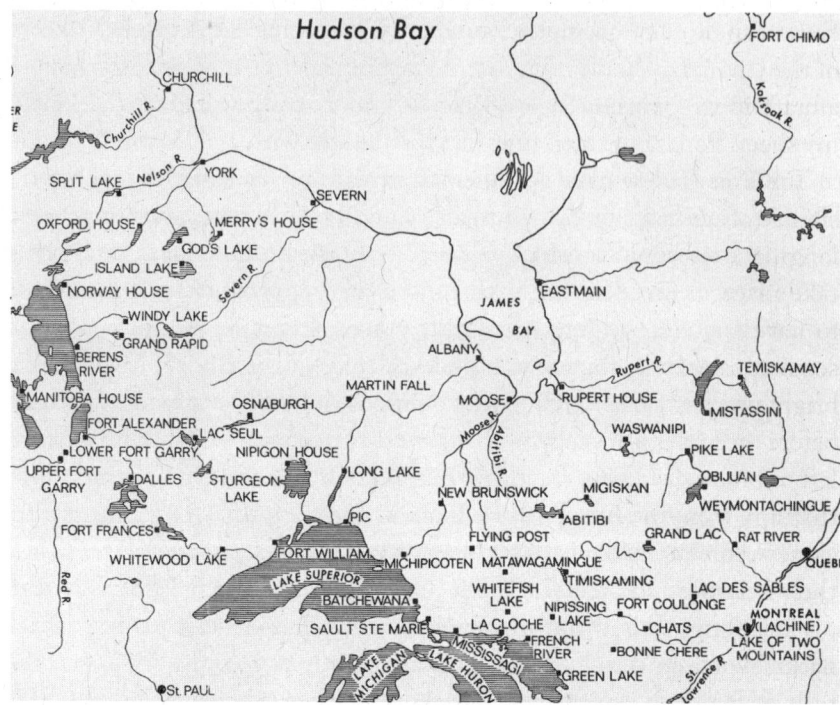

Part of a map showing the location of York Factory and some other HBC posts, 1832. It includes the area between Montreal and York Factory that Hargrave would have traversed during his career with the HBC. Courtesy of the Hudson's Bay Company Archives (HBCA), Archives of Manitoba, The Hudson's Bay Record Society 30, end map, N 8139.

Autumn receive at the principal Establishment from the Factor a supply of the goods brought in by him, and which it is the duty of the Clerk to exchange in Barter with the Indians immediately around his post for the Skins of the Animals which they procure by hunting during the Winter. The Barter is conducted in this manner. A Beaver Skin is the Standard and other skins are valued in proportion, such as 2 martins make 1 Beaver, 2 red foxes 1 beaver, 10 muskrats 1 beaver – also 1 Silver Fox=2 beaver, 1 Sea Otter=4 Beaver &^{c} and the Goods are also valued accordingly – i.e. a blanket of a fathom in length = 6 Beaver or 60 Muskrats, a Gun = 12 beaver, or 6 Silver Foxes, or 3 Sea Otters – &^{ccc}. The Trade is beneficial to all parties as the Indian supports his family on the carcass of the Animals he kills, clothes and ornaments them with bartering these skins for

European production whilst the White by bringing them to the Markets of the Civilized World realizes a most lucrative profit. This hasty glance I am afraid will scarcely be intelligible to you but I can spare it no more of my sheet. For more particular information see McK.

The hints I may have hitherto dropt in my correspondence of a possibility of my visiting Britain again may be interpreted rather as a heart longing after my native Land than as conveying any hope that this will take place, at least for many years to come. When I allow my feelings to have any voice in judging of this question an affirmative is the consequence, but when brought to the bar of reason and probability, – the bright prospects of imagination die away, a long and uncertain course lies before me and under this conviction these fond breathings of the heart are left to pine away under the sickness of hope long deferred. I cannot think that any who leave their native Land after coming to years of maturity can ever divest themselves of the ties which are insensibly wound round their hearts by the recollections of "early loves & friendships." Tis true my relations are now in Canada and a wish to visit that country is the natural consequence, but when I ask myself where is my Home – the blue hills of Scotland are present in my mind with all their attractions. My future situation in this country I have reason to believe, will ere long be at a great distance from where I presently am. An opportunity of distinguishing oneself in the service is of course the ruling principle of every one ambitious of promotion in it, – and as there is at present an opening on the other side of this continent I have volunteered my services to go next season to Fort Vancouver on the Shores of the Pacific. At that place there is every chance of seeing something of the world, a trip to the Sandwich Islands, a voyage to Canton in China, or a coasting Tour down along the shores of Spanish Main, would be extremely interesting, and to procure the situation of Super-Cargo for instance in any of the Coys Coasting Vessels would I flatter myself be far from difficult. All this I must however own is only an *air built castle*, the great difficulty to surmount is the getting rid of my present situation, where from the number of years I have filled it, I am considered more intimately acquainted with Colonial affairs and off course more fit for transacting them than any stranger who might succeed me. This I believe will eventually prove a stumbling block to my scheme; tho my offer of services on the Columbia was most flatteringly received, yet this difficulty was mentioned to me as one hard to get rid of – Next June will however bring the matter to the test. At all events address me by letter exactly as heretofore, all communications to my address when sent to York Factory being sure of reaching me in whatever part of the country I may be.

JHargrave

I Closed at YF – in
August or Sept[r] 1826

York Factory 5th September 1826

Rev[d] W. Rattray[11]
Private   Rev[d] & Dear Sir

The ship[12] from England not yet having made her appearance, and expecting soon to set out on my voyage for the interior, I do myself the pleasure of leaving a few lines in the London Packet[13] for you which will

---

11 Reverend William Rattray (1791–1851) was ordained a minister in 1815 and after serving in Coupar-Angus and Moniaive became the first and only minister of a second United Associate Congregation in Selkirk. This congregation originated with members of the congregation of Midholm living in the parishes of Selkirk and Yarrow who wished to have a more convenient place of worship. Rev. Rattray resigned in 1825 from this office. In 1830 he became the first United Secession minister of the Ebenezer chapel at Swalwell, in Whickham Parish, Northumberland, England, where he served for twenty years. Information obtained from Helen Elliot, secretary of the Old Gala Club in Galashiels, Scotland, e-mail messages to editor, 29 August, 30 August, and 12 September 2006.

12 The *Prince of Wales* was one of the HBC ships that sailed annually between England and Hudson Bay. The fleet of two or more ships sailed from the Orkneys to Cape Farewell, Greenland, and then through the narrow, ice-filled Hudson Strait, hugging the north shore to avoid the worst drift ice. Once through the strait, the ships broke convoy at Mansel Island and proceeded either southward to James Bay or westward to Churchill and York Factory. Catchpole and Moodie, "Archive," 128. The *Prince of Wales*, under Capt. John Davison, arrived 7 September at York Factory after leaving London 30 May and departed from York Factory 20 September arriving back in London 26 October. Houston et al., *Naturalists*, 153.

13 A parcel or package of instructions, correspondence, or other documents. Packets were sent on HBC ships to fur-trading posts each spring from

be forwarded should the vessel arrive this season. It is with a grateful heart to the Supreme Ruler of events that I am enabled to say I have enjoyed the best of health since I wrote you last season, and that I have been preserved in a course of life peculiarly exposed to danger while many around me – several under my own eyes – have been untimely summoned to their last awful account. This last year in the part of the country where I past the winter has been marked with a series of hardship and misfortunes – such indeed as has not been experienced by the oldest inhabitants. Around the Colony of Red River for many 100 miles the face of the country is perfectly level (bearing evident marks indeed of having been once covered with water) and to the South, West, and North as far as the sources of the Mississouri,[14] and up to the very base of the Rocky Mountains, entirely clear of timber – and is thickly covered with immense herds of Buffalo which pasture in these extensive plains. In the neighbourhood of Red River these animals form the entire subsistance of a large body of people denominated Freemen chiefly composed of Canadians[15] and Half breeds[16] – who live by the chase – and from their attachment to a wandering life could never be prevailed upon to settle themselves in the Colony. From some unknown cause the Cattle[17] entirely deserted that part of the country in the commencement of winter, the season proved unseasonably severe, and the wretched freemen about the beginning of February found themselves upwards of 200 miles from the nearest Settlement without the means of moving from their Encampments. To support their lives they had eaten up their horses and dogs – vainly hoping that the cattle would still make their appearance, – till driven to the utmost extremity those who were capable of walking set out for the Settlement,[18] many of them through the strong impulse of self-preservation forsaking their families or leaving their aged Parents or

---

the Governor and Committee in London. Packets destined for London returned by ship in the fall. They were transported in packet boxes, which were wooden boxes that could be locked for security.

14 "Mississouri" was an early nineteenth-century spelling of the Missouri river.
15 French-speaking *Canadiens* from Lower Canada.
16 Children of mixed marriages of Europeans and Natives.
17 Refers to buffalo or bison.
18 Red River Settlement.

younger relations to their fate. On the news of these misfortunes reaching the HB Coys Fort[19] in the Colony every exertion was used to rescue them from their desperate circumstances, and so prompt and efficacious were the measures adopted by M[r] McKenzie[20] the Coys Factor that upwards of 500 lives were saved which without such assistance would certainly have been lost. The Protestant clergymen Mess[rs] Jones[21] & Cockran[22] – likewise the Catholic bishop the R[t] Rev[d] J.N. Provencher[23] were most active in their benevolent exertions – Subscriptions of money and grain were raised among their respective congregations and through their united zeal many were also snatched from the Jaws of destruction. From the most correct accounts we could procure not above 15 perished from hunger and the severity of the season. Many of the poor creatures arrived at the Coys Fort utterly incapable of walking – some with Frozen feet, others so emaciated that they looked like shadows rather than men.

19   Fort Garry.
20   Donald McKenzie (1783–1851) was made a chief factor in the HBC in 1821 and was sent in 1823 by Gov. George Simpson to restore order to the company's affairs in the Red River Settlement. His "firmness, sound judgment and energy" were credited by Simpson with mitigating the devastating effects of the flood of 1826. Van Kirk, "McKenzie, Donald."
21   David Thomas Jones (c. 1796–1844) was a Church of England missionary who succeeded John West in 1823 as the Anglican missionary and HBC chaplain at Red River. Jones and his co-worker, the Reverend William Cockran, were both low Church, and eventually modified their liturgy to attract Red River's Presbyterian, Gaelic-speaking settlers. Johnson and Bredin, "Jones, David Thomas."
22   William Cockran (1796/7–1865), the third Church Missionary Society missionary to be sent to Rupert's Land, arrived at the Red River Settlement in 1825. The principal challenge facing Jones and Cockran was the evangelization of the large numbers of country-born descendants of British fur traders, largely Orkneymen, and native people, migrating from the trading posts of the interior to Red River after the amalgamation of the HBC and the North West Company in 1821. Foster, "Cockran, William."
23   Joseph-Norbert Provencher (1787–1853), a Roman Catholic priest, had been sent by Joseph-Octave Plessis, the bishop of Quebec, in 1818 to establish the Roman Catholic church at Red River. In 1822, as there was yet no diocese in the northwest, he was consecrated titular bishop of Juliopolis, the former episcopal see of Galatia (located in what is modern-day Turkey). Lemieux, "Provencher, Joseph-Norbert."

Only known sketch of the 1826 flood at Red River. The flood was one of the most devastating in the history of the settlement. Pencil on paper sketch by Peter Rindisbacher. Courtesy of Glenbow Museum, 58.42.18.

Groups were to be met on the roads to the settlement where the husband utterly helpless was dragged along on a piece of Buffalo Hide by a Starving dog – followed by the wife all in rags and carrying in her arms a wretched baby wrapped up in a tattered Blanket – and half dead with cold & hunger. Indeed I never witnessed such scenes of human misery, – yet happy would it have been had their calamities ended here – but it pleased Providence to try them still further – and to spread its trials through a wider circuit. From the end of October till the middle of April the rivers and Lakes are in these latitudes frozen up and the ground covered with snow generally upwards of a foot deep. This last season the fall of snow was extraordinarily heavy and no general thaw was experienced till after the beginning of May, at which period the weather changed suddenly – a powerful sun in a few days converted the immense body of snow that covered the face of the country into water which pouring into the river all at once, tore up & bore away the ice upwards of 12 feet thick – finally overflowed its banks more than 20 ft high and the whole of the settlers Houses which were built along the banks for about 20 miles – became a prey to its devastations. The body of the Stream was covered with masses of ice mingled with wrecks of houses and household furniture, while the wretched proprietor took refuge with his family in woods that border the River. With the assistance of Canoes some might have saved themselves from the increasing flood – their cattle however must have perished – had not fortunately 8 or 10 large Craft belonging to the Coy – (which had been newly repaired for the annual voyage to the Coast on the opening of the navigation) – been at Fort Garry & were immediately employed in removing those that were in danger to the higher parts of the neighbourhood. So sudden indeed was the rising of the waters that I recollect one morning of going with 3 Boats[24] to the assistance of about 60 families & 200 head of cattle enclosed on little more than an acre of ground and who the evening previous had considered themselves in perfect safety. By incessant exertions day & night in about one week the whole of the population were removed to a spot the highest within our knowledge & which on the water attaining its height was not above 1 ½ feet above the surface of the Stream. The whole face of the country as far as the eye could reach was an universal lake – many of the inhabitants had been taken from the trees or from Scaffolds erected among the branches – yet amidst all this devastation not a single life was lost. The loss of property has been immense, – to many irreparable, – our old servants who retired from the service to the Colony having laid out their little all in establishing themselves comfortably, – and thus in one instant have seen the fruits of a long servitude in the Indian Country swept from their grasp. So universal indeed has been the ruin that when I left the Settlement on the beginning of June from the forks of the Red & Assiniboine Rivers to Lake Winipeg the most thickly inhabited part of the Colony I counted only 29 houses or rather ruins – all the rest had been swept away. I am since informed that on the waters abating the greater part of the settlers have left the Colony for Up Can[a] & the U.S. totally disheartened with their loss, and that those who remain only do so to make preparations for their departure also. Dreadful as this visitation has been, – yet it is mercy itself compared with what has been experienced among the American & Indian Settlements on the Mississouri. By recent

24 These "freight" or "inland" boats for nearly half a century from the establishment of the Red River Settlement in 1812 formed the backbone of the HBC inland network. They were more seaworthy than canoes, with twice the carrying capacity. Later in the 1800s, they would be known as "York boats." Dennis Johnson, *York Boats*, 3, 30.

advices from thence we are informed that the whole of the Mandan Villages established on that River and composed of indians who had applied themselves to cultivation and who were making rapid advances in civilization under the benevolent superintendance of American Citizens – have been swept away by the height to which that river rose, & that the greater part of the inhabitants had perished. An American Military Establishment at the Falls of St. Anthony on that River has likewise been swept away – the whole Garrison – about 60 Souls being also drowned. These accounts add that the total number of lives lost in that quarter is about 2000. I do not place implicit reliance on the above melancholy information although; the gentleman from whom I had it had no doubt regarding the fact, – one thing however I fear is but too true, that that place has suffered still more than the Colony of Red River in consequence of the greater magnitude of the Mississouri, and the same level surface which also distinguishes that tract of country. High the waters there must have been, as many accounts united in saying that it was from the immense overflow of the Mississouri and the falling of a portion of its waters into the Assiniboine & Red Rivers, which raised the latter to the destructive height they attained last spring.

Our promising little School for Native Children in Red River[25] I much fear will be endangered by these calamities which have swept that country, as, should the Colony be broken up, the Missionaries may possibly be removed to some other quarter where the Natives can in general benefit more generally by their labours than what the few wandering families around Lake Winipeg can possibly do; in which case a number of the children will be withdrawn by their Indian relations, and thus the dawn which has opened on their minds be again quenched in the darkness of Indian Superstitions. Anxiously do I hope that the propitious beginning which has been already made among the surrounding tribes may be carried on to the eternal benefit of succeeding Generations, and that the light which yet glimmers in a corner may, under the blessing of the Almighty, ere long with heavenly brightness spread its healing rays through the palpable darkness which yet broods over this Northern Continent. Numerous Tribes yet unknown & unheard of by Christian Europe, cover the

---

25 The school was established in 1820 by John West, HBC chaplain and Church of England missionary, the first Protestant missionary to tour Rupert's Land.

North West of America, extensive tracts, yet unexplored even by the venturous Canoe of the Trader, are covered with human beings who have never looked upon the face of a White, what a field does not this open to those who like Brainerd[26] can leave every enjoyment which this world possesses so that they may win Souls to Christ. The prosperous beginning made among the South Sea Islands shews the advantage arising from a previous unacquaintance with Europeans and how much deeper root the seed of salvation takes in the heart when that is the first present made by their white brethren to these children of simplicity – Much information I trust will be given to the world regarding these unknown corners of this continent by the enterprising traveler Capt Franklin[27] who is now on a voyage of discovery from the mouth of McKenzies[28] River to the westward towards Icy Cape. All that country beyond the Rocky Mountains as far south as the Columbia River is little known even to our Traders and with the North & West Coast between McKenzies River & Nootka Sound we are utterly Strangers. The Russians have indeed Settlements in Norfolk Sound & entered their trade for some distance inland but never so far as ever to be met with by the HB Coys servants. The Natives are numerous, stationary, and collected in Villages, advantages to a Missionary not to be found on this side the Continent. To the east of the Rocky Mountains the condition of the Natives both in a temporal and moral point of view is rapidly improving. The Coys attention to their comforts is most praiseworthy – necessaries of life such as clothing & ammunition being given gratis to such as are not capable of paying for these indispensible articles, – and that great bane of indian morals – liquor has been gradually diminished till this season a resolution has

---

26 David Brainerd (1718–47), a Presbyterian missionary to the Seneca and Delaware Indians of New York, New Jersey, and Pennsylvania, who gained posthumous fame through the publication of his diary by Jonathan Edwards, the Massachusetts religious philosopher.

27 Sir John Franklin (1786–1847), a naval officer, Arctic explorer, and author. In 1826, on the second of two overland Arctic expeditions, he and his party explored 370 miles of uncharted coast west of the Mackenzie River delta. Impeded by ice and fog, they covered little more than half the distance to Icy Cape before Capt. Franklin decided that, with winter approaching and his men suffering from exposure, he had no safe choice but to return. Holland, "Franklin, Sir John."

28 Mackenzie River.

been past by the Council at this place that *none* be ever after sent into the interior beyond Lake Winipeg even for the Coys Servants. As an article of Trade however great the sacrifice to them as merchants it is utterly abolished throughout the country. These are no small beginnings, – I hope yet to be able to write hereafter still more cheering news

It grieves me to say that I have not this season received any letters from my parents through some mistake in the Montreal Packet. I am under much anxiety at this disappointment but trust for the best. They are now both aged and it melts me to think we must soon sunder on this side the grave. Soon may we be divided, – I firmly trust however it is only for a season, – to meet again in a state of being where anxieties are at an end and where all tears shall be wiped away from off all eyes. May god bless & preserve you my dear Sir is the sincere prayer of yours most truly

JHargrave

P.S. Should you favor me with a Sheet next Spring please write about the beginning of February by which means your letter will reach London and be forwarded by the Packet via Canada which takes its departure from England about the latter end of that month. It will consequently reach me on Lake Winipeg or at this place in June.
JH

York Factory – Hudsons Bay
6th Sept – 1826

Private
M^r. Jas. Mitchel[29]
Dear Uncle,

The vessel from London which brings out this place every summer the Goods required for the Indian Trade and by which we hear from our friends in England, not having yet made her appearance, and being in daily expectation of setting out on my voyage to the interior of the Country – I leave a few lines in the Packet for you which will be forwarded should the Vessel arrive. I have the satisfaction to say that I still enjoy

---

29 James Mitchell, an uncle of James Hargrave through marriage to his mother's sister, resided in Galashiels, Selkirkshire, Scotland. A Mitchell is listed as blacksmith and farrier in Galashiels in the *Combined Pigot's Directory of Scotland 1825/6*.

excellent health, and tho' not making Gold "in goupins"[30] am perfectly content with my share of the good things of this life. My income admits of my indulging every innocent wish, and of laying by now and then an odd hundred or two, which, should I be spared, will help to lay me snugly up in a quiet corner when I return an old & weather beaten Bachelor to Scotland some 10 or 15 years hence. A Bachelor I yet am, – and till I see the fair haired lasses of Scotland again a Bachelor I am determined to remain, – tho' when that time comes I fear these giddy nymphs that skip about my native vallies will be apt to turn up their pretty noses and tell me my day for catching their fancies is gone bye – that I scent of the Wigwam and have forgot how to court them in Broad Scotch. Well after all, – such treatment will only be what I may merit for deserting them in my youth and after traveling over half America without finding a face or mind to my fancy try for coming back perhaps "twa-fauld o'er a rung"[31] to throw myself upon their compassion, – and beg them "for pities sake to take me." – But leaving jesting to one side let me look about me for some news worth sending to you from this distant country tho' these I believe are extremely scanty. What is it to you whether few or many Beavers be caught in such a District – what the hunting of Buffalo or Bears, or what,

30 As much as can be held in two hands when placed together, a "double" handful, and extended to indicate a considerable quantity, especially in phrase *gowd in gowpens*. *Dictionary of the Scots Language (DSL)*. Sir Walter Scott, one of Hargrave's favourite authors, refers to "gowd in goupins" in *St. Ronan's Well*, an 1823 novel in the Waverley series. Or Hargrave may have known of a Mother Goose rhyme *If I had gold in goupins*.
   If I had gold in goupins,
   If I had money in store,
   If I had gold in goupins,
   My laddie should work no more.
   He should have a maid to wait upon him,
   Another to curl his hair;
   He should have a man to buckle his shoe,
   And then he should work no mair.

31 "Twa-fauld o'er a rung" means "doubled over a staff." DSL. The Scottish poet Allan Ramsay (1686–1758) imitated an ode of Horace in his poem *An Ode to the Ph – – (1721)*:
   Be sure ye dinna quat the Grip
   Of ilka Joy when ye are young,
   Before auld Age your Vitals nip,
   And lay ye twafald o'er a Rung.

whether the profits of our Trade be increased or diminished, – yet when I cast my eye over the "uncoes"[32] I have to narrate – the subjects of Duty – Sport or Interest comprehend all that furnishes what we call *news* in this extensive Wilderness. No doubt were I comfortably seated by your fire side with a smoking bowl of good Punch between us I would spin a yarn which would run through many a December evening and of which your incredulous "lugs"[33] would not believe one half of the ferlies[34] which should compose it, – yet unfortunately for my correspondents when I sit down to attempt committing these "hair breadth escapes by flood & field"[35] to paper – infallibly the whole scene shifts from before my minds eye & I can think only of the days when I used to ramble about Galashiels Hill or "dander"[36] about the banks of the Tweed with my fishing rod or a Book. Indeed so much does my fancy run upon these times which are gone bye – that were I to pay a visit to Scotland again I would certainly be found by the side of some of my favorite eddies for trout, – or possibly be even so foolish as to trust my now somewhat bulky carcass on a pair of stilts though a sound ducking should be the consequence.

I am sorry that I cannot give you any news of my old parents this season – their letters of last spring not having through some mischance come to hand. This is the first year since I entered the Indian Country that I have not heard from them, and were it not that there is every probability of their letters having been left in Montreal by oversight I should be apprehensive about their welfare. Indeed no letters from any of my relations in Canada have reached me this summer which leaves me entirely in the dark as to their health & circumstances. I believe I mentioned in my letter to you from this place last year that Joseph & Ruther[37] were settled in the State of New York and were getting on tolerably well. I have never received a single letter from either of them however therefore

32 Scots for news. DSL.
33 Scots for ears. DSL.
34 Scots for unusual or strange sights; wonders or marvels; novelties or curiosities. DSL.
35 James appears to be making a reference to Shakespeare's *Othello*, i, 3:
    Wherein I spake of most disastrous chances,
    Of moving accidents by flood and field,
    Of hair-breadth 'scapes i' th' imminent deadly breach.
36 Scots for to stroll, to saunter, to walk aimlessly, idly, or uncertainly, to wander. DSL.
37 Joseph and Ruther Hargrave were James's two older half-brothers, the sons of Joseph Hargrave and his first wife, Janet Rutherford. Joseph was born in

cannot speak with any certainty as for their affairs. John & Andrew[38] are now tall lads, steady, and will in time should they be spared become wealthy independent farmers as these things go in Canada. Poor fellows! I trust they will prosper as they have been dutiful children to our old parents, – and now manage to perform all the labours about the farm, the old folks (as well they may) sitting quietly down to enjoy the fruits of their by-past toils. Marys marriage I have also mentioned. Her Husband is a respectable young fellow and they are prospering extremely well.[39] Jane by her last letters was still single – tho' if I be well read in female epistles would appear by hers to have little objections to change her name also.[40]

Please present my love to my Aunt my Cousins and my venerable Grandmother should she still be spared among you. My Cousin Alexander[41] I trust is now a skilful workman and is getting on well. I hope my fair Cousin Effy[42] has this year favored me again with a postscript to your letter. I am afraid she would consider my letters dear of postage else I should have given her a sheet also. I certainly would be glad to draw her into a correspondence as from the neat specimen she gave me last year I should be highly delighted with her descriptions of little chit chat occurrences in your neighbourhood. Let her letters even be half filled with questions about this country I would cheerfully answer them all for the pleasure of hearing about what only young minds can think of – yet which are the dearest news from my native land. God bless you all my dear friends & believe me yours affectionately

JHargrave

    1785 and Ruther in 1788. After Janet Rutherford's death, Joseph Hargrave Sr married Jane Melrose around 1797.
38 John and Andrew Hargrave were James Hargrave's two younger brothers, born in 1806 and 1808, respectively, in Roxburghshire, Scotland.
39 James Hargrave's sister, Mary, was born in 1800 in Roxburghshire, Scotland, and married James Ross at Beechridge, Lower Canada, in 1823.
40 Jane Hargrave, James's younger sister, was born in 1805 in Roxburghshire, Scotland, and remained unmarried.
41 Alexander Mitchell was the son of James Mitchell.
42 James Hargrave refers to his cousin, Euphemia Mitchell, as Effy and Euphie. She was the sister of Alexander. In his 1828–29 Journal, Hargrave mentions that Euphie is yet unmarried and is living as nursery-maid in the family of his former teacher, Robert Fyshe, in Galashiels.

3 January 1826 – 24 March 1827 · *67*

Fort Garry[43] 4th Dec[r] 1826

J.G. M[c]Tavish[44] Esq[ui][r][e] &[ccc]
Sir

Herewith enclosed I beg leave to hand you the Req[uisitio][n] for Red River Outfit 1827[45] which has been made out with much care and is considered by M[r] M[c]K.[46] as not more [than] equal to the wants of the Colony for ensuing season. I also enclose you a Statement of our freight Account as far as it is applicable to York Store which may probably be useful previous to the arrival of the Accounts in the spring. I notice P[er] the Invoices forwarded last summer a charge of 3 Jars Linseed Oil 3 Gall[ons]. ea[ch]. which through some oversight have not been sent. These you will perceive I have included in our charge against Y[ork]F[actory] – also 5 P[iece][s47] blue corded Strouds[48] furnished A Nolin[49] upon your order. M[r]

43 Fort Garry was built around 1821 at the forks of the Assiniboine and Red Rivers. It was demolished after the flood of 1826 and replaced in 1831 by Lower Fort Garry. Subsequently an Upper Fort Garry was built in 1835 at the site of the old Fort Garry.

44 John George McTavish (Mactavish) (c. 1778–1847) was made chief factor at York Factory in 1821 at the union of the Hudson's Bay Company and the North West Company. He was the son of the impoverished last chief of Clan Tavish and was recruited into the North West Company in 1798 by a distant relative, Simon McTavish, whose spelling of his last name he adopted. Van Kirk, "McTavish, John George."

45 A requisition or order for goods to be supplied from London via York Factory. An outfit year ran from 1 June to 31 May.

46 Donald McKenzie (1783–1851) was Governor of Assiniboia at this time.

47 A "piece" was a ninety-pound bundle used to transport goods in the fur trade. Voyageurs typically carried two at a time but would sometimes manage three or even four. They were attached to a band around the forehead and supported on the backs of the voyageurs.

48 A coarse woolen cloth used in trade with the Natives.

49 Augustin Nolin was the Metis son of Jean Baptiste Nolin (1742–1826), an old Indian trader who in 1819 had sold his home, buildings, and property at Sault Ste Marie and moved to Red River where Selkirk had promised free land and discounted trade goods to him. Jean Baptiste Nolin was given three choice pieces of land in Assiniboia; his son, Augustin Nolin, received one and his son Louis was on the payroll as interpreter. Augustin Nolin was one of a handful of private traders who were in effect licensed by the HBC during the 1820s and 1830s as the company found them useful for the conduct and servicing of its own business. Robert Coutts, *Road to the Rapids*, 80.

Fort Garry, ca 1822. It was built at the forks of the Assiniboine and Red Rivers. Pen and ink on paper, mounted on cardboard, by Peter Rindisbacher. Courtesy of Glenbow Museum, 58.42.4.

Logan[50] has been supplied at this place with 4 kegs Dem[erar]^a Spirits 9 1/8 Gall ea = 36 ½ Gall. That Gentleman has been charged here with the kegs, filling &^{c} also the freight – and the Rum has been charged against YF which quantity you will please take for the Coy out of that be[l]onging to M^r L[ogan]. in your Stores. Mr Nolin states that he is charged at YF with 5 kegs Gunpowder which he did not receive, and has requested me to mention this in order that it might be rectified.

50 Robert Logan (1773–1866) was a fur trader who had left the employ of both the NWC and the HBC before settling in Red River as a merchant by the 1820s. In 1823 he was appointed a councillor of Assiniboia and in 1825 he purchased a windmill which powered the first grist mill in the Colony. Over the years he engaged in the wholesale trade, was an outfitter to the fur brigades, and became one of the busiest importers in the district. Rea, "Logan, Robert."

Through some mistake last fall the whole of the Goods sent up on frat [freight] P Swan River Boats to be stored at Norway House has been forwarded to this place with the exception of 2 P[s.] These Goods consisting of the following articles

  10 Bags Ball
  5 "   B Shot
  10 "   BB d[o]
  24 Kegs Gunpowder
   & 19 Rolls Twist Tobacco

———

in all 68 P[s] have been safely placed in Depot here and will be sent out next spring to Norway House by the very earliest opportunity

With much respect
I remain Sir
Your Mo[st] Ob[edien]t. H[um]ble Servt
JHargrave

            Fort Garry 4[th] Dec[r] 1826

J.G. M[c]Tavish Esq[r]
Private
Dear Sir

 Having finished every thing in the way of business that occurs to me as of importance to send you P the packet I now do myself the pleasure of running you over a few pages composed of whatever I think would interest you to inquire about were I personally smoking a pipe for an hour with you by your fireside at York. Our voyage hither was expeditious and agreeable. The weather fine, a good crew, and, thanks to you, abundance of most excellent cheer. We reached this on the 16th Oct[r] and landed our passenger the Divine[51] in high good humour. Both Finlayson[52] and I

---

51 Reverend David Jones was the passenger in the boat which was manned by five men from the MacKenzie's River District. HBCA B235/a/8.

52 Duncan Finlayson (c. 1796–1862) was an HBC clerk at Red River from 1826 to 1831. His career with the HBC spanned 44 years after he sailed from Orkney in 1815 with his brother Nicol. He was a favorite of Governor George Simpson, married Simpson's sister-in-law, and rose to be the governor of Assiniboia. He combined a high standard of personal conduct with a sincere concern for the Native peoples in Rupert's Land. Friesen, "Finlayson, Duncan."

John George McTavish, 1821. The HBC chief factor took Hargrave under his wing and mentored his future nephew-in-law for many years. Courtesy of Archives of Manitoba, MacTavish, John George 1 Collection, N12800.

made it a point to show him the utmost deference, and attention; and altho' we had both occasion to draw largely on our patience at times, yet I am happy to say our stock never failed us, – and for once I flatter myself I succeeded in pleasing him.

We found on arrival the Colony completely recovered from the Inundations of last spring. The Scotch & Blues[53] who now compose almost the whole of the inhabitants had all their houses rebuilt – all was quietness and good fellowship, and I will say it without even meaning a compliment to any one that the prudence and judgment with [which] affairs are now conducted here has left the Coy almost without a single enemy within the bounds of the Colony.[54] The harvest of course could not be expected to be productive. Wheat was blasted by frosts in September, but Barley

53 The "Blues" was a term frequently used at Red River to refer to retired fur trade officers and their families.
54 Francis Heron (1794–1840), an Irish fur trader stationed with Hargrave at Fort Garry at this time, wrote in the post journal: "A Red River settlers maxim was 'to provide for the present day, and let tomorrow provide for

& potatoes have come to perfection, and as the Colonists have plenty of Cattle – their wants are amply provided for, and I trust there will be found a sufficiency of seed wheat for next spring. The large bands of beggerly Swiss, Meurons[55] and Canadians which M^r McKenzie unkenneled last summer have lightened this place of a galling burden, and if the same system of emigration be followed up in putting to flight such large clouds of cormorants who still skulk about the lass[e]s in the neighbourhood the expense of this colony to the Coy will be diminished by one half, – and a fairer opportunity will be afforded of trying the practicability of the benefits expected from it than has ever yet occurred. Butter is the only article of Colonial produce which can be expected this season, the Req^n of that article has been completed, and from the care taken in examining it when purchased, I trust will be found worth encouragement. The Outfit of this season has in the primary articles been found equal to their wants – especially blankets and Cloth. Our demand this season has accordingly been framed on such experience and I think is the truest estimate for their supplies that has yet been handed you. The full req^n of Robes & Leather will however be required, as upon the certainty of receiving these depends the correctness of the other demands. Shirts & Cottons Calicoes & flannels were found much too short and the quantity this year asked for is considered moderate for the demand in these articles. The tin ware arrived too late, the sales being commenced long before [Augustin] Nolin reached this. A large proportion is consequently still on hand, and the quantity asked for this year has been reduced a little compared with our last supplies. Of Iron Works (Axes and Hoes) I think we will have a sufficiency for next year, and have therefore asked for none. I have set

---

itself.' – the more enlightened now have resolved to pursue a more provident line of conduct." HBCA, B.235/a/8.

55 Men of a regiment of German and Swiss mercenaries raised in the Napoleonic wars under the name of Col De Meuron. They were taken to Canada during the war between Britain and the United States and disbanded in 1816. Lord Selkirk took 140 of them to his colony in 1818. Nicholas Garry thought the de Meurons "little better than a lawless banditti and, almost to a man, Drunkards." Regarding the Swiss colonists: "The Colonists have been ill-selected, Captain de May, Lord Selkirk's Agent in Switzerland, having more considered Quantity than Quality, (he receives a sort of Head Money). The greater part of the Colonists do not appear to me to be fitted for the cultivation of the Country. Many of them both male and female were discovered to be bad characters." Garry, "Diary," 163.

down the full quantity of Rum stated in the minutes, but I think 100 kegs will be sufficient even should the Petty Traders[56] be supplied in that article here, – if not, 60 would answer. By the way, the Req^n is formed on the actual wants of the colonists without including the demands of these Gents the Petty Traders, and if they are turned over to this place, it will have to be proportionally increased.

On reaching Norway House last fall I compared notes with M^r McLeod[57] as to the Goods freighted to that place during summer for Outfit 1827 – He was at that time busied in getting them transported down from the Old Fort to the New Establishment, and it was found impossible to examine them personally, his Statements of Receipts however I examined and found them to agree exactly with your Schemes with the exception of some Spirits left by M^r A Stewart[58] from Ath[abasc]a: Outfit '26 there being only 20 Kegs instead of 28 as stated in your Scheme, – also with the exception of the 68 P^s sent in to Red River. Touching the correctness of these receipts I have not the least doubt, as M^r McLeods attention to that department of his duty appeared unremitting, his papers were arranged with a good deal of system, and if care and assiduity may ensure correctness I think you will find these matters conducted much to your wish. He was dreadfully annoyed by your Letter P Nolin, and if things occurred as he states them, he really does not appear to merit the blame. I shall not however presume to bias your mind on the subject but leave his account of matters to speak for itself, as he talks of laying the matter before council rather than submit to bear the fault of others, – more especially when these faults may impose a forfeit of 20 add Pounds.

On passing Joe Bird[59] I inquired regarding the piece belonging to Mr Thomas[60] which was amissing last fall, & which you thought might have been received by himself when on board the Prince.[61] I[t] seems however this was not the case; I also took an opportunity of overhawling his Bag-

---

56 Private or free traders.
57 John McLeod (1788–1849), HBC chief trader, had taken charge in the summer of 1826 of Norway House and oversaw the substantial rebuilding of that post. Van Kirk, "McLeod, John."
58 Alexander Stewart (c. 1780–1840), was chief factor from 1826-30 at Fort Chipewyan in the Athabasca District.
59 Probably Joseph, the son of retired Chief Factor James Bird.
60 Probably Thomas Thomas (c. 1766–1828) who had retired to Red River in 1819 after rising to be governor of the Northern Department in 1814.
61 The *Prince of Wales* supply ship for the HBC.

gage while on a portage but no such piece was to be found. Joe reached this on the 1st Novr with every thing in good order.

Nolin presented claims for payment of the passage of Madame Ross[62] & family from YF hither, but as nothing regarding this appeared on his Bills Lading this matter was left to be settled with yourself, we being perfectly ignorant of what had been promised him except from his *own* statement, which I really did not consider a sufficient voucher in a matter where his own interest was concerned. By the way, you recollect I questioned the truth of his story regarding the 12 packs furs carried off by Larante,[63] and it is now *proved under his own hand* to have been a wretched fabrication resting on the following facts. On leaving this for the States Larante took with him a quantity of Summer Bears, Wolves, staged minks[64] and refuse [musk]rats, which had been at various times rejected as entirely of no value by us during last winter & which when tied up with all his other Baggage did not equal half the no: [number] pieces stated by Nolin. After his departure he offered the whole to McDermot[65] and some of the other petty traders in the plains for a small supply of provisions but they were found such a parcel of rubbish that even McDermot

62 Sally or Sarah Ross (c. 1798–1884), the Okanagan wife of fur trader Alexander Ross, followed her husband east in 1826, reaching the Red River settlement that summer after the disastrous flood. She and her children spent the winter at Pembina before settling at Red River for the next fifty-seven years. Daniels, "Ross, Sally."

63 "Jacco" Larante was mentioned by George Simpson as a free trader in 1822. Fleming, *Minutes*, 411.

64 Minks grow two coats of fur a year which differ in length, density, and colour. A "staged" summer pelt is worth very little compared with the winter skin.

65 Andrew McDermot (1790–1881) had retired in 1824 as a trader with the HBC and opened a store just north of the HBC reserve at Fort Garry. The company considered it desirable to have stores run by private individuals to supply the settlers' demands for articles it did not provide. McDermot was allowed to import goods in the company's ships via York Factory. He acquired his own brigade of York boats to carry goods between York Factory and the Red River Settlement. In an attempt to keep furs from going to the rival American post at Pembina, North Dakota, the HBC gave McDermot a special licence to engage in the fur trade, and he resold his furs to the company at a profit. His friendship with Governor George Simpson secured him contracts with the HBC for freighting goods, exporting tallow to England on company ships, importing rum, supplying Upper and Lower

who is proverbially known to be brisk at a bargain refused to take them for any equivalent knowing that they would be refused by the company. The whole of these facts could be supported by affidavits did these malicious slanders of our Prince of baboons merit such a serious refutation. The only Petty Traders these [this] season are Ross[66] & M[c]D, Nolin, & Grant.[67] Bourke[68] I believe is doing a little also for himself, being already ousted out of the firm of Ross & Company. With the exception of Grant, who winters beyond Brandon House, all these are exercising their talents at chicane between Red Lake [Minnesota] & Pembina, and a violent opposition in miniature rages among them, with all its usual accompaniments of billingsgate, backbiting, and trickery. I trust the upshot will produce something as substantial in the way of packs as did last year.

    Fort Garry with firewood and provisions for horses, and importing cattle from the United States. Hyman, "McDermot, Andrew."

66 Alexander Ross (1783–1856) moved to the Red River colony in 1825 after Governor George Simpson found him to be redundant to the HBC. He found the settlement in a state of starvation and took to the plains near Pembina with Andrew McDermot to keep himself and his family supplied with fresh meat. Ross, whom Simpson always thought lacked loyalty to the HBC, traded meat and corn with the Americans, Indians, and settlers. He began to run York boats from Red River to Hudson Bay in 1826. Labelled a "petty trader" by the HBC officers, he shipped company goods out of the colony and brought in, both on his own account and for the HBC, trade goods and general merchandise. His brigades attracted the influential men of the settlement and Cuthbert Grant was among those who joined him. Pannekoek, "Ross, Alexander."

67 Cuthbert Grant (1793–1854) retired from the HBC in 1824 and settled near the colony at the village of Grantown. He transported goods for the HBC on contract from York Factory to the Red River, and from the winter of 1824–25 was allowed to trade as an independent under licence from the company. This trading, like that conducted by Andrew McDermot, was designed to keep American fur traders out of the territory covered by the HBC charter by providing a company-controlled market for furs not directly taken by the HBC. In 1828 the HBC appointed Grant warden of the plains of Red River at an annual salary of £200, to prevent "the illicit trade in Furs within that District." Woodcock, "Grant, Cuthbert."

68 Possibly John Palmer Bourke (c. 1791–1851), an Irishman, who retired from HBC service in 1823 and from 1824–c.29 was principal clerk to the governor of Assiniboia, later at Pembina for the colony.

In the way of domestic news there is little to interest. A profound peace reigns throughout the Colony. Those who arrogate to themselves the exclusive title of the Godly hold their love meetings, their evenings of exercise, and their seasons for social devotion without let or hindrance, – where they are edified by the detestable holdings forth of a Garrioch,[69] a Corrigal,[70] or a Hawer[?]. Those of the unregenerate who are still staunch to the inspiration of their ancient household Deities the bottle and the sex enjoy these blessings to surfeiting, and bless the kind hearts of those who have brought these gifts of the gods within the compass of their cash. Slander herself seems to have buried her hatchet and Scandal to have set the notes of her trumpet to a psalm tune. In plain terms the reign of my bourgeois[71] exhibits an instance of what Hume[72] calls the *beau ideal*[73] of good government – none of its incidents furnish materials for history.

\# We have as yet heard nothing from the neighbouring Posts. The old Borgne[74] by all accounts is in most wretched plight, his body covered with ulcers, and his temper whetted to tenfold asperity. The Doctor is discarded, his want of skill trumpetted forth to man, woman, and child, – while the old boy has taken his own cure into his own hands. The consequence I doubt will be that before spring the title of Fort Dauphin[75] will be in the market. I understand Govr Simpson had a narrow

---

69 Probably William Garrioch (1787–?), an Orkneyman who joined the HBC in 1807 as a potential schoolmaster. He worked in the fur trade until 1822 when he retired to live next to his father-in-law, William Hemmings Cook. In 1823 he taught school in the Red River Settlement and by 1825 was a schoolmaster for the Church Missionary Society.

70 Probably retired Chief Trader Peter Corrigal, who arrived with his family at Red River in 1822 and established his family on two 125-acre lots above Image Plain near the 1846 site of St Andrew's Church. Pannekoek, "Probe," 84.

71 Donald McKenzie.

72 David Hume, Scottish philosopher.

73 French for beautiful ideal. The model of excellency formed by fancy.

74 John McDonald, also known as McDonald le Borgne (1770–1828), a chief factor with the HBC, was from 1823 to 1827 based at Fort Alexander, managing the Winnipeg River district. In 1827 he was granted a furlough on account of extreme ill health and settled in Upper Canada where he died the following year. Brown, "McDonald, John."

75 An apparent reference to McDonald's stint in charge of the NWC's Fort Dauphin department from 1808 to 1810.

escape on leaving that place last fall, his canoe having swamped at the first rapid. Nothing however appears to have been lost, and his papers to have sustained but little damage.

Among ourselves we are passing a very agreeable winter. Through good management M^r McKenzie had secured our usual winter stock of provisions in the fall & at the ordinary prices, – a fortunate hit, as plain provisions are now extremely scarce, and the cattle at a great distance.

I have indeed found Finlayson to be the man you described him. He and I are on the very best terms, and it shall be a study with me to cultivate his friendship. There is no danger of any coolness arising between us out [of] our relative situations, we both understand each other perfectly, and it shall be a point with me to give him every information regarding business here, both because it is my duty, & because I would be more flattered by seeing it conducted in the system I have helped to introduce than by any mean & sordid pride arising from witnessing the errors of a successor.

The season has hitherto been unusually mild, with no snow & the rivers open till near the end of last month. This I fear will prevent our Packet getting forward to Nor[way]. Ho[use]: at the period you expected, every thing has however been got in readiness, and should it be practicable, the plan of 2 Packets, settled on before I left York, will be acted upon.

I have now touched on almost every thing which I imagine can either amuse or interest you, perhaps more; I will not however apologise for my long & rambling sheets, being well aware of the tediousness of your winter evenings and having the vanity to think that my quota of uncoes will help to while away some of them.

With sincerest wishes for your happiness
I remain
Dear Sir
Yours Mo: truly & affectionately

JHargrave

You recollect that our man St Denis[76] made some stir at York last summer about an overcharge of a Bill to his account as p[ai]^d to Osterlag[77]

---

76 A charge to the account of Jacques St Denis was made 1 Nov 1825 in favour of Dr Ostertag for 15 shillings. HBCA, B.239/d/289. In the York Factory Abstracts of Servants' Accounts 1825–26, Jacques St Denis is listed as being

for Medical attendance, and stated that such had been done without his consent or order. I made it a point to enquire regarding this on arrival, and now find that every word I then said on the subject was perfectly correct. I have the authority of M^r McKenzies repeated information to say that St Denis sent for Osterlag of his own accord, that such attendance was of no benefit to him that he (St D) at various times requested M^r McKenzie to pay him, which was accordingly done upon such order, – and moreover it is M^r McKs opinion that Dr Hamlyn[78] on his arrival in the Settlement paid Osterlag himself without ever imagining that any charge had been brought against the Coy for the same. Under these circumstances is S^t D: not accountable for the money thus thrown away through his conduct. The plain matter of fact is that the fellow is a gabbling half-witted fool – a laborious man enough when kept in his own place; but when allowed the privileges of a rational creature sticks neither to truth nor reason. As a specimen of his usual veracity he asserted a few weeks ago that he did not receive a Dozen articles at YF tho' charged £12 for the same, and publishes aloud that he is grossly cheated by the Coy. Formerly something could be made of him, but since his arrival from York he is good for nothing, is careless and disobedient, mad for marriage tho' deeply indebted sells his clothing to the Settlers for cash, and squanders the proceeds on ribbon and gewgaws. In short the only cure now for St Denis is an Annual voyage of 6 months and a good dry basting when inclined to exhibit his usual sauciness – neither of which is very practicable within these bounds. Indeed no man should ever winter here more than 3 years. They are constantly running among the Colonists, become lawyers and politicians, – and acquire habits of idleness, pride, and insolence totally incompatible with the character of a dutiful Engagé.

---

    age 30, a middleman from Pointe Claire with nine years service in the Red River District and a contract to 1827. HBCA, B.239/g/5.

77 A Lutheran physician from Wurtemberg, Germany, known variously as Louis/Lodowick/Ludwig Ostertag/Ostertog(g)/Osterlag. He came out with the Swiss colonists in 1821 to Red River and married a sister of the artist Peter Rindisbacher in 1824. He was engaged by the HBC for a number of years to provide medical care at Red River and the nearby districts and died in St Louis in 1832.

78 Richard Julian Hamlyn was one of two doctors in Red River in 1830. Governor George Simpson had no confidence in either of these men and sent for Dr William Todd to deliver his wife's son in 1831 at Brandon House.

Fort Garry 20*th* January 1827

J.G. M*c*Tavish Esq
Dear Sir

Your kind favor of the 8*th* Dec*r* reached me three days ago P our men from Norway House, and as the second Packet will be immediately starting I take the liberty of tagging a few more pages to the budget I sent you under date the 4*th* Dec*r*, altho' little of moment has since occurred. A Packet from Lac la Pluie[79] reached this the day before ours left for the Bay, and as it was filled with despatches to your address, you must be better acquainted with the southern news than we could be from the few crumbs which fell to our lot, and as that is the only one which has yet visited us, my portion of *nouvelles*[80] for you must still be purely domestic. Our holidays are over and gone, unmarked by any incident at all worthy the pen of the historian. As usual a substantial dinner called together our Notables of the Colony both clerical and particoloured, but the days are gone by when such assemblies were enlivened by the song and the dance, the soul drenched in wine, or the carcass snugly consigned to oblivion below the board. Wonderful indeed are the conquests of psalm singing and amazing its power in giving an edge to the blunted conscience. Grey headed topers[81] will now with precision minute down to you the day and hour of their *second birth*, and the venerable fathers of Seraglios[82] hold forth in homilies of endless duration on the gift of continence, platonic love, and the wiles of the Sex. Beelzebub[83] lurks in their Kerchief so sly & Appolyon[84] shoots darts from their merry black eye. But enough of such dotards as will tell you gravely that the high-way to hell runs through the mazes of a Highland Reel, – and who imagine that they forsake their sins

---

79 The HBC had built their first Lac la Pluie post in 1818 on the north bank of the Rainy River near Rainy Lake to compete for furs with a nearby NWC fort. After the 1821 merger, only the HBC Lac la Pluie House continued in operation. It was renamed Fort Frances in 1830 after a visit by Governor George Simpson and his new wife (and English-born first cousin), Frances Simpson. The post traded with local Ojibwa for furs, wild rice, and isinglass (a collagen substance obtained from the swim bladders of sturgeon and used in the clarification of wine and beer).
80 French for news.
81 Chronic drinkers.
82 Large harems.
83 The devil or Satan.
84 The destroyer.

when they are no longer capable of pursuing them. There is still a portion of our society possessed of so much sense as to despise such chimeras else our condition were more to be pitied indeed.

Tranquility still reigns throughout the land: – provisions I trust will equal the consumption, and the winter gives every promise of an early spring. Dependence can now be duly placed on cultivation; the buffalo appearing to have entirely left the neighbourhood of Pembina, driven away by the legions of *brûlés*[85] that hover in that quarter. These thoughtless beings would now be starving but fisheries this season are more than usually productive, and from these they principally draw their subsistence. In the way of Brandon House[86] cattle are also extremely rare. [Cuthbert] Grant was here during the holidays, and by his account there is no prospect of Pemican[87] from thence. He is however doing pretty well in the way of Furs, the high waters having covered the country with myriads of musquash.[88] The Americans are now established all along the line, evidently petty Traders & private Adventurers. They are reported from all quarters to be extremely liberal in their goods, having reduced their made beaver to 3 rats and giving a 3 point Blanket for 18 musquash,[89] – with other articles in proportion. I should be inclined to doubt the truth of such extravagance, were it not confirmed by a multitude of evidence both from Pembina & Riviere la Souris entirely independent of each other, and agreeing exactly in the principal particulars. Our own petty Traders are entirely disheartened, and instead of opposing them by lowering their prices, lock up their goods in their Store, and allow the furs to pass on to

85 Bois-brûlés (lit. "burnt wood") was an informal French term for the children of French Canadians and their Native wives.
86 Brandon House was erected by the HBC in 1793 on the Assiniboine River, and named for Douglas Hamilton (1756–99), 7th Duke of Hamilton and 4th Duke of Brandon.
87 Pemmican comes from a Cree word *pimican* meaning manufactured grease. It was dried meat, usually buffalo or bison, pounded into a coarse powder and mixed with an equal amount of melted fat, and occasionally saskatoon berries. Cooled and sewn into bison-hide bags, pemmican could be stored and shipped with ease to provision fur traders. Foster, *Canadian Encyclopedia*, 1639.
88 Muskrat.
89 In 1826–27 eight musquash were worth one made beaver in the Red River district, and a three-point blanket, six made beavers or forty-eight muskrat skins. Warkentin, "Western Interior," 252.

the Americans. Such a state of things however cannot continue long, as ruin must soon follow such unexampled proceedings.

Grant had returned to Brandon two days before the packet arrived, he will therefore have no chance of receiving your letter till spring. I perceive by his detailed Account from YF a charge of 6 com[mon]: Guns which I believe he did not receive, as Nolin reported that he had left them at York to be sent up P Joe Bird & by whom they did not arrive. Should you find this to be the case the information may still be in time to allow of correction without difficulty. That bundle of shrugs & grimace Nolin has by neglecting his own affairs when so busy about those of others – reduced us to some difficulty in the way of ammunition again this season. The large supply sent in from Norway House led M^r McKenzie to think that he could make up his deficiency without hurting the Colony, so furnished him with 5 kegs, but when 24 was found to belong to McKenzies River, the remainder by that time was shrunk indeed, and we now find ourselves with little more than 4 kegs in Fort Garry. These however shall be husbanded with care, and even should they run out before spring rest assured that the Depot for Outfit '27 shall be held sacred, and forwarded to your disposal at Norway House immediately on departure of the ice.

The packet of Accounts has been found full and complete. By its assistance our business here I trust will be closed for the year with as little difficulty as usual. I have examined the Invoice and found it in general *comme il faut*,[90] though mine is a microscopic eye – too apt to discover motes in the sun beam; besides you have so often bantered me for my attention to petty charges that I dread the idea of recurring to them. For all this however you must allow that more placable subjects than I would open their eyes at seeing that miserable little shell of a Skiff we came up in last fall charged against us the enormous sum of 12 Guineas! – a thing that before we had proceeded a dozen miles in it was half full of water, and which from its decayed state we never could repair, but had constantly to be baling during the whole voyage. I readily grant that this fidgetiness about trifles is more becoming a counterskipper who measures out tape by the yard than an Aspirant to the character of a liberal minded Trader; yet with this consideration full before me I cannot help reflecting what attention must be paid to minutiæ before our pitiful 25 PCent will cover such a sum, for God knows we have taxes enough upon it already! If this feverish anxiety be a fault in me it is one for which I have as usual

90 French for correct.

much to say in defence. I have as yet only trifles to be exact about, and I am afraid that in learning to overlook such, I might learn to view with indifference more important matters. A Host of Mercantile Axioms also range themselves on my side, and the single reflection that from copper roots springs the Golden *Plum* is enough to bear me up against a whole torrent of irony. Have the goodness only to examine Cadotte[91] on the subject of the Boat, and on his report of its soundness I am willing to let the question rest.

I believe I mentioned in my last the little prospect there is this year of procuring you any pickled Cabbage, from the total neglect of that plant last summer, – none having been cultivated. I shall however do my best in getting carried into execution the plan I alluded to in regard to the Pot Herbs, but it I fear would not be possible to get cabbage by the summer boats of next seasons growth. The seeds arrived in safety and are an acquisition, as our stock P the Outfit was very insufficient, and of course much older. I shall not omit comparing notes with the Professor[92] regarding an Ox for you. The price of a passable one at present here is £7– and of a cow £6– in the spring perhaps they may cost a little more. Your suggestions in regard to Rations Joe Bird &c shall be implicitly attended to. I omitted to include in the Req.n 6th epsom Salts: as it is my bourgeois' universal specific for all diseases you will please add that quantity to next years Outfit should you be able to spare so much. Mr McKenzie tells me that he received last summer from YF a Doz[en]: Windsor Soap which P the copy of his Acc[oun]t sent seems to be omitted. This he desires you will please order to be placed to his debit. Little Louis[93] shall be forthcoming at Norway House next spring. He is at present in good health, and seems to be getting rid of that constitutional disease to which he was formerly subject.

I have pored not a little over Booths Bookkeeping[94] and have drawn from it many new ideas on the subject. It is a most excellent Text-book

---

91 Probably Laurent Cadotte, a guide who is mentioned as wintering at York Factory in 1829–30. HBCA, B.239/a/141.
92 Probably Alexander Ross, who was a schoolmaster before he became a fur trader.
93 Probably Louis Guiboche, alias the Little Pigeon, c. 1785–? In 1826 he was described as a "Free Canadian Trader." Fleming, *Minutes*, 442–3.
94 Benjamin Booth in 1789 published *A Complete System of bookkeeping by an improved mode of double entry*, which contained much innovative improvement and was suitable for large-scale business management.

for reference, and though not wholly applicable to business in this country throws a light over the art in general mostly new to me.

I expect to be with you at Norway House early in June – meantime believe me
Dear Sir
Most truly & affectionately Yours

JHargrave

Fort Garry[95] 29th January 1827

My dear Parents

A Packet conveying Government Dispatches having reached this place today on its way to Montreal, I seize the opportunity it affords me of sending you a few lines to inform you of my welfare. I am happy to say that I still possess my usual good health, and am fully content with the lot which providence has appointed me in this distant and wild country. In this however do not misunderstand me; I never should choose such a place as a permanent one of residence – a country to live and die in: – no, indeed. My ruling object, and which is the object of every one who comes hither, is to provide a competency for old age, and then retire to enjoy it – either in Canada – or in Britain. It is however true that many spend their life here, I believe, almost every one of them against their inclination. This arises from their having formed connections in the country in their younger years which they find themselves incapable of breaking when the time arrives that they could retire. The leaving abandoning of a family, of whatever color they may be, is a severe trial to the feelings, – and which no man of principle will ever attempt; – to bring them with him especially the wife to the civilized world will lay him open to almost as painful sensations, – the consequence is that many who have set out with the firmest resolutions of again returning to their native land have, by getting entangled in this manner, at length abandoned all their former resolutions – and with a heart yearning for a sight of their friends again

---

95 In 1827, James Hargrave was stationed permanently at York Factory. Although he had been appointed to winter at York Factory in 1826, Hargrave was forced to return to Fort Garry in October of that year because Duncan Finlayson was in delicate health. They departed York Factory with Rev. David Jones by boat for the Red River Settlement on a cold and stormy 21 September 1826. HBCA, B.239/a/136.

– bury themselves alive, as I may say, in the forests of this country; – cut off from almost every thing that in youth they considered as desirable in life. Having the view of this capital error so clearly before me you will imagine that I should steer clear of the shoals in which so many hopes have been wrecked; – such is my determination, and in as far as any can answer for his future conduct, such will I do. By thus prudently regulating my course I may trust to revisit my native land in a creditable manner, although my circumstances will doubtless render that period still a distant one. My last Engagement with the Company expires next June, at which time I purpose renewing it, when I have no doubt of an increase in Salary. I am now generally known in the country, and I may say without vanity my character is respected by every one whose good opinion I value in it. With such views before me it would not be presumption in me to expect farther advancement – my conduct still continuing to merit it.

You will no doubt perceive by all this that my expectations are much changed since I left Lasalle[96] 6 or 7 years ago. They are indeed. When I first resolved on joining the Fur Trade my wishes extended no further than merely gaining a trifle to commence [the life of a] Settler in Canada which I then imagined might be done with £50 or 60 pounds, and on this resolution was founded my prospect of rejoining you – in 2 or 3 years. A further acquaintance with the world however pointed out more eligible views of life – With the share of education you had so kindly bestowed on me I perceived I might aspire to a more comfortable sphere in life than a scene of toil among the woods of Canada, and at the same time be enabled to assist you more effectually than I could have done according to my first views of life. These new ideas I have followed, and were it not that I am unavoidably kept at this distance from you, life to me would be happiness unmixed. But I need not dwell on this topic. Far as we are from each other, it ought to be gratifying to us all that our path through our present state of existence is sweetened with such a portion of happiness, and though I may never see some of you again, I know that I have the benefit of your prayers, and firmly believe that the blessing of the Almighty upon the good man also gladdens the path of his children. May I always by my conduct show myself worthy of such parents!

96 Located at the southeast corner of the island of Montreal and bordered on the north by the Lachine Canal which opened in 1825, LaSalle was named for the area's first seigneur and French explorer, Robert René Cavelier de La Salle. It became a municipality in 1845.

I have much more to add, but my time is limited and the Packet will be leaving this early tomorrow. I trust my brothers John & Andrew are still behaving themselves as worthy lads. Tell them from me that in whatever situation of life they are placed an unstained character is their greatest honour, and that whilst they preserve this, let them be ever so poor they will always meet with the approbation and regard of all those whose esteem is worth coveting. Give my love to my Uncle[97] and family – and kind comp^{ts} to my old friends around you. Rest assured I will let slip no opportunity for writing you – meantime I am
Dear Parents
Your affectionate son

JH

P.S. All my letters & Journals are written entirely for yourselves, and I trust that they are never shown to your neighbours or such as come

---

97 James's uncle, James Hargrave, a younger brother of his father Joseph, was born in 1756 in Roxburghshire, Scotland and emigrated from Scotland in 1812 with his family. Robert Sellar made notes of conversations he had with old settlers in preparation for his 1888 oral history book, *The History of the County of Huntingdon and of the Seigniories of Chateaugay and Beauharnois from their First Settlement to the Year 1838*. In these notes he described the purchase of land in Beechridge by Joseph and his brother James Hargrave:
> In 1813, 14 & 15 settlers came to Ormstown [Williamstown in the source from which he got this information; see below] looking for land & went to Milne [James Milnes, Esquire, one of the agents in the Seigneury of Beauharnois], who refused to concede. Notwithstanding they settled on them & were not molested until Oct. 1821 when they were summoned to attend at Beau[harnois]. Hon Jas Richardson [actually John Richardson, executor to the estate of the late Seigneur George Ellice], seemingly in great anger, called them land robbers & trespassers, & were not worthy of obtaining deeds, but if they w[oul]d comply & sign an obligation to pay certain am[oun]ts. They w[oul]d get deeds of con[cession]. otherwise they w[oul]d be deprived of their improvements & ejected at once. They complied. The following has to sign obligations for following am[oun]ts.
> Jas Hargrave 50 pounds
> Joseph Hargrave 12 pounds

gaping for news when they hear of such coming from this country. Did I think they were to meet any other eye than your own there are many things in them I should have left out, therefore I hope my dear parents you will not expose to the sneers of gossips the unvarnished expressions of your son.

JH

Fort Garry 30th Jany 1827

M^r. Ja^s. Ross,[98] Montreal
Dear Brother

A packet from Capt. [John] Franklin of the Land Arctic Expedition passing this on its way to Montreal affords me an opportunity of telling you that I am in my usual good health, and trust this will find you all as I would wish you. I have not one iota of news that can at all interest you, – this place which suffered so much by the floods last spring, has greatly recovered from its recent devastation and the Colonists are passing their time in peace & plenty. I hear however from the Northward that serious warfare is raging among the natives, whole bands with their families having been cut off on both sides. To us these things sound so common that I never imagine the details at all worth communicating. Happily we only hear the thunder at a distance, remark that it is foul weather somewhere & pass on – for the natives around us are more inclined to make war upon the Muskrats & Sturgeon than among themselves. I return to York Factory again next summer from which place I will write you at more length in the fall, – though short as my letters may be you are now several in my debt, which circumstance I trust you will recollect in mea-

---

Sellar, *Notes and Conversation*, vol. 4, 166. Sellar apparently obtained this information from an appendix to the Proceedings of the 1832–33 session of the Lower Canada House of Assembly. See Appendix, Journals, N.n 22d. March. The yearly rent to be paid was 25s. in cash and five bushels of wheat.

98 Hargrave's brother-in-law, James Ross (1793–1846), was born in Dalkeith, Scotland and emigrated to Lower Canada after the end of the Napoleonic Wars. In 1823 he married Mary Hargrave and bought a farm in the Jamestown concession in the Chateauguay River Valley. He spent much of his working life on the construction of the Rideau and Lachine Canals and later on the railways while his family was raised on the farm.

suring me out your quantum of Nouvelles next spring. I enclose a letter for my father which you will have the goodness to forward to him by the earliest safe conveyance. Give my love to your *Cara Sposa*[99] Mary and to Jane should she be in your neighborhood.
Good bye – My dear Sir
Yours affectionately JH

Mem° The two foregoing letters are put under one cover and addressed thus – "M^r Ja^s. Ross Montreal. To remain, till called for, at the HBCoys office Lachine."[100] Should this packet not be called for before next fall – to request M^r. D[onald]: Ross to return it under cover to me. It is sealed with my initials & crest, the Rein deer head.

---

99 Italian for Dear Spouse. James wrote his friend William Lockie that he had learned Italian after he came to Rupert's Land in order to while away the long winter evenings by reading Italian literature and because he disliked translations, particularly of poetry which he thought could not be translated. In 1827 he ordered, from Britain, pocket copies of an Italian-English dictionary and Italian grammar, preferably cheap and second-hand "if they can be got." Letter to Mr J. Claves from York Factory, 30 August 1827.
100 The HBC's North American headquarters was located in Lachine, near Montreal.

[Letterbook]
N⁰. 2
Rough Copies Letters by
JHargrave
from 24ᵗʰ March 1827 @ 1ˢᵗ Decʳ 1827

YF 23 July 1827[1]

My dear Father

    I was much gratified by receipt of all your kind letters, (both those of last and this season) about 3 days ago, and as an opportunity offers just now for sending you a few lines I have sat down to scribble. I have reason indeed to be grateful for the preservation of all your lives during the long period since I heard from you in 1825 and I can say with truth that the joyful news your letters contained afforded me more happiness than any thing else I have experienced for these two years last past. I know you will also rejoice to hear that I still preserve my usual good health, and that from the sober and easy lives we lead in this country I have every reasonable hope that many happy years are still before me. We may however all calculate in vain – the young are as exposed to the dart of death as the aged and hoary head – and may this consideration wean my affections from an over anxiety about the fleeting objects of pursuit in this world, and fix them on that state of existence where sundered friends shall be reunited – and where tears of affliction shall be changed into songs of joy. My dearest father, let us not murmur that providence has seen meet to cast our lots so far asunder, – distance cannot weaken affection, and tho' absent in body In spirit I am often with you. To think of your happy fireside, to figure to myself your little circle engaged in your evening devotions, and to be convinced that in the sincere petitions of your hearts to the throne of Mercy the absent Wanderer is not forgotten – pours consolation over my sometimes melancholy mind. I have besides many other reasons for thankfulness. You are all well and providence has at length crowned your industry with comfort and independence. My brothers I am proud to find are worthy and honest lads – my sisters in understanding and prudence have equalled my fondest wishes, – all these are motives for rejoicing.

   1 Hargrave and Duncan Finlayson had arrived back at York Factory by boat from Red River on 28 June 1827, in fine weather. HBCA, B.239/a/136.

A 1987 photo of the homestead that Joseph Hargrave built for his family in the late 1820s in Beechridge, Lower Canada. Photograph by Malcolm Sissons.

You mention the desire which Ruther expressed that you should remove to his neighborhood[2] where were also several of your old Scotch acquaintances – and that you deferred deciding till you should hear from me. I must say that I cannot view this scheme with much approbation – and the following are my reasons. You will be removed to a greater distance from me – my letters will often miscarry before they can reach you and yours will hardly ever come to my hands – the Company having no Agents in that quarter. The greater part of your present property you will have to sell off – mostly for less than it cost you before you can move, – and wherever you may pitch upon you will have as it were the world to begin again – at least it will require much time and expense before you will be able to find yourself as well situated as you are at present. There is

2 Ruther Hargrave and his brother Joseph were shepherds in Scotland and emigrated to Lower Canada in 1817, staying for some time with their uncle James Hargrave in Beechridge before buying property near Waddington and Lisbon, respectively, in St Lawrence County, New York on the south shore of the St Lawrence River.

I fear but little prospect of any of these inconveniences being remedied by Ruther or Josephs assistance; at least it is but a slender proof if any, to find them craving payment of some old small debts out of any little money I may send to my mother and which was solely designed by me to be laid out in procuring comforts for herself alone. It is true the company of old companions must prove pleasant to you – but such pleasure would be purchased in my opinion at too high a price – and besides I am now old enough to have learned myself by experience that most friendships in this life continue longest when there is no necessity of requesting their aid on meeting with difficulties. 'Tis not every where believe me that you will meet with such worthy characters as your neighbors the Struthers.[3] They took you by the hand when you were houseless and Strangers, – their assistance ever since has never been awanting and that most disinterestedly; – have any of your blood relations done more? have many of them done so much? – No – my dear parents, if my opinion has any weight with you I beg you will not leave your present situation for any in prospect however inviting. You can visit old friends from where you are – and such visits will yield more pleasure than a permanent residence among them even should the change be obtained by no sacrifice whatever.

I am happy to find that you purpose setting about building a new house. Your old one must now be a perfect ruin, and nothing conduces more to comfort that [sic] snug and warm lodging. Your new one should be divided into 2 rooms – one end as a Kitchen, the other as your sitting and sleeping room. Let it be furnished well – and strong and substantially built: should you not be able to muster as much money as will finish it to your wish let not this stop you, as my purse shall be open to defray whatever you may find necessary to your own comfort.

xxxxxxxxxxx

The above letter has not been sent. I was obliged to write a few hurried lines instead under the same date.

---

3 The Struthers family owned a farm near the Hargraves on the northwest side of the Beechridge concession of Williamstown, a large triangular region on the northeast side of the Seigneury of Beauharnois. William Struthers (1774–1831) and his wife, Hannah Derick, had a number of children including James (1799–1863), Philip (1801–1862), and Margaret (1803–1893). James Struthers married Martha Dewey (1799–1874), the sister of Melinda Dewey, in 1820.

York Factory 20th July 1827

My dear Mother

It was indeed with much pleasure that I received both your kind letters last spring on my way hither from Red River where I spent last winter, and you may well imagine how glad I was to find that you were all in good health after such a long time as has passed since you wrote me in 1825. My own health is still excellent, the climate of this country is so good and our way of living so very conducive to health that out of all the Gentlemen belonging to the Company in this country, *not one* who remained in it has died since I came here in 1820. It is true that all our lives are uncertain – but it is also true that the hour of death is hastened or retarded by our own conduct and the course of life we pursue in this world. With my present experience had I my course through life to choose again I know of none I should prefer to that which I have already adopted and my worldly affairs are prospering far beyond what I could have reasonably expected. I am happy in my own mind – I trust I have reason to say & that such happiness is planted on a foundation which cannot be shaken. Indeed when I read over your letters my heart swells to reflect that we are so far asunder and that I am deprived of the happiness of seeing you and telling you all that I feel; but my dear Mother let not grief prey upon your mind, – it is the will of providence that we are thus separated – and it is our duty rather to rejoice at the blessings we enjoy which are not a few – than allow our hearts to be oppressed with melancholy by the few privations which we experience.

I received your kind present of the pair of mittens which are really very handsome, and as coming from you my dear Mother they are more prized by me than the richest present could have been coming from another. I think you say they were made by Peggy Struthers[4] for which kindness I feel much indebted to her. Were it possible I would send both you and her some little keepsakes from among the curiosities of this country, – but the Canoe which goes down to Montreal is required to travel so expeditiously that no parcel larger than a letter is allowed carriage in it. The same rule is observed at Lachine and indeed had it not been the kindness of a Clerk in the Office there with whom I was acquainted, my letters would not have reached me this season also in consequence of the mittens being put under cover with them. It is therefore too great a risk to

---

4 Margaret (Peggy) Struthers of St Remi, Lower Canada, whose parents had a farm near Joseph Hargrave, Sr in Beechridge.

run – and you will hereafter only send my letters alone in the parcel. Any thing else it is impossible to get forwarded.

You will receive in this letter a Bill for £10 Sterling which I send you as a little present, and it is my *earnest desire* that you expend it all in procuring comforts for yourself and my father. In my letter to Jane I have mentioned what I wish you to purchase with it – and should she not be living with you at present you can open the letter for her and read it. I was happy that my former Bill came so conveniently to pay the expenses of my sister Janes sickness – but it vexed me much to find that part of the little I sent you was taken from by Joseph in payment of the remainder of what he claims from my father. I shall not give such conduct its proper name, – but I cannot help saying that had I known what part of that money he would have taken that part I would not have sent. As it regards my poor brother Joseph himself, I frankly forgive him, – for I fully believe he has no will of his own. I feel for his condition and I wish him all the benefit he can reap from money so acquired. For the present Bill of £10 Stg – you will rec^{ve} about £11..2..2 in the money of Canada. I have written to Ross about it & he will get it cashed for you, – should he be out of town I have also explained to Mary how she will be able to get money for it, – but should they be both absent when this reaches you – John can easily take it to Montreal, and any Merchant in town will give him the money for it – as it is signed by Govr Simpson[5] whose name is now known to all Mercantile Men in Canada. Now my dear Mother do not imagine that I pinch myself by sending you this trifle. Very far from it indeed. The interest of the money I have already saved is yearly more than the above sum – and did I think that your little wants required more at present the double of that money would be as heartily at your service.

Nothing has astonished me more than what you mention of Normans having attempted his own life. Such is often the end of a habitual course of drunkenness. I understand he has lately made himself very busy in my affairs. I laugh at his attempts and hold all that he can do in too much contempt to allow it occupy a moments thought. I once had an esteem for him, believing that he had done me much service from the best motives. I have now learned that these motives were the very contrary. I fear they will yield him less pleasure but a benefit done where nothing but harm

---

5 Sir George Simpson (c. 1786–1860) was governor of the HBC for forty years until his death.

was meant merits no return of Gratitude from me. I despise his conduct too much to allow it occupy another line of my letter.

I need not talk about news as I have this year again sent you my Journal of last winter which contains enough of such matters. I remain here ensuing winter where I have every prospect of passing my time most agreeably. I will write you by every opportunity I can find – for nothing gives me more pleasure. At present I must close with assuring you that I am
My dear Mother
Your very affectionate son

JHargrave

York Factory 2nd August 1827

Mr Wm Lockie
Stouslie – Roxburghshire
North Britain
My Dear Lockie

Your most kind and interesting letter of 15th February last reached me on the shores of Lake Winipeg in the beginning of June by the Packet from England Via Canada, – and altho' the summer duties of my Situation employ every minute from day break till dusk, – yet the pleasure of addressing you is so enticing to me that I have begun at this early date, and shall from day to day *eke* one line to another at every leisure moment I can procure till I shall have overrun you the Annual Sheet. Your information regarding public affairs was most interesting to me, and gives me a more lively idea of the condition of the great Body of the People in my native country, than any thing I could have gathered from the public prints – I trust in every succeeding letter you will continue your hints on this subject; but still dearer to my feelings were the little sketches you favored me with, of my old School fellows & acquaintances who are still around you. The prosperity of my old Comrade "Rob the Elder"[6] I rejoice to hear of; tell him, I hope yet in some future year to beat up his quarters and to spend one delicious evening in recounting our antient feats at foot

---

6 In his 1828–29 Journal, James refers to having received his annual letter from William Lockie, his former schoolmaster in Stouslie. He mentions having received news from Lockie about old schoolfellows, including a Walter Scott of Boonraw, his elder brother Robert, "a farmer along with his father 'the Elder.'"

ball on Stouslie Green. To Miss J: Ormiston[7] I beg you will remember me in the kindest manner & tell her I am sorry to find that she is still single._x Such I am certain is her own fault, – and give her a hint from me in the old saw of "making hay while the sun shines." True it is, its edge turns also towards myself, – for alas! I have forsook the flowery path of love for the more rough one of ambition – in all likelihood never to find my way back into its delicious recesses. Should ever I see Scotland again this may yet be amended, – but no, – my country-women used me scurvily enough when my cheek was smooth & skin white – A tawny and sun burnt wanderer has therefore little to hope. I will however encourage the day-dream that paints my return at least for a season to my native fields – and let me beg that you will every season furnish my fancy such food as your last letter contained in a copious allusion to names – incidents – and local changes around you.

I can say nothing now regarding the requisite equipment of an Emigrant for Canada, as it is more than 7 years since I left it, and all that I then knew I believe I have already written you. Business in that country is as much at a Stand as in Britain, to single men – wages are low and money extremely scarce; such will therefore be at present little benefited by a change if they find employment in their native country. A Middle Aged married Man however whose family can be of assistance to him on a farm and who can muster wherewith to plant himself down on a Lot in Canada will, if he is industrious, still do better than at home: Money indeed he cannot expect to make, – but he will fare better, and live easier, than he can do under a master in Scotland. I have heard from my parents this spring, they have now been 8 years in Canada, and their present condition is such as an industrious man might promise himself after the same number of years residence. My father mentions that he has about 50 Acres of cleared and enclosed Land under Cultivation which he considers enough & reserves the remainder of his woodland for furnishing occasional supplies of timber as he may want it. They have a good dwelling House, Barn, & Stables, 1 Horse, 2 yoke of Oxen, 3 cows, 2 calves, 11 sheep, Hogs, fowl, Bees &^{c} &^{c} – and on the whole are now in easy circumstances. He landed in Canada with scarcely a Guinea in his pocket, and the whole is the produce of his own industry – aided by my brothers

---

[7] In a similar vein, James mentions in the 1828–29 Journal the deceased R. Ormiston of Drinkston whose son Andrew, "my Comrade & School fellow," is a shepherd on the farm his father used to let.

John & Andrew, and some remittances of money I have made him from this country. They are all in good health, – happy & contented. The old folks are indeed much failed, – but my two brothers John & Andrew are steady, sober, active lads and are now more than equal to the duties of the farm, while my old parents are passing the evenings of their days in ease & plenty. You can imagine their different condition had they remained in Scotland. My old father writes me that he has not an ungratified wish in this world but to see me once more before he leaves it. They had received your letter & were anxiously looking out for you – I have informed them of what you said to me in your last, – and no doubt they will be sorry to hear of your detention – and once under my fathers roof – *whatever be your circumstances*, you might then depend on having reached harbour. I would not however over-persuade you, weigh well your present condition & your prospects for support in old age – if these admit of a rational hope that you can spend your days in your native country without other aid than your own or your childrens help the change is the less necessary. If not, the alternative presents, – unwearied industry for 4 or 5 years, – and after that your head is above water for the remainder of your days, – should providence bless you with health. Weigh these alternatives well & let me hear your decision.

I do not think you will consider too much of my sheet occupied by the subjects I have touched on, – I shall now turn to the theme which interests you most unconnected with ourselves – the country & its inhabitants. What can be said on this subject in a small letter is so unconnected, and gives such an imperfect notion of things as they are that I really know not how to take it up. Imagine to yourself a country – the whole face of which is covered with a thick forest, a country of such an extent that the whole of the British Isles would form only a contemptible speck on its surface – fancy this immense tract intersected with rivers of such magnitude that in comparison our famed Scottish Streams of Tweed,[8] Etterick or Teviot shrink into diminutive rills – indeed bearing the same proportion to the majestic Streams of this land as the rivulet which passes your cottage does to the Teviot at Hawick. Throughout the whole of this part of the Continent, say from Canada Northward to the Arctic Circle

---

8 The substantial Tweed runs north of Hawick eastward through the Borders in Scotland for 100 miles to its mouth at Berwick-upon-Tweed in England. Its tributaries include the Ettrick to the west of Hawick which joins the Tweed near Abbotsford and the Teviot which runs northeast through Hawick to join the Tweed at Kelso.

& from Hudsons Bay westward to the Shores of the Pacific, – no white men are to be found but such as are connected with the Fur Trade (except the small Colony of Retired Servants on Red River) – nor no established village or town beyond the Picketed Forts formed by the Traders for the purposes of Traffic. The Natives are thinly spread over the face of the country, – and are divided into tribes more or less powerful. Each Tribe speaks a different language or at least a different dialect of some original tongue and the greater part of them are constantly in a state of warfare among themselves. The principal Tribes on the eastern side of the continent I have formerly mentioned in some of my letters; They have attained to a certain degree of civilization, are in general friendly to the whites, – and have become so habituated to the use of European Commodities that they now cannot do without them. To the westward of the Rocky Mountains and to the North of the 50° of Latitude the country is yet unexplored – the natives in the interior parts have never seen the face of a white, and are treacherous, warlike, & hostile to all intrusion on their territories. The Columbia River which empties itself into the Pacific about Lat. 45° has been established upon for about 20 years – and the natives are much improved from what they were when first visited – yet what do you think of the following description sent me this spring by an intimate friend who was sent thither last year – and which I *know* to be a true picture taken from life. – "Does any one wish to view man in his natural state? – let him visit the Columbia, – there he will find a Being so nearly allied to the Brute that his reason is perceptible only in the efforts absolutely necessary for the support of his animal existence – a leaf even does not cover his nakedness, – but there he stands as he was ushered into the world – his Sex exposed to the glare of open day – not a blush upon his front. He is as unconscious of shame as he appears to be ignorant of his own fallen degraded nature."[9]

---

9 Possibly Edward Ermatinger (1797–1876), who spent three years on the Columbia with the HBC but was no expert on Pacific Northwest natives. Ermatinger was at York Factory in 1824–25 before being posted the following year to the Columbia district. His son later quoted Ermatinger reminiscing about the chief of the Chinooks in a similarly dismissive vein: "I remember old King Comcomly once marching into Vancouver, with all his naked aids and followers, rigged out in a British general's uniform. But His Majesty had thrown off the pantaloons before he marched out – considering that they impeded his progress." Ermatinger, "The Columbia River," 204–5.

This place from which I write is situated on the shores of Hudsons Bay at the Mouth of Hayes River[10] a stream above 3 miles broad, and is surrounded by low swampy Marshes covered with a stunted growth of Pine Trees & Willows. The Climate during summer, that is from the beginning of June to the end of August, – is much warmer than in Scotland, but from the immense clouds of Mosquitoes and the constant change of chilling fogs & burning sunshine is with truth considered both the most disagreeable & unhealthy season of the year. During the other nine months the earth is bound up in impenetrable chains of frost, the ice on the Rivers & Lakes from 5 to 9 feet thick, – and the forest only pillars of ice. During most of the depth of winter it is dangerous to go out even a few miles – without a thick clothing of Deer Skin & Duffle[11] – should any part of the skin be exposed to the air it is immediately frozen, – and many instances occur of lives being lost notwithstanding all the care that experience can teach. Quicksilver is often hammered like a mass of lead, – and the thermometer has been frequently registered at 50° below Zero on Fahrenheits Scale.[12] It lies in nearly the same latitude as Siberia in Russia, – and the climate & nature of both countries are nearly the same At this place I am now to be established in all likelihood for several years to come, and to those unacquainted with the country such a prospect could not be considered a cheering one. My sentiments are very differ-

10 The Hayes River, from 1821 to the 1860s, was the avenue by which nearly all fur traders, soldiers, European settlers, and early arctic explorers entered the British North-West. Moving inland from York Factory, boatmen and their cargoes followed the Hayes River upstream nearly to its source, then travelled by way of the Echimamish and Nelson Rivers to reach Norway House at the head of Lake Winnipeg. A 400-mile track of lakes, rivers, rapids, and falls, interrupted by thirty-four portages, it required two to three weeks for upstream passage, depending on weather and water levels, but considerably less going downstream to the bay. Dennis Johnson, *York Boats*, 53–4.
11 "Duffle" referred to a coarse woolen fabric with a thick tufted nap woven for warmth that was originally made in the Belgian town of Duffel.
12 James noted some years later in his entry for the York Factory Post Journal of 19 January 1836 that the freezing of quicksilver at that time threw into question the exactness of the thermometer readings at York Factory for the preceding five years. Meteorological journals were kept at the depot with three daily recordings of weather conditions, temperature and wind conditions. HBCA, B.239/a/149.

ent. We have yearly communications with England, and of course possess many European luxuries & refinements which Inland Winterers cannot obtain. Our lodgings are commodious, elegant, and impenetrable to the howling blast which raves around us during most of the year. Our short days are whiled away in easy employment at the desk, – and we beguile the tedium of the long winter evenings by a Game at Backgammon, Chess or Whist – enlivened by a bottle of wine, or should the pensive mood prevail a well stocked library furnishes food for the mind in profusion besides which I have annually a chest full of Books Newspapers & Reviews from London, containing every thing most attractive in the literary world. This Depot is the headquarters of all the Fur Trade north of lake Winipeg, – a mercantile education for this country can only be completed here, and by a perfect knowledge of the business, the higher ranks in the service can only be attained My appointment has been urged & procured by some of my warmest friends. Should providence bless me with continued health I have little anxiety about futurity my course now being strait before me, fully pointed out, and every season bringing the period of attainment nearer to hand.

York Factory 30th Augt 1827

Dear Uncle –

With much pleasure I duly received your kind letter of April last and was glad to hear of your prosperity. My old & bowed down Grandmother[13] has at last paid the great debt of nature, and however long her life has been spared, it is a warning voice that even the longest pilgrimage in this scene of care must at last terminate in the same way as the shortest. Indeed long life when considered in connection with the pain & trouble attending it is scarcely to be desired, – and he who can look forward to a future state with hope and consolation may view the terrors of his last hour with indifference – whether these meet him in the flower of life or when the knees begin to tremble and the Grasshopper becomes a burden. This information will weigh heavy on my dear old mother, however it may have been anticipated in the common course of nature. Tho' they never could have met again in this world, still the affectionate mind is soothed by the thought that the same sun shines upon both, and that providence has still permitted the beloved object to enjoy those imperfect scenes of pleasure to which we attach value in this state of existence.

13 His maternal grandmother.

May we all after having used our zealous endeavours to fulfil the duties incumbent upon us here, meet again in an hereafter, where the gloom of the grave shall never again overshadow us.

I had letters last spring from my father and it gives me the truest pleasure to find that they are all well and that they are now completely above the pinching wants of life. I understand that they have about 50 Acres of cleared & enclosed land – a horse, 3 or 4 cows 2 yoke of Oxen Calves Hogs Sheep &^{cc} and the labours of their farm being managed by my brothers John & Andrew, whom I am proud to say are sober & industrious lads, – the old folks are now enabled to spend the evening of their days in quiet and ease. How different would have been their condition had they remained in Scotland! – penury & want with years would have crept upon them, – and from the few opportunities, there, for the children of poor parents to raise themselves in the world, I could never have been able to alleviate their condition in my native country. I believe my entreaties persuaded them mainly to the step which they took and I am truly happy to find that my views & hopes connected with an Emigration to Canada have not been disappointed. However fortunate they may have been, I would not however be inclined to press others in their circumstances to follow their example. So much depends on industry – moderate expectations, patience and steadiness, – the want of which so often occasions misery where the man of small desires & frugality would find all his wishes exceeded, – that I should by [sic] shy in enticing strangers from their native land who on meeting with the first hardship would immediately blame me for holding out fallacious and empty hopes – in their opinion never to be realised. I can merely say for myself that I have reason to rejoice in the fixed plans I laid down for life, – others who have views of leaving their native country will also use their own discretion in choosing for themselves, – on the whole – happiness, ease & plenty can certainly be found in Canada, – this earth presents no spot where the contrary is not also to be experienced. I rejoice to perceive you have found your condition in Scotland so far favorable as to prevent the necessity of change. Affairs certainly look gloomy, at present, – but I trust that with time they will improve to the advantage of both rich and poor. There is a degree beyond which national suffering can never sink, and as nothing is stationary – the lowest spoke in the wheel however it may change its position can only ascend.

I need say little about myself. – Year follows year, in the same routine, – my circumstances are easy – my prospects for future days are as flattering as those of most young men at my years – and I am happy to experience that my ambition is not so insatiable as [to] long after what cannot be attained. My time for half of the year is at my own disposal, spent in exercise, hunting, fishing, or reading – the season of active employment is spent in the Counting House or the Store and tho' duty often presses so heavy as to tire the staunchest industry, – when the busy season is over quiet & ease again are ours. In this pursuit I expect to spend the most active days of my life, – I have often *heard* of more pleasant and more lucrative situations, – but I am content with small things and have no desire of a change. I shall now give the remainder of this sheet to my Cousin Effy – as postage is to[o] high to admit of sending her a separate letter. I had however almost forgot to say that you need not hereafter pay the postage of your letters to me on putting them into the post office in Scotland as the Company in London now settles this matter for us. All your future letters you will direct in the following manner – "Ja[s] Hargrave, Hudsons Bay House, London" – under which address they are certain to reach me in safety. & now to the more enticing part of my letter.

My dear Cousin, –
That part of my Uncles letter written by you I have perused with the utmost pleasure, – and let me tell you never apologise for weak minds and want of matters of importance – let them be all such as I have yet seen, your undisguised thoughts conveyed in the first words that came to the tip of your pen – & should you write me quires you would find in me a partial and attached reader. To your inquiries about this country I shall say as much as this small corner of the sheet will allow. You have never seen one like to it. It is all covered with trees so close together that there is no traveling through it except up & down rivers, and except at our Forts, which are many hundred miles asunder there are no people but indians – whose language you could not understand a word of. Their dress and appearance are so strange that I cannot describe them as there is nothing in Scotland to which I could compare them. These people all live by hunting the wild animals of the country such as Buffalo (that is the wild cows) Deer Beaver &[c]& – besides the rivers abound in large fish, some weighing upwards of 200 lbs that they catch in nets, – and the marshes and lakes are swarming with Geese and Ducks which are also shot by the Indians in great numbers. They are all armed with guns, bows & arrows, scalping Knives and Axes but are very kind to White men who need not fear to meet with them however defenseless they may be: – indeed the

indians have save[d] the lives of many white men when starving for want of provisions while traveling through the country – and I have myself been most hospitably furnished with food by them when for want I was reduced to kill and eat the Dogs I had for hauling my sledges while on a winter journey – and for this provision so kindly furnished they expect nothing in return. In a word although we call them savages and although they are pagans in the truest sense of the term, yet the most of them with no better education than what the light of nature, teaches lead more innocent lives, and better fulfil the duties of fathers, sons, brothers & sisters than many who in the civilised world call themselves Christians.

I shall tell sister Jane the news you send her. She like yourself is still single – Mary has now two children and her husband & she are prospering very well in the world. You say that Peggy Grey[14] is still single, – waiting for me – I am indeed sorry for it – as should she and I ever again meet I am afraid we would find ourselves both so changed that we should not know each other. In short this will be in days when the so cherished pursuits of youth will be looked back to like a dream that is half forgotten. I wrote twice already to Ja^s. Lees[15] but as I have never heard once from him I shall not again take up my pen to address him. He pledged himself to answer me, I find however that promises & performances are often two very distinct things – in many instances considered as not at all having any relation towards each other. Ja^s Sword appears also to have sunk into silence, – & is two letters in my debt, but till I hear from him I shall take care that he shall not owe me a third. As the Coy in London now pay all postage of letters from Britain to us in this country I wish you would write me a letter yourself next season instead of adding a postscript to that of my Uncle addressing it in the same manner as I have mentioned above. I cannot promise to send you a sheet in return the expense of a ship letter being very great, but a postscript like this shall always be tacked to that for my uncle. I really would be glad to see you all again, and when sitting writing these words – how sincerely I wish that the hand which traces them were at this moment clasped in those of my

14 In his 1828–29 Journal, James writes that "Old And^w Grey is dead some time ago, also George Greys wife. My Old 'Chere Amie' Maggie, is yet single, a sure prize for me, my uncle says, *should I yet retain the sentiment of 12 years ago*. I however consider it a *merit* to have thoroughly *changed* them."
15 Possibly James Lees, listed as an English teacher in Galashiels in Pigot's 1825–26 Directory.

friends whom I am now addressing. At this distance, however warm my language it can only mean the kindest *friendship* and so I shall conclude, my dear girl, with assuring you that I am yours with sincere love & affection. God bless you all,
My dear friends:
Yours affectionately

JHargrave

York Factory 1st Nov' 1827
To Miss M: Struthers
My Dear Miss

Being so occupied last fall when the express Canoe to Montreal started, I have been obliged to delay till this date returning you my thanks for the pretty pair of Mitts you were so kind as to make me two years ago – and which only reached me last summer. Believe me that I shall long preserve them out of regard both to the Maker and the Sender. It particularly pleases me to find that I am not yet forgotten among those with whom I have passed a most agreeable winter, – and whenever I may visit Canada I shall take the first opportunity of telling you all so: at the same time will convince you that I never send a commission where a young lady is concerned that I would not a thousand times, more gladly execute in person, than by *proxy* – I understand you purpose on such an occasion to form a party of Old Bachelors & Old Maids: Set me down by all means as one of them; tho' I much fear that the next news I hear from you is that you have disqualified yourself for taking a seat among such a choice collection of musty characters. It is nothing but the difficulty of pleasing your nice eye which keeps such a tight & blooming lass as I left you, in a state of single blessedness. Even at the risk of losing the authority of making such a queer collection do smile a little more kindly on the young Beaux around you. For my own tardiness in these matters I have much to say in apology. You rail against all Squaws, – and tho' I am a little more lenient and kind hearted I must confess that the voyage of life is likewise in my eye – a much too serious an affair to be embarked upon in an Indian Bark Canoe: – I have also as you partly know been rather unlucky among *fairer* faces, – and so from various reasons there is much probability that I shall refrain from ever tempting my fortune again in a search so discouraging & unfortunate. Were I at this moment with you in person I could I flatter myself find many amusing stories for you but they are too nonsensical &

too long for a letter, – I shall therefore collect a budget till I again join the circle around your Winter Stove, & with kind regards to your worthy parents your brothers & sisters
I am with great esteem.
My Dear Miss Struthers
Yours ever truly

JHargrave
To
Miss M. Struthers
Lasalle

York Factory 1st Novr 1827

My Dear Mother

    A packet for Montreal will be leaving this soon, and as I well know how happy every letter from me makes you I with pleasure sit down to fill you a sheet. I have enjoyed my usual good health since I wrote you in July last and am spending my time at this place very agreeably. The Winter has just set in, and the weather here is always excessively cold throughout that season, but we have most excellent lodgings well heated with Stoves, and so carefully built, plastered painted & ceiled that not a breath of air can penetrate them. Every one of us has a room to himself, and when tired with chatting in the public Hall during the long evenings – I return to my own apartment and spend my time in reading or writing. I am while now addressing you snugly seated by myself in my room, a couple of mould candles burning on the table while around me are lying Books, Newspapers &^{c} &^{c}. A warm & comfortable Bed – with the Blanket turned down & the curtains ready to let fall – fills one side, – into which I tumble as soon as my watch points 10 OClock – and there listening to the storm howling over the waste around us, I reflect with a thankful heart on the many blessings providence has bestowed on me, – put up a petition that Your days may be lengthened out in happiness – that we may [be] allowed to meet again in this world, – and when passed from time to eternity that we may all be reunited beyond the Grave – "a family in Heaven!" My dear Mother, – to write in this manner would be called weakness and enthusiasm by many, – I trust however in God that I shall never be found ashamed of my religion, – and altho' I would refrain from giving occasion to scoffers were I writing to many, – oh how delightful it is to pour out the mind in full confidence into the bosom of a mother! To think of you & of all your tenderness to me even when I was a stubborn and wayward Boy softens me sometimes – to tears; – almost every evening thoughts of you all are the last on my mind – they even mix in the dreams of the night, – and morning brings back to my mind recollections of my *Home* and of all that is there dear to me.

This country has its advantages and disadvantages: – Here the public ordinances of religion are few times met with in comparison with the opportunities in the happy Island of Britain, – but in the solitudes of this land, the mind is insensibly led to meditation & reflection, from which the best results sometimes arise to many who would have drowned in the bustle of civilised society "the still small voice" of the conscience. Among the young Gentlemen who are in this country – many are as every where else vain and frivolous – but not a few are worthy & good men, – whose company & friendship are worthy of being sought after. Among the first class I endeavour to live on an easy & good humoured footing, – but it is from among the last that I select my companions; – where I seek for a friend to whom I can open my mind in confidence, – strengthen good resolutions by mutual encouragement, – and take counsel from each other in our conduct and actions through life. Of these I have been so fortunate as to find a few – when we meet, which is often not for years – we meet as brothers – they are all my own countrymen, – and – I need not describe the pleasure we take in talking about our Native land & the days of other years.

Along with this I send you a letter I received from my Uncle Ja^s Mitchell last fall, which you will find contains the melancholy intelligence of my venerable Grandmothers death. This in the course of nature was certainly to be expected, and tho' nature will have its course & the heart be melted at the heavy news – yet when we reflect on the well spent & blameless life which had been lengthened out to such an unusual span – we have also reason to rejoice in the hope that the emancipated soul freed from the cumbrous load of frail mortality, – has at length rejoined that Almighty power which first breathed it into dust, – among the spirits of just men made perfect. – Let us not weep as for those who die without hope; – this world possesses little of itself to bind us to it, to live well is better than to live long and the death-bed of a pious christian is fruitful in sources of consolation to those who have yet to continue their pilgrimage through the snares & temptations of this world. My uncle Ja^s Melrose[16] is also no more. Death cuts us down one by one: – they cannot

---

16 A brother of Hargrave's mother, Jane Melrose.

rejoin us, but we shall all go to them: – may that awful day find us prepared for the predestined change!

My dear Mother, I am loth to lay down my pen, and yet what can I say more: Glad would I be to see you again, – but few families are permitted to enjoy the privilege of remaining unbroken through life. Such is our fate yet though we cannot all be around you we are in many respects highly favored above many. Let me entreat, my dear mother, that you will now in the evening of your life take some relaxation from the painful cares that have occupied most of your days. I declare there is nothing on this earth would yield me more heartfelt delight than to cherish your old age and the little money that I last sent you let me beg that you will use it as I requested in my letters of last fall. I know you will find these comforts of benefit to your health and in order that you may never want them I purpose settling on you during the remainder of your life an Annuity of the same Amount as I sent you last year, and which you will always receive in my Summer Letters. Do not hesitate at this, – as if I was leaving myself bare, – I have abundance; & it is only my bounden duty to share it with those to whom I owe the means of earning it.

* I enclose under cover with this a letter to Peggy Struthers thanking her for having made me the Mitts you were so good as [to] send me last summer. I had no time to do this when I wrote you last, so I now send her a few jesting lines to laugh at in return for the many messages I have had from her through you. Send it by some one who will deliver it to her in safety. With kind love to my Uncle & family and with best regards to your worthy Neighbours W. & Alex: Struthers.
I remain My Dear Mother
Your very affectionate Son

JHargrave

YF November 2nd 1827
Dear Father,
Although I wrote you fully by the Canoe of last fall I cannot omit any opportunity of sending you a letter, as I feel by the pleasure I have in writing to you, – what you will experience in reading it. I have just been reading over yours of last spring and I assure you that any advice from you will ever be grateful to me: – At all times and in all conditions the paternal injunctions of such a father will ever be received by me with welcome regard: – Your opinions regarding the doctrines of a church to which you consider I might adhere in this country I fully agree with. The funda-

mental doctrines of all the protestant Preachers here are far from being of a legal description, and the doctrine of Salvation through the merits of the Saviour alone, forms the foundation of all their Sermons. While in Red River I accordingly attended church every day & I trust have been much benefited by this teaching but have not joined as a Member of the Church. My hesitation may be wrong, but it is not occasioned by any dissatisfaction with their doctrines nor did it arise from carelessness, – but when I considered the unsettled life we lead here, – and the changes in our residence almost every year I felt a dread in the want of preparation, and knowing that I should not return thither – I considered it wrong to enter into communion with a Society from which I was so soon to be separated. These are bad reasons I own, but I could not prevent myself from being motivated by them: – I especially dreaded the danger of approaching unworthily. In this country, from its very nature, we inevitably lead a course of life differing much from the steady and sober course of those who are placed in civilised society, and from that reason above all others I should never wish to spend the whole of my life here. On the voyage especially the men must labour every day, it being quite impossible on most occasions to allow a single hour to be lost when we run the risk of being stopt by the rivers freezing up, hundreds of miles from any habitation; and although the Sabbath is pointedly observed at the Establishment, during all the time we are traveling little difference can be made. At this place much attention is paid to the moral conduct of our servants. Sermons are read by one of us every sunday when every person in the Fort must attend, and bibles & religious Books are every year sent out to us from London by the Company which are distributed to every person who can read throughout the country – so that none need be without the Sacred Volume who wishes to possess it

    It need not vex my brothers John & Andrew that I have not written them this time; easy as writing is to me in comparison with them – yet when they growl at my seeming indolence they ought to consider that for every letter they write in a year I write fully two hundred. Under these circumstances they ought rather to give me credit for those which I do send them. Time has rolled on so fast since we last saw each other that they must now be tall lads – almost as old as I was when I first came to this country – tho' when I think of them it is always as the little ragged rogues whom I left scrambling like squirrels among the logs that they were cutting up. They are now at that period of life when it is natural for them to think of providing something for themselves with an eye to their future condition in life. This they should do on your own farm and among yourselves. They should provide Oxen Cows and Sheep and in doing this you can assist them as much as you choose out of your own Stock without any regard to me in these matters; as what I have given you I always considered in the light of a free gift, without any idea of ever looking for repayment. Consider me as having no greater claims upon you than themselves – and assist them as you may see meet, out of your own Stock in the same manner as if you never had had the aid of a single shilling from me to procure it. They ought never to think of hiring themselves to gain money as labourers; they have ever been their own masters, and by continuing so they will be enabled do more both for you & for themselves than were they working for another. They have served a good apprenticeship to the Axe, and if they continue steady and industrious they may yet expect to make themselves independent and even wealthy farmers. Of all things let them beware of getting attached to liquor. There are many instances around them of the ruinous consequences of this vice: – I am certain they have never known one, given to drunkenness, who has prospered in the world: – and when they see a poor creature dragging thro' life in poverty, hanging about taverns to catch a glass of rum, in charity, from some passing traveler, – when they see this poor wretches family in rags and owing to the pity of a neighbour the food which keeps them alive – when they see all this & which they may see almost every day – let them reflect on the inevitable end of this abominable vice and take warning, lest such may one day be their own. I hope better things of them, and I merely point out this as one of the most dangerous rocks they will meet in the voyage of life – in the full hope that their own good principles will enable them to steer clear of it. I have little room to say any thing to my dear Jane. She seems like myself – shy in making a choice for life; – I trust she will shew the same prudence in her selection that she has done in taking time to make it. If it is at all convenient, she should now remain at home with you. – A good mistress & a residence in a sober family is difficult to procure; – any other situation is both disagreeable and *dangerous*. I have written a few lines to Mary: – she has made a most judicious choice for herself – I am proud of her conduct, – and indeed it is one of my dearest pleasures to observe the good conduct of them all. Of such relations I shall ever feel pride in calling myself their Brother.

P.S. By the way, I received a letter last Spring from my cousin And[w] Hargrave[17] which I would have answerd had I not learned by your

17 The son of James's uncle, James Hargrave.

letters that he had gone down to Quebec. Should he be by this time returned tell him I received it and feel much gratified by his kind remembrance of me.

JH

Great and general attention is also paid to the condition of the poor natives around us. That great destroyer of their happiness – rum – has been discontinued in most parts of the country, – and every where it is no longer used as an article of Trade. These simple people are still sunk in the darkness of heathenism, and although much attention is directed to their spiritual improvement both here and by the Heads of the Company in England, much time will yet pass away before their darkened minds can be illuminated by the truths of Christianity. In Red River however, a large school of Native children from mostly every Tribe in the Country is supported by the Missionaries in order that these children when grown up may carry to their different countrymen both the arts of civilised man, and the glad tidings of Salvation. In the course of time I fondly hope that this judicious plan will be blessed to eternal benefit of millions. In their present condition they are harmless in their conduct, but their imperfect notions of religion are deplorably benighted. They all however have a belief in a future State – have distinct ideas of right & wrong, – virtue and vice – in which state they believe that those who lives good lives in this world will be happy – and the bad miserable. A good man, in their idea, must be honest & charitable, a kind father, a dutiful son a skilful hunter & a brave warrior. In the world of spirits they imagine they will pursue the same course of life they do here, – the good being placed in a country abounding with game & every thing they now value, while the bad will be exposed to all the hardships they dread in this life, to hunger, cold and misery. They believe in two great Spirits, the Origin of good and evil, but considering the Good One too merciful and kind to do them harm, they address all their prayers to the bad one in order to avert the evils which they imagine he has the power and will to inflict upon them. These their rites of religion they often observe with much solemnity, especially when about to undertake any important action, a hunting excursion, a distant Voyage &^{c} –

This account I have drawn out to such a length as to leave little room for my own matters. These however can be summed up in a few words. I am passing a cheerful pleasant and easy winter, – am happy in my own mind, and were I sure that you all were in the same condition I would

have nothing farther to wish. That such may be your present state is the earnest prayer of
My Dear Father
Your very affectionate Son

JHargrave

York Factory 2nd Novr 1827
My Dear Mary,

By a round about conveyance I have found a chance of sending letters to our parents, and cannot close up the packet without putting a few lines to you in it. I am still "hale an' hearty" – passing my days most agreeably – sometimes with paper & pencil in hand, with a drove of satellites about me I am bustling through the Stores, making up assortments of Goods, – sometimes mounted on my high three footed Stool at the Desk, as grave and starched as a Don – eftsoons I throw aside the Ledger, the Starch & importance of the Counting House, – and wrapped up in Leather, Duffle and Fur, with my fowling piece in hand I sally out on my Snow Shoes on a shooting excursion, make a turn of 15 or 20 miles – call at an Indian Tent on my way to have a jest with these simple denizens of the desert, – wish the old folks luck among the game and the young smirking squaws luck in finding a husband – smoke my pipe – and then with a light heart and a heavy Cargo of Partridges [ptarmigan] again wend my way towards the Fort. There you have a picture of my labours and of my amusements. Simple they are and admit of little variety, – but in such a way the winter slips over unperceived and indeed nowhere in the civilized world have I felt time less irksome than what I do here. It seems but as yesterday when I first set my foot in a Canoe to become a Wanderer in the Waste and yet Eight Suns have nearly told their course since you and I separated. How many more may yet run ere we meet again is what I even dare not guess at – but let us keep up our hearts and look at the bright side of things, – we are all well, have much to be thankful for, and should we be spared when we do meet again, that day will be one of the happiest in my life. But falling into this train of thought seriousness creeps over me before I am aware. I however sat down to write you a cheerful letter and so avaunt care – not a single subject for melancholy shall this sheet convey to you. What do you think? I am become a most inveterate Snuffer, as well as Smoker. A portly Silver Box is presently posted at my elbow, to which I apply with all the devotion of a lover almost every minute. To make you open your eyes, know that I consume 12 pounds every year – that is a pound each month, or more than half an Ounce a day!!! Do not scold me for could you but at this moment feel the delicious smell that issues from my Box as I now open it, no olfactory nerve could resist the temptation. But this is enough of nonsense.

I have not written this time to your husband, though the packet will be addressed to him, imagining that when this reaches you in the Spring he will probably be absent, but should he be at home, I must make this sheet serve for you both, as even my flighty pen could hardly find wherewith to fill another one for him.

God bless you My Dear Mary! – give a kiss from me to my little Nephew & Niece[18] – when I get them in my arms how I shall cram their pockets with Gingerbread and Coppers, – and make them stare at their "Indian Uncles" long stories about Windigoes and Manitous the Ghosts & Spirits of this land.

With kindest love

I am

Your Affectionate Brother

JHargrave

---

18 William (1824–1904) was born in Montreal when his father James Ross was working on the Lachine Canal, and Jane (1826–1916) was born in Ottawa when her father worked on the Rideau Canal. William spent his life in the Chateauguay Valley as a farmer.

[Letterbook]
N°. 3
Rough Copies Letters by
JHargrave
from 2ⁿᵈ Decʳ 1827 @ 1ˢᵗ Augt 1828

YF Jany 29ᵗʰ 1828

My Dear Mother

My accompanying letter dated 1ˢᵗ Novʳ last has lain by me for these three months without my having an opportunity of forwarding it, – but as the packet for Montreal will now leave this in two days, I have opened my first letter to enclose you a few lines in addition to say that at this date I am in as good health as your affectionate heart could wish – May this also find you as well as my fondest wishes desire. It is needless for me to search for news to amuse you from among the strange things of this land; the place where I am I have already described in my former Journals and in this country century may follow century and still the face of nature be the same. Our winters here are much colder than with you in Canada: when we sally out on a hunting excursion which is usually twice or thrice a week we are literally loaded with clothing five or 6 fold thick of leather Blanketing & flannel. Could you see me in this trim I really think you would not know your own Son. Hunting is our only exercise out of doors, and altho' I only at first took to it out of regard to health I find that practise brings back all the eagerness with which I formerly used to follow Hare Snaring in Scotland. John formerly used to dun me about a Gun, should he now have got one I will *wad*[1] him five Guineas the first time we meet that I beat him as a marksman. Our game here is principally partridges Rabbits & foxes with now and then a White Bear, but these last Gentlemen are rather surly Customers when pursued so closely, and for all my boasting of my Skill as a Shot, I find it most prudent to keep on good terms with Bruin, who is always such a good neighbour as never to molest those who leave his skin whole. In the spring and fall however we have myriads of Geese Ducks and Swans – with large herds of Rein Deer, so that at in all seasons, whether we take to the woods or the River, the Hunter has as much Game as he chooses to point his Gun at. I often wish when returning to the Factory with a load of fowl that you could benefit by the produce of my Hunting. You have now I trust a sufficiency

---

1 To pledge, wager, or bet. DSL.

of provisions, yet I know it would gladden you to have a dish now and then of "your Jamies" procuring.

My Dear Mother It is needless for me to say more. Let me entreat you to take care of your health, as you love to add to my happiness. To soften the weary path of age to my old parents has been my fondest wish since I left you, Oh let me have your united care to lengthen out this delightful duty to its utmost span. Procure and use good warm clothing, – spare no expense in providing good and nourishing food, and beware of labour above your strength or of exposing yourself to catching Cold or getting wet. Wherever my purse can be of service to you for such purposes, command it; with the whole heart of the owner. Depend on receiving ensuing summer what I have mentioned in my former letter, and that you may have health & happiness to enjoy a continuance of the same as long as happiness can be united with the burden of age is the earnest and daily prayer of
Your Most affectionate Son

JHargrave

York Factory 1st July 1828
Miss Jane Hargrave
My Dear Jane

Your kind letter reached me about a fortnight ago, and it was with sincere joy that I was informed of both your and all our familys health and happiness. I know it will afford you the same satisfaction to find that I am still as well and hearty as ever, as jovial a Batchelor as ever turned the Weather Gage of Thirty – free of Wife, incumberance or anxiety. Now don't at these words bristle up in defense of the Sex, and cry out "Oh the insensible and hard-hearted man!" – consider it may be that the fault has not here *always* [been] on my side; and what is still more likely, that were I in the Civilized World, and had a fair view of supporting a family with comfort, it would require very little of the dexterity of your Sex still to throw *Glamour* in my eyes, – that is to say should they consider me – a shaggy fur Trader, – still worth the noosing. But this is enough of *Badinage* – let us talk of similar matters more seriously. I catch your hint of that bug-bear, *single* five and Twenty, – and my dear lassie, – and far from wishing to make a jest of what you so jestingly talk of, tho' I "jalouse"[2] it goes nearer your heart than you desire I should see. This is natural, and

2 Suspect, surmise, guess. DSL.

let me tell you candidly, nothing would please me more than to hear of you making a respectable connection for life. That is the important hinge on which the happiness, aye use, of female existence depends, and I am convinced from the tone of all your letters that you have ample discretion and good sense to make a prudent choice. I see however where the Shoe pinches, and now assure you that it has ever been my intention to give you the same assistance in "providing yourself" as I gave to Mary, – whenever you may require it; – that is to say provided you make as prudent and respectable a choice. A wealthy match I do not insist on, but I entreat that you select a husband of an unspotted character, steady, industrious, as near your own age as may be and of a family with as unstained a character as himself. Our own family has been and is still a poor one; but I am proud to say that dishonesty, fraud or dissipation could never be coupled with its name. This is the true point of honor with the poor, and ought to be guarded as vigilantly by the same fear of disgrace as would deter a lady of fortune from forming a match with her footman. To return to our subject, whenever you hint to me that my assistance is alone wanting to settle you in life, and that I find by our parents letters that they approve of your choice, depend on receiving from me immediately the same sum that I gave to Mary.

 I can fully see the laborious life you must have at home, and shall give my mother a hint to try and keep our worthy old father within reasonable bounds in his anxiety to get his farm labors forward. I have ever been of opinion that out door work generally should never be laid upon women: – their duties are those of the dwelling house; and except as reapers, hay makers – or such half-play – the drudgery of outdoor labor is altogether unfit for the Sex however poor they may be.

 I have this season sent my Mother a present of fifteen pounds,[3] part of which will go towards paying for their new House,[4] but do see & keep at least Six or Eight pounds of it out of my fathers claws to purchase tea, Sugar, Wine &c for him & my Mother. I say this because I fear that he will consider these as so much money thrown away, should the purchasing of them interfere with the payment of some part of his "*Onstead*:"[5] now I know that these comforts are essential to them both, however he

---

3 The equivalent of about 1,000 pounds sterling in 2007, using the retail price index. Officer and Williamson, "Purchasing power."

4 The houses of Joseph Hargrave and his brother James still stand in the village of Sainte-Clotilde-de-Chateauguay, Quebec.

5 The houses and buildings forming a farmstead. DSL.

might appear to laugh at them, and the fag end of his building expenses can be squeezed out the produce of his farm. Indeed I should imagine from what they say that the rem[aining]^y Eight or Nine pounds will pay for the whole of the Building.

You will perceive that this letter has been written wholly for *yourself*, and tho' you may shew it to our mother, the Boys and our father will laugh at you should you let them see how I have been lecturing you so keep it to yourself.

Remember me kindly to Peggy Struthers – I wrote her a few lines last winter to laugh at and trust she has received them.
God bless you, My Dear Girl: –
Your loving brother

JHargrave

York Factory 1st July 1828

My Dear Mother

It is unnecessary for me to say what was my delight on finding by the receipt of your letters a fortnight ago, that you were all spared in good health: You can well imagine it by the joy you feel on receiving mine: my time is busily employed during summer and I am already sat down to assure you that I am as hale & hearty as ever, tho' my letters cannot be forwarded for two months to come.

I am happy to find that the little money I sent you last year came so seasonably, and that what I wished you to purchase with it has proved so beneficial to your comforts. I feel hurt however by the blate[6] manner in which you ask a little more to help you out of debt with your house. Believe that I speak from my very heart when I say that you do me a favor and a kindness when you point out where my assistance can be of use towards your own comforts, or where it can save you a minutes uneasiness. Nothing that ever you can ask would ever be looked upon by me as unreasonable: *ask* therefore, and ask with confidence; for you can only hurt me by begging it. You will see by a letter I sent you last winter fro[m] this place that I had already settled the sum of £10 Stg, – upon you annually, and to help you out of debt in building your house, I send you this year a present of 15 instead of £10 – the half of which you can spend that way, but the other half I entreat may be laid out as you did the last in getting little comforts for both yourself and my father. Along with Sugar &

---

6 Bashful, diffident, sheepish. DSL.

Tea, I wish you would also get 3 or 4 Gallons Port Wine; to take a glass of it each day,: – it being, when taken in moderation, extremely nourishing and good for the health. You know the text, – "Drink no longer water but use a little wine for thy Stomachs Sake"[7] and as every word of Scripture is valuable, this precept rightly interpreted may be called the golden rule for using that which mans extravagance so often abuses. It can only be got good in town, and from a Spirit Merchant, not a Tavern Keeper, as these last always have the worst liquor & sell at double the price the Wholesale Merchant asks. The best should not cost you above 10 Shillings Halifax[8] the Gallon. Never taste rum; it ruins the health.

I have had a very sensible letter from my Sister Jane. From it I think I can gather that my father is rather too severe upon women in making them work at hard out-door labour. Her health appears still to be tender, and labor beyond her strength, under a burning sun may prove dangerous to it. *Between ourselves*, try and prevail with him to leave her to perform the indoor work alone: He has been so accustomed to wield the Rod of a *Grieve*[9] in Scotland, that I fear when anxious about the prosperity of his little crops – he has little sympathy for the weaker power of women when occupied in the rough duties which properly belong to *man*. The indoor matters of the family are too much now for you, she must at all events manage there in part, and my experience says that women know right well how to persuade men that their own duties are enough for them, – without taking any share in mens labour, – so that I have little doubt you will be able to lighten poor Janes toils without letting our old worthy father perceive that he has at all been unwittingly too severe.

I am really sorry to find your fears about me have borne so heavy upon you last winter. You were right in supposing that I had given an explanation about my Engagement & views in this country in the letter from Red River which you did not receive: That letter I believe is yet in the Office at Lachine but as the packet was addressed to "Ja^s Ross to remain at the Office till called for" as he was not in town and as John may have asked for letters to my fathers address alone, the Gentleman[10] in the office could not have known that such were under the cover to my brother

---

7 King James Bible, 1 Timothy 5:23.
8 By 1832, Halifax currency was worth 10 per cent less than English sterling. Evans, *Emigrant's Guide*, 83.
9 Overseer on a farm, farm bailiff. DSL.
10 James Keith (1782–1851), as superintendent of the Montreal department, ran the HBC office at Lachine, Lower Canada, from 1827 to 1835, and again

in law. I shall explain this matter in a fuller manner to John so as that I hope he may yet be able to recover them; in the mean time I shall add regarding myself that I am now like all the rest of senior clerks under no regular Contract with the Company, – but act in their employment at a Salary of £100 Sterling[11] P Annum, and stand next to promotion, on the first vacancies that may occur in the higher ranks of the Service. I am so little bound by Contracts, indeed so completely my own master, that if I choosed I could leave the country to-morrow: should I do this however, or even should I go to the civilized World for a single winter, I would lose ground in the service, and the certainty or even the risk of losing the near prospect of upwards of £300 P Annum, is what I am certain you would not advise me to, more especially as my fortune is yet but very slender. The sum Total of my affairs is, that in this service I can gain a comfortable sum to support me in the evening of my days, my wishes are not too ambitious, and a few years with the income of those immediately above me would satisfy them & enable me to join you with a competency for life how then can I throw aside at once these hopes & return to Canada little richer than I left it, and having lived so long without being obliged to work with my hands I am certain I now could never become inured to it. On the whole, do not press me further on that subject My dear Mother I beseech you my own wishes are painful enough to resist, and when I see your grief gall is added to my cup – otherwise so delicious. Could I say when my turn for promotion would arrive, at once I would name the year I would see you, but this none can do, – I am perplexed between providing for my self and the desire of again joining you; unhappily the one desire counteracts the other; both can only be accomplished with time and under the guidance of a kind providence, that brings us often happiness out of what we have considered full of difficulties & of sorrows. To his care I commit you, and may he in his mercy bind up the bleeding heart and wipe away the tears of a most affectionate Mother.

By One passage in your letter I was particularly struck. It would appear you had met with some part in my last years letters, where you have thought that I begged you not to *forget* me. I must have expressed myself very differently from my meaning, or else you have misunderstood my expression. The words I think you allude to were in my letter of 23rd

---

from 1837 to his retirement in 1843. His resignation from the HBC became effective in 1845. Goldring, "Keith, James."

11 About £6,700 in 2007 currency, using the retail price index. Officer and Williamson, "Purchasing power."

July '27 from this place where I observe "in the sincere petitions of your heart to the throne of Mercy I was convinced the absent wanderer would not be forgotten," – and mentioned this as one of my chief sources of happiness. No, my dear Mother full well I am persuaded you will never forget me. What I rather dread is that you allow your fears about me to render you unhappy, by giving too easy belief to the ignorant stories of people around you about this country. This place is now my fixed residence and here there is less danger than I would meet with were I living in the middle of Montreal. Give ear to no report about the adventures of the Indian Country. Not one in ten that you will hear is true, and where truth does appear it is almost invariably mixed up with fables.

I this year again send you my Journal, and by it you will see how happily I live; – indeed, as I have often said, were it not that I am absent from you & the griefs & fears that you entertain in consequence of my absence, my life is as happy as my heart can desire. Try and gather comfort; shake off these apprehensions about my safety here; and believe me that when I assure you there are not the least foundation for them I speak the real sentiments of my heart, and not with the view of deceiving you into false happiness.

God grant my dearest mother that many happy years may yet be added to your life, and that I may in time have the joy of again seeing you in this world is the sincere & earnest prayer of your
Most Affectionate Son

JHargrave

P.S. I will omit no opportunity of writing you.

York Factory 3rd July '28

My Dear Father

I have after several unsuccessful attempts procured a few leisure minutes to set down and answer your affectionate letter of 3rd March last the perusal of which gave me great pleasure. I rejoice to find you are still in good health, for which we ought all to be doubly thankful both because you are now well stricken in years, and also for the comfort & peace which surrounds you after the toilsome days you have passed through ere you attained them. Long may your days be lengthened out; – to add to their pleasures is really the most substantial happiness that my heart can experience. It pleases me to find that you have now set about getting yourself a new Dwelling House, and to help you a little I send a Bill for a few pounds to my Mother: – but mind only part of it is for that purpose, – at least one half must be kept to get wherewith to spend a comfortable winter around your new fireside. How I wish it to be laid out I have explained in my letter to my mother.

It makes me smile to see what a Politician you are now become, with your petitions to Parliament and your sending of 2 lawyers to present them. Were I with you I am certain I should take an active part in getting the object presently in view forwarded, as the interests of the Presbyterian Church in Canada have in my opinion been too much neglected, and it must be owned the Church of England has been rather too grasping in the matter of the Lands allotted by Gov[ernmen]^t for the Support of the Gospel. I have had this spring, from some of my friends who went down from this country, a bundle of the Montreal Herald Newspaper, the Editor[12] a Countryman of our own; and I am happy to see that great exertions are made by him in placing this subject prominently before the eye of every one concerned. I perceive by the latest dates that is, about the middle of last April, there is every probability of their gaining their object. I observe it is also proposed, and of which I highly approve, that the whole of the Presbyterian Ministry in Canada should be regularly organised into Presbyteries & Synods subject to the General Assembly of our Scottish Kirk. As a staunch Seceder,[13] I know you will cock your eye at my talking of this union, but really I think that all differences between Seceders & The Kirk should be made up when they meet together in a strange country. The great & almost the only point at issue is that of *patronage* a mode of presentation unknown *out* of Scotland: – Having therefore the choice of your own pastors, and acknowledging with the Kirk one system of doctrine, as contained in the good old Confession

12 Archibald Ferguson was editor of the *Montreal Herald* from 1824 to 1833.
13 Ebenezer Erskine (1680–1754) was the chief founder of the Secession Church or Associate Presbytery, formed by dissenters from the Church of Scotland, after he was suspended from the ministry in 1733 for preaching on lay patronage (in 1712 "lay patrons" had again been given the right to "present" or appoint ministers). This church split again in 1747 into Burghers and Antiburghers over the issue of the Burgher Oath, which required holders of public offices to affirm approval of the religion "presently professed in this kingdom." The Burghers in 1798 and the Antiburghers in 1806 each split into separate "Auld Licht" and "New Licht" factions, the latter being more theologically liberal.

of Faith, I can see no reasonable grounds for our countrymen worshiping asunder in a foreign land. Indeed what you say of the union of the presbyterians of both Upper & Lower Canada & of their petition to the Church in Edinburgh, leads me to think that in the woods of Canada you own as brother in religion every one willing to subscribe to the ritual of our Scottish Church by whatever name his former Society was called in Scotland. Look back and tell me candidly if you do not think that there was really too much of prejudice and ill temper in the manner that Antiburgers, Burghers, Reliefs[14] and Kirkmen[15] used to look upon & talk of each other in former days? For my part I really think so, and in Canada would give the hand of fellowship to every one of them who adheres to the good old fundamental doctrines of the Kirk as explained in the Confession of Faith. Calling of names has done much harm, and really there is often as much difference between the opinions of two Seceders as between those of individuals of all the above mentioned Societies. I thank you for recommending the Books you mention in your letter: – the most of them I have already seen, and will read the others whenever I can get hold of them. I am this year getting out among others D^r McCries life of John Knox[16] a book I am certain would interest you. The courage, the constancy, the Soundness and the perseverance of that great Apostle of the Scottish Kirk is most deservedly celebrated, and every successive year spreads his name wider in the world, and adds deserved honour to his valuable labours. I promise myself much pleasure in perusing the life of this venerable reformer, one of the most honored Characters in my eyes that our native country has ever produced.

To return to our own affairs. My mother mentions some lands in your neighbourhood being for sale as a good bargain, and wishes my opinion on purchasing them. Should they be *Kings Land* I would likely approve of it, but I suspect they are like most all around you held from Seigneurs, a mode of holding property not at all to my taste. Any little money I possess, I have placed at interest, which brings me in fifteen or twenty pounds annually, should I lay it out on land I would loose this interest,

---

14 Members of the Relief Church, which was formed in 1761 by three dissenting ministers of the Church of Scotland.
15 Members of the Church of Scotland.
16 Thomas McCrie (1772–1835), a Scottish historian, writer, and preacher, published the *Life of John Knox* in 1812, for which he was awarded a Doctor of Divinity from Edinburgh University in 1813.

the land would scarcely be of that much use to yourselves; & besides when I return to Canada I will have many opportunities of making good bargains, having the ready money in my pocket. In the hope that this will be in time to spend many a pleasant evening with you and my other dear relations around both your and my own fireside
I remain
Dear father
Your Mo: Affec^te Son

JH

YF 4th July 1828

Mr John Hargrave
Dear John

Your kind letter of last March is now before me and I am sat down to scribble something in return, what that must be is yet to be thought of, – and I am as usual so surrounded with business that I scarcely have time for a moments reflection. I can see, even by the stout strokes in your handwriting, that you are now become a strong fellow, and I am rejoiced to find that you are as steady and industrious as you are healthy. Now don't be angry at me & think that this a hit at your penmanship, for you really have improved much since I had you under the birch at Midholm.[17] You do well to attend the night Schools as you mention, for should you even not learn any thing new, a brushing up to your old learning in arithmetic you will find extremely useful. I see you have at length set seriously about getting a new dwelling House, which you now must surely be much in want of. Get it strongly & neatly finished off, with plenty of good furniture in it, and I shall trust to sister Jane for its being kept clean and tidy – or as we say in our Broad Scotch "well redd up".[18] You should also have a garden before it, neatly enclosed with railing, and planted with all the Small fruit Bushes you can find in the woods such as gooseberries Currants &^c. This would be an excellent place for our good old father to amuse himself in during the fine weather, and where he could be as *prossy*[19] as he pleased, in planting rows of cabbages and laying out Beds of

17 Midlem or Midholm was a village in the parish of Bowden, Roxburghshire, just east of Selkirk.
18 Tidy, well-in-order. DSL.
19 Prossie or prowsie: stuck-up, conceited. DSL.

Carrots and Onions. You have made a very good bargain in getting your House built at 4 Dollars[20] a week, but take care at the same time that the mason performs his work well. Those who work at such a cheap rate are usually but indifferent tradesmen. The inside should be divided into two apartments, one as a Bed Room the other as a Sitting Room for passing the day in with your Stove in the partition between them, – which will keep them both warm & comfortable. The kitchen should either be behind or at the end of the house with a door opening into it from the Sitting Room; and on no account have your Pots & Kettles in the same room that you eat and pass the day in.

I am my dear John, so surrounded with busy people at present that I have really not time for writing you a long letter; – You will therefore excuse me this time, and do not measure my affection for you by the number of pages I write you, for I can assure you there are few days pass but I think of Beech Ridge[21] and the ragged little rogues I left there, no doubt now so changed in person that were we now to meet I should scarcely know them.

Before concluding, I shall say a few words on the subject of my letters from Red River. I assuredly sent them forward made up in one parcel, under address as follows – "M^r. Ja^s Ross Montreal to remain at the HBCoys Office at Lachine till Called for," and as they were forwarded by what I thought the safest conveyance (Captn Franklins Govt packet) it is strange how they have got astray. You may however have only asked for letters to our father, and if so, those under the above address would not have been given you. After this when you call for letters always ask both for those to our father & also to Ja^s Ross by which means you are

20 The 1834 publication notes that the dollar is worth five shillings Halifax. Buchanan, *Information for Emigrants*.
21 Beechridge (or Beech Ridge), the location of the Hargrave family home in Beauharnois Seigneury, southwest of Montreal, was described with a somewhat jaundiced eye by a later visitor in the 1860s, while writing about a neighbour of the Hargraves: "There was nothing about the place, or its vicinity, that one could have supposed would have had any attractions for a mind so poetic and so keenly appreciative of the beautiful in nature. To our own eye, though we saw it in winter, the locality seemed a dull and dreary solitude, fitted rather as a place of endurable exile than for a pleasant summer retreat. It was inland and the landscape, unrelieved by hill or dale, was fringed by the grim, gray primeval forest." Croil, *Life of Rev. Alex. Mathieson*, 93.

sure of getting all. Indeed should James have called at the Office since you wrote me I am persuaded he will have received the parcel I sent from Red River, – as I cannot see how they could have got astray.
Your Aff[ectiona]*te* Brother

JH

YF 18*th* July 1828

M*r* A. Hargrave
Dear Andrew

I have just finished reading over for the tenth time I believe your letter of last spring, and I must own nothing pleases me more than perusing all your little stories about your farm, your labours, and your plans. We indeed have reason to be thankful for the comfortable situation our family is now in, compared with former days in Scotland. Every one of you is his own master, you sit down & rise up as you please, and every stroke of your Axe, turns to your own advantage, instead of toiling for a scanty pittance under the severe eye of a master. I think it was in the fall of 1817 – when coming over from Midholm to Lindean[22] I went down to my father who was working in the *haugh*[23] on the west side of Lindean Mill, between it & Bridge-haugh. He was then thinking of leaving Scotland, and we began to talk about the chance of bettering his condition in America. While speaking he looked round on the field about him, and observed "I would be perfectly content with my lot were I owner of a park like this. That would be enough for all my wants." He was at the time toiling hard for the gains of another, and this wish of his sunk so deep in my mind, that I believe I may date from that moment my fixed resolution to leave Scotland, and do what I could in a foreign land to improve our situation in the world. With that view I advised & urged him to come to America, with that view I followed him, with that view, I came to this country when I saw that by the trifle I gained as a teacher in Canada I could not hope to attain my object, and it is for that purpose & to obtain this object – that I send to him & my mother whatever I can spare out of my salary. Providence has greatly prospered me, and I firmly believe that the blessing which has been upon my undertakings and my course

22 A small village lying two miles northeast of Selkirk.
23 Level ground, generally alluvial, on the banks of a river, river-meadow land. DSL.

through life has been granted to the earnest prayers of one of the best and worthiest of fathers. How can I be otherwise than happy then to find you all talking of the plenty and comforts you enjoy and to see as through a glass by your letters, that every year you improve in what renders this life desirable in a temporal point of view.

Write me always about your farm matters, your crops and your Stock. I hope that before next season you will have had your new house finished, and are into more commodious lodgings. The old one by this time must be a perfect ruin, and the new one become absolutely necessary. I see you like the rest are anxious to know when I am going to return to Canada. You ask a question my dear boy, I really cannot answer, as it may be in a year or two, or it may be more, – this matter does not rest entirely on my wish, or rather the undertaking would thwart my views in life so much that I cannot venture on it without the certainty of great inconvenience & hurt to my prospects in life. Should I however go down soon it could only be for a few months, and then to return again here for some years longer: this would give little pleasure, as the pain of separation would embitter the happiness we all would have when together. You recollect our old Stories about going to "poose[24] our fortunes" – such is my aim in this country, to leave the pursuit now, would spoil very flattering prospects indeed, and instead of a fortune I would return to you little richer than I left you. Let us all however be content and providence I hope will one day bring us together again, meantime I am
My Dear Andrew
Your Aff[ectionate]. Brother

JHargrave

YF 19th July, 1828

M^{rs}. Mary Ross
My Dear Mary –

I need not tell the pleasure I experience in receiving & reading your annual letters, you yourself can well imagine it I know from what you feel on receiving mine. I have just been reading over again yours of 9th March last, and I cannot help admiring the neatness of your language, as well as feeling affected by the Sisterly love which breathes throughout it.

---

24 "To pouss one's fortune" means to take steps to improve one's financial status, to push one's fortune. DSL.

Little time have I at this season for sending you a return worthy of your one, – but that little shall be well employed, and I know that, short as my letter may be, you will believe my affection for you to remain as warm as if I had written quires. Regarding myself I have little to say: at this place I fill the situation of General Store Clerk, a duty of the most arduous labour during summer: – the situation however (I can say it to you without ostentation) is one of much respectability & trust, and is considered one of the most confidential Offices confided to the Senior Clerks in the Service. In a year or two I have reason to hope that promotion in the Service, and a high increase of Emolument will be the reward of my present labours. I need not add that there is little chance of my leaving this place for any other in the country; – indeed from the few Clerks presently in the Service, I really think I could not be spared from hence even for a single winter, without great inconvenience to the business and consequently much hurt to my own interest, for you have now seen enough of the world to know, that the prosperity of an individual is exactly in proportion to the use, value, and certainty of his services. This feeling & this alone, prevents me from asking leave of absence for a single winter to see our old parents. I know what inconvenience my absence would occasion. I know too that my chance of promotion would be retarded by the inconvenience of that step and consequently that the period of my leaving the country altogether would be placed at a much greater distance. A single word to the Gov[erno]^r this summer would have obtained that permission, for Govr Simpson is one of the kindest & most considerate of men, but by the rules of the service, another with justice would lay claim to the merit of having performed those duties belonging to me during my absence. I feel for the anxiety of our old parents, – I have written much to them this summer on the above subject & I trust my poor mother will see the propriety of my remaining here for some time longer & will try to acquire resignation to my absence: my health is as good as ever, and you will laugh at me when I tell you as a proof of my resolution to return again at no very distant period that I am yet a bluff bachelor, free of wife or other encumbrance, and that in this land at least I am *determined* to keep myself so. – This sacrifice however is not for the sake of Melinda.[25] I have heard more than enough of her indiscretions to destroy every such thought had such ever existed, – which *she knows* was never the case. As for Stuart he is welcome to the reward of his ingenuity in getting rid of

---

25 Melinda Dewey, a neighbour of the Hargraves in Lower Canada.

me as a competitor for such a worthless prize, I will abide by the alternative which my good fortune has presented me with in exchange.

I am happy to hear that my little nephew William shows such an early attachment to his book. My Dear Mary let his education be taken care of, and there is little fear of his prosperity hereafter in life! I send down to little Jane a present of a few pairs of garnished shoes this season which I hope will fit her. I have entrusted them along with this letter to one of my most valued friends in this country a M^r. Cumming,[26] who goes down to superintend the HBC^{oy}s affairs at the post of the Chât at some distance up the Ottawa River from where you are. He will send them down to the office at Lachine where they will remain till you should call for them. I have nothing to send to William, but will try & procure something curious for him another time, should I again find an opportunity for forwarding it. I am really pressed for time & must close with assuring you that
I remain
My Dear Mary
Your Loving Brother

JHargrave

YF 21st July 1828

M^r. Ja^s Ross
Dear Brother

Tho' it is far from being likely that we will be *personally* acquainted for several years to come, I assure you it is with the feeling I experience in addressing a known & tried friend that I sit down to write you a few lines in return to your kind letter of last spring. Few I fear they must be for I address you from the very focus of business, while upwards of a hundred Voyageurs tongues are clanging in my ears joined to the creaking of Bales Presses,[27] the noise of hammers and all the other discordant sounds of a crowded Depot. I am rejoiced to find that you succeed so well in procuring contracts for which the many public works now going forward in Canada

---

26 Cuthbert Cumming (1787–1870), HBC chief trader, moved from Swan River to the Chats in the Montreal Department in 1828.

27 Fur presses converted the bulky furs into easily handled cargo. About sixty beaver pelts, piled on four binding cords and sandwiched in burlap or muslin, were pressed and tied into each compact ninety-pound bale.

affords such favourable opportunities. The Rideau Canal[28] especially is a work worthy of the patronage of the British Nation, and countenance & encouragement from the Gentlemen entrusted with the completion of it affords no doubt to those in your line every chance of being well recompensed for your undertakings. The Bridge over the Ottawas at Hull[29] is really a stupendous idea, as I well remember the beautiful falls of the Rideau which I passed some 9 or 10 years ago, and can well conceive what difficulties the architects had to contend with. Who is this McTaggart?[30] We have files of the Montreal Herald[31] every season, and I see he often employs his pen in it, much to the amusement of its readers. I understand he holds some situation in the engineer department.

I need not attempt looking round me for subjects to interest you among the transactions of this country. Every white in it pursues his own interest, for such alone is the object of his residence here: – in the dull routine of business what is there to attract the attention of a stranger? And as to the Natives he who has once seen an indian, has seen every thing that is interesting in that part of our species. Their mode of life appears every where the same, making allowance for the changes occasioned by the various productions and nature of the country where they reside. When I first came to this country I could have written whole quires regarding this primitive race of people, – but their ways have now become so familiar to me that I cannot touch on the subject with the least hope of interesting. So good bye to it.

28 In 1826, Lt Colonel John By (1779–1836) of the Royal Engineers was assigned the task of creating a navigable waterway from Kingston to Ottawa through a wilderness of rough bush, swamps, and rocky terrain. After completion in the fall of 1831 with many lives having been lost during its construction, the Rideau Canal opened for navigation in 1832.
29 The first truss bridge over the Ottawa River was completed in 1828. Known as the Union Bridge because it connected the two Canadas, it had eight spans, including one of 212 feet across a cauldron known as the "Big Kettle." Robert Drummond (1791–1834) was the principal designer of the drystone construction bridge which, after a span washed out in 1836, was later replaced by a suspension bridge.
30 John Mactaggart (1791–1830), an engineer and author, was the Clerk of Works on the Rideau Canal construction. He was also partly responsible for the design of the Union Bridge across the Ottawa River.
31 The *Montreal Herald* was founded in 1811.

Your Object seems to be to procure a competency whereby to commence Settler preparatory to which you have already secured a farm ready to set down upon. I came to this country with that object also, and still have occasional visions of a snug house in the woods with flourishing crops around it, while a sweet wee lassie sometimes forms part of the imaginary prospect; but alas these are creations of the fancy. My hand has now become so conversant with the pen that the hatchet or plough would despise its guidance, I must therefore stick to my present pursuits till they produce me enough to render all other aid unnecessary. This I have strong hopes of accomplishing in time to admit of spending many happy days yet among my friends, *and* when I rejoin my dear sister & you, after being so long separated among these will be *some of the happiest.*

I must however close this sheet, – the produce of at least a dozen continuations. It shews my desire of chatting with you, and indeed does little else; but I write to those I know will excuse a hurried page & who will look to the attempt & design more than the performance. By the way, I wrote you from Red River in the winter of 1826/27 by a Packet fro[m] Capt Franklin to the British Gov' and addressed my letter to you as usual to remain at the HBCoys Office at Lachine till called for, – tell me whether you have ever received it.

Yours affectionately

JHargrave

YF August 1st 1828

Mr Willm Lockie
My Dear Lockie

I am never more affected with the force of that simple & expressive comparison in Scripture "As cold waters to the thirsty soul so are good news from a far country."[32] I would say that these words never come home to my heart with such power, as when my annual packet of letters are put into my hands each successive spring. After those of my revered parents I feel my heart gladdened by the sight of your well known hand, and were you a witness of the avidity with which I devour the well filled pages, your time in tracing them I am convinced you would consider most charitably spent. Of all treats of this nature your sheet of last spring was most

---

32 "As cold waters to a thirsty soul, so is good news from a far country." *King James Bible,* Proverbs 25:25.

to my taste, and it is not to flatter you that I acknowledge I have read it so often over that I have it mostly by heart. It really was an epitome of every thing which interests me in my native land, and the information it communicated relative to public affairs & to literary subjects was peculiarly gratifying. In return most heartily I take up my pen to reply, tho' much I fear inadequately, as the bustle of a crowded Depôt presently surrounds me and placed as I am in its focus, receiving and answering incessant applications on business every minute, I would find it difficult to abstract my mind from the mental labor of the day and turn an undivided attention to softer feelings and more attractive recollections. On your indulgence I rely, & should I omit an expected paragraph or touch lightly on [what] to you may be an interesting subject, believe that notwithstanding all such, I am still the same, and that the heart dictates altho' the pen may lamely describe.

In reply to your warm inquiries after my dear parents I am truly happy to say that both they and the rest of the family were by letters I had, dated in March last, in good health and comfortable circumstances. The following extracts from their letters may give you a more graphic description of their condition and occupations than I in my own words might be able to produce. My brother John writes "We had a very good crop last year, only where the ground was low it was not ver[y] good, because the season was so very wet. We have had very little snow all winter until now: we did not get any thing done to the house last year (a new house they are building) because one of the oxen was sick for most part of the summer with the horn distemper: we had to saw both his horns out by the root but now he is almost as good as ever. We have got a yoke of young oxen two year old this spring & four Cows & 10 Sheep. We expect the mare to have a foal in the month of May. We have given the house to a Scotsman of the name of Mr Fenton[33] to build: he is engaged with us for four dollars a week we are going to make it thirty feet long & 24 ft wide. We have got out most part of the Shingle Wood and we are now busy in getting logs to the Saw Mill." My mother writes, speaking of some little trifle I sent her last season, "I received your kind gift which you were pleased to send me and I was very proud of it I can assure you. I have laid it out as

---

33 Possibly Andrew Fenton, who is listed in baptismal records for his children as a farmer in Williamstown in 1833 and as a mason in Dundee in 1836 and 1838. http://www.swquebec.ca. See online database of nineteenth-century Southwestern Quebec Church records.

you bade me, in bed clothes and a coverled, a feather Bed *like any lady* and flannel shirts for your father & me, and he often says we have the best bed in the place, and a great coat & Bonnet & some pounds of Tea and Sugar. I am a great tea drinker now: A *fore* I came here I durst not taste, now it agrees well with me. I was likewise furnished with money for to loose my webs from the river: we had a *cleadin*[34] in for your father & your two brothers, and a gown for Jean & me." Brother Andrew says – "Our old father has taken your advice in not working so hard as he used, but he cannot leave it off altogether. he still thrashes the barn, and when he sees any body he knows passing the road he must have them in to take a drink of milk and have an hours *crack*[35] with them. That is just his pleasure, – and it is likewise pleasing to John & me for at his age it is time to quit work." The Old Boy writes himself, & a long screed of doctrine he gives me – "We presbyterians have agreed both Upper & Lower Canada and have signed 3 petitions, one to be laid before his Majesty and another to be laid before the parliament, & the third to be left at Edinburgh to send us ministers among us, and there is two Lawyers to present our petition craving that we may have the same right for the support of the gospel with the land which government hath alloted for the Clergy – But the Bishop & his underlings, claim the whole of it: And we about Beech Ridge have agreed to have a Minister to preach gaelic & english & all the inhabitants between the head of the French Settlement to Norton Creek have signed to support a minister but the Roman Catholics, and the place of public worship will be the burial Ground near your uncles lot.[36] Now Son, I had a great desire to purchase some books to send up to

34 Clothing. DSL.
35 Talk, gossip, conversation. DSL.
36 The Gaelic-speaking minister finally materialized in 1837. In the mid-1830s, Beechridge's 150 Scottish families were primarily Highlanders who had left Scotland in 1802 and then relocated from Chambly in 1816. It was not until 1837 that the Beechridge congregation was "fitted up" with a Gaelic-speaking minister, Rev. Thomas McPherson. A little earlier in the decade of the 1830s the two non-Gaelic-speaking Presbyterian ministers in the Beauharnois seigneury, Rev. James Anderson at Ormstown, and Rev. Walter Roach at South Georgetown, took turns trying to tend to the spiritual needs of the Scottish community in Beechridge. Campey quotes Roach describing their plight in 1836:
   In their zeal and anxiety to obtain a Minister they have swelled their subscription list to the amount of £75. But alas would it ever be realized? And yet … as must such a congregation be continually destitute

you, but I find what you have said that they will not receive bundles into the packet & I shall name them & you can purchase them by the Ship that goes to London, the first is Marshal[37] on Sanctification, the second is the Marrow of Modern Divinity,[38] with Boustans Notes,[39] the third is Boustans four fold state[40] and the 4th is Booth's Reign of Grace,[41] and, if you please to add, Truths Victory over Error by Mr Dickson[42] professor of divinity at Edinburgh." Now only think of the good old man recommending The Marrow of M^n Divinity & the Four fold State to the study of a head so over jaded with Bills Ladings Invoices & all the intricacies of Tariffs that on an evening which stretched out on a Sopha in the silence & solitude of my bed room a chapter of the Evangelists is the deepest reading in Divinity which my mistified ideas can comprehend.[43] Such is still the man; as you know him I have selected these extracts to show with

    of pastoral instruction. The people in that quarter have in a special manner a claim on our sympathy. Surrounded by Roman Catholics and infested with Methodist preachers from the States, and many of the younger families displaying much ignorance in the doctrines and scriptural facts of the Bible. Yet bound by all the hereditary attachment characteristic of Highlanders to the Church of Scotland, they claim an interest in our endeavours and in our prayers.
    Campey, *Les Écossais*, 72–4.

37 Walter Marshall (1628–1680) wrote *The Gospel Mystery of Sanctification* published in 1692.
38 *The Marrow of Modern Divinity* was first published in London 1645–49 by an author known only as E.F. Authorship is sometimes disputed.
39 Rev. Thomas Boston (1676–1732), a Scottish church leader, published an edition with notes of his own in 1726.
40 In *Human Nature in its Fourfold State*, Thomas Boston expounds on the biblical teaching about the four "states" of God's relationship to humankind: innocence, sin, grace, and glory.
41 Abraham Booth (1734–1806), an English Baptist, wrote *The Reign of Grace, from its Rise, to its Consummation*, published in 1768, on the importance of grace.
42 David Dickson (1583?–1663) was the author of *Truth's Victory over Error*, first published in 1684 by his translator, George Sinclair, as the latter's own work.
43 Hargrave might have sympathized with the views of Agnes Deans Cameron upon examining an old library book she found at Fort Simpson: "The lengthy titles of the books of this vintage, as for instance, *Death-Bed Triumphs of Eminent Christians, Exemplifying the Power of Religion in a Dying*

how much propriety it may be said of him "that even his failings lean to virtues side."[44] I must however quit this fascinating subject – which has already engrossed a large portion of my sheet.

Your notices of my old friends & school fellows is a most interesting passage and I am happy to find that such among them as merit prosperity, have it. Should I visit Scotland again, it assuredly will be one of my first objects, on returning to that quarter I yet remember so well, to search out & renew my intimacy with such as deserve regard, whatever their circumstances in life may be. The falling off among some, my present experience has taught me to bear with equanimity: – I certainly had calculated on warmer feelings in the breast of Sword; and it appears had calculated erroneously; I shall however to adopt his own language, hereafter consider him as a *casual acquaintance*, and as such, desire that his name may hereafter occupy no portion of our correspondence. For my part, one of the chief & most refined pleasures to me in this scene of existence is the unrestrained intercourse of congenial minds: – To find one worthy of such confidence is indeed rare, but I trust the defection of some, and the unworthy motives discovered in the services of others, will only bind me still more strongly to such as I have proved worthy in word and in deed. I have long ago curbed the open liberality of youth, which is so apt to fling open its arms & its confidence to every fair profession, old friends like old wine every year become, of more value to me, and what though some bottles burst and are lost I have still enough to rejoice my heart and to cheer the evening shades of existence.

Now to your Queries. But Oh! for a fireside chat of only one evening, and I would pledge myself to a better answer, than what a ream of letters could contain. Your anxiety regarding the course of religion and morals in this country I am happy to be able to meet, if not by an unexceptionable statement, at least with what contains much worthy of commendation. Of Course, spread as we are over such an immense surface, and

---

Hour, bring to mind the small boy's definition of porridge – 'fillin', but not satisfyin'." Cameron, *New North*, 181.

44 Oliver Goldsmith (1728–1774), Irish poet and prose writer, in his poem *The Deserted Village*:
Careless their merits or their faults to scan,
His pity gave ere charity began.
Thus to relieve the wretched was his pride,
And even his failings lean'd to Virtue's side.

liable as every one is to removal from one quarter to another almost every season, no regular congregations of professing christians can be formed; yet the Gentlemen at the head of affairs both in England & this country, ever solicitous for the welfare of the Servants both spiritual as otherwise have used their utmost efforts to overcome the difficulties which the nature of the country opposes to the establishment & diffusion of religion. At all our Forts by an established Order of Council, public prayers are weekly made by the Gentleman in charge, a sermon is read, and serious instructions suited to the understandings of the hearers is bestowed on them. Such assemblies consist of the Coys Officers & Servants their families also every native that may happen to be at the Fort & who could understand the instructions used. Missionaries could be of little benefit either among Whites & Natives, from the thinness of the population & the migratory life they lead, but in the Colony at Red River established for & composed of our old Retired Servants & their half breed families, two Clerical Gentlemen of the Reformed Church,[45] as well as 2 more of the Romish persuasion[46] are established, and I must say that both parties live in good neighborhood, and their only rivalry is who shall do most for the welfare of their respective congregations. Both of these Churches teach Schools of native children & their present labors I trust will be of vital importance to the cause of christianity among the poor & ignorant natives. From this you will gather that the human species here is extremely scanty considering the extent they cover. The Whites (the only part of all possessed of civilization, taking Christianity & the arts of life as a criterion) are only to be found at the Coys Forts, which are separated at least by 2 or 300 miles from each other, & the number at each never exceeds 20, at most, not one/4 of that number. The poor natives are however in general most friendly to the "palefaced Strangers" and no danger is apprehended in consequence the weak force that could be opposed to their hostility. My information regarding the domestic habits of the Indians is more limited than what might be expected from a 8 y[ea]^r residence among them, and I can enter little into detail regarding the arts they employ in hunting the fur animals of the country. Beaver are either caught in Steel Traps,[47] Shot, or dug out of the holes they burrow in, about the

---

45 David Jones and William Cockran.
46 Joseph Norbert Provencher and Joseph Nicholas Dumoulin.
47 The steel trap was invented by an American, Sewell Newhouse, in 1823, allowing hunters to set and bait dozens of traps with castoreum and then

banks of rivers. This last is a most laborious operation, occupying often three or four days to get at a single family of these animals. Porcupines are always shot likewise the marten or sable, the mink, the Lynx & the otter. Foxes are either shot or caught in Steel Traps. The hunting of these last I am intimately acquainted with, having last winter for amusement & exercise kept 3 or 4 traps set during the whole season & which I visited every day. The Trap is formed much like that for rats used in Scotland, but larger stronger & having 2 Springs, one at each end of the jaws instead of only one as in the rat trap. They are set in the following manner. A hole is dug in the snow in a smooth open spot, about a foot deep & 20 in. square, in which the trap is placed with its jaws expanded, & the latch or pallet so easy of motion that the least weight falling upon it causes the trap to spring. Arranged in this manner, a sheet of paper is then placed over the trap & the snow so smoothed around & over it, that to both man & beast, unacquainted with what is below, nothing unusual is seen. The bait consisting of some fresh meat chopped up into small pieces, is then scattered over the surface & all around, the scent of which attracting the fox, he begins with eagerness to gather the delicious prize, till stepping unawares upon the concealed Trap it springs & catches him by the leg where he remains alive till the hunter makes his daily rounds & knocks him on the head. When once a fox is attracted to the spot & it is not aware of some danger he is inevitably sure of being caught; indeed I never saw an instance of it missing. It sometimes happens however that his acute sense of smelling warns of the danger & instances are known of these cunning animals having dug down in the snow at the side of the trap, till getting below it, turns it up with his snout when it springs & then with safety to himself *at his leisure devours the bait*. Even when caught, the hunter is not always secure of his game, as in leaping about & dragging the trap he sometimes breaks the bone of the leg, the limb in consequence freezes as Hard as a stick, and the animal gnaws it in two & frees himself. An instance occurred to me of this last winter. On visiting them one day I found one of the traps sprung, the snow all around covered with blood, & the foot of a beautiful Silver fox left between the jaws. I had my gun with me, and as I was able to trace him by the bloody track I set off in pursuit. He had taken to the bank of a river down which I followed him several miles. Many times I found where he had attempted to

---

collect the beavers. This was a much more efficient, if crueler, method than trying to spear animals around their lodges.

hide below an overhanging tree or burrow in a snow wreak, but judging his concealment insecure had again left it. After proceeding 3 or 4 miles in this manner I at length found poor Reynard snugly *derned*[48] under a tree root, shivering with pain & gnashing his teeth at his approaching enemy. He again took to flight but it was only for a few yards & a single shot laid the poor wretch extended lifeless in the snow. The Skins of the Silver foxes are very valuable, selling in London for from 8 to £20 each. Of all instances of skill however I have witnessed among the natives in hunting, that of the Esquimeaux in pursuit of the seal during winter, is the most ingenious. These animals dig out or widen holes in the fissures of the ice and on a fine day come up through them to bask in the sun on the surface. They are very timerous keep out from shore, are most acute of hearing, and never stray to any distance from the margin of the hole into which they plunge on the least apprehension of danger. The Esquimeaux has learned from experience to overcome all these difficulties. He starts armed with only a spear from a side where the breeze comes to him from the Seal so that a sense of danger cannot be conveyed by smell, and crawling sometimes on his knees sometimes on his side & using adroitly for concealment every little inequality on the surface of the ice, he ordinarily is enabled to get within 100 yards before perceived by the seal. The animal then gazes around, and prepares to plunge into the water, but is attracted by the antic gestures of the hunter who nods his head flings up his heels & to the life imitates the action & cry of the seal – in short deceives the real one into a belief that a neighbour phoca [Latin for seal] is coming to visit him, a deceit well assisted by the Esquim[au]ˣ dress which is entirely formed of that animals skin. Proceeding in this manner he draws nearer, and nearer still observing all the motions of his game till when within 15 or 20 y[ar]ᵈˢ he suddenly launches his spear, and almost to a certainty strikes his prize. In this state the Seal would still escape by diving, but finds himself unable to move from the Spear being fixed to the Esquimaux body by a line, and holding by which the hunter secures his booty at leisure. The skill discovered by this Tribe in hunting forming arms & implements of the chase, as well as in the various arts employed to resist the rigour of their dismal climate, is in my opinion far superior to that evinced by any other nation in North America. To enter into detail however is needless, without specimens, Drawings &ᶜ I could not explain so as to be understood, and I must perforce let this topic of native arts and

48 Hidden, concealed. DSL.

skill remain almost a dead letter till you & I in some future year meet over a bowl of real farintosh[49] Toddy, or if your southern County cannot afford this incomparable blood of John Barlycorn[50] we shall try what inspiration there is in a ½ dozen Bottles of port. By the way I well recollect the ordinary whisky of Hawick was most execrable stuff perfect aquafortis or liquid fire & I trust for these credit of their far-famed Gill, (not unknown even this extremity of the globe) that they have regenerated the brac of our national liquor.

I am particularly interested by the hints you give of your professional labors. Like a man viewing the surrounding landscape from the top of a high mountain, I can in this country more take in at one view the various features of my native land and her hundreds of useful institutions. Among the most praise worthy in my eye is her School Establishment, aided as it is so nobly by the universal desire of education even among the poorest of her children. Above every class in the community in the Scale of usefulness in my estimation Stand the Teachers of youth. To them is committed the formation of the National mind, and according as their duties are well or ill performed, in the same degree will each succeeding generation improve or degenerate. On the faithful performance of these duties depend the success of the preachers instructions, the Magistrates institutions, the internal tranquility & innocence of the country, and in fine the character the nation at large will maintain in the estimation of the world. Lowly and obscure then as may be your labors, in this light they stand forward alike honorable to yourself & to your native land – pittance for which you toil when the future value of these labors are considered appears trebly contemptible, and I am truly happy to learn that there is a probability of your soon being raised above want by having a yearly salary allowed you.

Now for a little to what I would wish to hear of in your next. Let public & literary matters by all means specify as much of it as the last. Your remarks are so just and the conclusions you draw, so sound, that I derive more information from them than from all the files of papers which every

---

49 A kind of whisky formerly distilled in the village of Ferintosh on the Cromarty Firth near Dingwall. It was characterized by its strong peat-smoke flavour. The term was often used of whisky generally. DSL.
50 John Barleycorn is the personification of barley and of the alcoholic beverages made from it, beer and whisky. Hargrave may be referring to Robert Burn's poem, "John Barleycorn." In Cunningham, *With His Life*, 333–5.

autumn litter our rooms. Every notice how trifling soever it may be to you, which regards names & places formerly familiar to me will always be interesting; of these what ever you can drag into your service. What proportion is there in solid inches or [illegible] between the old Scottish measures & weights & the English ones lately abolished by Act of Parliament.[51] Let me also have if you please a list of the old Scottish Names for all the different divisions in weight & capacity.

Is Douglas of Cavers lineally descended from the antient & powerful family of Douglas on the Borders; is he, or who is considered, the head of that honorable name in the present day. These & such topics will be food for many an ideal visit to my native land another season. X (Monument in Edinh?)

On glancing over a few hints which I jotted down on again reading your letter before I began this sheet I perceive I have omitted some of your minor queries, which I shall now answer in the order they come. I have examined every mem° regarding my correspondence with you since I came to this country, and from them aided by an imperfect recollection I am almost certain I wrote you in the years 1821 & 1822. The first was either written from St Marys on Lake Superior or Fort William, & the other from this place. Should you not have received them they must have miscarried. I think I have regularly written you once a year ever since I entered the Indian Territories, also twice I believe from Canada making this my 10th Letter. The distance which separates us is I believe upwards of 3000 miles – but I say this almost from a rough Guess with little other authority. This to you may appear the journey of a life, it however has been 3 times doubled by me since I left you, and the voyage were the day come for undertaking it would not cost me two anxious thoughts. The number of civilized people within my every day reach, is, as above hinted, very limited indeed. This place, the head Depot of the Trade, does not contain above [illegible] adults & within a circle of 500 miles around it, that number is not doubled – The number of all classes of whites in the country, (that is to say not natives) I should name below a thousand & indeed there is scarcely a European east of the Rocky Mountains & north

---

51 Until the middle of the nineteenth century a wide diversity of weights and measures were used in Scotland. Standardization took place from 1661 onwards, and in 1824 an act of parliament imposed the English versions of Imperial measures and defined the proportions of older measures to Imperial measures.

of Lake Superior, but whom I personally know. I think this comprehends the most of your queries.

17th Augt. I almost forgot to mention that by the arrival of the Ship[52] fro' London the other day I had a letter from a female cousin in Galashiels, who gives me a hint that a renewed correspondence with Miss A. Wilson would be now very satisfactorily received. Excuses of friends opposition &^{c} are made for former silence, & a mode pointed out by which I might yearly hear from her. This is now too late; the sparks of former feelings I confess are yet alive, but both our years are now too far advanced to admit of an apology for the romance of visiting Britain merely from youthful attachments, ruinous as such a procedure would be to my best interests in this country. In short I am now by time & circumstances forced in my turn to the defensive side, – my answer however shall at once be to the point, – she shall never have it to say – nor indeed would my still unabated regard for her allow me to give the remotest cause for complaint, that I have by tantalizing conduct blasted the hopes of happiness in one for whom I have ever avowed the tenderest sentiments. This newly opened mode of intercourse by the way makes up for the slight inconvenience arising from the former *very doubtful* one being closed *by Sword*. I have scarcely room left to say a word to my kind friends & old comrades around you. My best wishes are with them, & assure them from me that I yet purpose to make the round of my old haunts before I retire from active life, in what quarter soever of the globe I may fix on for laying up the battered hulk of an old Northwester. When that time comes I shall make it a point to enquire out every one to whom the renewed acquaintance of "little Jamie Hargrave" would as I conceive be acceptable.

Read as much of this as you please to our worthy friends Geo[rge]: & Esther Aitken, & tell them that I have had several inquiries from my old parents as to their situation & prosperity in life. To this add an assurance of both my parents & my own undiminished regard. Remember me also most kindly to Geo: Reid, John Reid[53] & R. Scott.[54] Also to whomever you may consider I would personally be a welcome Guest. – To Mrs Lockie I beg to express the kindest feelings arising from "Auld lang Syne", and

---

52 The *Prince Rupert*, under Capt. Benjamin Bell, arrived in York Factory 17 August after leaving London 3 June.
53 Possibly the "Little Johnnie Reid" of Baghall, a shepherd at Deloraine on Etterick, mentioned in Hargrave's 1828–29 Journal.
54 Possibly the Robert Scott mentioned in Hargrave's journal of 1828–29.

to your rising family I desire to be known as the old pupil & one of the most attached friends of their worthy parents. May their course in life ascend above the "narrow rural vale"⁵⁵ even with all its simple attractions, or at least may their path through it be strewed with *gowans*⁵⁶ instead of briars. God bless you my Dear Lockie
Your unaltered friend

JH

---

55 A line from a poem by Robert Burns called "Address to Edinburgh." In Cunningham, *With His Life*, 1–4.
56 Common daisies. DSL.

[Letterbook]
N°. 4
Rough Copies Letters by
JHargrave
from 25th Augt 1828 @ 11 July '29

York Factory 25th Augt. 1828

Miss Euphemia Mitchell
My Dear Cousin

    I have been favored with your kind letter of 3rd April last which reached me about ten days ago, and I assure you have been quite delighted with the perusal of all your little stories, expressed as they are in such neat & correct language. I promised last year not to tax you with the postage of a separate letter in return, but there are passages in yours which unless I write you yourself for reasons you will perceive I must leave unanswered, and as these are among its most interesting topics, I trust you will excuse my breaking my promise for this once for the pleasure it will give me to open my mind to you without reserve in regard to these subjects I allude to. I was a good deal diverted by your candour in what you say regarding rumours of your marriage, and approve highly of your prudence in taking time to make a proper selection of a companion for life. In this however there is a good medium. Be neither too hasty nor too fastidious. Heedlessness &c imprudence almost inevitably are productive of ill sorted & unhappy matches; on the other hand, a too fanciful scrutiny of a lovers person or means in life who to much merit may add some trivial faults, will often lead young maids on in single blessedness to a period in life when they are too apt to consider any husband better than none. I have however too high an opinion of your good sense to think you stand in need of any such advice, and what you say on this subject is entirely according to my idea of how a young woman should act in this matter, which is in reality the grand hinge on which the happiness or misery of their future life depends.
    I own I was a good deal surprised at what you tell me from Miss A. Wilson, and how highly soever I might have been delighted by her favorable remembrance *some years ago*, circumstances *now* render it altogether useless to commence a correspondence with her again. On this subject I will open my whole mind to you, and firmly trust to your good sense & discretion for its remaining a secret with every one from whom I wish it

concealed. I will candidly own then that when I left Scotland, gloomy & uncertain as were my future prospects for life I entertained such sentiments for her as would have induced me to disregard every consideration in comparison with the happiness of calling her mine & taking her along with me. Her refusal was firm & decided, as to leaving her native land, altho' allowing me to hope a more favorable answer had I remained in Scotland. I left her & it with regret, compelled by fortune & other feelings. In this country when my prospects in life brightened & my circumstances became such as I once had no hopes of, a favorable chance offered for my return to Britain for a few months. I had no inducement to the voyage besides my recollections of her, much more favorable matches as to fortune & what the world would call more prudent, I as situated in this country might have aspired to, yet I chose rather to renew my proposal to one I still esteemed above all, – which if answered favorably would have led one to Britain the following year. Next Spring bro' no answer, and hope being thus extinguished I allowed the opportunity of seeing Scotland again pass without seeing it. The reason for her silence which you mention I am willing to believe just, it is however not the less unfortunate & destructive of all future correspondence between her and me. On receiving no answer to my letter of 1823 I concluded all future hopes at an end, & having no longer any wish to see my native land when such hopes were quenched, I then & have since changed my views of life so much that consistently with them it would be a weak *hankering* after what can never be accomplished for me to again open a correspondence with Miss Wilson. I have no expectation of visiting Britain again for many years to come, and may consequently never have the happiness of seeing her again, I *fear* however that the remembrance of one, once so dearly esteemed by me, may be more difficult to blot out than my future relations in life may render expedient. Have the goodness to tell her from me that with feelings as warm as ever I return her my kindest love, with every wish for her future happiness. You may indeed shew her the whole of this letter, and should parts of this explanation prove disagreeable to her, I can with truth add that it has been made with much pain also to me, in order that our unfortunate acquaintance may to her no longer be attended with anxiety & suspense. Having adopted this course, which is indeed one of necessity more than of choice, I cannot expect to hear from her personally, but in your letters no part will interest me more nor be more often perused than whatever information you may here after give me of the condition in life of Miss A Wilson.

To satisfy your inquiries so judiciously made, regarding this country, will always give me the greatest pleasure; though the short Carnets of a letter can do it but very inadequately. You will no doubt hold up your hands in amazement when I tell you that there are no Ministers in this Country with the exception of two about a thousand miles distant from this, no Schoolmasters at all, also excepting these two Clergymen, and that many now in years in the remote quarters of the North have not heard a Sermon from a pulpit since they left Britain in their youth. This you will consider a bad and wicked state of society, but making allowance for circumstances I must say that I doubt whether the same reverence for sacred things be more generally shown now in Scotland than that exhibited by the Whites in this country. At all the Coys Establish[ts] the Sabbaths are regularly observed, the Gentleman in charge officiates as Clergyman by reading a sermon or portion of the Bible to all the Whites & natives who can understand him & who receive much benefit from such instruction, every parent also attends to the education of his children and the consequence is that as many have educations in this country generally as is often met with in the civilized world among the like number of inhabitants. We are scattered over an immense territory, to which the whole isles of Britain are only a diminutive speck in comparison, not above a dozen Whites are at every Fort which are usually many hundred miles asunder, solitude however & absence of temptation preserves society from most vices, & indeed I in this country lead as happy, safe, comfortable & I trust blameless a life as I could have done had I remained in the land of Cakes.[1]

I am happy to say that I have had letters from my parents & friends in Canada as late as last March when they were all in good health & happy. Sister Jean[2] sends her love to her cousin *Euphie*, and is like yourself still single, tho from my experience in maids letters I am inclined to think she like yourself thinks there is "a providence in these matters" but that patience is requisite to wait duly upon it. Mary as I have already mentioned has some years ago changed her name to Ross, and is most happy in her present condition in life. Her husband is a steady active Tradesman, at present a Contractor to a large Am[oun][t] in some national Canal[3] now forming in Canada, & there is every probability of his retir-

1 Scotland, famous for its oatmeal cakes.
2 Jane Hargrave.
3 The Rideau Canal.

ing from active business in a few years with a comfortable competency. Our old parents have every wish gratified as regards the necessaries of this life, & it is one of my purest pleasures to hear of their continued welfare every succeeding spring. You may show this letter also to my dear aunt your Mother. She will laugh at some parts, but I know such will not be one of derision. Show it to none else but her I have said so much about, & never lend it out of your possession. Write me again a separate letter next spring & I will as usual answer it by giving you half of my sheet to my Uncle.

Excuse my hurried frases, the departure of the Ship[4] loads me with public business & I am sorry I have made this letter no more interesting. With kindest sentiments of regard
I am My dear Cousin
Yours Affectionately

JH

York Factory 29th Augt 1828

M^r. Ja^s Mitchel
Galashiels
My Dear Uncle

I received about a fortnight ago your kind letter of 7 Ap^l last and am truly glad to hear of your welfare, which I trust by this time is increased by the recovery of my Cousin Mary. I also had one from my Cousin Effie, and I am both surprised and delighted by the sensible and correct manner in which she writes. I have had a good deal of experience now in correspondence and I must say few letters have pleased me better than the one she last sent me. Now this is not by way of flattery, but is a really well merited expression of truth. I feel much interested by the little history you have given me of old acquaintances about Lindean, a place to which my mind first turns when I think of Scotland. The Marriage of Wilson to Miss Milne astonishes me not a little, and his increased starchiness in consequence is quite amusing. What Turkey Cocks we Mortals are when the sun shines on our plumes!

I last spring had as usual a whole Budget of letters from my dear parents and friends at Beechridge, and I am happy to say that the information they gave me was as pleasant as I could expect or desire. The old

---

4 The *Prince Rupert* departed for London 21 September that year.

folks are still both in good health, and as sister Jane also John & Andrew are all with them, the labor of their farm costs them little toil or anxiety. They express themselves perfectly happy & contented, and indeed desirous of nothing further of this worlds riches. Jane manages the indoor matters & my two brothers see to those without so they themselves are relieved from most of what once lay as duties on their own shoulders; yet so accustomed are they to labor as a mode of passing the day, that they cannot contrive to leave it off altogether. As a specimen I shall extract a few lines from brother Andrews Letter. "Our old father has taken your advice in not working so hard as he used, but he cannot leave it off altogether. He still thrashes our barn, and when he sees any body he knows passing the road he must have them in to take a drink of milk and have an hours crack with them. That is just his pleasure; – and it is likewise pleasing to John & me, for we can do all that is to be done, and at his age it is time to quit work." The last season they had very good crops of Wheat, Indian Corn, Barley pease, Potatoes, pumpkins, & Turnips, and the Stock of Cattle Sheep, & hogs which they now possess furnish them with Beef pork & mutton all the year round. They are anxious that I should return & settle beside them, but this tho' I should desire it in many points of view is yet in others very inconvenient to me. The course in life I am presently pursuing will in the prosecution of it bring me in, not only my present wants, but allow me to lay aside what will support me in comfort and ease in old age should providence see meet to lengthen out my days so long: – to relinquish this & commence Settler would ruin all my prospects here, present me with toil & anxiety in a new occupation for comparative ease, good living, and content in one with which I am now fully conversant. Guided by these Motives I have hitherto declined listening both to my own wishes & their persuasions, convinced that such a step would be more hurtful than beneficial to all of us. To your kind inquiries I am sorry my strongest reasons for not visiting Scotland may also be drawn from what I have above mentioned. I may indeed for a season have a chance in a few years to go home in the vessel which annually visits us, spend the winter in London and Edin[burg][b], and again return hither in the Spring. This furlough is usually granted in rotation to the Coys Officers here, also when their personal affairs call them home; but it is always attended with the expense of a few hundred pounds, a sum which I have little wish of laying out, when the want of it must lengthen my residence in a foreign Country. Occasionally indeed the public Service calls some of us to England, and in the department of business I am employed in, I may have a chance of a visit without much expense to myself. Should this occur, depend upon it that I shall not omit beating up your quarters in Galashiels like one dropt from the clouds.

I regret to hear that business in Scotland is yet so dull, & that in consequence of it, so many are under the necessity of leaving their country. I agree with you that in a foreign country the mind is never so happy as in the land of ones nativity, and I am far from being an advocate for emigration when a living is to be had at home. My own case is indeed an exception: – fortune more than friends has opened a path to me in life, I am yet a single young fellow without incumbrance & could make the circuit of the globe without inconvenience. My mind is therefore at rest and knows not the yearnings of his who placed in a strange land, repines without hope for the friends which he can never expect to see again. I must however draw to a close so with kindest love to my Dear Aunt & all your family I am My dear Uncle Your Aff: Neph[e]^w JH

York Factory 29th Augt 1828

Revd W. Rattray
Rev^d & Dear Sir

Your kind yet melancholy letter[5] of the 23rd June last reached me on the 15th ins^t, – which I have several times perused with no common interest or sympathy. Believe me I deeply feel for the trials which you have experienced, – trials the intensity of which none but a husband & parents heart can fully appreciate. It is indeed in these gloomy scenes of our earthly pilgrimage when the support of our holy religion is felt as the only stay to the bowed down & fainting pilgrim, and excuse me for saying that never in my own experience have I witnessed the consoling effects of true religion on the mind more thoroughly exemplified than in the resignation with which you have been enabled to bear up under the chastenings of the Almighty. From some expressions indeed, I am inclined to think that you search your heart and try your feelings by even too rigid & unsparing a rule. The duties of a Minister of the Gospel are indeed a solemn & awful charge, and a heart devoted to them is what our God

---

5 According to James Hargrave's Journal for 1828–29, Rev. Rattray had written to him from the Orkney Islands in June 1828 to say that he had lost both his wife, Anna Allan, and three of their five children. Since leaving Selkirk in 1825, he had travelled in the north of Scotland through the Secession Church, preaching as occasion offered.

requires of him who would undertake to publish his Glad Tidings to a careless world. These duties however I should think far from being interrupted by the deep attachment in the head of a family to the little world of love around him, and a parents yearnings over his little ones is what he has condescended to select among ideas suited to our comprehensions, in illustration of the love he bears to the human race. Instead then of stern punishment for estranged affections I should interpret these afflictions dispensations of his providence as fatherly chastenings, trials indeed that prove the heart & the reins, but in which the mercy of a father is yet visible, in leaving you still a part of those darling pledges of affection whilst he has withdrawn others to himself, away from the dangers which necessarily beset them in this state of existence.

I know it will gratify you to hear that my now aged parents are yet in good health when I heard from them in last March, and that all our family are both in prosperous circumstances and are conducting themselves with propriety in their adopted country. The old folks are now indeed become very frail, and the evening of their day fast approaches, but it gladdens my heart to think that plenty of ease surrounds them at a time when they would have felt most the weight of poverty. Jane, John & Andrew are all with them & manage their little property under the eyes of my father without his being obliged to take an active part in their daily labors. I have always a letter from each of them & I shall take the liberty of giving you a few extracts from them which will afford you a more graphic idea of their condition that what I could convey in my own words. Brother Andrew writes "Our old father has taken your advice in not working so hard as he used, but he cannot leave it off altogether. He still thrashes our Barn, and when he sees any body he knows passing the road he must have them in to take a drink of milk & have an hours *crack* with them: – that is just his pleasure, and at his age it is time to quit work." My old mother writes speaking of some little trifle I had sent her. "I received your kind gift which you were pleased to send me and I was very proud of it I can assure you. – – – – – I have laid it out as you bade me in bed clothes and a coverled, a feather bed *like any lady*, and flannel shirts for your father & me, and he often says we have the best bed in the place, – and a great Coat & bonnet & some pounds of Tea & Sugar. I am a great tea drinker now; – *afore* I came here I durth not taste, now it agrees well with me. I was likewise furnished with money to *loose* my webs from the River: we had a *cleadin* for your father & your two brothers and a gown for Jane & me – and shirting for us all." I will not attempt an apology for thus copying trifles which to many would sound ridiculous. I know I am writing to an old & respected friend, who can appreciate the feelings which gave utterance to these little garrulous details, and who can perceive the true motive which makes me dwell on their broken english with delight indescribable. My fathers letter is filled with an account of the measures now taking in Canada to secure a maintenance for the presbyterian Church out of the Lands allotted by gov.[t] for the support of the Gospel. The Episcopal Es[t]ab[lishmen]:[t] appears to consider these Grants exclusively its own, & very unpopular measures have been used in asserting its right to Church Lands in Upper Canada in Counties where the inhabitants are nearly to a man presbyterians. A firm & very proper stand has however been made to this rather grasping spirit, and it appears that the English Gov.[t] has decided in favor of the aggrieved class. He complains much of the want of worthy preachers; – Sectaries[6] of the most strange & extravagant opinions are in abundance, Jumpers,[7] Ranters,[8] & hundreds of other nameless enthusiasts, but the pure & practical preacher of the Gospel is in many places unknown. The presbyterians throughout both provinces appear to be bestirring themselves to remedy this,[9] petitions are forwarded to Edin[h] requesting assistance in the good cause, and a general spirit of union & good fellowship seems to pervade in that land where the European checks on conscience are unknown the

6 Dissenters from an established church, especially Protestant nonconformists.
7 So named from their acts of jumping in church services.
8 Nineteenth-century Primitive Methodists were also known disparagingly as "Ranters."
9 In 1833 fourteen ministers of the Church of Scotland were sent out to the Canadas by the Glasgow Colonial Society and by some presbyteries. Four were settled in Lower Canada. Rev. Walter Roach was ordained to the pastoral charge of Beauharnois, St Louis, and Chateauguay. He wrote a letter back to the Glasgow Society soon after his settlement in 1833 in which he describes the Scotch settlements he found: "No part of the Lower Province is more thickly peopled with the Scotch than the banks of the Chateauguay, which, taking its rise in the State of New York, winds its course through upwards of sixty miles of the most rich and fertile lands of lower Canada till it falls into the waters of the St. Lawrence a little above Montreal. The country is wholly peopled by French-Canadians, with the exception of my hearers, from the mouth of the river to Georgetown, sixteen miles up. Georgetown, Ormstown, Portage, Huntingdon, Hinchinbrook, and Trout River, all following one another in regular succession upwards unto the boundary line which separates the State of New York from Lower

whole of the various classes of presbyterians by whatever name they were formerly distinguished in Scotland. This is as it should be. When beyond the influence of those civil forms & disqualifications which in their native Country so painfully separate Christians of exactly the same doctrines, – they in a foreign land reunite like the branches of a stream which an island had divided.

Of myself it is unnecessary to say much. I left Red River Colony above a year ago, and am now appointed to the situation of General Store Clerk in the Depot at this place, a situation from which I do not expect change for several years to come. My duties throughout the year are arduous & the charge one of much responsibility, my health however is good, I am fully acquainted with the routine of the business, and the duties I have to perform are quite agreeable to my inclination.[10] I have every reason to be contented, and I trust I am so. When I left Scotland I had little expectation of bettering my circumstances, at least beyond the lot to which I was born; – whatever advantages my present easy circumstances present me with, I therefore owe under the blessing of providence, to the kind liberality of my parents, who with much difficulty & privation to themselves procured me an education I had no reason to expect from them. To them indeed I owe every thing and I trust I shall never be found forgetful of all that they have done for me.

I am sorry that from the early departure of the vessel for England this season & the consequent pressure of business, I have not been able

---

Canada, are all of them wholly peopled with Scotch, with a few exceptions of Americans.

To the eastward of Chateauguay are the settlements of Laprairie, La Salle, Beechridge, Russelltown, English River, Hemmingford and Gore, which are more or less peopled with Presbyterians. On the westward again are Beauharnois, St. Louis, the back concessions of Georgetown, Ormstown, Godmanchester, La Guerre and Dundee, settled in the same way, excepting the former, which is chiefly by Canadians. The farther up this beautiful river just so many more are the Scotch families."
Gregg, *History of the Presbyterian Church*, 472–6.

10 Robert Miles, chief trader at York Factory, reported that five officers and 46 servants wintered 1828–29 at the factory, together with three Indian lads, a young orphan boy, a dumb [mute] Indian with one arm, fourteen women, and six children (not including the families of chief factor McTavish and himself). One of Hargrave's duties was to provide each fall and spring supplies from the sale room to these inhabitants. HBCA, B239/a/141.

to touch on such a number of topics as you had reason to expect, But another year may amend this hasty sheet. When you please to favor me with another letter please address the same as formerly to "JHargrave York Factory, Hudsons Bay House 3 Fenchurch St. London" – or should you be near the Orkneys where the Vessels for this always touch *en passant*[11] "to the care of J. Rae Esqr[12] H.H.B.C^{os} Agent Stromness" will get it forwarded to me without fail. From the month of Feby to May is the usual time for writing from Britain: after that date no opportunity for forwarding letters occurs till the following season: – I shall next fall expect to hear again from you: I have few correspondents in Scotland, and a letter from the land of my nativity is in this country like meeting with an old friend.

With best wishes & sincerest regard –
I remain My Dear Sir
Affectionately yours

JH

York Factory 21st June 1829

Private
J.G. McTavish Esq[13]
Dear Sir

The white Govr[14] reached this yesterday, and Mr Miles[15] having given me a perusal of your letter, I have lost no time in equipping the engaged Indians, the Boats are now under repair (Sunday as it is) and I hope we will be able to start them early tomorrow with the whole of Athabasca

---

11 French for in passing.
12 John Rae (1772–1834), a factor on an Orkney estate, became in 1819 the Orkney agent of the Hudson's Bay Company at Stromness. He was the father of John Rae (1813–93), Arctic traveller and HBC doctor, who solved the mystery of the Franklin expedition and the location of the last navigable link in the Northwest Passage.
13 McTavish was away from York Factory to attend the Council meeting of the Northern Department held at Norway House 22 June 1829.
14 A "Governor White" is listed as a guide wintering in 1829/30 at York Factory. HBCA, B.239/a/141.
15 Robert Seaborn Miles (1795–1870), an Englishman who was Chief Trader at York Factory from 1828 to 1833.

Outfit at this place. By the outfit Scheme Ath*a* was to have its Quantum of Tob[acc]*o* from L Depot,¹⁶ but lest some unforeseen demand may have broken in on this arrangement, and as the Outfit otherwise did not complete the Cargoes I have made them up with 15 Rolls add[itiona]*l*, – which I trust will meet your approbation. The enclosed copies of the Bills Lading are made out for your self, the usual copies for Nor. Ho are forwarded exclusive of these.

I have been busily employed ever since your departure in getting the mem*os* you left me completed, and have all the whole pieces made up to the extent required, except 7 kegs mixed Sugars having run short of both. I believe however there will be enough to meet the demand from the number on Contingencies. Wilson¹⁷ had the misfortune to cut his arm severely which has retarded us something, but is now nearly better.

[Alexander] Ross has not yet cast up, but on his arrival I shall arrange as well as possible with him, – as many pieces & as few sales as he likes. The Req*ns* of Messieurs the petty Traders I have put on the file, but had the curiosity to capitulate those now on hand say [Augustin] Nolin, [Alexander] Ross, [Andrew] M*c*Dermot [John Palmer] Bourke & find their am*t* in essentials ab[ou]*t* treble what can be afforded P the Outfit Scheme, – Nolin bearing off the lions share having asked abt d[ou]ble that supply alone. They shall however all sleep quietly till your arrival. May this be soon & in safety is the earnest wish of
Dear Sir
Yours with highest regard

JH

YF 26 June '29

Private
J.G. M*c*Tavish Esq
Dear Sir
   Tho' we are looking out for you every hour I take the liberty of chancing a few lines with Statements of Mess*rs* Ross & Cooks¹⁸ costly Cargoes

---

16 Refers to Norway House depot.
17 William Wilson is listed as a cooper wintering at York Factory 1829/30. HBCA, B.239/a/141.
18 Possibly Joseph Cook (c. 1788–1848), a son of former Chief Factor William Hemmings Cook and his wife Mary (Mith-coo-coo-man E'Squaw). He had retired from the HBC in 1824.

– the latter of whom is now Starting. Ross reach^d this on the 23rd, Cook yesterday, & both delivered their downward Cargoes in tolerable order. The professor[19] received a few Supplies for himself from the Store and tried me on all sides to get his men into the shop. I however parried all his logic, and he started yesterday just as Cook hove in sight. The latter goes off today with the tide having tried the same course for his men with the like success. Indeed they are themselves more content with this than if their men had been paid, as it affords them a hold on these ragged Colts which after parting with their wages they find they no longer possess. The mere trouble would have been no consideration with me, but equipping about 30 hands and melting down the Bundles of Cash & Orders their pockets were stuffed with, would have made a serious hole in our Shop supplies, much to the hurt of the Companys Regular Servants.

Wilson can now work a little & has filled 250 kegs Rum which were finished yesterday. He this day begins working up the Staves Ross brought down which will help out the number in the end of the Season. 300 kegs *at least* will be required P the Outfit Scheme. The Rum will be quite sufficient, there being 14 puncheons[20] still untouched after the above quantity was completed.

We are all pulling together finely, with a longing glance up the River now and then, from whence momentous things are expected.
Yours Mo. faithfully

JH

YF 1 July 1829

Miss Jane Hargrave
My Dear Jane

It was with much pleasure that I received all your letters the other day and was never more delighted than to find that you were all as well as I could wish you. As to myself I am well – in excellent health – and prosperous circumstances; – which few words comprehend every thing that I can say regarding myself. My residence is now fixed at this place, in all likelihood while I remain in the country, and altho' the duties I have to perform are sufficiently heavy, I get through them with ease to myself and satisfaction to my employers.

19 Alexander Ross.
20 A large cask of various capacity.

You will find by the enclosed Bill that I have not forgot my promise of last year. I am really happy my dear girl that you at length have met with an opportunity of settling yourself in life in a way that prudence approves as well as that affection points out. Your conduct I heartily approve of, and as a proof you see I entrust you with this money altho' you have yet neither mentioned the name of your intended to me nor spoke at all on the subject to our mother. I have believed every thing on your word, and I feel convinced that you are incapable of throwing yourself away on a person unworthy of you. When matters are conclusively settled between you, give my love to him & tell him that I shall be happy to hear from him by next Springs packet. The enclosed Bill is for Eighteen pounds Sterling for which you will receive Twenty pounds in the currency of Canada when it is presented at the HBCoys office at Lachine. This is the exact Sum I sent to Mary: you are both alike dear to me, the conduct of you both while single having given me unmixed satisfaction, and I consider my money could not be more meritoriously laid out than in assisting to settle for life two young women who have so well fulfilled the duties of sisters and of daughters. It will be needless for me to give you any cautions as to the proper time for drawing this money. Should *you unfortunately not need it* as soon as you expected, it would be difficult for you to retain in your hands so much untouched for any length of time, my only request is therefore that you will not draw it until you are *certain* of immediately requiring that assistance for which it is intended: & besides take particular care of the Bill, as if it is lost, the value of it is lost to both you and me, it being charged to my account when drawn and my signature on the bank authorizing the payment of it to whoever may present it at Lachine.

Our old mother will alone feel the want of you, but she must try and get a servant girl at a moderate rate to help her in the household duties. I again send her this year the usual present, and I trust that it will be laid out entirely for her ease and comfort. Their new house by this time must be near finished. It appears to have cost them a good deal of hard labour, as well as not a little cash. It however could not be better laid out than in this undertaking as it will be a comfortable retreat for the rest of their days.

I shall with pleasure remember you to Cousin Euphemia. I heard from them all last year and they were then in their usual good health. My uncles letter I shall enclose to our Mother.

I have at present little time my dear Jane for writing, and my letters are consequently short and hastily written. I know however your good nature will make allowance for all this, and believe me still
My Dear Sister
Your very affectionate brother

JHargrave

[The following letter has been crossed out and presumably not sent by JH.]

YF 1 July 1829

M^r. John Hargrave
My Dear John

Few letters of yours have given me more pleasure than your last of 22nd Feby. I am happy to find you all well, happy at the comfort and plenty you enjoy, happy that industry good behaviour and contentment render you also happy. You appear to have had a busy season of it last summer, and I am certain you will reap the reward of your labor in the comfort and satisfaction your new house will give to both you and our parents. It will be a shelter to them for the remainder of both their lives. One great object still is to have it well furnished and "weel red up".[21] Our old parents, however anxious they may be to get your little labours forwarded, have not now the strength, nor can they bear the fatigue of keeping every thing in its proper place. *Should Circumstances therefore render it necessary* they should engage some young girl as a help to our mother, as the indoor work, much more any of your farm labours, is now much too heavy for her advanced years. From what I gather and of all your accounts of your building I[t] seems to be snug substantial & roomy. The plaster should be allowed to dry well before you go to live in it, as nothing is more unhealthy than a damp new house. The plank ought also to be well seasoned else the heat of your Stove during winter will make them shrink and twist very much. It is an excellent plan to get your shingle roof painted. It will last two times longer, and the expense of paint & oil cannot be great. Spanish Brown is as good as any you can use: it ought

21 Tidy, well-in-order. DSL.

not to cost more than 25/ P Cwt in Canada, and boiled Linseed Oil for mixing it not above 4/ P Gallon.

  Cwt paint and   Gall. Oil ought to be sufficient to cover the whole of your roof & doors. White paint should be used for the Windows and Ceiling of your Room, also the walls over the plaster on the inside. This will cost about 5^d P[er]U[nit][?] and 20 U [?] should be sufficient. With this finishing off, your dwelling will last without repairs for 20 years.

 Regarding myself I can as usual say little. My health is as good as ever, and altho' the busy duties of a Depôt, keep me at harder work with the pen than I ever experienced before, I am happy and contented with my employment. I can at present indeed make little money, as my Salary, tho one of the highest in the country, goes little beyond £100, one half of which is all that I can usually lay bye, yet in my present situation I stand among the foremost for promotion, the first step of which would raise my yearly income to above £400. Of course I cannot say when this will be my lot, but my friends flatter me with hopes in one, two, or three years at the farthest. I can then lay up fast what will prove sufficient to keep me independent either of farther exertions myself or of being obliged to others for aid, during the remainder of my days. Previous however to my leaving this country forever, I purpose applying for leave of absence for a season to spend among you a few months, as I feel I could not bear to think of never seeing some of you again. It is not in my power to fix this time when I shall visit you, but whenever I am certain you shall know a year before hand.

 I am greatly pressed for time my dear John, and can add nothing more at present but that I am
Your Affectionate brother

JH

                   YF 6 July 1829

My Dear Parents
 You can well imagine with what joy I received all your letters a few days ago, and how thankful I was to find that you were still blessed with good health and comfortable circumstances. I am myself as well as ever, – happy and contented – altho' this season I have scarcely time to tell you so. The Canoe for Montreal sets out from this in four days time, and the business I have to get through before it takes its departure is so

great that were I multiplied fourfold, every part of me would find ample employment. I am therefore obliged this season to write you all together, and although this is only a poor return for the long and kind sheets I had from you all I know you will excuse what I find it utterly impossible to make more worthy of you.

My health is as usual excellent, and I get through the load of writing and store business which falls to my share with pleasure to myself and satisfaction to others. I can indeed as yet make little money, but I have no fears on this score, as my turn for promotion approaches fast, and then I can make up for the scanty earnings of by gone years. Now while saying all this do not imagine for a moment that I complain of poverty & regret the trifles I send you. Very far from it indeed, for I declare I consider these presents I make you as the most valuable use to which I can turn my earnings, and know that they return with tenfold blessings upon me, in the blessing of the Almighty on all that is dear to me, and in the delight of feeling that I have attempted to perform the duties of a Son to the kindest of parents. The reason I thus mention my money matters is to prevent you from imagining that I purpose remaining always in this country, and to persuade you that as soon as I can secure as much as will keep me above want for the remainder of my days, I will return & join you never more in this world to separate again.

I am really well pleased to find you have got on so well with your new house. By my brothers' account of it, – it must be substantial, roomy and comfortable – and will be a fixed home for you during the remainder of both your lives. Your cleared ground seems also to be sufficient to maintain the family throughout the year, and if so, you should cut down no more timber, – as in a short time wood will become of much value around you, – fuel will get scarce – and those who have laid bare their farms will then find the expense of passing a long Canadian winter. My uncle in my idea appears to have taken a very inconsiderate step by selling his last farm & removing to another. He is now far advanced in years, and can never hope to see another farm so much improved as his last. The money also appears to be still due him, and may find some difficulty in procuring it. He indeed appears to have thrown aside a crutch that would have supported him for the rest of his days – and set out in pursuit of an empty shadow – "a rolling stone gathers no moss."

I this season send my Mother my usual present of £10 Stg to provide something comfortable through the ensuing winter. My former letters have so fully explained my wishes on this subject that I shall not repeat what I then said. Lay it out wholly in defraying your own wants, and I shall never think it misspent.

 I am really squeezed for time at present My Dear Parents and am heartily sorry that I cannot write you so much as you must expect and I wish. I have besides no journal to send you this season, occasioned by want of time last winter for writing one. It is begun, and will form part of my letters next year should we all be spared.[22] I shall omit no chance for sending you a letter, as I know even a single line will give you satisfaction being a proof of my welfare.
May God bless & preserve you is the earnest prayer of
Your Most Affect.te Son

JH

P.S. I enclose you a letter from My uncle Ja.s Mitchel of Last Year. I have heard neither from J. Ross nor from Mary. I have no time for writing them just now.

---

22 See Journal below.

[Letterbook]
Nº 5
Rough Copies Letters by
JHargrave
from 13 July 1829 @ 24th June 1830.

York Factory 20th Octr '29

My Dear Mother

The unusually busy season I passed last summer prevented me from writing you as fully as I could have wished and I know you must have expected; so it [is] with much joy that I embrace the present opportunity of again letting you hear from me. My only news are indeed that I am hale & hearty as ever and tho' this can be said in a few words I know how important they will be considered by you. [The rest of this paragraph was crossed out by JH but is included here]. To be prevented from hearing of your welfare & letting you hear from me is indeed what I regret most in my lot in this country. We are indeed far asunder, and the distance is rendered still more irksome from the few occasions afforded for keeping up our correspondence. When the usual day arrives for receiving your letters every pursuit is thrown aside, I shut myself up in some corner of our Stores, and there for hours pour over the precious packet which has been put into my hand. Those of last spring were bro[ugh]t down to me by my friend Mr Finlayson,[1] and tho' I had not seen him for Eight months and had been roused from my bed in the night time to receive him, yet no sooner was your packet put into my hands than I fairly took to my heels and left him to find out the way to my room in the dark, where he at length found me rejoicing over the happy news of all your safeties. I have little of what is called news to tell you of – from this out of the way quarter of the world. Our occupations & amusements are so unvaried that what I have told you before regarding them is all that I could repeat on the subject. My respected friend Mr [John George] McTavish under whom I have always been at this place, went last fall to England from whence he returns again next spring. His absence I regret much, as his conversation & society was one of my greatest pleasures. He is a Gentleman of a very respectable family in the west of Scotland, was educated in Edinburgh, and came abt 25 years ago to this country where

---

1 Duncan Finlayson was chief trader at Red River at this time.

he has resided ever since, and where he now holds the highest rank next to the Governor. To his friendship I owe the whole of the success that has attended my course through life, and on it I rely as my main support in succeeding years.

My letter to you of last summer was written before I received my usual letters from Scotland, the news contained in which I know will be interesting to you. My uncle Ja^s Mitchel with all his family are in their usual good health. They still reside in Galashiels where he is doing very well. They complain much of never hearing from you and I perceive you also think that they never write you. My cousin *Effy* says – "My mother, father, and all the rest have their kindest love to you and wish you to present the same to your parents when you write them for we have not had any letters from themselves these two years. We have written to them since that, but received no answer." I suspect neither you nor they address your letters properly, and on that depends every chance of their reaching their destination in safety. Yours to them should be addressed – "Mr Ja^s Mitchel, Galashiels, Selkirkshire North Britain[2]" and when put into the post Office the package should be paid from Mont^l to Quebec. You should also mention to them some person in Montreal to whose care their letters to you ought to be addressed, otherwise they will always miscarry. They tell me that Mr Inglis[3] of Midholm has become a Bankrupt for about Two Thousand pounds He has been put out of his place, and all his property sold at public [illegible]. Poor Mr Rattray died last year.[4] The letter I sent you last summer was the last I had from him – pray take care of it. He was an excellent man, and a pious christian. I had also a long letter from our old friend Lockie. He is still flourishing the *Taws*[5] at Stouslee,[6] and has now a much larger school than when I was one of

---

2 After the Acts of Union of 1707 which united Scotland and England into Great Britain, Scotland was sometimes known as North Britain.

3 Probably Rev. James Ingles, minister Midholm United Secession (listed in Pigot's 1825–26 Directory).

4 In fact, Rev. William Rattray was admitted in 1830 or 1832 to a ministry in Swalwell, Northumberland, England, and died in Durham in 1851. Helen Elliot, secretary of the Old Gala Club, Galashiels, Scotland: e-mail messages to editor, 29 August 2006; 12 September 2006.

5 A leather whip divided at the end into strips, formerly used to punish children. DSL.

6 Another form of Stouslie.

its inmates. George & *Etty* Aitken are both well & desire their kindest comp[limen]^ts to you, also Geo Reid. They are all still living in Stouslee. "Nell & the Eyre" is also alive tho' now much failed. Markets are low, and the circumstances of the poor much improved since we left our native country. I omitted to mention that Cousin *Effy* desires me to inform Jane that M. Adams her old acquaintance has got married to Thomas Gray who was at Lindean Mill. Effy is still single, and appears by her letters to be a shrewd sensible Girl.

Even at this time I cannot command so much leisure as to write a separate letter to all my Brothers & Sisters. Those with you will of course see all that I do write, and even were I enabled to give each of them a sheet I could merely repeat over the few scanty news I have gathered into this. This I will however try to make up for ensuing summer, and every one of them shall hear from me next opportunity. It is indeed a great chance whether this letter will reach you before those I will write you next summer, but as there *is* a chance, I cannot omit risking a sheet by it. In the fond hope that this will find you all in as good health as it leaves me

I am My Dear Mother
Your Most Affec^te Son

Jamie

YF 22 Oct^r '29

My Dear Father

By a packet going this winter in the direction of Montreal I sit down with delight to run over a few lines for you & my mother knowing that you think you never hear too often from me. I have great cause to be thankful in being able to say that I am still preserved in health & strength, – the Greatest blessings this life possesses, as without them all others are tasteless. May this my Dear Old father find you as well as your Son can wish. I am sorry to hear by your last that My Uncle[7] has left your neighborhood, and gone down towards Quebec. It is a most unadvised Step, which I am

---

7 His uncle, James Hargrave, moved to the Inverness/Leeds area in Megantic County in the Eastern Townships of Lower Canada. As in Beechridge, a substantial number of Highlanders also settled in this area. A large influx of Arran settlers to Inverness began in 1829 with the collapse of the Hebridean kelp industry and the clearances of estates to make way for

certain he will regret in a short time. The labor of 10 years is disposed of for a trifling sum, and that sum still unpaid, – whilst he sets out bending over a Staff again to take up his lodgings in the woods. I could not have thought him capable of so weak a resolution, and I fully believe that the Scheme is Walters[8] – not his. The character of that young man is a bad one, – I judge of him by his conduct to that poor girl he betrayed and left, – and I fear that he will contrive to get whatever payment is made on their sold Lot into his own hands, and if so his old fathers share in it will be but a scanty one. At all events, let me advise you to keep clear of their transactions with McRae.[9] He is your neighbor, and they may very likely propose to you to advance them either money or something else to be paid you out of McRae's debt to them: thus making you the drawer in of what they may find it inconvenient to get hold of. By all means avoid this, my dear father, they have undertaken a scheme for themselves, and at their own risk, so let their own wits help them out of whatever difficulties may attend it. Your little farm has been too well earned by the sweat of your brow to allow of its comforts being at all diminished in amending the false steps & blunders of others. Neither lend nor borrow is a maxim that is of use in 9 cases out of 10 in money transactions with the people around you.

You complain much, and with reason, of the want of proper Ministers of the Gospel among you. This I trust will however be soon remedied, as the General want of them throughout Canada as I perceive is noticed in

---

sheep farms. Both Congregationalists and Presbyterians built churches in Inverness. Less is known about the source of other Scottish settlers to the area, according to Campey, *Les Écossais*, 78–86.

8 Walter Hargrave (1800–1873) was a son of James Hargrave, Sr. In 1826 he married Mary Russell and they went to live in Inverness, Megantic County. He later built a chapel on his land and when it burned down he gave the ground to the Wesleyan Methodists. He became county magistrate and for years court commissioner and agent for Crown lands. In 1854, he and his family moved to Ripon, Wisconsin. *Pedrick Genealogy Notebooks.*

9 See Appendix, Journals, N.n 22d March. Alexander and Duncan McRae are shown between James and Joseph Hargrave in the list of people who as squatters on land in Beechridge in 1821 had to pay their debts to the Seigneury of Beauharnois in order to obtain deeds of concession to the properties. The Beechridge Presbyterian Cemetery records indicate the Highlander McRaes were natives of Kintail, Ross-shire, in Scotland. Alexander died in 1885 aged ninety-one and Duncan in 1866 aged seventy-seven.

the Newspapers I have received from Edin*ᵇ* this season, – and steps are taking to send out proper labourers to that neglected corner of the Vineyard. You have much reason to complain of the wandering preachers who presently frequent the settlement around you; most of them are uneducated enthusiasts who full of impureness themselves feed with wind the hungry flock they have the presumption to call together. With none of these could I *join*, and indeed a strong argument in favour of a regular Church Government where the Teacher is answerable to superior authority, is that these Teachers are men who have made the sacred office of a Minister of the Gospel their study for a long time before they are permitted to fulfil its duties, – and then permitted only when *from examination* their knowledge & talents are found adequate to the task. The independents, the Baptists, too many of the Methodists, and the whole swarm of Jumpers, Ranters, Shakers,[10] with a crowd of other enthusiasts have teachers whose blind zeal is their only guide, and who like hoodwinked men among snares plunge on with a recklessness that endangers both themselves & all those who are so weak as to place themselves under their guidance. Too many of these are around you, and usurp the place of the pure & practical preacher of the Gospel. Your old friend M*ʳ* Rattray I often thought might be induced to cross the seas to your Settlement, and this season I purposed mentioning it to him, but I deeply regret to find by my letters from Scotland that last winter closed his earthly pilgrimage; and the worthy servant has gone for his reward. I enclosed you last summer the last letter I received from him, and by it you will see that he had not received a settled residence ever since he left Selkirk but had been employed on preaching throughout the Secession Church. He was a truly worthy & good man. Inglis of Midholm has become Bankrupt and is degraded from his Office of Minister. This man I never liked, so I shall say nothing more of him lest I express myself uncharitably.

 I have nothing of moment to add regarding myself. This place is a fixed residence for me, where month follows month without one story occurring worth telling. I like my employment well, tho fully as busy a one tho' not so laborious as that of my brothers with their hatchet. I can as yet lay

10 The Shakers were an offshoot of the Society of Friends (Quakers), who originated in Manchester, England, in the early eighteenth century. The name *Shakers*, and the variant, Shaking Quakers, originally pejorative, was applied as a mocking description of their rituals of trembling, shouting, dancing, shaking, singing, and glossolalia (speaking in strange and unknown languages).

bye little for a future day, – for altho' I am sufficiently economical not to be a miser, yet my expenses leave only about £50 in my pocket at the end of each year. My hopes of preferment are now however strong. I stand at or almost at the head of the list of Clerks, – & will ere long have such an income as will allow me to save from £200 to 300 each year. I am not over ambitious of Riches, and when I reach the point of being able to support myself in ease & independence, this country shall hold me no longer. I much wish to see you all, and should a chance at all offer, will come down some season & spend the winter among you. Do not build hopes however on this as it can only be after I obtain promotion, & that period can never be fixed. – Meanwhile with earnest prayers for your preservations
I am My Dear Father
Your Aff. Son

JH

YF May 26th 1830

J.G. McTavish Esq
Dear Sir

    I have little to say at this busy season, yet I cannot think of M^r [Robert] Miles starting without a few lines to you from me, however trifling & uninteresting. I have just finished the Budget for Nor. Ho. and I would fain think you will find by it that the public business has been assiduously attended to since you left us. To enter into detail on this subject would draw on you a merciless pra[i]sing without communicating further information than a five minutes glance at the usual papers will convey to you. I shall therefore rein in my pen on its so well known track, and leave Invoices & Schemes[11] to plead their own cause. We have passed the byegone winter quietly & snugly together, with every comfort & enjoyment that this coast admits of. The winter has been a severe one, – much more so than any thing I have yet seen here, & it was only on the [missing date] Inst when the river opened before the Fort. Tho' our fall hunts in Geese & much more so in Deer were but scanty ones, yet on the whole we have had more than usual luck in getting hold of provisions: the partridges were amazingly numerous towards spring, the fishery yielded its usual quota, and from some Herds of Deer which passed the winter around us, and which in the spring had almost taken the fort by storm, Mr Miles has

---

11 Scheme distributions were plans for the distribution of supplies held in inventory. Scheme indents were used to determine the need for new supplies.

secured not only a well garnished ice house, but wherewith to cram every mouth in the Fort for many weeks in succession. I have never seen them so numerous since the spring of '22. Mr Miles accompanied by Mr Ballenden[12] purposes starting on the 1st prox. and I shall anxiously look out towards the end of the month for some arrivals to vary the macadamised tenor of our vegetation.

What shall I say more: – Madame[13] and all the little Madroulikins[14] both old & new are well & happy paying all spring a visit to the river side to see when the road shall open for you. I have my own wishes also, – the principal points to your safe return. May it be as I wish it! I might touch on many other topics, but *Arrête*,[15] as old Battoche used to say; my health all spring has been ailing, – the blues sometimes settle down on me, – so I sha'nt trust my self with the chance of welcoming your return to the Country with a Growl.
God bless you!
Yours faithfully as ever

JH

York Factory 10th June 1829 [sic][16]
My Dear Lockie
You cannot have regretted more than I do myself the necessity I was under of leaving unanswered till this date your excellent Letter of 28th

---

12 John Ballenden (c. 1812–1856) entered the HBC's service as an apprentice clerk in 1829, and after serving at both York Factory and Red River, was promoted accountant at Upper Fort Garry in 1836. Van Kirk, "Ballenden, John."
13 Nancy McKenzie (c. 1790–1851) was the daughter of NWC fur trader Roderick McKenzie and an unidentified Indian woman. She was married to J.G. McTavish, probably in 1813, according to the custom of the country and they had as many as seven children, all daughters. In February 1830, however, while on furlough in Scotland, McTavish married Catherine Turner, thus taking the unprecedented step of casting aside his mixed-blood wife without first making provision for her. Hargrave had not yet heard of the marriage when he wrote this letter to his mentor. Van Kirk, "McKenzie, Nancy."
14 The children of Nancy McKenzie and J.G. McTavish.
15 French for stop.
16 This should be 1830. Hargrave assumed the management of affairs at York Factory during the month of June 1830 while Robert Miles was absent at

Feby last. Tho' written about the period I requested it unfortunately did not reach the Coys House in London till about a week after the departure of the spring packet so that instead of the beginning of June it was the middle of August before it reached me by the annual Ships to this port. I had delayed addressing you till it should come to hand trusting that I might still find an opportunity between the arrival & sailing of the vessels – but from an unforeseen pressure of business every moment was so occupied in my public duties that during the whole of that period night was to me changed into day & sunday added to the rest of the week. My correspondence in Scotland is now not a large one, yet small as it is, not one letter got I written last season to that quarter of the world. To make amends for this unavoidable silence, I have sat down during 'the quiet season' here to fill a sheet in my fullest style by way of peace offering to those feelings of friendship I know I must have put to the proof tho' I trust without injury to their foundation. I have read with much interest and deep regret the account you give of the horrible acts committed in Edinburgh last winter by those demons Bourke & Hare,[17] and have seen much besides on the subject in the files of Scottish papers /which were

---

Norway House. In the York Factory Post Journal of 31 May 1830, he listed the tradesmen and labourers attached to the factory: armourer, baker, two blacksmiths, blacksmith's assistant, two boatbuilders, two carpenters, three coopers, tinsmith, tailor, hatter, storeman, four sawyers, cowherd, mess butler, mess cook, mens cook, sailor, fisherman, interpreter, five labourers, and three invalids. The thirty-five servants were considerably fewer than the forty-six servants that Robert Miles had noted as wintering over in 1828–29, perhaps a reflection of Governor Simpson's cost-cutting measures. HBCA, B.239/a/141.

17 William Burke (1792–1829) was a criminal notorious for a series of murders committed in Scotland in association with William Hare, another Irish immigrant. In 1827 Burke was living in a lodging house in Edinburgh kept by Hare. Because the growing need of doctors and students for corpses for dissection could not be filled legally, body snatching and resurrectionism were rife at that time in Scotland. When one of Hare's lodgers died, he and Burke sold the body to Robert Knox, a leading anatomist, for £7 10s. Helped by two women, the men lured travellers into one of their houses, made them drunk and suffocated them. In nine months they disposed of the bodies of fifteen victims at prices ranging from £8 to £14, but the disappearance of the sixteenth victim was noticed, the police traced the body to Knox's cellar, and the four were arrested. Hare turned king's evidence,

forwarded to us by the Ships. I am ashamed to think that such enormities could be perpetrated in my native land, and not less so to find that the public authorities allowed to escape him who in my eyes was the most hardened & brutalised of the two. The Magistrates it appears to me failed in their duty by prematurely making promises of safety to Hare in order to secure evidence against his associate in crime, when afterwards such evidence was procured as would have convinced any Jury of their guilt without this mean expedient of bargaining with infamy; – was not this doing evil gratuitous evil in order that good might come? They themselves evidently perceived this, and tried to shuffle out of their engagements, but the Council for the criminals were too true to their cause & so the Master Villain escaped. The public feeling seems even to have called on the relations of the victims to come forward as private prosecutors – no doubt a novelty in Scottish Criminal Courts, but yet strictly legal, – but here again the fatal pledge proved a shield – at all events – the demands of Justice were again left unsatisfied. This I consider the real spot of infamy in the case. The deep feeling of execration so universally evinced on the horrid tale bursting on the public ear must be to neighboring nations a proof of the moral purity of the Scottish Mind, but the inefficient satisfaction to outraged humanity will I fear also leave a contemptible idea both of the activity of the city police & of the energy and efficiency of our public authorities. If ever an Edinburgh Mob did right in seizing on the sword of Justice when the lingering arm of Law allowed Villainy to escape – no period in my opinion has occurred since the Porteous[18] lesson

    making Burke's conviction possible. He was hanged in Edinburgh on 28 January 1829. Hare was safe from prosecution, but public hatred drove him from Scotland.

18 John Porteous (c. 1695–1736), captain of the city guard of Edinburgh, was associated with the riots of 1736, which provided the plot for Sir Walter Scott's novel *The Heart of Midlothian*. A riot broke out on 14 April 1736, at the execution of a smuggler who had won popular sympathy in Edinburgh by helping a friend to escape from prison. Porteous, who was accused of giving the order to the city guard to fire into the crowd, and of firing himself, was brought to trial and sentenced to death. After his execution was postponed, an armed mob broke into the Tolbooth prison in Edinburgh, seized Porteous, and hanged him from a signpost in the street on 7 September 1736. The government in London ordered an inquiry, but no one was ever convicted of the murder.

so fit to teach robed authority the extent of duty it owes to the power which entrusted public safety to its protection: – perhaps 'tis as creditable to good order that no ebbulition of private feeling burst forth, – yet still I might have rejoiced to hear that the giant arm of public vengeance had swept the wretch from among men whom trammeled justice still allows to insult humanity. The impunity with which Knox[19] has escaped I attribute also to this supineness in legal authorities. In fact the profession of Surgery has risen far above the level I conceive is its right in society, and thousands of young men are so educated who on stepping into the world can find no employment thanks to the tranquillity of Europe, and are obliged to take to some other road in life. This over supply in the profession is really a matter deserving of consideration among our rulers. It is confessedly notorious that only by illegal means can the demands for "subjects" be satisfied at present, and I perceive that last spring a Bill was in course through Parliament to authorise their appropriating to the dissecting room the bodies of those unfortunates who died in Hospitals & Poor Houses unclaimed by friends.[20] This to me is horrible: – must the poor & broken down soldier, the stranger, the Widow who has outlived her family, – her sons perhaps fallen in the defence of their country, – must these go to supply the unfeeling demands for human carcasses so confidently & arrogantly made. – first perish say I three fourths of the profession! Why is there not some regulation proposed as to the number of students in these Gentlemanly Chambers, when for those who issue from them the good health of men & the good sense of nations furnish such inadequate employment? At least, however, why is it not proposed

19　Robert Knox (1791–1862) at the time of the Burke and Hare scandal was curator of the museum of the Royal College of Surgeons and one of the most gifted and popular lecturers in anatomy the University of Edinburgh ever had. Knox was an actor and showman by style and depended upon having corpses available. The practice of resurrectionism, or grave-robbing, to procure bodies for the medical schools was rife in the period and it was some of Knox's students who first made the liaison with Burke and Hare. It was never proved whether he knew or suspected that the victims had been murdered. His supposed part in the incident earned him the wrath of the Edinburgh mob and his house in Newington was surrounded and stoned.

20　The Anatomy Act of 1832 expanded the legal supply of cadavers for medical research and education by allowing unclaimed bodies, in particular those of people who died in prison or the workhouse, to be used for dissection. Donors could also provide the bodies of their next-of-kin in exchange for payment of the costs of burial.

in the very first clause of this horrid bill, that those who have lived by knowledge so acquired to in the end leave their bodies for the instruction of their successors. Surely they who laugh at the prejudices of humanity in the mouths of others, – can feel no hesitation when the same argument is applied to themselves & that with tenfold justice. Enough of this, – I trust in God however the good sense & feeling of my country men will arrest this Shameless Bill in its course, whatever may be the outcry raised by these human Cormorants. Let them thin their ranks, instead of thinning the Graves of the dead.

I feel deeply obliged by your clear & methodical responses to the queries of my last. The Tables of Scottish wt^s & measures in particular are interesting. The hints on literary topics I have also perused with much delight. An attachment to books is in me I take it a sort of hereditary taste; tho' my early poetic dreams has changed the ancient family tone from polemics to the more ornamented & imaginative productions of intellect. British News & British literature are to us here the great source of amusement & the topics of conversation. Tho' an economist on principle I am lavish in my expenditure on Books. Within these few last years I have procured the whole of the Waverley Series in 40 odd Volumes,[21] the Life of Napoleon in 9 Vols Octos[22] also Robertsons[23] Blairs[24] Popes[25] Miltons[26] & Byrons[27] Johnston's[28] Works. Next Season will bring me an addition to the extent of £20 to 30 pounds. Among these are McCrie's

21 The author was Sir Walter Scott (1771–1832). A recent project entitled *The Edinburgh Edition of the Waverley Novels*, the first critical edition of the novels, lists nineteen titles in this collection.
22 The author, Sir Walter Scott, was so impressed with Napoleon that he visited Waterloo and met with Wellington, after which he returned to Scotland and wrote this nine-volume work which was published in 1827.
23 Probably William Robertson (1721–1793), a Scottish historian and Presbyterian minister, whose writings were the earliest popular histories within their respective fields and were highly esteemed by his contemporaries.
24 Probably Robert Blair (1699–1746), a Scottish poet, whose poem "The Grave," achieved great popularity and influence.
25 Alexander Pope (1688–1744), the most distinguished of the classical poets of the Augustan age in England and the most accomplished verse satirist in English.
26 John Milton (1608–1674), the greatest English poet after Shakespeare.
27 Lord George Gordon Byron (1788–1824), English poet and satirist.
28 Probably Samuel Johnson (1709–1784), English poet, critic, essayist, lexicographer, and the greatest clubman of eighteenth-century London.

"Life of John Knox" (an name by the bye to which I think our native country has not yet done sufficient honor) also Jamiesons[29] Scottish Dictionary, The family Library[30] a series of Biography by the best living authors, french & italian works &*c*. The latter Language is acquired since I came to this country, I commenced the study as a means of occupying a long winter evening and am repaid with usury by the rich mine of literature the possession of that key has unlocked to me. I have indeed a distaste to all translations, poetry especially can *never* be translated.

The last letters I had from my Old Parents, were dated last April, but expect to hear again from them before this leaves me, & if so, will add a postscript on that subject. When they last wrote me, they still enjoyed their usual good health, with all the comforts that their limited wishes desired. They have a good lot of Land, as much cleared ground, well enclosed as produces in abundance all the necessaries of life; a substantial roomy and well furnished, stone house, a Barn, Stables & Outhouses, with Horses, Oxen, Cattle, Hogs & all the other inhabitants of a Barn Yard. *They have plenty*, and that plenty is their own. Every Stroke of their axe, adds to their possessions & their comforts, without the drawback of Rents, Taxes or Bankers Accounts. I will own to you mine old friend, that these comfortable circumstances of my aged parents, is to me one of the purest sources of pleasure. I feel proud in saying to you that the assistance my situation in life affords me of aiding them, has raised above the anxieties of poverty a worthy pair who even if I owed not a drop of blood to them, I would as much esteem for their honest simplicity & purity of life, as I can do, related as I am & owing as I do to their care of my early improvement, every thing that I possess. This part of my conduct I look to with unmixed pleasure – pleasure which gold otherwise employed can never purchase. Mary would term this boasting; I know you so well that I need not point out to your kindly feelings a purer source for my pride than empty vanity. The account of my journey from lake Superior hither which you mention I am sorry to say I can now recall so lamely that every feature of interest has been blotted from it. Eight years of a busy life my dear friend, works sad freaks in the memory, & having no Notes

29 Rev. John Jamieson (1759–1838), minister of the Secession Church and philologist, published the *Etymological Dictionary of the Scottish Language* in 1808–09, with a supplement in 1825.
30 John Murray (1778–1843) published a series of books from 1829 under the title *The Family Library*.

Part of a bill of lading for the Prince Rupert for goods shipped by Hargrave, chief trader in 1835. Courtesy of the HBCA, Archives of Manitoba, HBCA, B.239/z/22/34.

by me of those days I can now call up nothing regarding that period at all worthy your notice. Since 1827 I have resided at Head Quarters and so constant are my duties that during all that time I have not been 5 miles distant from the Stockades of the Fort. My summers are spent in the General Depot, from the end of June till the month of Augt inst[ant] supplying Goods for the Trade to the various Divisions of Boats[31] which

---

31 The largest of these "York boats" were over thirteen metres in length with a beam of three metres, propelled by eight oars and carrying up to 100 pieces of freight. Smaller boats with six oars were widely used, carrying up to seventy pieces of freight, depending on water levels and the difficulty of the route. The most famous of the inland brigades was named the La Loche Brigade, manned largely by Metis from Red River, who undertook an arduous four-month journey of 3000 miles starting from Red River in spring, going via Norway House to the Methye Portage where freight was exchanged for furs from the northern districts of Athabasca and Mackenzie, then carried via Norway House to York Factory, just in time to meet the

come from inland each Summer to receive them, & no sooner is that completed than the Vessels from England make their appearance & the landing of the Cargo shipping the Homeward lading, with making out the requisite papers & accounts strain every moment till the end of September, when both the Ships for home & such inlanders as wait their arrival alike take their departure and leave us in solitude for the winter. Then our Bundles of papers from England are untied, then are our trunks of books torn open & one sweet Holiday of a fortnights duration is spent in prowling over these precious fruits of civilization. About the middle of October winter again sets in. The Rivers are frozen up Rain Sleet & then Snow & Drift confine us within Doors, – Our winter Counting House is arranged & down we sit, each to wind up the writing part of his department of Business. This employment occupies us till about the month of February such is the quantity of what is to be done at which time the period for taking the annual Acc^t of Stock arrives: – This fills my hands till about the Month of June, and so charged with these various cares the year rolls round. This unceasing application & confinement is no doubt trying to the constitution, and even the most healthy feel the effects of it in the long Run. Thanks to my breeding, my stamina & appetite which could once digest a bicker[32] of Brose,[33] are yet sound; and a mess of Scotch porritch & milk is still one of my favorite breakfasts. I believe I have already described to you our usual bill of fare here which is really luxurious compared with what falls to the lot of the middle ranks in Britain. Notwithstanding our busy occupations we have for all that our seasons for exercise & amusement. Every Saturday during the winter is devoted to walking or hunting, and wrapt up in treble folds of Duffle & Deer Skin we brave with impunity all the terrors of an Arctic sky. Of the extremity of these *words* can convey you no idea: none without

---

annual supply ship from England which would carry their furs to London. The boats would be reloaded with mail and merchandise for the company's stores at Red River and the brigade would arrive back there early in October. Johnson, *York Boats*, 30, 71–3.

32 A vessel for containing liquor for drinking, properly one made of wood; a porridge-dish; a bowl. DSL.
33 A dish made by mixing boiling water or milk with oatmeal or peasemeal, and adding salt and butter. The mixture may be only roughly stirred up so as to leave lumps. Oatmeal brose had sometimes the addition of the skimmed fat of soup. DSL.

H.B.C. Bill of Fare, York Factory, 1838

IT will be of interest to our readers to learn that the food provided at the H.B.C. officers' mess was varied and substantial. Beef, potatoes, and pork were raised on the "plantation," as it was called in those days. Country provisions, venison, fish, geese, rabbits and partridges appear to have been plentiful. The menu reads as below:

1838 Dec.	Breakfast	Dinner
1	Fried fish	Soup, stewed partridge, pork chops, potatoes, cheese.
2	Beef steak	Soup, roast beef, potatoes, pudding, cheese.
3	Fried fish	Soup, stewed rabbit, boiled partridge, potatoes.
4	Fried fish	Soup, venison pie, broiled partridge, potatoes, tart.
5	Fried fish	Soup, roast beef, potatoes, cheese.
6	Fried fish	Soup, roast pork, curried partridge, potatoes.
7	Fried fish	Soup, salt beef, potatoes, pudding, cheese.
8	Fried fish	Soup, roast venison, beef steak, potatoes, cheese.
9	Beef steak	Soup, roast beef, pudding, cheese.
10	Fried fish	Soup, stewed rabbits, partridges, potatoes.
11	Fried fish	Soup, venison pie, venison steaks, potatoes, tart.
12	Fried fish	Soup, roast beef, potatoes, cheese.
13	Fried fish	Soup, roast pork and partridge, potatoes.
14	Fried fish	Soup, salt geese, ducks, potatoes, pudding.
15	Fried fish	Soup, roast venison, curried partridge, potatoes.
16	Beef steak	Soup, roast beef, potatoes, pudding, cheese.
17	Fried fish	Soup, roast partridge, stewed rabbits, potatoes.
18	Fried fish	Soup, venison pie and steaks, potatoes, tart.
19	Fried fish	Soup, roast beef, potatoes, cheese.
20	Fried fish	Soup, roast pork, potatoes, cheese.
21	Fried fish	Soup, salt geese, curried fish, potatoes, pudding.
22	Fried fish	Soup, roast partridge, stewed rabbits, potatoes.
23	Beef steak	Soup, roast beef, potatoes, pudding, cheese.
24	Fried fish	Soup, roast venison, potatoes, cheese.
25	Fried fish and beef steak	Soup, roast beef, geese, potatoes, mince pies, pudding.
26	Fried fish	Soup, roast beef, potatoes, cheese.
27	Fried fish	Soup, roast beef, potatoes, boiled ham and tongues, mince pies.
28	Fried fish	Soup, boiled pork, potatoes, peas, suet pudding.
29	Fried fish	Soup, roast venison, potatoes, cheese.
30	Fried fish	Soup, roast beef, potatoes, pudding, cheese.
31	Fried fish	Soup, curried rabbit, roast partridge, potatoes.

On Sundays only, wines, madeira and port were served, whilst porter and spruce beer were supplied during the week.—*C. Harding.*

HBC Bill of Fare, York Factory, 1838. As a chief trader, James Hargrave would have eaten these provisions that year in the HBC officers' mess. Reprinted, with permission, from *The Beaver*, September 1923, p. 453.

---

feeling it can conceive that air to the lungs could impart the same sensation as a shower of frozen snow to the naked skin. Game here is abundant tho' all of the smaller kind. White partridges or ptarmigan, is our principal object of pursuit during winter, and these are so plentiful that scarcely a Saturday passes without our each procuring as many as we can carry home. They are of our usual Game the only fowl which remain in this cold latitude during winter. Geese, Ducks, & Plover all seek a more southern sky. The partridge feeds on the seed of the dwarf willow which abounds in the marshes all around us, and are usually so tame that they may be approached within Gun shot before they start. Of Birds of Prey 2 or 3 species of hawk remain throughout the year also several kinds of Owl, among which the white one is the most curious. The usual prey of these birds is rabbits & partridges & so bold is the white owl that when pressed to hunger he will sometimes dispute with the hunter the game his gun has brought down. One of our Tradesmen last winter had shot a partridge & while in the Act of picking it up a white owl which had eyed his Movements from a distance pounced upon him before he had secured his bird in his bag & fairly carried it out from among his fingers. The poor knave however with all his sagacious look (& his head is like a periwigged Lawyers) had not the wisdom to make off with his prize, but sitting down at a short distance to discuss his windfall a second shot from the hunter conveyed both the spoiler & the spoil into the fatal bag. They are about the size of a Turkey, are of a pure & beautiful white, & are really a curiosity to the Amateur in Natural History, being only found I believe here & in the northern parts of Russia. They kill their game with their talons which are four in number, fully 3 inches long strong, & as Sharp as needles. Without knowing their mode of defense it is dangerous for the hunter to pick up a wounded one, as he defends himself nobly & if he catches hold will make his talons meet through the hand never quitting his advantage while life remains.

 I have looked round & round me for subjects of merit to you, and the above is all I can pick out worthy my present notice. I shall now turn to such remarks as I have made from your last favor & to which the Above topics have not proved an answer. I rejoice to hear of your continued prosperity in your professional avocation, always a delicate & precarious one, – much more so when it depends as in your case on the breath of public opinion. You hint at another side School in the parish: where is it situated & who is teaching? It really says little for the Gentry around you, that nothing fixed or permanent is allowed to such praiseworthy institutions. You never mention to me the number & circumstances of your little family. I think the last hint you gave me was that you had them still around you. I believe I recollect a boy & Girl, a little fair haired lassie, the writer if I mistake not, of a manuscript copy of verses yet in my possession. How have you planned for William,[34] and is his sister settled in life or is she still single? I like these little anecdotes: they place me among you. I am glad to hear of your intimacy with Mr Scott[35] and have certainly no objections to his perusal of my letters to you. Though I had not the pleasure of an acquaintance with him, I recollect his name well and the high character he bore in his profession. His compliment on my mode of writing & inquiry now performed is a curious coincidence with

---

34 Presumably William Lockie's son.
35 Possibly George Scott, parochial school master at Cavers and Minto (listed in Pigot's 1825–26 Directory).

one of my old recollections. I remember well of having seen a manuscript of his writing in the possession of an old friend, a Mr Adam Laidlaw[36] of Prieston,[37] and also of having attempted to form many of my letters after that copy. All my letters to you are the productions of the ordinary quill, & his observation as to their clearness & regularity I fear me is more flattering than they merit. at least more than this one deserves. The truth is, since I became a hack in business, expedition has been the only point I aim at, and my style of writing, that part of my education which least pleases me. I partly owe this to my first teacher, Jardine of Hawick, part perhaps to inattention to the subject myself in my youth. Our Clergyman[38] in Red River Colony has I believe an original notion on the subject of writing. He tells me that the character of an individual may be known from his mode of forming the letters; and for my pains in combating this to me heretical opinion, extracts from my poor fist the evident marks of obstinacy in argument. In fact – writing to me is something like countenances, no two exactly the same; – the Scholars resembles the Teacher, such as a son may a father, yet still every man has his own peculiarity, the root of which is of too subtle an essence for my metaphysics, – perhaps originating in the quality of his nerves & the formation of his hand. But let us return from this – to us all – professional digression. You seem to apprehend an approaching state of anarchy in our native country, an event regarding which I would humbly say, – God forefend. I can see no symptoms of it in the public prints, and I would fain hope that the dread has been occasioned by the agitation of the Catholic Question[39] which at the date of your letter engrossed the attention, not only of parliament, but of the whole nation. It is now settled, that bone of contention round which angry millions have disputed for these 30 years last past. I know you a staunch churchman – a protestant, – but yet a man of liberal mind, – and I believe you will not think less of your old pupil when he avows

---

36 Possibly minister Rev. Adam Laidlaw, Kirktown Established Church (listed in Pigot's 1825–26 Directory).
37 Prieston lies about three miles east of Selkirk in Bowden parish.
38 Either Rev. David Thomas Jones, who was HBC chaplain from 1823 to 1838, or his assistant from 1825 to 1838, Rev. William Cockran.
39 The Duke of Wellington and Sir Robert Peel, against their earlier judgments, introduced and carried a major Catholic Relief Act in 1829, removing many of the remaining substantial restrictions on Roman Catholics in the United Kingdom.

the pleasure he felt on hearing that exclusion made no longer a part of the British Constitution. I imagine to myself the stare with which you read my words, but I assure you they are the conviction of my mind & founded on all the experience which reading & observation has enabled me to acquire. Depend upon it the pope of Rome is in this age no longer an object of dread, and that step of the British Government has dried up his influence over England for ever. Wellington never deserved so much for his victories in war as he has merited by his conquests in peace. But I will not enlarge on this point: – 'tis likely I am combating shadows when I suppose that you would countenance a system which went to keep Catholics a band of servile Helots to British protestants, the staple of their ranks in war – in peace their hewers of wood & drawers of water. – Write me fully next time on all the passing topics of conversation regarding public affairs. I like to hear what the world at large think of what we only learn through the biased sentiments of editors, – most of them in the pay of one side or the other. I will at this time say nothing more, leaving the remainder of my sheet to be filled up when I shall receive my parents letters about the end of this month, – when I also expect yours of this season.

YF 23 June 1830

Miss Jane Hargrave
Dear Jane

The whole of your kind letters reached me 2 days ago, and I am already set about saying something in return foreseeing well that ere five days be over my head I shall be so busy that writing letters will be quite impossible. I am hale and hearty as ever, and it is the pleasantest news I have heard since last season, to be informed that the whole of you enjoy your wonted good health. With what you tell me of your own private affairs I must say I am not equally pleased. You have sadly mismanaged the money I sent you, and having trusted you so far as to leave it entirely in your hands & only to lay on you the single injunction of not drawing the money till you were *certain* of wanting it for the purpose it was sent, I must say I did expect you would have attended to what I said more punctually than you have done. The whole is now gone except as you say eight dollars – and only the *tenth* part of what I expected you would have hoarded up for a time when it would have been so necessary – instead of which you have disregarded the only request I made on the subject. You have indeed the excuse that you have not spent it on yourself but rather in a way that you might have expected I would have approved. This excuse may be good if I saw it on all sides; but from every thing I can learn from the letters I have had this spring I fear my poor father is preyed upon in his building schemes by some poor needy creatures around you whom he had engaged to raise his house. I sent you & them last spring upwards of 30 pounds Halifax. They told me their contracts for finishing their building were far within that sum, instead of which they & you have got from me within these two years nearly 50 pounds Halifax, most of which for any thing I can see have gone to satisfy masons & carpenters and yet the dwelling remains unfinished. This seems to me a strong proof that on beginning their undertaking that [they] had made a very erroneous calculation of the Cost, or else that some needy sharpers around them, finding that they had money within their reach, have by some plan or other screwed it out of their fingers. The whole of this affair I cannot see through and as it now appears to me, have much reason to disapprove of their expense & of your giving up the money I sent you for a different purpose. I did expect also that you would have said this time something more regarding the disappointment you have met with, and the reasons for your conduct throughout in the affair. These matters with me are as safe from the ears of the world as if you never had spoken them; as your elder brother and as one who is interested in all your welfares I did expect it, and – I have been disappointed. You hint at reasons of which I can make nothing: – and when left in the dark it is natural to fear evils are greater than what they may be in reality. This is also one part of your letter which does not satisfy me.

After all this – I must however say that I am *not angry* with you, but rather that I am in doubt and fear worse things than what actually may be the plain matter of fact. You write well and sensibly – and had you told me a plain downright story of all your little affairs & that between ourselves they had been as safe as they now are in your own keeping & perhaps I might have seen many reasons to excuse what I now find fault with. On the whole, My Dear Jane, I have yet confidence in your good sense, and trust you will next time put more confidence in your brother & open your mind more freely.

I have nothing to add about myself but what I said above that I am well. I will again remain at this place & with all the heavy labour I undergo like my situation extremely.

Good bye My Dear Sister & Still believe me
Your Very affectionate brother

JH

York Factory 23 June 1830

Mr John Hargrave
Dear John

I was very glad to hear on receiving your letters a few days ago that you were all well, except our old father, who I hope is ere now quite recovered from his accident. I am also happy to hear that you have got into your new house, tho' I am sorry to find that it has cost you so much money and so much trouble. It is however satisfactory to learn that you have succeeded in getting out of debt to strangers in consequence of this building, and I trust that hereafter you will calculate better the expense of your plans before you undertake them. You are now my Dear John getting up in years, and will likely soon wish to settle yourself for life. Your purpose of taking another Lot I think a good one but beware how you run yourselves in debt in any such step. This lot if got without expense will be just the way of providing for yourself: – a log house built on it & a clearing made, could I think be all done within yourselves without employing strangers who would assuredly squeeze out of you all the money they can. I hope however that whenever you may wish to set up House yourself, our old parents will not be left without help. They are both far advanced in years and cannot themselves work the farm they now occupy. Your or Andrews assistance will always be required, and I have confidence in you both that they will be taken care of.

Regarding myself I never can find much to say. I am not likely to be removed from my present situation while I remain in the country, and altho' the work I have to do is as Heavy as I can well get through, I am however in good health and am pleased with my employment. You complain that you can not now get a journal from me, but for writing one as well as writing letters I have no time. I however send a book[40] in which I began one two years ago, and which for want of leisure to write as well as matter to write about I was obliged to leave unfinished. It will however help to eke out my stock of letters this summer & so I shall parcel it up with them.

I promised you all a letter last time I wrote, and tho' they may be found short, believe me it arises from the crowd around me & the interruptions I am liable to, – not through want of the will. Believe me I shall always remain
My Dear John

---

40 His 1828–29 Journal.

Your Affec Brother

JH

York Factory 23rd June '30

M^r· Andrew Hargrave
Dear Andrew

 I received your kind letter two days ago with great pleasure, and am truly happy to hear that you are all so well, and so comfortable. Our poor fathers accident in returning from a visit to our brothers I lament to hear of, but fondly hope that it will be followed by no serious consequences. What you say of the condition of Joseph & Ruther with their families I am also happy to learn. Their large families must at present indeed be a burden to them, but a few years will soon go by, & their sons will be able to help them most materially. Joseph especially has a whole troop of them, and I am not a little rejoiced to find that Annie[41] has turned out so much better than I once feared. Our old feuds of former days you can assure her I have long ago forgotten, and when I visit Canada will assuredly call upon them all. I thank them both for having had the kindness to name one of the little rogues after me, and hope yet to see him a clever and industrious farmer. This indeed seems to me the only way in which my name will be continued: – I am yet single, and in all likelihood will make no match in this country, so that by the time I set up housekeeping in Canada I may be so attached to the life of a bachelor, that it will be an over hard task for the sex to noose me. We however shall see. I like well to hear that Ja^s Ross and Mary have resolved to settle down upon their farm. You say they are in your neighborhood, and it must be pleasing to our Old parents to have so many of us around them in their latter years. I always hope to be permitted to see them also again once more: we have long been separated and now nothing could give me so much pleasure. I indeed have no hopes at present of being able to leave this service entirely and settle among you but I have a strong wish to visit you for one winter in the course of 2 or 3 years. To sit down as a Settler in Canada one must lay ones account with not a little hard labour or else there must be such a sum of money in the pocket as to hire & maintain servants. – This I think I have not yet got hold of. Can you tell me what it would require to purchase a farm of 400 acres one fourth cleared, – with a good house &

---

41 Joseph Hargrave Jr's wife, Nancy (Annie) Dobson.

offices upon it? Knowing this I think I could make a close calculation of what I should want in all. For work myself I now could never think of it. The pen is so different from the Axe that I would feel as awkward at the one as you can do at the other.

I can say nothing about myself but that I am well and that I shall be always your Aff. Brother

JH

York Factory 23rd June 1830

Mr. Ja^s Ross
Dear Brother

I had the pleasure of receiving your kind letter a couple [of] days ago, and rejoice sincerely to find that you & Mary with all the little Madroulikins are well & happy. I think your resolution of sitting down on a farm & turning to the best advantage the money you have acquired in Canal contracts is a truly wise one, both for your own comforts and for the improvements of the little ones. I hear your lot is within a days traveling of my fathers and in that neighborhood I purpose also to settle myself whenever I can believe I have a sufficient sum to keep my head above water for the remainder of my days. This must be however without farther labor than is necessary for healthy exercise. The difference between the pen & the axe is so great that I now could never work my self into any chance of using the last to advantage. What sum do you think is necessary to purchase a farm of say 400 acres with about a quarter cleared having a good house on it also Offices &^{c} &^{c} exclusive of all live stock or farming utensils. You see by this that I am already beginning to think towards a roosting place for myself, – tho' I fear my purse is yet too light for anything like the position my habits would make me comfortable in. I still live a bluff bachelor, & so my house keeping would be the smaller, – yet I suspect you will add not the less expensive. Well we shall see about mending these matters when I again get among lasses whom I can flatter in my native tongue, – tho' I dread a fagged out and rough North Wester will have but slender influence over their fancies. *Mais Nous Verrons.*[42]

Mary has been lecturing me not a little about not writing you both last season. Now I have many things to say in my defense. First she has Now a much more legitimate subject than myself to scold, who is bound to bear these matters "for better & for worse"; and besides in the next place she

---

42 But we shall see (French).

takes it for granted that the fault is all my own. Here I catch her by the ear & tell her that in this she decides too hastily. Time was so precious with me last summer & will again in 5 days be the same this year that every letter I then receive will remain unanswered till long after the Montreal Canoe be started. This was the case last year & the only few lines I wrote my parents & which were designed for you all, were scribbled over, between sleeping & waking after a fagging days work of 18 hours during which every mental & bodily power was kept to the stretch. Seriously talking I know not where to address you, your letters not having got to hand; & when a thing is difficult to be done, with the head confused & the eyes heavy you know how small a feather will turn the Scale. Believe this my dear friends, believe any thing rather than that it was from my want of regard for either you or her. I shall always remain
Yours affectionately

JH

York Factory 24th June 1830
Mrs Mary Ross
My Dear Mary

I received your very kind letter a few days ago, and I assure you it gladdened my heart to find that you & James with all the little family were well. You seem to have taken to heart my not having written you last summer, but believe me it was occasioned by any thing rather than want of regard for you both. You little know the busy life I lead here else I am sure you would have excused my seeming neglect. The situation I hold is attended with such a mass of labor both mental & bodily that I have often, about the time I should have written you last year dropt asleep through mere fatigue & want of rest, with the pen between my fingers & my head lying on the page I was writing. After lugging through a day of 18 hours labor in this manner I am sure you will own, that I had need of repose, and will think that the six hours I had for rest would scarcely allow of much being devoted to the indulgence of my own private feelings. I besides did not know where to address you, and thinking that you might be near our father or at least visiting them during the winter I purposed their letter as a general one to serve you all. Jane I had to write, about some little affairs such as I once had occasion to speak of to yourself, – and I regret to find that she has not quite followed my injunctions on the subject. I have given her a lecture in consequence, but for all that, you can assure her that I love her as much as ever, and that I still

believe she may have many reasons to excuse herself, had she thought proper to entrust me with them. For all that I have said above about my busy life I am however happy & in good health. True it is confinement & toil have quite reduced my former rotundity of person: I am now thin as a Whipping post yet tough as wire, with an appetite that could still digest a "bicker of brase" were such a luxury of our younger days to be procured among these swamps. I thank both you & Ja^s most kindly for having complimented me with a name in your family. I myself seem little inclined to perpetuate it, and look forward with much composure to the Cauldrife[43] life of an Old bachelor. From such resolutions however many sudden conversions are often made. You have now a small & increasing family & I think that you have resolved most wisely to settle yourselves comfortably down on your farm. Single men may ramble about, but a family prospers best when rooted to one spot. I fondly hope some year or other to pop in on you when you least expect me & assure you all in person how much
I am their Affect^ate

JH

York Factory 24 June 1830

My Dear Mother

You can well imagine so that I need not describe the pleasure I felt on receiving all your most kind letters, and in learning that you were yet all alive, happy and comfortable. No doubt both you and my poor father are far advanced in years, and this life to us is not for ever; but yet you both have the recollection of a well spent life to sweeten the approach of its end, and still both may be graciously spared many years, to allow your children the pleasure of smoothing the path of declining years. Keep up your heart my dear Mother, and do not let your fears overcome you either on account of yourself or me. We are all under the protection of an indulgent Father who can bring to us joy and gladness out of sorrow & weeping as waters once flowed for the refreshment of His people Out of the barren & flinty rock. I sincerely hope & trust that we may be allowed yet once again to meet in the land of the living. My dear fathers accident I am sorry to hear of, but fondly hope that nothing serious will follow it. Your journey to visit Joseph & Ruther must have been most fatiguing to you both, yet I am glad to hear that you went since it has afforded

---

43 Chilly, indifferent. DSL.

pleasure to you & them. I am particularly pleased to find that Annie has turned out so much better than I once feared and will this season write Joseph & her thanking them for their kind treatment of you. This letter you will find enclosed with the others & I hope you will get an opportunity of forwarding it. Both he & Ruther seem to be comfortably situated, and whenever I may get to Canada I will assuredly visit them both. Tho' I do not write owing to the distance, the difficulty of getting letters sent to them, and the little time I can here call my own, – yet for all that, they are not forgotten by me. I am also glad to hear that you are now so comfortably lodged, tho' the building has cost you so much more than what was first calculated on. The money I sent you for yourself I certainly expected would have been at least partly required to clear it, but I was surprised to find that Jane's little marriage portion had also been found necessary. I hope my father will hereafter better weigh his undertakings before he allows himself to get involved among some of these hungry cormorants that roost about you. I have written Jane on the subject & scolded her a little, for I think she deserves it, having broken the only injunction I laid on her when I sent her the money. She will yet find as well as I have done that money is more easily scattered than gathered. It is now however over, and on the whole I am glad you have a comfortable & durable house to put your heads in, – for I am certain you needed it. To help you out in laying up a stock for winter I again send you my usual Bill of £10 and as your building schemes are past I think you will be able to use it in providing yourself with the little comforts which I have always wished you to procure with it. I need say nothing about myself but that I am well and in the same place & at the same desk as when I last wrote you, – and what more can I add? I wrote you & my father last October and hope you have received the letters. Comfort your self, my dear Mother with the knowledge that I am often with you in spirit though absent in body, and that I am as well in health as you could wish me. May you long enjoy the same blessing is the earnest prayer of
Your most Aff. Son

JH

York Factory 24th June 1830

My Dear Father

I have read with great pleasure your excellent letter of last spring now before me, and rejoice that you have been spared to address me again after the serious accident you met with in returning from the United States. I trust that ere this time you are perfectly recovered from its effects. It is also most gratifying to learn that you have at length got into your new house and that you find yourselves so Comfortable in it. The expense has been large beyond what I expected, but that I do not regret since the dwelling pleases you so well, – yet I could have wished that poor Janes little portion which I sent her had been spared. I fear you are all of you too simple & single minded for some of the knowing rogues around you and from your wanting so much as Janes Bill, I suspect that the Tradesmen you employed have sadly imposed on your honest simplicity. In trying to repay Jane, *borrow not one shilling* from *any one* to do it: a debt due to a child is more easily borne than one owing to a stranger: rather let me know how much you cannot make up and leave the rest to me. I never regret what is for your benefit, when I can see that it is so spent; but really I have strong suspicions that either your bargains have been badly made or else that you have been imposed upon to your hurt.

You have also you say reason to complain of me in not answering you on the subject of the books you were pleased to recommend to my perusal; – on this subject I will now reply to you with the same scrutiny this complaint is made, for I cannot rest under the belief that my aged father should remain unsatisfied with any part of my conduct. Tis very true I have not yet procured any of the Books you mention, and it is also true that I have the means to purchase them. To comprehend why I have so delayed take a look at the life I lead. From five in the morning till 11 at night throughout the summer my hours, minutes, nay moments are devoted to the duties belonging to my station, and which duties require the utmost stretch of thought and exertion of body – of which I am capable. The few remaining hours of night are all too little for repose, – and so the summer passes over. Winter has also its toils. From Day light till bed time I am at the desk, buried in papers & accounts, forwarding my own duties or directing others. In each week five days are so occupied, Saturday is passed in hunting or walking; absolutely necessary for the preservation of our health. The Sabbaths throughout the year are indeed our own, but when the mind is jaded with mental tasks through the week, how can I enjoy the deep & abstract subjects you recommend to my attention. On these sacred days, doubly blessed to me for then I can lay down my worldly cares, – I find the greatest relief in the perusal of my bible. This book is never absent from my room, and there is a freshness in its simplicity which fatigued in mind as I am, I can relish far beyond all the elaborate work of human reason. These last require too much exertion of thought, I cannot bring my wearied mind to undergo the labor of weighing the arguments or fathoming the depths of the Four Fold State whilst a chapter of the Evangelists refreshes me by the purity of its doctrines & the ease with which I can comprehend its simple precepts. All the arguments of the works of man on the subject of religion only go to support the truths of the blessed gospel, or else they ought not to be read: – Of most of them I can more easily understand their texts than their comments, so while I can drink from the fountain, why tire out a wearied body in searching for beautiful prospects & clear pools in the streams which flow from it? These no doubt are to be desired when the mind can go in search of them, but you will perceive by what I have said that I have little time for speculating on any subject. For all this I am not however blind to the benefits of a faithful guide in many of the dark parts of the sacred volume. The books you mention might strengthen my faith and I believe the whole of their doctrines are pure. Whenever I can indulge myself with the task of comparing their arguments with my own, I will procure them were it only because you recommend them: But placed as I presently am I hope you will now agree with me that the Simplest food, the milk for babes – the book which he who runs may read, – is also the book most fitted for my closet table.

I have little more to add, my dear father. You mention your age as 75 years,[44] – mine is now 32, – yet often the young head is laid low when the white hairs of age are spared. The consideration of this is never from before my eyes, & let our daily prayers be that, whenever the appointed hour may arrive, we may not be found asleep at our posts. That long & late this house may be to you, and that your rem[ainin]g years may yet be brightened by the sight of *all* your family around your Table is the fervent prayer of
Your Most Aff. Son

JH

---

44 This would make Joseph Hargrave's birthdate about 1755, not 1749 as stated in the Hargrave family manuscript.

[Letterbook]
N°. 6
Rough Copies Letters by
JHargrave
From 25th June 1830 @ 7th July 1831

York Factory
Hudsons Bay   25 June 1830

M^r. Jos^h Hargrave
My Dear Brother

   I was very happy to learn by our fathers letter of last spring that he had been paying you a visit during the winter, and I was highly gratified to find that both you and Ruther were in such comfortable circumstances. We are so far asunder that we cannot expect to receive many letters from each other, but I was so pleased by the account which both my father & mother gave of your & Annie's kindness to them & of your remembrance of me that I cannot resist the desire of sending you a few lines, and trust to fortune for their getting on. I assure you their letters spoke highly of the manner in which they were welcomed by you both, as well as of the comfort & plenty which both you & Ruther enjoyed on your farms. They will have told you of my situation in this distant corner of the world, so that what I may say further will perhaps be already known to you. The spring after we came to Canada, I engaged with the Canadian Fur Coy[1] as Clerk to go into the Indian Country and remained in their service till they united with the Hudsons Bay Coy – an Association of British Merchants who trade into Hudsons Bay, and who have now the sole right & authority from the British Government over the whole of North West America. In the service of this United Coy I had the good fortune to be retained, and have, since I entered it, been advanced from one situation to another, till I now fill the post of Depot Clerk at the Head Quarters of the Trade. My duties are sufficiently laborious; and my Salary, tho' the highest given to Clerks in the service, not more than 500 Dollars yearly – yet I like my situation very well and altho' I cannot yet lay aside much money I am certain of receiving in one or at most two years more an yearly income of above three times what I have now. I will then have the means of providing for old age, and should my life be spared, will return to settle among you all in Canada. I am yet a single man & pur-

---

1 The North West Company.

pose remaining so while in this Country; but I am glad to hear that both you & Ruther have each fine & numerous families, so the name runs no danger from the shyness with which I avoid matrimony. My mother in particular mentions that you & Annie have a family of five as fine little fellows as she ever saw, and further that you have complimented me with giving my name to one of them. I feel much your kindness in this, my dear brother, and hope to find the little knave a good axeman & a steady lad when I visit you all some future year. Give my love to Annie, and my little nephews, & also to Ruther & his family. I should like to hear from you both, I know Annie is a good penwoman, and hope she will write me next season. If you can get a letter for me sent down to our fathers before the end of next February it will get to me by an express Canoe which leaves Lachine as soon as the ice breaks up, & will reach me here in June next year. At any other time letters cannot get forward, there being no chance except by this Canoe. God bless & prosper you my dear Brother & believe me always
Yours most affectionately

JH

P.S. Address your letters "J. Hargrave HB Co York Factory Hudsons Bay."

YF 22 July 1830

Private
J.G. McTavish Esq
Dear Sir
    Mr Clarke[2] is about starting with the Light Canoe for Canada, and as a letter by that conveyance may have a chance of reaching you this fall, I do myself the pleasure of adding a few lines for you to the Budget,

---

2 John Clarke (1781–1852), a chief factor who had been in charge of the post at Lesser Slave Lake from 1824 to 1826, then in charge of Swan River district at Fort Pelly until 1830. He left York Factory 31 July 1830 for Canada with a crew of "seven Goers & Comers from Montreal and two retiring Winterers." HBCA, B.239/a/141. In his 1832 Character book, Governor George Simpson portrayed Clarke as being "a boasting, ignorant low fellow" showing "total want of every principle or feeling allied to fair dealing, honour & integrity ... He is in short a disgrace to the 'Fur Trade.'" Brown, "Clarke, John."

having the vanity to think that you may expect to hear from me. I purposed writing you by last winter packet to Moose, – but seeing that no other was inclined to make use of the opportunity, I was restrained by motives which I know you will believe to any thing rather than neglect on my part. I chanced a few lines by the spring Canoe to Nor. Ho. which I believe may reach you with this. I little thought last fall when bidding you farewell on board the Prince Rupert that it was likely to be one for ever, and was never more surprised than this spring when I found the change that had been made in your winter Quarters.[3] I rejoice at it, – as one which will afford you a quiet life in comparison with the moiling years you have spent here, – yet I fear me that many in this Department will learn to appreciate the value of your former services by the want of them. As regards my own private feelings, I must learn resignation. I have been so long with you, have benefited so much by your instructions, and have been borne up by your friendly arm in so many rough gales, – that I now may be expected to walk alone. But believe me, that whether I may ever again see you or not, – the remembrance of all your kindness to me can never pass from my mind.

You will have heard through other sources of the gnawings a miserable faction have this season been making at your conduct both public & private;[4] – I will not hurt your feelings by a repetition of the wretched malice: – suffice it to say their puny efforts at detraction met with the firmest opponents in Gov.r S[impson]. & Mr Christie.[5] They have both shown the most friendly interest in every thing connected with your name or your affairs.

Your personal property left here was partly disposed of by direction of Gov.r Simpson, & the proceeds am[oun]t[e]d to £22 add placed to your

3 John George McTavish, upon his return from Scotland with his new Scottish wife, was posted at Moose Factory, headquarters of the Southern Department.
4 Although he had been well liked for his kind and generous character, his cruel abandonment of his native family led to severe attacks upon his character, particularly by John Stuart and Donald McKenzie, that hurt him deeply.
5 Alexander Christie (1792–1872) was an HBC chief factor and administrator. He was in charge of Moose Factory from 1826 until 1830 when he was transferred to York Factory. Three years later he was placed in charge of Red River and was appointed governor of Assiniboia. Bowsfield, "Christie, Alexander."

credit. I enclose you a list of the Articles sold. Some wearing apparel, which was not offered for sale, & several Books for which no purchasers could be found, still remain. Of all these I will send you a list by the winter Express, my busy life at present preventing me from collecting all your little matters so carefully as I could wish. This property I shall pack up, and it will remain here till your wishes regarding it are known. Mr Christie thinks that it might be sent home & from London forwarded to you at Moose with little difficulty. It will certainly be of more use to you that way, than any thing which can be realized for it here. There is also a long Case remaining in the Biscuit Room over the Provision Shed, which I think you brot from F^y William, – also a painting of the Late M^r McTavish[6] hanging in your Room. These will be preserved with the rest till your instructions regarding them are received. Several of your most valuable Books I have not seen since your departure, among others The Modern Drama in 6 Vol 8vo & Russels Modern Europe.[7] Perhaps you took them with you.

Excuse I beg of you the hasty style of this sheet, I could say much, but time is denied me, surrounded as you can well imagine I am at this season. I am glad such a steady, plain upright Gent^n as Mr Christie has been found to succeed you here: – I shall do my best to second him in whatever I can be of use. We have now most of the summer business over, – and from the additional number of working hands expect to get through it without the grinding labor of former seasons.
With the deepest respect & regard I am
Yours most faithfully

JH

Poor George[8] is sadly disappointed in not getting back to you as he expected, – On Service.

---

6 Lachlan Mactavish, the impoverished last chief of Clan Tavish, who had died in 1796.
7 *The history of modern Europe: with an account of the decline and fall of the Roman Empire; and a view of the progress of society, from the rise of the modern kingdoms to the Peace of Paris in 1763. In a series of letters from a nobleman to his son*, by William Russell, 1741–93.
8 George Thorn was a butler at York Factory.

YF 8 Novr 1830

J.G. McTavish Esq
Dear Sir

The winter packet for the south, being ready for starting as soon as the unusually mild season will allow it to get under way, I add my puny sheet to its contents freighted with whatever I can select for your amusement out of the uncoes of this quarter. Your sloop for Ungava[9] unexpectedly cast up last month at 5 f[atho]m Hole driven back they say by boisterous weather. It is consequently laid up here, and the crew pass their winter at York & on the winter Road. About the usual time the Two ships[10] from England arrived here, – the Old Commodore[11] quite on his beam ends from Gout & other ailments. So much so that he never got ashore during the whole time of their stay. They delivered their Cargoes in high order, the portage La Loche Boats arrived in good time & the Prince sailed on the 17th Septr with Mess[ieurs]. McLeod[12] & Rae[13] – the only passengers home this season. Our stores certainly are now sufficiently crammed. All the usual stowage room was filled to overflowing & both fur stores had to lend their aid in getting housed the surplus. The invoice at YF last is upwards of £55,000. The Reqⁿ of this season has consequently been bro^t down to near £22,000 & one ship is expected to bring the whole next season. The goods of this year are materialy improved both as to quality & cheapness, – and all, such as will be sooner or later turned into an advantageous equivalent. I am grinding away among them, with the same [illegible] and in the usual style of arranging matters, our honest bourgeois great aim being to keep the business in the same state of regularity it was left. We have also had a good addition to our working hands

---

9 The *Beaver* was driven back near Mansel Island off the Ungava Peninsula at the entrance to Hudson Bay.
10 The *Prince of Wales* went to James Bay and the *Prince Rupert* to York Factory.
11 Capt. Benjamin Bell.
12 John McLeod went on furlough in 1830–31, taking his two eldest sons to school in Scotland.
13 William Glen Rae (1808–1845), a brother of John Rae, returned to Europe on leave of absence for medical advice. He later became chief trader at California in the Columbia District from 1841–45 and committed suicide at Yerba Buena (present-day San Francisco).

in Mess T. Simpson[14] & Rae[15] – and get through the routine with less difficulty & a shade more of good humour. Last winter indeed bore so heavy on me that towards spring I was fairly wrought out and had this summer got permission to visit Canada next season for the benefit of health, – I now however find myself so much recruited as to hope, if I do not retrograde, that I shall not need this trip. I am most happy also in having found in Mr T. Simpson a most agreeable & intelligent companion, whose conversation helps me to while away seasons yet peculiar to York atmosphere & which formerly were wont to prey so on the spirits.

The Gun you were so good as [to] procure for me came safely to hand, and I am highly delighted with it. It is acknowledged the best which has been sent here this season, tho some nearly double its cost has been brot out. The want of the books has caused me no inconvenience, – I having laid my hands on such a stock in the fall from one or other of my acquaintances as will serve for the winter.

I have now got the whole of your property collected which remains here undisposed of and enclose you a note of it. It will remain in the store waiting your directions regarding it. Mr Smith[16] last fall sent me out a Leather Capot trimmed with fur designed for you, desiring me if possible to get it forwarded. This I shall try & get sent on to Michipicoten[17] next summer by whoever goes down to Canada in the Express Canoe. The present Conveyance is too precarious a one for any thing beyond the weight of a letter.

You will have heard ere this of the result of Winter Road Bubble.[18] Never was wreck more complete. The thaw last spring found the Goods

---

14 Thomas Simpson (1808–1840) was a cousin of Governor George Simpson and entered the HBC as a clerk in 1829. In 1837–39 he was engaged in Arctic exploration with P.W. Dease; he was killed in Iowa in 1840.
15 Richard Rae, a brother of William Glen and John Rae, was serving as an apprentice clerk at York Factory that year.
16 Edward Smith (d. 1849), the HBC chief factor at Fort Simpson from 1823 to 1832, went on furlough between 1832 and 1834.
17 An HBC fort on the Michipicoten River which runs into Lake Superior. It was on the route to Moose Factory on James Bay.
18 The HBC planned to build a winter road between Norway House and York Factory so that the Red River carts could run over it. The road was never finished.

strewed along the Road from the forks of hill River to the Head of Oxf[or]ᵈ Lake, – beyond which not a Pˢ got on till embarked in Boats. Abᵗ third of the whole was embarked this spring from Fort Daer[19] yet even these escaped not damage. The Stores were so low that the whole got flooded by the thaw. They froze up again – & bales & Sugar kegs had to be dug out with ice Chisels. Near 150 Pˢ remain in the swamps all summer below Oxford covered with bark, – the mild weather having overtaken them while in transit through the "lower Section". Next spring can only tell the damage, as not a scrap of paper reachᵈ my fingers of the upshot & we are indeed still ignorant here of what has been saved – what remained behind. Its Conductor[20] was really an object of pity: – his men gave him out as having had *la tête tourné*[21] – all spring. He retorted with charges of rebellion & processes for theftdom. It still however goes on in a small way – 200 Pˢ being again tried this season.

Elsewhere little occurs of moment. My friend Barnstone[22] tells me he has given notice of leaving the country & comes out next spring. He seems disgusted with the service, or rather that part of its executive to which he has lately been subjected. I deeply feel for him. A high toned

19 Fort Daer was an HBC fort on the west bank of the Red River at the mouth of Pembina River on the site of the present town of Pembina, North Dakota. It was named after Lord Selkirk, who was also Baron Daer.
20 Colin Robertson (1783–1842), a Scotsman, was at Oxford House from 1828 when he was put in charge of the scheme for a winter road to the Red River settlement. When Simpson visited him there in 1830 he reported: "Robertson has be deviled the Winter Road, incurred much expense, destroyed a great deal of provisions, damaged most of the [pieces], 150 still remaining in the woods. Killed 6 of the Oxen, in short has made an infinite jumble of the business and confused and confounded every thing connected with it. He goes to Swan River." Rich, *Colin Robertson*, cxii.
21 French for mad, crazy, (literally "the turned head"). *Tourner la tête* means "to make mad," according to Larousse.
22 George Barnston (c. 1800–1883) was an HBC fur-trader and naturalist. Like Hargrave, Barnston joined the NWC in 1820 as an apprentice clerk and was taken into the HBC following the union of the two companies in 1821. The records for the period 1825 to the mid 1830s reflect his frustration and unhappiness with his career. In 1831, while he was in charge of Fort Nez Perces, a sharp dispute with Governor George Simpson over his next appointment and rate of advancement caused him to resign. He rejoined the service in 1832. Brown and Van Kirk, "Barnston, George."

– delicately sensitive soul such as his can ill brook the bully-ragging treatment which sometimes it is the lot of poor Subalterns to endure, he has again the world to begin: and thus eleven years of life, the prime of life, are sacrificed in the pursuit of a shadow.

I have made out for you a sort of comparison between this & last outfit which Mr Christie will enclose for your information. It will give you some notion of how things go forward in these matters. With this Gentleman I feel myself perfectly happy. Few could have succeeded you & acted with such prudence. He has had the judgment to see the advantages of your system of business, & the firmness to adhere to it. We understand each other perfectly, – & for this judgement of me I owe him the more gratitude, as I had once discovered symptoms of the mole under my toes. It may however get itself squeezed in its hole before it undermines me, should it still continue its scratching.

I have nothing farther that can amuse you – so God bless you! Yours most faithfully –

JH

YF 12 Novr 30

My Dear father

A packet which leaves this in a few days for the South gives me an opportunity of forwarding you a letter, and tho as usual I have little matter to interest you unconnected with myself I know the very sight of my handwriting will be satisfactory to you, especially when I can add that I am hale & hearty as ever. The last time I wrote you was in July which letters must now have reached you. Since then I have remained here employed as usual in managing the Depot business of York Factory. Since my last, the vessels from England arrived here by which I had letters from Scotland, among others from my uncle Ja^s Mitchel. They were then all well, and were still residing in Galashiels. A number of families left their neighborhood last season for Canada, among others Ja^s Gray of Lindean Mill[23] – by whom they sent you a letter. This will inform you more in detail of their circumstances, should it have chanced to reach you.

---

23 James Gray is listed under Corn and Flour Mills in Pigot's 1825–26 Directory.

I have in my former letters & journals said so much of this place that any further account of it can add little to your information. In my residence here, – and the observation applies to the country at large, what I feel most the want of is the absence of a Church Establishment – when one day in the seven could be devoted to spiritual improvement, by the means best adapted to that important end. No doubt, we have the aid of books, but there is something in the regular call to a place of public worship which fixes the attention more on the duties of the day than what can be done in a private dwelling house – where other matters are too apt to thrust them upon the attention & entise the mind aside from the duties of the day, – often too willing to be entised. This circumstance, added to the long absence from all that are dear to my affections, is the only thing which I feel irksome in my path in life, – otherwise it is bountifully strewed with pleasures & with enjoyments far beyond what my hopes could once have ever aspired to. It is the general opinion in the civilized world that Missionaries are alone wanted, to change a heathen into a Christian Country, to civilize the wild inhabitant of the woods, & change the indian wigwam into a Christian Temple. I once had strong opinions also regarding the efficacy of this, but experience has proved them in my eyes to be only a weak tho benevolent wish for the welfare of our Red Brethren – at least till several Generations have passed away under the continued application of the means of improvement. An Indian grown to maturity can never be brot to comprehend the doctrines of the Gospel, – his mind is too narrow – his understanding too limited & prejudised by his own superstitions, ever to receive & understand the truths of a pure & abstract system of Religion. To accomplish this, the attempts at conversion must commence from Childhood, Civilization in all the departments of a settled life must lend its aid, and even under this slow & gradual advance, several generations must pass away before the native Savage can be transformed into the enlightened & pious Christian. Of the truth of this I feel convinced – and it is with a melancholy feeling that I mention it as applicable to the immense regions over which the British Coy I serve extends its sway. To live & die in such a country could be the wish of only those who have shaken off all remembrance of more favored Climes or who have by their own folly bound a burden on their Shoulders which they find impossible to carry elsewhere. My eyes are open to this grand error, and I trust to benefit by the example of too many of those around me. That this period may arrive while I yet can receive a blessing from my aged parent on this side the Grave is the earnest prayer of

Your Most Affectionate Son
P.S. Make my kind Compts. To old Mr Barber   JH

YF 12 Novr 1830

My Dear Mother
   By the southern winter packet I again chance a letter for you in hopes that it will inform you of my welfare next summer, long before the usual time of writing by the summer Canoe. I still remain at this place employed as usual, nor is there much likelihood of my being sent elsewhere for some time to come. My health this season is excellent and that comprehends all I can say about my self. Last fall I had a letter from my uncle Ja^s Mitchel. They were all well in April last, and mention having written you by Ja^s Gray who with his family were then about leaving Scotland for Canada. My Cousin Effy says "I think my aunt will need a few days warning to have the White Cake ready she promised to Old James as big as the Mill Stone." I have not received a letter this season from Lockie, – and from the abundant occupation I have through summer, I had not time to write either my uncle or him. I am sorry to hear the reports you mention of Lockie. I trust they are exaggerated, but his not writing you, when he had such an opportunity *if he knew of it*, was certainly a neglect I could not have expected. I long expected that he purposed coming to America, but I believe his circumstances are too low to bear the expense. I have refrained from advising him to this step as without something to begin with in Canada, a new settler has many hard years of poverty to struggle with before he can call himself independant, – and the adviser often receiving any thing but thanks for his advice. It is one of my Greatest pleasures to think that you yourselves are now above want, and are entirely your own Masters. Of all things now, beware of getting into Debt. Borrow from none, lend money to none. Whatever I have given you or may hereafter send you, is freely yours, but I need not describe how painful it is either to crave money from others or to be craved your selves when it is not convenient to pay. Your little farm now produces enough to support you. You have a good house which will be a comfortable home for the remainder of your life, I trust to my brothers John & Andrew that they manage your little affairs under my fathers eye, and you may depend on my yearly Bill to help you in pocket money throughout your life. Jane I hope has been repaid the money she advanced you last year, at least in some way or other. She ought not to expect money in return for that must ever be scarce with you but there are many things

else which will be useful in a family that you can let her have. Borrow from none to repay her. John mentions a plan you had to take another lot in your neighborhood. This is very right. They poor fellows have a good right to look out for something for themselves now, and they both should take lots, and prepare for an establishment in life. It should however be near you, for whether single or married I hope they will continue to help you through with the work of your own farm, a task which is doubtless now far beyond your own strength. My father can aid them in stocking any new lot for themselves out of what he has, for I wish him to consider every thing he has as his own & entirely at his own disposal. He should put his wishes on this subject to writing & keep the paper by him: – I know we Scotch, have a dread about making wills, but since I have mingled with the world I have seen the good of it.

 I have little time for adding any thing further my Dear Mother. The packet starts in a day or two, & I have so much to furnish for it that I am now writing you when the clock is striking midnight. May God bless & preserve both you & me till we meet again is the earnest prayer of your loving Son Jamie.

YF 20th May 1831

J.G. McTavish Esq
Dear Sir

 As tis likely a packet will be sent you this spring by the Govr from Nor Ho: I chance a few lines for that conveyance in acknowledgment of your kind sheet of 29 Jany last via the coast. That by way of R[ed]R[iver] has not yet reached me. All your property here I have together in the Store & will agreeably to your wishes forward them this fall to you by the English ship. In copying the list of Books sent you I perceive I had omitted Old Ostervald[24] – he is however in company with the others, also one or two more which I have since found bearing your name. The capot I shall make up in a parcel & get to Michipicoten by the fall Canoe for Canada.

 I am grinding away here as usual & have matters nearly in a state ready for commencing the summer business. My honest Bourgeois & I arrange most admirably, and all in my department goes on exactly in the same channel it has so long been accustomed to do under your eye. To

---

24 Perhaps Jean-Frédéric Ostervald, 1663–1747, a Swiss Protestant pastor, lecturer, and author. Ostervald's *Bible*, a revision of his French translation, was long well known and much valued in Britain.

keep matters in this state is my greatest ambition& when Mr C[hristie]. remains to conduct the Store business & I may have a hand in seeing it done, – I can venture to say your footprints will not be lost sight of. Our Stock of Goods is really an overwhelming one. The Yellow Store Garret is filled with Reserve Bales – & the Shops are crammed with every thing that can tempt money from the voyageurs pocket. The quality of all is unusually good, and bear evident marks of a careful selection. The Trade however I trust will be as sparsely supplied as formerly, for since the Rat uproar has sunk it is found that your Estimate of Outfits is ample for all the necessary demands of the interior. The Govr seems to be impressed with this opinion – and the last & next Req{n} on England have both been very carefully gone into, so as that not an article may be asked for but such as is absolutely wanted.

There is little news worth noting from the interior. Another vessel the Isabella has been lost at the mouth of the Columbia – crew & part of the cargo saved.[25] The Trade wears the usual aspect, only rats hae sunk to a low ebb. I had a long rigmarole of a letter from Monsr Joe[26] – about his property here – commissions on commissions & the upshot of all, to produce hard cash from old Clothes, I slipt, out of his fingers "as slick as a Gut". He is ranting about an Encyclopedia & a Telescope he says were lent you, but for my part his words are the Antipodes to Gospel in my ears. I cannot wonder at the state of your feelings regarding the stuff of last summer. As to our man of puff & strut here – he is an ass, & altogether below your notice, but it went to my heart the same mawing inclination among some whose lips should have been shut by every feeling of Gratitude and old kindness.[27] Man is positively a selfish animal, and I now firmly believe that an "honest man" is as difficult to be found as a grain of Gold in a bushel of sand. We have passed a tranquil winter here, – sometimes diversified by a sulky day now & then but then periodical fits I allow to glance by without note. Mr. T. Simpson left this for R R. in March, but I hope to have the pleasure of his company again in a few

25 The brig *Isabella* had participated in British maritime trade and commerce from 1825 to 1829 when she was purchased to become the annual supply ship for the HBC's Pacific Northwest fur trade operation. She was sunk in 1830, only a year after another shipwreck at the mouth of the Columbia River.
26 Probably Joseph-Norbert Provencher.
27 Hargrave may be referring here to Robert Miles, Chief Trader at York Factory at that time.

weeks – when we shall pass some delicious hours in setting the affairs of Europe at rights. Your kind attention in forwarding the Sheet of News was highly gratifying. I devoured it.

I had a letter from Barnston dated July last. He seems bent on coming out this spring. Indeed the other side the Mountains seems rather at cross purposes – & most remain only because they cant do otherwise. Another chance of writing will probably offer by the fall Canoe which I shall try to improve by adding to the slender stock of nouvelles this contains. With deep regard & meantime I am Dear Sir yours Mo. faithfully JH

George [Thorn] begs me to add his humble thanks for all your kindness to him. Poor fellow! he was almost crying when he mentioned your name. His property by Massan[28] came to hand in safety. I am sorry to mention the loss of poor old Valois.[29] He was killed last Holidays by the accidental discharge of a gun he was using for foxes. In him the Co – lost an honest hard working servant.

YF – 6 July 1831

J.G. McTavish Esq
My Dear Sir

Your kind favors of 10th Jan & 28 March have both reached me in safety, – and altho' our busy season is now in full tide I seize the occasion of Mr A. Stewarts[30] departure to reply to such points of your letters as may be of interest to you, deferring a more lengthy yarn till our winter packet.

---

28 A man named Massan "& another Indian" left York Factory 10 December 1829 to go to Cumberland House in charge of the inland express. HBCA, B.239/a/141.

29 Alexis Valois was listed as a labourer at York Factory in 1829/30. HBCA, B.239/a/141. Alexander Christie informed Governor Simpson in a letter from York Factory 10 February 1831 that "Valois met his untimely fate on the 27th Decr while arranging a set gun For Foxes – he unhappily received the shot in his right breast, which must have produced immediate death, as a few hours after he was from here, the corpse was found, about 40 paces from the Gun." HBCA, B.239/b/89b.

30 Alexander Stewart (c. 1780–1840), a chief factor, was appointed to Albany 1831–32 but was granted leave due to ill health. He retired from the service in 1833.

To meet any chance in spring, I had written you on the 20th May via Nor. Ho. but as I believe none occurred, that sheet will likely come to hand along with this. Previous to receiving yours via R.R. of 10 Jan. I had packed up every thing which was supposed to belong to you here in readiness for forwarding in the fall. A List of this I enclose with remarks. On the arrival however of Gov[r] Simpson, I mentioned the subject of your prop[erty]: here to him & he was of opinion that it should remain here another season, – the reason for which he said he would explain to you. Are all the other articles in Case #3 – with Nelsons[31] portrait to be handed over to M[r] Christie?

The £3.-.- paid by Rod M[c]Kenzie[32] for china has been written back with his concurrence. Gov[r] S: says he had rather misunderstood your wishes regarding this article knowing you had purchased a quantity of Crockery from Capt. Matthy[33] he had concluded that this china formed part of it, – accordingly had made no distinction in the disposal of it. The whole [illegible] of both earthen & China ware had been offered by him to Nancy, and that part sold was only such surplus as she considered she had no use for.

I have looked into your acc[t] summary '29 & find various credits to a/. of the Gent[n] you mention but whether for M[r] Pellys[34] paintings is unexplained. I enclose you a Note of these – also the number of [illegible] paintings still here. What is to be done with these?

---

31 Horatio Nelson, 1st Viscount Nelson (1758–1805), was an English admiral famous for his participation in the Napoleonic Wars, notably in the Battle of Trafalgar, a decisive British victory where he lost his life.
32 Roderick McKenzie (c. 1771–1859), fur trader and politician, had been promoted to chief factor in 1830 and spent the rest of his working life with the HBC in charge of the English (Upper Churchill) River district, with headquarters at Île-à-la-Crosse, Saskatchewan. Arthur, "McKenzie, Roderick."
33 Probably Capt. Frederick Matthey, of the De Meuron Regiment.
34 In 1823 the interim governor of Assiniboia, Andrew H. Bulger, had commissioned from Peter Rindisbacher a series of six watercolours depicting Bulger travelling by various conveyances and meeting with Indian delegations. Robert Parker Pelly, Bulger's successor, saw copies of the series and ordered a set, which he took with him to England in 1825. There he had oil copies made, depicting himself in Bulger's place; from them coloured lithographs were produced and sold as sets in Britain, where John Franklin's

The Letter left in YF Will Box addressed (under cover) to Gov.r Simpson I now enclose.

The clock here has been proved your property by the entry to your a/ of the payment to Geo Flett,[35] which you mention & Gov.r Simpson has given directions for its value being passed to your credit.

I forward by M.r Stewart a parcel to your address cont[ainin]g the Leather Capot also the Scheme P Indent '29 & some rough Copies of Calculations of YF made works since your departure up to the latest date. These papers had become waste & I do not think will be wanted here.

The Tongues for M.r Smith[36] will not be lost sight of. I did my bit at scattering the Thermo[meter]s. but Geordie[37] is Lynx eyed & some still remaining here had been ferreted out by him.

Barnston is now at Nor Ho. on his way to Canada. I am really at a loss for his motive of action. I cannot think he wishes in heart to leave the service & yet he has given in his resignation in such a way as shuts up all chance of intercession in his favor. His fate in the country is decided. Poor fellow I am afraid 'tis a noble mind wracked. I mentioned to him what you say regarding his pistols.

George – poor lad begs to be mentioned in every letter I write you. I have scarcely ever seen so attached a servant. He has received the property you sent by the Canoes in good order & correct to the list you enclosed me. His fiddle & Images[?] he begs you may dispose of as you may consider best.

This is a hasty scrawl, but I'll make no apology for it. The correspondence you honor me with must show me as I really am, the faster I write

---

expeditions were creating a market for them, and in the northwest, where "Pelly's picture books" also sold well. Rindisbacher received neither credit for his originals nor remuneration from the sales. Harper, "Rindisbacher, Peter."

35 Possibly George Flett (ca. 1775–1850), who came to the HBC in 1796 and worked as an inland labourer and boatman under the jurisdiction of York Factory until 1810. From 1810 to 1822 he worked at Moose Lake, near Cumberland House, first as assistant trader and then as clerk. Flett retired at Red River in late 1823. The Flett family acquired thirty-four acres of land in the Point Douglas area and George Flett received thirty pounds annually from the HBC.

36 Perhaps Edward Smith at Fort Simpson.

37 Perhaps George Thorn.

the fresher are my words from the heart. I am this season in excellent health & spirits and get through the routine with a good humour formerly unattainable by me, & have yet great hopes of retrieving the character of a good natured man. Meanwhile, as I now am – depend on me as
Thine most faithfully

JH

The Bills &ᶜ you enclosed me have all been regularly passed to your credit here in the Off[ice]. Shop.

[Letterbook]
N°. 7
Rough Copies Letters by
JHargrave
From 8th July 1831 @ 25 July '32

YF 8 July 1831

My Dear Father
    Your kind letter of March last reached me a couple weeks ago together with all those from my mother Brothers & Sisters. This season is with me so busy a one – and so little can be said worth either writing or reading – except that I am in even better health than usual, that I really have lost hope of writing sheets in return for every one they have sent me. I know they all expect this from me, but tis I fear impossible for me to accomplish it. This one however is designed for you all – and if I can find time to add a few words more to them on other sheets also – I will do it.
    I rejoice to hear that your accident of last year has produced no serious effect on your health – and that you are still hale and hearty under the burden of nearly four Score Years. My dear old father the remembrance of you is as fresh before me at this moment as it was the day we parted, and were it in my power without bringing on my worldly affairs such ruin as I know you would be the first to advise me to avoid – I certainly would have seen you this fall. This I had settled last season & purposed to pass ensuing winter with you all, – but at this present time, an opportunity of advancement to a secure & lucrative rank in the service has just given my friends in this land the power of rewarding my long & heavy services. The success of their exertions I cannot know till next spring as the Sanction of the Company in London is required to secure my advancement, – but this I have the strongest hopes of, and if obtained, will afford me the long wished for opportunity of laying by something for old age. On the whole – I feel myself on the eve of reaping the harvest of all my by past labours for *eleven* long years. The fruits of which will, carefully gathered, raise me above want for the remainder of my life. At this period therefore you will perceive that my absence from this place where my services every year become more valuable to my employer would have any thing but a good effect on my fortunes. All this I tell to you my dear father to whose care of my youthful education I owe all – in order that

you all may rejoice with me at my anticipated success: – but I beg of you in the most earnest manner to preserve what I have said a profound secret among yourselves till you hear from me again, – The reasons for this are many, part of which will be obvious to you. I hope & trust you will follow my wishes in this.

Your kind parental advices are ever welcome to me, and were I to visit you, they would form my greatest reward for the journey. I am sorry to say that not one of the Books I wrote for to London has been sent me, in consequence of my letter having been mislaid, but I hope next year will at length remedy the disappointment. I have at present Blairs[1] & Tillotsons[2] Sermons which contain an excellent body of practical divinity & doctrinal exposition. Browns[3] Bible is my exposition of dark passages in the sacred writings. For works of controversial divinity I must own I have no taste. My opinions I trust are established in the faith of the Church in whose bosom I was born & educated; and I am of that turn of mind as to find little pleasure or edification in puzzling the mind about the subtler points of difference about which polemic writers have made so much noise in the world, – my collections also containing several works of higher reading primarily History & Poetry, – the last such only as is written by the best authors. Robertson, Scott, Johnston, Milton, Young[4] & Addison[5] &c are contained under this head, – names that are an honour to the land that produced them – and whose works contain the wisdom of antient times written with the elegance & taste of modern days. These form my principal closet companions.

1 James Blair (1656–1743) was a Scottish Episcopalian clergyman, missionary, and educator, best known as the founder of the College of William and Mary in Williamsburg, Virginia. In 1722, Blair published *Our Savior's Divine Sermon on the Mount*, a five-volume collection of his sermons from 1707 to 1721.
2 John Tillotson (1630–1694), Archbishop of Canterbury, was famous for his sermons and writings and was a favourite of American colonists. He was instrumental in James Blair's reception of a charter to establish the College of William and Mary.
3 John Brown (1722–1787), Scottish divine, was author of *The Self-Interpreting Bible*, otherwise known as *Brown's Bible*.
4 Edward Young (1683–1765), English poet.
5 Joseph Addison (1672–1719), English essayist, poet, and dramatist.

This is enough however on this subject – as before I close I should add a few more words regarding myself. I am this season in sound & robust health and again remain for the ensuing year at this place from whence indeed there is little immediate prospect of my being removed. I am perfectly happy & from the improved prospect I now have of providing a competency for more mature years I am perfectly *content* with my lot in life & look forward with confidence to being able in a few years to sit down in Canada at ease for the remainder of my days. That your days my Good old father may be lengthened out to see this period is the earnest prayer of
Your affectionate son

J. Hargrave.

YF 10 July 1831

My Dear Mother

Your affectionate letter found me a couple weeks ago at this place enjoying the same good health that I am so happy to find is also possessed by you all. We are certainly a family favored by providence far above many, and tho' our lots have been cast in distant lands yet since ever we separated our condition in this world has every year improved. It is peculiarly pleasing to learn that you have at length got into your new house and that you find yourself so comfortable in it. Do not however think my dear mother when I lectured you all so much last year that it was because I regretted so much money being laid out for this purpose. Far from it. I only regretted the risk you ran of getting into debt, and as you have avoided this, I fully approve of every shilling you have spent.

I this year send you again my yearly Bill for £10. Stg – which will be cashed at LaChine as usual, – and as I perceive that you every year want some of this to clear up old scores I shall not this season lay you under the necessity of acting differently from what you may think I wish you to do with it. I give it as a free present from myself to you – and however you may please to dispose of it – I know it will be turned to the most useful account. May you long my dear mother be spared to my prayers so as that I may have the pleasure of repeating many times this to me the most pleasing way in which I can spend my money. I am sorry however to perceive that your kind heart disquiets itself by imagining that the trifle I send you causes my residence to be the longer in this land. For this suspicion there is not the least grounds. Every young man who by his education can raise himself above manual labour & who inherits no fortune from his family, however he may prosper in life, – must spend the active part of his days say between 20&45 in providing for the wants the latter parts of his life will require. What I call providing is to gather a sum of money the interest of which will amount to £200 or 250 pounds yearly. On this I could support a family with less I will not leave business till I can see my chance of accomplishing my object within the time I have fixed for continuing the pursuit. My present income, as I have always said, however I might save it, will not suffice to grow rich upon, – and it is only the hopes of advancement & increased gains which keep me in this land. I have now strong hopes that my day of reward is at hand, – & if so – I can then begin to lay up for old age. How these hopes arise I have explained more fully in my fathers letter, – but I beg of you all that you say nothing on this subject to any one till I am able to assure you more certainly of my good fortune. From all this however you will see that no trifle which I have sent you – could ever have kept me a day in this country longer than was my own desire, – and it also explains my backwardness in leaving the service even for a single winters visit to Canada. I hope the time will yet arrive when I being able to call myself *Independent* – will set down among you in Canada – with the happiness of finding you all alive & well to share with me in my good fortune.

That you & all my relations may be preserved to see this come to pass is the earnest prayer of
Your most affectionate Son

JH

Make my kind Compts to Mrs Struthers. I am truly sorry to hear of the mournful loss she has sustained. The Death of Stuart – however melancholy, was I fear me the consequence of his own irregular habits. God keep me from such a life and such an end.

JH

YF 10 July 1831

Mr John Hargrave
My dear John

Your kind Sheet of 7th March last is now before me, and I rejoice to see by it that you are still all well & prospering in the world. Our old parents are now indeed much failed – but it is truly pleasing to me to find that they are happy & contented, – and at their advanced period of life have their wants & necessaries so well provided for them. This I must say they owe mainly to the dutiful conduct of yourself – of Andrew & Jane. The gratitude they express for the little assistance I send them is in my opinion more justly due to you, – as what I give is more like the rich mans present than the poor widows mite – whereas your labor & time wholly goes to the support & prosperity of the family. Continue to do so – my dear brother & believe me that the remembrance of this dutiful conduct of yours will in after life be the most pleasant parts of your conduct in life when an old man and a father you look back over the works of the years that are gone. You do not say whether you have taken lots for yourselves, as you formerly purposed doing in the letters of the former year. This I think you should not neglect. Both you and Andrew are now fast rising into life, and I should like to see you both beginning to provide *something* for yourselves, which I think could be done without injury to the labours upon our fathers little farm.

You have sadly mistaken my meaning in regard to what I said about the expense of your new building, as I am far from thinking that money could be mispent in accomplishing so proper an object. What I was surprised at was the high sum you had found necessary over the moderate estimate you mentioned in your letters of 1829. When I compared this with your actual expenditure – I of course concluded either that you had been overreached in your bargains – or that you had not made use of your well earned knowledge in arithmetic, which you recollect I took such pains to flog into you at Midholm, – and I perceive that the increased am^t has been occasioned partly by the one cause partly by the other. As to the building itself I have ever been of the same opinion that nothing was more required by you – and whatever it may have cost you – the comfortable dwelling it now affords you more than repays all the trouble & expense it has occasioned you.

I should like much to see you all again were it only for a couple days but this my dear brother, fortune has ever denied to us. Of all our family I am the only one who has attempted realising our old stories about "poosing our fortunes"[6] and tho I will never reach the wealthy state that our Childs dreams used to run on, – yet I trust to make in my present situa-

---

6 Also *poussing*: taking steps to improve one's financial status, pushing one's fortune. DSL.

tion what will make me independent of the world through the evening of life – should providence see meet to lengthen out my span so long. I am this season in excellent health & still remain at my old quarters on the Shores of Hudsons Bay.

Were I with you I could coil you long yarns about the wonders of this land, but these will not be compressed within the limits of a single sheet, – we shall therefore leave them till we meet, & in the mean time
I am My Dear John
Your affectionate Brother

JH

YF 10 July 1831

Mr And. Hargrave
My Dear Andrew

I may say with you that I have read your last kind letter several times over, – and after I had got into the thread of the discourse was highly interested with the news you gave me; – but in this it was sometime before I could succeed. I found your name on the *first* page & puzzled through & thro' it without knowing where to begin till I hit on the expedient of trying it in Pat's way – and la! made out the whole of your little stories by beg[inni]^{ng} at that place that should have been the end – & reading backwards.

I regret to hear my dear Brother that you consider my father is failing so fast. He himself writes cheerily – and I trust your melancholy forebodings are more occasioned by your anxiety about him than from the frail state of his health. You urge me strongly to come down, – but I fear much whether this would have a beneficial effect upon either him or my mother. Violent emotions at their age must ever be hurtful – & both Joy & Grief I feel by my self would attend both my arrival & departure. I have not yet the means to sit down as a settler in Canada, – I have served long & wrought hard to attain to this, – fortune seems now to promise me something like a reward for my toils, shall I therefore set at nought the labours of nearly half an active mans life & throwing prudence to the winds follow both your wishes & my own, whatever may be their effect on my fortunes or on the health of those that are most dear to me. I really consider that it is & will be more satisfactory to both our old parents & to you all to know that I am well, happy & prosperous – than to purchase a short lived joy by a lengthened & deep Grief. I do not mean however by all this to say that I have no hopes of visiting you soon. Fortune may yet give me an opportunity of seeing all sooner than we expect, – tho' I can at present point out no particular period for this.

It is sad to hear of the ravages death has been making among my old acquaintances among you. Poor Struthers is gone to whose kindness you all owed so much on your arrival in Canada. Norman is also no more, – by whose means I am now in this land tho' my prosperity in it was certainly not the motive which induced him to lend me a hand in getting into this path of life. His fate is assuredly a dreadful one – and whether his end was his own act or not, tis plain to me that his dissipated habits shortened his days. Poor fellow!

I can say little more my dear Andrew, continue in the steady course of life you have been brought up in – and sooner or later I have strong hopes we will all yet meet together in joy in this life. To hear of your welfare your good fortune & good conduct will ever be the best of news to your absent brother. I am well & happy & that you may long continue so is the prayer of yours most affectionately

JH

YF 10 July 1831

Miss Jane Hargrave
My Dear Jane

Your kind letter of 18th March is now before me and I am sorry to find that you have taken so much to heart what I said in my letter of last year. Your desire to assist my father I was far from finding fault with, – I only feared that by your doing so you had hurt yourself at a time when the few pounds I sent you would have been peculiarly useful. I am sorry my dear lassie to find that you write so despondingly about your own prospects in life. Let your conduct be ever such as it has been – creditable to your family – and care not for the rest. Should your present hopes fail you still keep up your heart, I will sooner or later lay up the storm beaten hulk of an old North Wester in my adopted Country, and should I then find my dear Jane still a *spinster*, why I am still & likely to be for life a bold bluff batchelor – so hang it we shall set up Housekeeping together you shall manage these things for me and we shall be the happiest & merriest Old Boy & Old Maiden the parish can produce. – & so there is a prospect for you! Seriously however, as I have formerly said to you be neither over anxious nor too difficult to please. Those who have a horror of a single life (poor silly flies dancing round a Candle *say I*) are ready to throw themselves away on the first offer whatever may be the character who makes it, – and the over nice allows youth & life to slip through their fingers while they wait in vain for that match which they think could alone give them happiness.

I grieve to hear of the melancholy fate of poor Stuart. His end was certainly hastened by his own irregular habits even should he have been guiltless of more direct attempts on his life. That poor beguiled lassie also who alone stuck to the side of his body after the many promises he had made her were quenched in the grave! How I feel for her! Now do not feel indignant at my expression of sympathy for *her*, for I declare that I never felt her so worthy of commendation as on reading your account of her conduct on this occasion. For her general behaviour I know there is no defense – but I declare I would take to my bosom tomorrow were she honest – the poorest of the sex who could love with such intensity of feeling – I have I may say searched the world & I could never yet persuade myself that I had found a female who could regard me in this light. Luck is the secret of my Celibacy, – & such I fear will continue it.

Your letter my dear Jane I have indeed read with great pleasure & the full account you have given me I am sorry I can repay only by these hurried lines. You all little know the mental toil I daily undergo when you call out for each a letter and that a long one. I have this season done my best – & succeeded better than I expected yet still I am not certain whether I will get a sheet for each of you. I however make no excuse for you, – for all advantages of time & number are on your side – so write me always – write me fully & tho you may not get a line in return believe me ever
Your most aff^{ate} brother

JH

YF 10 July 1831

Mr Ja^s Ross
Dear Brother

I had the pleasure of receiving your letter about 2 weeks ago and feel much obliged by the clear idea you give me as to the means necessary to begin a farmers life in Canada. I have measured my purse by all the different estimates you mention, & tho' I might cover some of them with my present means, yet I have little hopes that the speculation would to me prove a lucrative one. At this time I could muster upwards of £500 but from my inexperience in that sort of life, the great outlay required at the first step – & the innumerable other expenses such a course of life would entail on me – I fear that with my present slender stock of Ballast I would dread shipwreck almost before I had left port. I must therefore leave farming alone for a few more years – and steadily stick to my present pursuits the prizes in which are not a little dazzling to the eye – tho' a long residence in this land is necessary to their attainment. To resist such temptations however & to resolve on burying myself among the woods of Canada in the prime of life where, as I now am, my bread must be earned by the sweat of my brow, is throwing away the substance for the shadow, – even were the substance less palpable than reasonable hopes promise.

I am happy to find that you are so well pleased with your new pursuits and I have not doubt comfortable, easy and plentiful days will be the reward of the active & industrious course you have pursued and are still following. Happiness in this life I have long ago learned is more equally divided than the superficial observer could have imagined. I, as I have been bred, struggle for riches to produce me only the same quantum of happiness which is enjoyed by others possessing not half of what I aim at, yet from their more moderate desires & different habits of life are already in possession of what I now strain after.

I still remain at my old quarters, from whence there is little chance of my removal for some time. I enjoy excellent health, and tho' both my summer & winter duties are sufficiently arduous my employment suits my taste exactly. You may guess at the busy Days I pass – from the circumstances of having since the 1st Ins[t] issued out of this Depot Goods, Ammunition – Provisions &[c] equal to the consumption for one year of the whole indian population from north of Lake Superior to the Arctic Ocean – an extent of country ten times larger than both Canadas. All this has come thro' my hands & we were finished yesterday – the last inland Brigade of Boats start tomorrow. We are now preparing for the departure of the Montreal Canoe – after which the reins slacken till the arrival of the Ships from England ab[t] the middle of next month. This furnishes about 4 weeks bustling work – when we again get into winter quarters, begin active service at the Desk – which forms our dayly round till inlanders again find us prepared for them on the following month of June. Out of such materials nothing can be wrung at all interesting to

correspondents elsewhere unless that their friend here is as happy as he could wish & that he is theirs
Most affectionately

JH

YF 10 July 1831

Mrs Mary Ross
My Dear Mary

Tho' I have not heard from you this season, I will not follow your example of last year & set out with a regular scolding about forgetfulness – laziness and all that. I feel by myself that my dear Mary can never have forgot me, – whether circumstances allow her the means of telling me so or not. So there is a pattern of forbearance for you: let me see you take a lesson by it and learn to believe that something else may prevent your Jamie from telling you he is well besides indolence or indifference. I am glad to hear that you have at length got settled down on your farm, and are so comfortable after the rambling life you have lately led – which by the way must have given you a shrewd notion as to what is borne by a fur Trading Squaw. To talk seriously with you however, I should have liked to have heard from you this season, – more especially as to the health of our old parents. They themselves both assure me of their welfare but Jane & Andrew talk not so favorably of their good health. They are now certainly well stricken in years; but I should fain hope that their good constitutions have still some years of health in store for them both. They urge me much to pay them a visit but that situated as I am I *cannot* perform without paying a price for it the value of which they cannot conceive. I must therefore rest satisfied with knowing that they are above want, & that their condition in life is as happy as their children can make it. Our sister Jane gives me a long account of the changes 12 months have produced among my old acquaintances in Lasalle. I am sorry to find that these news are mostly melancholy and that several of those I left in the prime of life & strength have sunk into the grave. Truly when I look back over the dangers I have passed since we separated – and yet find myself well & prosperous – I have reason to bless that providence which has so visibly watched over me in all my wanderings.

Regarding myself I have as usual little to say. I remain at my old quarters & with the best of health am happy as the day is long. That this may find you my Dear Sister in the same condition is the sincere hope of yours Most Affectionately

JH

YF 1 Sept' 1831

Dear Uncle[7]

I had the pleasure of receiving a letter from my aunt Mary[8] last Month by the Vessel from London[9] and was most happy to learn that both she yourself and all the family were well & happy. She rates me roundly for lack of writing, & it would seem you all imagine that I have forgotten my friends in Scotland. This however my dear uncle is far from being the case. I have regularly written you once a year by the London Ship the only chance I have of sending you a Letter – with the single exception of last summer, during the whole of which my duties pressed so heavy on me that I found it impossible to write any of my friends – even my old Parents I had to inform of my welfare by a few hasty lines. You cannot imagine the busy life I lead – day & night throughout the summer are joined to each other – & till the moment the Vessels sail I do not get one day with another above 4 hours rest, even at this moment I write you near witching time of night & must be at the desk in little more than a couple hours hence. 'Tis not however to tell you of the laborious life I lead that I now write you – & only mention it as some apology for what you have interpreted into neglect on my part. My old parents I thank God were last March both alive & well – with all the family around them on their property in Canada. They are now easy in their circumstances & possess every thing which can contribute to their ease & comfort. Mary, the only one of us yet married, is settled in their neighborhood, & amidst a fine rising family is happy as heart can desire. My Brothers are now grown up & manage all the labours of their little farm, – the old folks enjoying in ease & peace the fruits of what they have labored so long & so successfully to obtain. They complain like yourselves of never hearing from you, yet say that they have written you every season. I fear that neither of you address your letters aright, at least from what I know of Canada, a

7 James Mitchell.
8 The wife of James Mitchell, Mary Melrose.
9 The *Camden*, a chartered ship commanded by Captain Robert Royal, arrived at York Factory 25 August that year and departed again 19 September.

letter from you will have little chance of reaching them out in the country unless addressed to the care of some person of their naming in Montreal. This I believe is the real cause of both your & their complaints. My Brothers Joseph & Ruther are both comfortably settled in the State of New York, about 100 miles distant from my father. Both my parents paid them a visit in the winter of 1829 '30, and they speak highly of their condition in life – far beyond what any of us could ever have attained to had we remained in Scotland. On returning my father met with a serious accident in the overturning of his Cariole by which his arm was dislocated, but he is now perfectly recovered from the effects of it, and enjoys as good health as he did 20 years ago. My mother also is happy & cheerful, & I believe desires nothing further in life but to get me to rejoin them – who am the only rambling branch of the family.

I am sorry to hear of my poor uncle Hectors[10] Death, your letter being the first intimation I had had of even their having left Britain. I do not think that my parents have heard of this, which will be heavy news to them, as they said nothing of it last spring. If they had gone to Canada my aunt & the family would have found a home in my fathers house.

I have always written to my old School Master Mr W. Lockie of Stouslie by Hawick till last season, but for these two years last have not had a line from him perhaps he is no more, but if alive and should you ever have a chance of seeing or hearing from him let him know that I regret his silence much. I hope at no very distant year to visit Scotland again, & when this happens my old friends will find that time or circumstance have made no changes in me – I am *Jamie* still.

As to my situation in life I am well as I could desire. My Income is at present so much as to allow me laying up what will be useful in old age – and in a year or two I have the strongest hope that it will be increased about fivefold. My prospects for life are indeed unclouded, and I am perfectly happy & contented. All this I owe to my Old parents – who with much hardship to themselves procured me an education which few parents would have struggled so much to procure for their sons. I also owe much to the Late Rev^d Dr. Douglas[11] of Galashiels – whose memory I will ever revere. He was one of the best men I have known.

10 Hector Elliot.
11 Rev. Dr Robert Douglas (1747–1820) served as minister at Galashiels from 1770 until his death. He obtained the degree of Doctor of Divinity from the University of Aberdeen in 1797 and occupied an influential position in

Excuse this hasty Sheet my Dear friend & believe that
I am Still yours Most affectionately

JH

YF 1 Decr 1831

J.G. McTavish Esq
My Dear Sir

 Our packet for R.R. will be leaving this soon & as a letter will reach you by Govr Simpson next spring I sit down to the concoction of something that way, composed of what first turns up. In my last of 6*th* July by Mr Stewart I mentioned that the Cases containing your property have here been retained by direction of Govr S: – Afterwards however he altered his instructions & they have accordingly been sent home by the Camden to your address at Moose & directed to the care of Mr Sec [William] Smith. N*^o* 3 in the list I enclosed you remains here agreeably to your wishes. The old clothes &*^c* contained in N*^o* have been taken out & given to George[12] as you desired.

 Time passes over me with a light footstep this season. I having of late improved greatly in health – getting *fat* & good humoured. So much for my own trumpet. The Store work lies as solidly on my shoulders as ever, but they are now accustomed to the load & I amble gaily on round the circle of the year – avoiding with careful eye the ragged corners of strife which so commonly present themselves within these bounds. My honest Bourgeois & I accord most nobly – & it is one of my greatest treats to get down with him at table with Division Schemes or infant Indents before

---

the Church of Scotland. In the year of James's birth, he published *General View of the Agriculture of the Counties of Roxburgh and Selkirk, with Observations on the Means of their Improvement.* He was instrumental in promoting the woollen trade in Galashiels, frequently lending money to the manufacturers. In 1811, he sold Cartleyhole, a 100-acre farm, for about £4000 to Sir Walter Scott, the newly minted laird of Abbotsford. The two men remained on intimate terms and frequently visited each other. Robert Hall, in his 1898 *The History of Galashiels*, described Douglas as "a man of eminent shrewdness, foresight, and benevolence" as well as tolerant and free from bigotry as evidenced by his visiting the houses of Dissenters as well as those of his own parishioners. Hall, *History of Galashiels*.

12 George Thorn.

us, – where every item is most sagely weighed; – while ever & anon our the conversation makes an unaccountable tangent to some favorite writer, or takes a glance at the Blue Hills in the Land o' Cakes. Soberly speaking however – we have been & are still deeply studied in bringing down the immense hills of property which inland dreams have built up in our Stores & the Req^n of this year has been pared down to about £13m – with strong presumptions that that of the following summer will not much exceed the same sum. The goods we have on hand are however of the best quality & fitted for the Trade; – containing not one item likely to degenerate into "old Stores" – while the low state of the market when they were procured will help to make up for the increased interest on idle capital. We however find ourselves contending another difficulty – in the crowded state of our Stores. Every garret in the new Buildings is groaning under its own burden, & the old Factory[13] has at length become so Crazy, leaky & unfit to be filled with property that it has been found necessary to commence rebuilding part of it. The middle front through which the gateway passed has been taken down & parts of an excellent store of 2 1/2 stories – 40 feet long & 30 broad – has been raised in its place. The lower flat – gives a noble packing room; – the second an outfit Room – while the third is divided into rooms for the purposes of our old apothecary & Stationary Rooms. To each end of this store is purposed to be added wings each 30 feet long on the foundations of the old Bastions & 2 stories high forming a continued front of 100 feet – the lower flats divided into 4 rooms entering from the New packing Room while the second flats will make 2 excellent Blanket & shop Rooms on the same level & opening into the Outfit Room. These changes go on without increased expense the whole materials being procured & put up by the men trained to such work under yourself. Our Bourgeois indeed feels in many points the loss [of] a conductor but in such undertakings he is perfectly at home himself – & the store now raised is really a substantial & commodious one.

The winter so far is extremely mild but little show of partridges. The Deer also have entirely changed their habits. More are next got in the fall – & hitherto our hunters have only fallen in with a few stragglers. The goose Hunt last fall was a fair average one. On the whole however we rub

13 The great depot building was started in 1831 with the erection of this two and one-half storey store to replace an earlier building. For further information on the history of the York Factory buildings, see Wilson, "Forts on the Twin Rivers."

on extremely well – something fresh always casts up, and symptoms of scurvy are rare in this establishment.

Severn was reestablished last fall with a small Outfit. We heard from there a few days ago – & I lament to add that we were informed of the loss of poor Pat Cunningham[14] who was drowned while on a [illegible] party at some distance from the House. It seems the boat had got adrift for some time before it was perceived when he plunged into the water & swam to endeavour recovering her. On getting hold however he found it impossible to enter loaded as he was with heavy clothes – & letting the boat go endeavoured to return ashore but sunk before he could reach it. Poor fellow his loss will be felt in this district. Lachlan Phelp[15] has charge in the mean time.

The winter road is at rest this season to afford time for raising a proper chain of stores along the line. Mr Lewes[16] gets on quietly & rationally & whatever the upshot may be, expenses will be kept as low as possible. We had a large supply of flour last season from RR – from which Inlanders now entirely supplied at Norway & the stock bro^t here is so large that our order on England last fall was curtailed by one half. Should next summer be equally productive, the English order may be discontinued for 32 without risk. A Years stock for York will always however be required on hand here to avoid the chance of Colony disappointments.

On Inland Topics I need not enter as you will hear more than I can even hint at from better informed quarters. I rejoiced to hear of the settlement the Govr made last spring in your affairs in the north, so proper & suitable to all parties.[17] He is a friend who does nothing by halves. The storm is now over, and an inaudible grumble is now the highest note of the exhausted volcano; – a fiery ordeal it certainly was to a feeling and

---

14 Patrick Cunningham (c. 1789/94–1831), an Irishman, was working as postmaster at the HBC post at Severn when he drowned in October 1831.
15 Lachlan Phelp is listed as a fisherman at York Factory in the winter of 1829/30. HBCA, B.239/a/141. In 1832, Phelp was replaced by Charles Leask.
16 John Lee Lewes (1792–1872) was an HBC chief factor at Oxford House between 1830 and 1835, during which time he was in charge of the construction of the winter road.
17 After McTavish's desertion of his country wife, Nancy McKenzie, because of his Scottish marriage, Governor George Simpson stepped in to settle affairs. Despite her expressed wish not to be forced to marry again, the dowry of £200 offered by McTavish soon enabled Simpson to arrange for

honorable mind. The prize in the struggle however is your own. & calumny in the end inevitably reverts on its author. They laugh who win.

 This now is passably well in the way of pra[i]sing for one sheet. You see I make liberal use of your kind invitation to an off hand letter: There [are] few to whom I sit down to write with equal pleasure, so my pen runs riot without an effort of mine to restrain it. I will use all occasions for similar scribbles without reserve. Meanwhile with kindest respect & regard
I am My Dear Sir
Most faithfully yours

JH

YF 15 Feby 1832

My Dear Parents,
 There having been no winter Packet to the southward this season I have been deprived of the pleasure of letting you hear from me; yet as we are now sending letters by way of the Interior to some Posts nearer to Montreal I shall chance a letter for you – which perhaps may have the good fortune of reaching you before those I shall write you next summer. I thank God I am able to say that my health still continues excellent, and I have not a reasonable wish on earth ungratified beyond the desire of knowing that you also are all still well and happy. I have many anxious thoughts about you my dear parents, far advanced as your lives now are, & the small chance there is of our seeing each other for several [years] yet to come. My earnest prayers are for your welfare, and the happiness I enjoy each spring when by your letters I find you are still preserved to me is such as to deprive me of sleep for one or two nights after. Oh how I look forward with anxiety to that time, and ever dread to open the letters lest my fears for your safety be realized! But we are all in the hands of our Almighty Father, and tho' he may never permit some of us to see each other again on earth I firmly trust we will again be reunited beyond the Grave "a family in heaven."
 I need say nothing further of my own affairs. I am still in my old quarters here from which there is little prospect of my being removed

---

 Nancy's marriage to a respectable company employee, Pierre Leblanc, then in charge of building Lower Fort Garry. She was baptized and the couple were married in the Roman Catholic church at Red River on 7 February 1831.

for some time to come. I can give you no further information as to my chance of advancement, the certainty of which will not reach me till next June. I have however small anxiety on the subject, as if not next season, I am eventually certain of succeeding should my life be spared. I hope next season to have a letter from either Joseph or Ruther. I have written them both since I came to this land, and tho' we can have no chance of keeping up a correspondence, I should like to hear of their welfare from time to time. My only letter from Scotland of last fall was from my Aunt Mary, written in April 1831. The whole family were still well, but they complain much of never hearing from you. They have written you several times within the last 4 years but not one letter from you has ever reached them. The whole of this arises from the letters not being properly directed: – In their last to me they mention that my uncle Hector [Elliot] & his family have gone out to America (I suppose the United States) about 3 years ago past, and that the [illegible] Robert[18] & 3 daughters had follow^d in 1830. Robert has since written them & informs them that my uncle Hector died in November 1830 but no mention is made of what they are doing or where they are settled. This is the only news my Aunts Letter contains.

I do not write letters to my brothers by this occasion, as this one I design for you all, – and indeed tis great chance whether it will reach you a week sooner than those I purpose writing you 4 months hence. If so, however it will serve to give you a days pleasure so much sooner, and allows me to assure you again that

I am
My Dear Parents
Your Affectionate Son

JH

YF 1 July 1832

Mrs Jane Hargrave
My Dear Mother

The whole of your kind letters reached me a few days ago, and I rejoice to find by them, that you are all still preserved in good health and are living in plenty and happiness. Since I wrote you on the 15th of Feby last I have also enjoyed my usual good health and in the situation I face & the duties I have to perform am happy as the day is long. This place where I have now been for 5 years is likely to be my fixed residence as long as I

---

18 Robert Elliot.

choose to remain in the service, and from the good health I enjoy at it, and the comfortable & regular life I am enabled to lead in comparison with those who reside at inland posts, I may say that there are few places in the Indian country I would prefer before it. I am sorry to say that the hopes I entertained of advancement in the service & which I mentioned to you last season, have proved premature; and that I still remain in the same rank & at the same salary as before. It has turned out that no opening did exist last season for advancement, consequently none has been chosen, but of this *I am sure*, that having once been chosen in this country as fit for promotion, as soon as an opportunity offers I stand next in turn to fill it – so my hopes of providing well in this service for old age are nothing abated, notwithstanding my present disappointment. I have since I came to this country up to this time gathered such a sum of money as has purchased me in the English Funds about £600 3 PCent consol[19] which yields me a yearly interest of about £18.-Stg – To this sum I add every season as much as I can save out of my present salary which gradually increases both the principal & Interest, so you see I do not entirely depend on hopes for procuring me something to support old age. Indeed on looking around me in life I see few paths in which I could have hoped to succeed better. My Character I am proud to say is unstained, my services I know are of high value to the Company I am loved & respected by all those who know me, & on whose services I rely for promoting my interests; and at my years, without a powerful friend or a Shilling to aid me on my entrance into life, there are few young men of my degree who are in better circumstances or have more cheering views of future affluence. Now, my dear mother, this explanation of my circumstances is entirely written for your own satisfaction, show it to none – read it to none: there are few even of my relations to whom I could have brought myself to lay open to their view the future of my affairs, the grounds of my hopes & expectations; to yourself & to my father alone I touch on them, and on your prudence I rely that not one word gets abroad in the world of what I have said to you on this topic. I have strong reasons for asking this of you.

The whole of your letter of this season interests me extremely. I have ever received your letters with delight, but this season you have given me more news and have improved so much in the art of writing a letter that

---

19 A government bond in Great Britain, originally issued in 1751, that paid perpetual interest and had no date of maturity. It was also called a bank annuity (short for consolidated annuity).

there are few of your former ones to compare with it, judging of it as a scholar judges. What you say of my uncle James & his family does not surprise me. I foresaw much of his present fortunes from the time I heard that he had resolved on improving his circumstances by a removal. 'Tis an old proverb "Two removals are as bad as a fire"[20] – and every years experience confirms to me its truth. You yourselves are now well lodged & well fed: this gratifies my dearest wishes. To add to the comforts you have, I again send you my annual Bill for £10 Stg for which you will receive the usual sum at Lachine, and which you may employ as best agrees with your wants; – only keep a *good lug* of it for yourself – for to yourself alone I give it. Make my kindest Comp[ts] to poor Widow Struthers, to her Daughter Marg[t] – to A. Struthers and to old Barber. They have been kind friends to you in your poverty, I will never forget such services tho you now no longer stand in need of them. I am sorry to hear of my poor brothers Ruthers loss. His small family will feel it severely. I hope next year to hear from Joseph – none of them have yet written me since I came to this land. I at this time can add little more, but that with sincerest prayers for your health & welfare I am with deepest affection
My dear Mother
Your loving Son

Jamie

YF 1 July 1832

M[r] Jos[b] Hargrave
My Dear Father

Your kind letter of 27th Feby last reached me a few days ago, and I assure you it was with a grateful heart to the Giver of all good, that I found by it you were all still preserved, were happy and contented with your lot in this life. I know it will be the most pleasing advice I can send you to be able also to say that I am still as well as ever, and am prospering in life as well as even your own kind heart could wish. True it is that the hopes I had entertained last season & which I mentioned to you, of advancement this season, have for the present been built on a sandy foundation. None have been preferred before me for none have been promoted, – and though my hopes have been deferred I have still the confi-

---

20 The proverb actually is: "Three removals are as bad as a fire." It is attributed to Benjamin Franklin (1706–1790).

dent expectation that in my present employment I will realize all that my views of riches in this life have desired. I may say it without vanity that I have preserved my name unsullied; my services to the Company I serve is of such value, and the friends I have acquired in this land who have the desire place these services in their true light are of such influence that I have no fears about my future prosperity in life. Keep all this to yourself my dear father: I would be ashamed of being considered a boaster – the report of it would do me much harm, and 'tis only to you and my dear mother for your satisfaction that I can bring myself to lay open thus far the views & hopes connected with my course through life. I am yet far from possessing riches – I may never possess them in the opinion [of] the world, but I thank God I possess what far outweighs them, an unspotted Character, Good health & Content.

I know well the person you mention who last winter wished to purchase a lot in the neighborhood of Ja^s Ross. His name is Mr Ja^s Robertson,[21] I have known him for 10 years in this land, and he is as worthy & upright a man as is in it, however much poorer he may be. When he left it 2 or 3 years ago he was at a distance from me, else I would have sent you a letter by him, knowing that he purposed going to your neighborhood, & from him I was well aware you could have learned more of me and of my situation in this land than I have been able to convey to you by all the letters I have ever written you. Should you have the means of letting him know it, I would wish to hear from him and as to how he is prospering in Canada, a country regarding which we had many conversations during the winter we passed together at Norway House.[22]

21 James Robertson, an Orkneyman, entered the service of the Hudson's Bay Company in 1805. For the outfits of 1821 and 1822 he was a clerk at Norway House. In 1823 he was appointed to Island Lake district where he was described in 1826 as a "steady good œconomical trader at the height of his ambition." In 1830 he retired from the Company and went to Canada. Rich, *Colin Robertson*, 239.

22 The Hudson's Bay Co.in 1814 established a post near the northern outlet of Lake Winnipeg and named it Norway House in recognition of the Norwegian labourers who were recruited to build it. Norway House was a key point in the Hudson's Bay transportation system. Furs and goods were collected at the fort from posts further inland for transportation along the Hayes River system to York Factory for pickup by HBC ships bound for England.

I can well feel what a privation it must be to you to be without the public ordinances of Religion in your neighborhood, – and highly approve of the exertions you and your neighbors are making to obtain them. Your parental advices to me on this subject, depend on it my Dear Father, are conveyed to no inattentive ears. We are far asunder, and our God only knows whether we will ever meet again in this world, but your letters since I left you, and the precepts you instilled into me in my boyhood, however they had to contend with the giddiness & folly of youthful years, will ever, by me, be looked back to with reverence & affection, and regarded as the solid basis on which inexperienced unknown & unfriended as I have been, I have yet been able to build up a Character and a hope of prosperity for myself. You have done your duty, more than your duty towards me, to you I owe all, may our God reward you by long and peaceful days in this life, and in that which is to come with the full fruition of happiness, through the merits of our blessed Saviour.

May God bless & preserve you is the earnest prayer
of your Most Affectionate Son

JH

YF 2nd July 1832

Mr John Hargrave
My Dear John

Your kind letter of the 18th March last reached me last week, and tho' half worried just now with the crowd & work which also come upon us at this season, I sit down at every spare moment to scratch a line to you in hopes before the Canoe again starts to have my usual number of sheets for you all. I rejoice to find that you are all still preserved in health, the greatest riches this world affords, and to find that you now have the means of living in plenty & comfort. Our good old father is now far advanced in years, and on you and Andrew must depend the whole labours of the family; and it must be consolatory to our Venerable parent to find you both such dutiful & obedient children as he describes you to me. True it is that both of you are now arrived at maturity, and are capable of guiding your own steps & managing your own business, yet the words of the aged ought always to have weight with the young, and when we are old ourselves I know of nothing which can give greater pleasure when reflecting on the days which are gone than a consciousness of having been done the part of good sons to them who may then be no more. Such conduct is the surest grounds for hoping to have obedient children yourselves.

When I think of you & Andrew tis always at first glance as the little fellows I left scrambling among the Logs at Beechridge. You must now however be fast approaching 28 years & he 26. At this time of life you ought certainly to be thinking of some establishment for yourselves. Begin by taking some snug Lot in your neighborhood, & when time serves get buildings & enclosures raised. Be prudent dear Brother in the choice of her who is to bear your name, – one raised in your own sphere in life is best, as near your own age as may be, – and what is *never to be overlooked*, the *decent industrious* daughter of serious steady parents. You will laugh at all this, but believe me tho I was giddy enough myself, 34 has taught me more sober views of such things, and besides has frequently proved them to my eyes by examples. I know you will see these hints from your absent brother in their true light. They are dictated solely by my anxiety about you and are written to give utterance to this anxiety than because I think you want them.

I like well to hear of the improvements which are going on around you. Your taking in a newspaper is an excellent plan; it will furnish amusement to our old father, and its contents will enlarge your knowledge of what is passing in the world both in Canada & Europe. The best in America for English news is the New York Albion, & for Canada affairs the Montreal Herald; – this last however has much fallen off since 5 years ago. We get here each Spring complete files or sets for 1 year of both, & in the fall have whole bales of British papers from London by the ship. Without them this desert would certainly be a dreary waste.

I can as usual say little of myself. I perform the same duties, write at the same desk, lodge in the same room as I have done for these 5 years last past. Time rolls round & brings me back every season the same faces to transact the same business which occupied the last, and so our years slip by. From such a quiet & unvaried round nothing can be drawn worth relating. I enjoy excellent health & am happy as the day is long – May this find you enjoying the same blessing, is the sincere wish of
Your affectionate brother

JH

I should see M^r D Finlaysons letter carefully forwarded to him. He and I have been as intimate as brothers for many years but we are now far asunder – not likely to see each other again for some time. He is an excellent friend & a worthy Man.

YF 4 July 1832

Mr And^w Hargrave
My Dear Andrew

I have just now read over again your very well written letter of 18 Feby, and I rejoice to find that the account it gives me of the condition of the whole of you is such as my best wishes could have desired. I am still stationed at this place which I like well and from whence there is small likelihood of my being removed for some time to come. My health is excellent, and tho even your axe does not fatigue you more than my pen at times does me, I have become so habituated to business that out of labor I extract more pleasure, than many could do from having their time at their own command. By all your accounts of your condition in life I perceive you are now above want, and with health and industry you are independent of the world. My most anxious wishes regarding you are therefore realized and from your steady & sober habits I have no doubt a long pleasant and happy life is before you. Our good old father is now fast declining into the vale of years: – cherish his old age my dear brother, let him want no comfort that your circumstances admit of procuring, and depend upon it that in future years your own heart will reward you for such filial duty.

I knew Mr Robertson well in this country and should be happy to hear that he had got comfortably settled in Canada. He is a plain worthy man, for whom I have much regard. I regret to hear that my old acquaintance Miss M. Struthers still bears her maiden name. – Tis all the fault of you young fellows who with all your advantages of a settled home & leisure, are as difficult to please in the choice of a Mate as we fur Traders who are ever birds of passage and in all our wanderings meet only with the brown faces, strange manners & strange tongue of the indian wigwam. Make my kindest regards to her and tell her that I hope before I reach Canada again to hear that the young fellows about her have learned better how to appreciate the value of an industrious and kind hearted Housewife. You say nothing of my other old acquaintance Melinda. Why all this reserve? I am certain that it arises from no ignorance in you at your present age of matters & things regarding every young woman within five miles of you. Should you not find mates for them both before I visit Canada depend upon it I carry them both off with me to this country where we North-westers know better how to value a fair face than you Pork Eaters[23] about Beechridge seem to do.

Make my best compts. also to Alex. Struthers. I regret to hear that he seeks for pleasure at the bottom of the rum bottle: – 'tis a dangerous amusement, and I fear poor fellow he will eventually find it so. Poor widow Struthers I rejoice to hear is still carrying on well, notwithstanding her heavy loss. Wherever you or John can be of service to her in her farm affairs I trust you will need no hint to remember the kindness of that family to you in bye gone years when you were houseless, friendless strangers in Canada. I hear nothing of how James Struthers & Martha are coming on. Let me have in your next a complete account of all those whom I know during my first winter in Canada. Meanwhile with kindest love I am

My dear Andrew
Your Affectionate Brother

JH

YF 4 July 1832

Miss Jane Hargrave
My Dear Jane

Every additional letter from you gives me a higher opinion of your good sense and discretion. Your last of 4th March I have read several times with great pleasure, and I rejoice to find in you my dear sister such prudent opinions of life and of your path through it. Continue to guide yourself by such, and ever depend on the best love and services of your affectionate brother. Your kind sheets found me as usual at this place up to the *lugs* in labour, in excellent health and the best spirits. I rejoice to find by them all that you are well and happy; a great consolation to me; when every new arrival from the interior informs some [of] my acquaintances of the decease or misfortunes of those who are dearest to them, or leaves others without any information at all regarding their friends in the civilized world. May you long My dear Jane be spared to send me annually such glad tidings.

I recollect perfectly the person [you] mention, named Robertson, whom you visited last spring. – and the conversation we had on Sal-

---

23 A term for a summer employee or voyageur who lacked experience.

lanside[24] hills regarding old Border feuds, the battle fields of which lay around us: I remember particularly pointing out to him Ancrum Moor[25] & Lilliards Edge,[26] as the scenes of some of these; and no doubt talked a great deal of nonsense about the feats of the Black Douglas,[27] & gallant actions of our Scottish forefathers, being a young foolish boy with a head crammed with all the old traditions of the borders. I have frequently since recalled this incident to mind, and often blushed at the recollection of what still appears to me as the vain boasting of a young enthusiast filled with dreams of the years that are gone. I shall feel great delight in meeting him in Canada, and trust to strengthen on better grounds the good opinion which he has formed of me from this old chance meeting. Make my kind regards to him & let me know in your next how he prospers in the world.

The regret of my uncle at leaving his old farm I cannot wonder at. I have ever been of opinion that such changes produce no benefit to those who make them and have always found that he who is not contented with the condition he is in will not be so in that which he desires. Remember me in the kindest manner to Marg' Struthers. You & she seem to be difficult to please in the choice of a match; indeed your neighborhood seems this season to have produced no weddings, a fault that I should be much disposed to amend were I to visit Canada soon.

I have little to say as usual of my own affairs. My health is excellent, my employment is entirely to my taste, and my purse if not yet heavy is sufficiently well lined to meet all my wants & wishes. At head Quarters I

24   Salenside is just south of Ashkirk in the parish of the same name, Selkirkshire.
25   The Battle of Ancrum Moor was fought in 1545 during an Anglo-Scottish war toward the end of the reign of Henry VIII of England. The Scottish victory put a temporary end to English depredations in the Scottish borders and lowlands.
26   Lilliard's Edge was part of the battlefield of Ancrum Moor (1545), in the parish of Ancrum and two miles northwest of Ancrum, Roxburghshire. There is a tradition that Lilliard, a maid of Teviotdale, made desperate by the loss of her lover, fought in the Scottish ranks till she fell beneath many wounds: and she has bequeathed to part of the battlefield the name of Lilliard's Edge.
27   Sir James Douglas (the Good, 'the Black Douglas') (1286–1330) was a Scottish soldier and knight who fought in the Scottish Wars of Independence and was knighted at Bannockburn by Robert the Bruce.

am ever in the way of procuring books & Newspapers the great sources of our amusement in this land, and our style of living & quality of our provisions far superior to any thing I had reason to expect from my original condition in life, or what I had experienced till I came to this land. As a specimen we have two or three kinds of the best wine at our table every day, venison, fowl &c in abundance and Malt Liquor at all hours what we choose to consume. Our only privation is the want of Vegetables for rearing which the summer is too short & climate too cold. Indeed a Bushel of potatoes or onions would to me at present be a greater prize than a couple Gallons wine. When I next visit you depend upon it my fathers garden which he is so prossy about will feel the effect of my longings for Melons, Squashes & Cucumbers.

I depend on hearing all the news of Beechridge from you next Spring. Meantime I am My Dear Jane
Your Mo: Affect. Brother

JH

YF 4 July 1832

Mrs Mary Ross
My Dear Mary

Your kind letter of 4th March last reached me about a week ago, and I rejoice to find that you & family with our Old parents are all still well and happy. My health this season is good as ever, my situation and employment the same as last season, and I am happy as the day is long. Canada will certainly be the place to which I retire from this service, and I fondly hope that this period will arrive so soon as to allow me enjoying the happiness of seeing you *all* again; meanwhile, separated as we are I rejoice to find that you are all prospering, and that our good old parents enjoy that comfort & plenty which it has ever been my most anxious wish to help them to obtain.

I am well acquainted with the Mr Robertson you mention. We have known each other for these last 10 Years, – and have ever esteemed him as an upright & worthy man. Had I had an opportunity of seeing him when he went down 2 years ago I purposed sending a letter by him to our old parents, for from him they would have learned more regarding me than any thing I can convey by letter. I would be glad to hear that [he] has settled in your neighborhood, and that he is prospering in life. Our parents and all of you have ever been anxious that I should soon return to settle among you, and I am happy to find by what Mr Robertson has said to you, that they are persuaded of the propriety of my continued residence in this land. Indeed to leave it at present would be sacrificing every hope I entertain of eventually making myself independent. There are degrees of rank before me in the service, which I know I am capable of filling & to which I do not feel it presumption in me to aspire, the annual income attached to which is what we once looked upon as a *fortune*: as I presently am I possess happiness, stand high in the regard of the Heads of the Company, and have plenty to provide for all my wants & wishes. When I settle in Canada, it will not be to *make* money but to enjoy in comfort, in a civilized country & among my friends the fruits of exertions in this country. I have ever looked to cultivating a farm as the best means of amusement & of more easily providing for the expenses of a family, but I trust before I bid adieu to the Indian Country to realize such a sum, as to be able to support such upon the Interest, should this mode of life not appear to promise so much happiness to me as some other.

I am grieved to hear of the loss poor Ruther[28] has sustained. A Small family without a mother to take care of them is an anxious charge to a father. Both he and Joseph appear however to be in prosperous circumstances, certainly far superior to any thing they could ever have expected had they remained in their native country. I can pick up little more regarding myself just now which can interest you, so in the hope that you will be spared to write me again many years
I am My Dear Mary
Your aff. Brother JH

Master W[illia]^m Ross
My Dear Nephew

Your kind little letter of last Spring I have read with the greatest pleasure, and heartily thank you for this attention to your absent Uncle. I hope yet to see you in some future year; meanwhile my dear little fellow be attentive to your book, and learn to be a good scholar, for this you will find to be of more value to you, when you become a man, than money or any thing else you can have in this world. Listen & attend to all your kind parents tell you for this is the way to become a good man, and if a

---

28 Ruther Hargrave's first wife, Agnes Goldie (1796–1829), died in Waddington, New York, leaving six children. Ruther later married Margaret Rutherford (1813–1895) of Madrid, New York.

man is not good he will never be happy or be liked by his neighbours. Be this & you will ever find me, Your Affectionate Uncle

JH

YF 4 July 1832

Mr Ja^s Ross
Chateauguay
My Dear Brother

I was favored with the receipt of your kind Sheet of 3^d March last a few days ago, and amid the usual turmoil of Head Quarters at this season I sit down to produce a few lines in reply however trifling may be their import. I have since I last addressed you enjoyed my usual good health, and been occupied in the Depot duties of this place, from which there is little chance of my removal for some years to come. As for myself I have no desire of a change; the Gent^n in Charge of the Factory,[29] a countryman of our own is one of the best & kindest of men, who treats me rather as a Son than an inferior and a more agreeable & good humoured person than whom I could not be placed under.

I have read with much interest the details you give me of the prospect of success in farming speculations in Canada. This I certainly look forward to as the occupation of riper years, but when the time arrives I will take to it more as a means of innocent & profitable amusement, than as a mode of improving my fortune. The fur Trade has been the department of life in which the prime of my life has been spent, and from this I trust to extract such a competency before my days decline into the dry & yellow leaf, as will keep me in comfort & independence for the rest of my days. I may indeed be unfortunate in the pursuit of that Will o the Wisp Riches, but I find present pleasure & some profit in the chase, and may as well as others be rewarded with a sleeve of Silk by aiming at the whole Robe.

I like to hear of your little speculations in Rafting[30] to add to the profit of your farm. Such a Merchandise is always certain of a good market as sure as the cold season returns, and your fortunate position as regards water communication is an advantage which those farther removed from large streams have no chance of competing with you.

29 Alexander Christie was chief factor at York Factory from 1830 to 1833.
30 Cordwood was probably rafted to Montreal. See Brisson and Bouchard, "Haut-Saint-Laurent."

Let me hear in your next how the Rideau Canal gets on, & how far it is from being finished. I saw something in the English Papers last winter of its being likely to be abandoned, a design for which I hope there is no foundation, as the benefits it would both render Gov^t & the Colonists are of the most important nature. Tell me also the proper address for letters reaching you should there be a post Office in Chateauguay.[31] At present I enclose yours with those for my parents and all are left at Lachine, by which arrangement, yours may be a month in Canada ere they reach you. That this may find you in the excellent health in which it leaves me is the ardent wish of
Yours Affectionately

JH

YF 20th July 1832
10 p.m.

J.G. McTavish Esq
Dear Sir

Mr Robertson[32] starts early tomorrow & I have just this moment heard from the Govr that a chance for letters reaching you will occur this fall from Michipicoten, so to work I have fallen to see what a few minutes near witching time of night will produce. The Govr informs me also of your infirm state of health, a reason which fully accounts to me for not hearing from you at Fort William, and I fain would hope that ere this may reach you your usual good health & strength will again be your own. Since my last to you of 1st Decr via R.R – little of note has occurred within our limits. The same duties as of yore; the same mode of executing them still wear round the circle of the year. The summer crush is now mostly over, the brigades are dispersing and a few moments sometimes occur for prying into the uncoes from Europe. Those from the north of this season wear no extraordinary features. Returns are respectable and

---

31 A post office opened the following year at Dewittville (in 1833). This would have been quite close to Hargrave's brother-in-law's farm.
32 Colin Robertson (1783–1842) had a major quarrel in 1831 with Governor George Simpson when the former brought his Metis wife to Red River and tried to introduce her into "society" in that settlement. He decided to retire and made plans to sail for England but in 1832, before he could depart, he had what was probably a stroke from which he never completely recovered. Woodcock, "Robertson, Colin," DCB.

the greater portion is now in our Stores waiting the vessel. Mr Smith[33] comes out from McKenzies R – likely to visit Canada, & the old smoking bog[34] of Winipeg has set off at a Tangent to take his place. Mr Cowie[35] accompanied by Mess: Lane[36] & Anderson[37] are gone to the Col[umbi]^a. Mr Robertson visits Canada instead of England: turned aside from his plans by bugbear colera. Dr Todd[38] has Swan River with Fort Ellice under his charge in consequence. The Americans are becoming troublesome in Fort de prairie & Mr Rowand[39] remains inland this season to make a crusade thro' the plain Tribes to bring them if possible back to the right faith. Bow River is also to be reestablished as an advanced guard on these intruders.[40] McKintosh[41] is off to his old haunts in Peace

33 Edward Smith went on furlough between 1832 and 1834.
34 John Stuart (1780–1847) took Smith's place as chief factor at Fort Simpson in the Mackenzie River district from 1832 to 1834.
35 Robert Cowie (d. 1859) entered the North West Company in 1811. In 1829 he became a chief trader in the Hudson's Bay Company and was employed at Lachine until 1830 or 1831. He was later at Fort Vancouver and Moose Factory and retired in 1846. Glazebrook, *Hargrave Correspondence*, 10.
36 William Fletcher Lane, b. ca. 1794 in Ireland, was an HBC clerk in New Caledonia from 1832 to 1845.
37 Alexander Caulfield Anderson (1814–1884) entered the service of the HBC in 1831 and spent the years from 1832 to 1854 in the fur trade on the Pacific slope. McLoughlin, *Letters*, 384–6.
38 Dr William Todd (c. 1784–1851), fur trader and surgeon from Ireland. From 1832 to 1843 Todd was in charge of the Swan River district, as chief trader at Fort Pelly.
39 John Rowand (c. 1787–1854), fur trader. In 1823, Rowand succeeded to the command of the HBC's Saskatchewan district with headquarters at Fort Edmonton. He was to manage the many responsibilities of the difficult charge successfully for the next thirty years. He was named chief factor in 1826 and a councillor of Rupert's Land in 1839. He was a nominal Roman Catholic and dealt well with the Plains Indians who frequented his post. They referred to him as "Iron Shirt" or "Big Mountain," impressed by his bravery. Van Kirk, "Rowand, John."
40 In 1822–23 Rowand assisted Chief Factor Donald McKenzie in the command of the Bow River expedition which found the fur resources of this southern region so poor that the idea of establishing a permanent post was abandoned.
41 William MacKintosh (also McKintosh) (c. 1784–1842) joined the NWC in 1802 and played a vital role in opposing the HBC's invasion of the Athabas-

River & is succeeded by T Isbister[42] under the surveillance of M[r] [Roderick] M[c]Kenzie of English R[r]. The outfits of this season – are larger than those of last but yet I think not beyond the demands of a fair trade would warrant. The Stores here are still flowing with Goods, but from the small Imports expected this season & the still smaller order calculated as wanted in 33 for o[utfi]*t* 34 I expect we will by & bye bring to a moderate compass the pyramids built up by inland Ignorance. We have now the main body of our new General Store completed, & the wings will be added this fall & next spring: – I think the solid substantial style in which it has been finished & the great convenience it affords for making up outfits in short time & with small labor would meet your approbation. Most of your old hands are still here & are our leading men. Drever,[43] Randall,[44] Poitras,[45] Bouvet,[46] Wilson,[47] Benoit[48] & Young Marion[49] with Smith[50] & M[c]Gregor[51] are still with us: – Young L.

---

ca country. Although named a chief factor after the amalgamation of the two companies, he held no important commands. Following his transfer back to Fort Dunvegan on the Peace River in 1832 his health began to fail and he resigned in 1837. Goldring, "MacKintosh, William."

42 Thomas Isbister (c. 1793–1836) an Orkneyman, who was HBC clerk in charge of the Island Lake district from 1832–34. He was killed by a bull in 1836.

43 William Drever (c. 1803–), an Orkneyman who worked between 1821 and 1839 at York Factory as a labourer, and then carpenter, joiner, etc.

44 John Rendall (Rendal, Randall) (1801–1877), an Orkneyman, was postmaster at Severn from 1832 to 1834. He had previously worked as a boat builder and carpenter at York Factory.

45 Medard Poitras was listed as a rough carpenter at York Factory in 1829/30. HBCA, B.239/a/141.

46 François Bouvet, from Montreal, was listed as a blacksmith in 1831. HBCA, B.239/g/11.

47 William Wilson was listed as a cooper at York Factory in 1829/30. HBCA, B.239/a/141.

48 André Benoit, from Longueil, was listed as a baker at York Factory in 1829/30. HBCA, B.239/a/141.

49 Narcisse Marion (c. 1807–), a Canadian from L'Assomption who worked as a blacksmith at York Factory from 1827 to 1835.

50 Edward Smith, c. 1800–, an Orkneyman who served as a blacksmith at York Factory between 1829 and 1846, with the exception of the outfit year 1837–38 when he went home.

51 Magnus McGregor was listed as a tinsmith at York Factory in 1829/30. HBCA, B.239/a/141.

Leblanc[52] has also been here for about 2 seasons & is now our Steward. He conducts himself well & is firm and steady in his duty: a favorite with our worthy Bourgeois: – His father & the family are all well in Red River: – George[53] is still our Butler as careful & steady as ever but his dam is a perfect Rabbit, – & the swarm of young ones she surrounds him with will, I fear, soon lead him towards some roosting place.

I had a letter this spring from my poor friend Barnston: He you will have heard has been making much stir both at home & with the Govr & I deeply regret to find that his communications are such as will little advance his interests. What a change in this fine young fellow within these last 10 years! His opinion of Govr S: is particularly unjust, & on the whole subject of his affairs in this country I fear he has allowed his mind to brood so long & so despondingly, as at length no longer is he able to form a sound estimate on the subject. Would to God I may be mistaken, but I dread an aberation of intellect on this topic. This opinion, I confide to your honor, – I would never forgive myself should his mind be more steady than I fear it, that it should have to bear also the suspicions of his friends as to its sanity. I have written him also by this conveyance, – but avoided the topic which apparently preys on his understanding. I trust to have a few lines from you by the winter Express – meantime with deepest remembrances of all your kindness to me I remain
My dear Sir
Most faithfully Yours

JH

---

52 Louis Leblanc was probably the son of Pierre Leblanc who married Nancy McKenzie after she was deserted by John George McTavish. His father was postmaster at Lower Red River at this time. Louis Leblanc is listed for the first time in York Factory Abstracts of Servants' Accounts, 1829–30, as a Native apprentice. HBCA, B.239/g/9.
53 George Thorn.

[Letterbook]
N°. 8
Rough Copies Letters by
J Hargrave
from 25th July 1832 @ 19 July 1833

YF 10 Septr 1832

Mr Jas Mitchel
Dear Uncle

    I have read with great pleasure your kind letter of 6th April last which reached me at this place about 3 weeks ago, and I rejoice to find that you are all still preserved in health & happiness amid the dangers and diseases which within these last 12 months have passed over our native land. I had also last June letters from my parents, brothers & sisters in Canada, written in March at which time they were all well & prospering in the world. My good old parents are certainly now much failed, and are sinking fast into the valley of years; – yet while thus loaded with the weary burden of frail and withering mortality, it is peculiarly consoling to me to reflect that their circumstances are easy, they are their own masters, and as they say themselves have nothing further to wish for in this world. Since writing you last season I have remained stationary at this place where I will also be the ensuing winter. My employment is still the same and in executing the trust reposed in me year follows year in quiet & happiness. The country around us is certainly a wilderness in the truest sense of the word. The climate is also the severest I have ever experienced, 9 months of intense & unremitting frost forms our winter, and the summer is a few weeks of alternate heat & drizzling rain. The severity of the cold is such that words could convey you no idea of it. Quicksilver in the month of June, when exposed in the open air freezes & becomes solid as lead, in this state it will bear to be hammered out into a plate or moulded into any shape. This I have myself seen & closely examined more than once. For all this however we contrive to bear with impunity the winters rigour & summers moisture. I have never had a day of sickness since I came here five years ago. You ask me whether I think not of returning again to my native country. This hope I assure you is never absent from me, but the period when this shall take place I find it impossible to fix. Embarked as I am in the voyage of life – a trading voyage – in which time is money, and assiduous application the root of success I can find as yet no opportunity to turn aside with safety from my present course & indulge my feelings in a tour of pleasure to the scenes so familiar to me of yore. Unless in some extraordinary instances of good fortune youth is usually spent abroad in climing to situations in which alone reward is to be obtained for years of hard application in business. This period with me is not yet arrived. My present income is still slender, tho' more than equal to all my wants; but prizes are now almost within my grasp which will reward the toils of former seasons; and there are situations in this land to which I have, if my life be spared, full confidence of obtaining the yearly income of which would by me have been considered a fortune when I left my native country 13 years ago. I feel confident in my ability to fill such with credit to myself; – and it is with a heart filled with gratitude that I reflect it is to my dear parents having strained to their utmost their slender means to give me an education, that I am enabled to raise myself above the life of toil & privation to which I awas born. To their credit I must also join that of the late Dr Douglases of Galashiels. The friend of my youth, *the worthiest* man I have known. The memory of this good man shall never be forgotten by me.

I regret to hear that that pestilence, the Cholera, has at length reached Scotland but it satisfactory to find by the last Accts we have that it is on the decline. The public affairs of Britain seem also in a precarious state from the agitation occasioned by the reform Bill,[1] but I rejoice to find that our latest dates inform us it has been passed into law, which I have great hopes will quiet the nation again. This measure of reform had become absolutely necessary, and if the people use with discretion the power thus entrusted to them I have yet great hopes that better times will arise in our native country. That you may all be spared to inform me of such in some future year is the earnest wish of
My Dear Uncle
Your affect^n Nephew

JH

---

[1] The 1832 Reform Bill of the British Parliament was the first of several that expanded the electorate for the House of Commons and rationalized the representation of that body. The first Reform Bill primarily served to transfer voting privileges from the small boroughs controlled by the nobility and gentry to the heavily populated industrial towns.

YF 6 Dec[r] 1832

J.G. McTavish Esq
My Dear Sir

Tis with great pleasure I embrace the opportunity which the present packet gives me to run you over a page or two regarding the every day subjects among which I have been occupied since I wrote you last July. The summer routine passed over quietly, the Brigades dispersed, and the vessel cast up about the 23 Aug[t]. The Gov[r] who with his lady had remained here till her arrival, took his departure immediately after for R.R. – also M[r] Berins[2] a young Gent[n] son of the Director of that name, who goes thro the country this season on a trip of pleasure and observation. I was sorry to observe that our valued chiefs health was much shaken, Grief[3] & a life of hard service have actually reduced him to the Ghost of what he was. He recruited much however in course of the fall, and his lady especially was quite cheerful again previous to their departure. A Drizzling stormy fall retarded much our labours in exchanging the cargoes of the Rupert which however was completed about much the usual dates, the northern furs reached this in good time & she took her departure on the 20th Sept[r]. M[r] Hutchinson[4] the only cabin passenger who goes home for a winter to recruit his health. The gross am[t] of the Cargo Rec[d] this season was some little above £14 m and our order for next shipment as you will perceive by the Minutes of Council is bounded by £10m. These Imports it is calculated will bring down the Stock on hand within the compass of the Reserve you always wished to have as surplus stock in case of accident, & which we carefully follow, say 100 P Cent all Amm[unitio][n] Iron works & fishing Tackle with about 25 P Cent on all articles required for trade or duties. The Req[n] of 33 will consequently be up possibly to ab[t] £18m tho' still not equal to a full outfit arising from some heavy goods being yet

---

2 Henry Hulse Berens (1804–1883), the son of Joseph Berens who had been governor of the Hudson's Bay Company between 1812 and 1822, arrived with a letter for Governor Simpson from Governor John Henry Pelly asking the former to give him all assistance in learning about the HBC operations. Simpson soon came to detest the brash young visitor. Galbraith, *Little Emperor*, 119.

3 The first child of Governor Simpson and his wife, Frances, died as an infant in 1832 while the newly wed couple resided in Red River.

4 John Hutchison was listed as a clerk in the McKenzie River District from 1823. Fleming, *Minutes*, 55.

over abundant. This subject forms my chief study in business, & from the advantages I derived thro' your lessons & the example you have left, – I think we will be able to balance the scales fairly neither overloading the Country nor suffering the Trade to languish thro' want of its essentials. The Colony of Red River alone embarrasses us: its wants we find it difficult to ascertain exactly one year forms a poor criterion for the following, arising from the various plans annually springing up for its benefit. On the whole however we get on well, and being allowed to ask for what foresight can suggest as necessary have little difficulties on the whole to encounter, – compared with the days when hands were tied down and a host of clambering throats in full chorus for that which was not. The winter road is expected this season to be ready for operation the following fall season. Substantial Stores & Stages are erected along the whole route the road thoroughly cleared & stumps grabbed out with Oxen & large sledges upon it for transport. The Govr is still struggling away with the sluggish mass in the Colony which may be considered capable of doing any thing in the way of improvement. Flax, wood, Tallow all form the subject of his plans. His exertions are unwearied, & coldly seconded as they are – deserve only the higher praise on that account. Really the force of things in that quarter to me is best demonstrated by the experiments of Galvanism. The electric wire touches a nerve. The [illegible] flourishes an arm, jerks out a limb – opens a mouth – all but breathes, take away the operating cause and back sinks the [illegible] carcass into its original state of repose.

Several alterations in the divisions of the country around Lake Winipeg have this season been made – Winipeg added to Lac La pluie, Brandon Ho- to Swan R^r & [illegible] to Isle à la Crosse. The outfits as you will see by the comparison sent you are full but not much on the whole beyond our average. Little can be said of trade at this season, but that is now so regulated as never to be much over or below par unless an ocean of Rats [illegible] down on our Stores.

My health this season is good & my spirits excellent. Work to me is now a trifle, – rather a pleasure. I find my services useful, and the kindness of the Govr who gives me more credit for these than I conceive they deserve, has raised me out of the despondency once too apt to beset me. To you who have ever been my truest friend I will mention that this season I have hopes of promotion, being [illegible] me first on the list for a Commission next spring. I may be disappointed yet for the home choice is free, yet I believe 'twill not be long, – and I say this much for your satisfaction who I know will rejoice sincerely at my good fortune to which I will award you have contributed so much that this is one of the few topics on which we have never conversed. One subject of [illegible] with this. I have written to my poor friend Barnston by this conveyance & beg you will please see my letter gets into the right road to him. I know not in what part of your Department he is.[5]

I long much to hear from you, to be assured of your health. I fondly hope it to be re-established so a few lines will repay all this prasing. We begin to think here you have forgotten us. My honest Bourgeois[6] & I are as ever on the best terms. We arrange most admirably. Happy in possessing his confidence & [illegible] with good health I now view with comparative indifference the taunt of malice & the sneer of envy, – which once gnawed so deeply here on my repose.

I could run this out to much greater length in politics & Whiggism triumphant, for a noble subject for a song of Jubilee. But I shall have mercy both on your patience & [illegible] Toryism. Should any additional [illegible] of the European world subsequent to the [illegible] in June last have reached you I will not scarcely add. Pray think of those hungering & thirsting for such precious food within these bounds. God bless you & may this find you as well as I could wish – as well as it leaves me, is the sincerest wish of
My Dear Sir
Yours faithfully & affectionately

JH

YF 10 July 1833

Mrs Jane Hargrave
My Dear Mother

The whole of your ever welcome letters reached me a few days ago, and afforded me the greatest delight & cause for the deepest gratitude to the great Author of Good to find that you had all been spared while so many around you had fallen victims to the pestilence which has desolated so many quarters of the world. 'Tis with the same feelings I know you will read that the same is my good fortune, and that altho' no unusual sickness has prevailed here, I have however had not the slightest ailment

---

5 George Barnston served at Fort Albany in the Albany District in 1832, the year he rejoined the HBC.
6 Alexander Christie.

since I wrote you last year. I still remain at the same place, and am occupied about the same duties as formerly; – nor is there much chance of my being removed for some years to come. I know you will be delighted to hear that the expectations I had of advancement in the service, which I had mentioned to you these two last years, have this season been realised. The Coy in London has this spring sent me out a Commission of Chief Trader, the income arising from which will in a few years produce me as much money as will be to me a fortune. The annual income is not a fixed sum but varies according as the Years trade is more or less profitable: For these many years back it has never been less than £400, and in several of them has exceeded £500. This is now my yearly Gains and possessing such, what cause for Gratitude do I not owe to you my dear mother, who together with my father, shared your last penny with me to obtain me the education which has been so useful & so profitable to me. Do you recollect, when at Lindean, you gave me a few pence to purchase some necessary book I required at Fyshes School, and which you had gathered through several weeks to procure yourself an ounce or two of tobacco? This act of kindness of yours will never be forgotten by your absent son while he breathes; – it has been a lesson of self-denial to me through life, – and has been the grain of mustard-seed to my fortunes. I may tell you further, that prospects of higher Rank and larger gains are still before me. A few years more will I trust raise me to a situation producing annually *double* the sum I mentioned above, and which is the highest rank any can reach in this land. My hopes for such advancement are *well* founded, if my Benefactors life be spared so long.[7] The proofs of what he is both able & willing to do for me are seen in what he has done for me already. Now my dear mother, as you love me, keep all I have said locked up in your own mind. To my father *alone* you may make known what I have told you, and to you two & in order to add to your happiness, I have *alone* made known to any in Canada the fortunate change which has taken place in my circumstances. Guard especially against telling to any what I have said about future prospects – or the amount of my present income. These are secrets nothing could tempt me to divulge but the desire of giving joy to my poor old mother.[8]

7 James is referring here either to Governor George Simpson or to John George McTavish.
8 The HBC directors were concerned to keep the financial status of the company private, and they considered it dangerous to allow information on officers' incomes to be acquired by outsiders, since such intelligence could

You will this season receive enclosed a Draft for £15 Stg – for which on its being presented at Lachine you will receive £16.13.4 in the currency of Canada. This is for your years pocket-money – a small token from your absent son of his remembrance, – the *interest* I owe you for the loan of your "Tobacco money."

I have little further to say my Dear Mother. I thank God that your years are still lengthened out, & pray from my heart that many may still be added to them so that I may be able to cheer to their utmost span the evening of your days. I am well myself as ever, without family or encumbrance, and when I have gathered what will enable me to support one with credit in Canada, this country shall hold me no longer. That you all may be spared to see that day is the sincerest wish of
Your loving son

Jamie

P.S. The within Bill is drawn in my brother Johns name who will receive payment of it for you. He must write his name on its back before presenting it as you formerly saw mine, without which it will not be paid.
In the packet with this will be found a letter for — Mathison from his relation Mr D. Finlayson & which you will send to him. Mr Finlayson enclosed it to me this spring from Fort Vancouver on the Columbia River where he now is – upwards of 3000 miles from this place.

YF 11 July 1833

Mr And^w Hargrave
My Dear Andrew

I have read with great pleasure your well written sheet of 11th March last and sincerely rejoice to find that you have all been preserved while so many were falling around you by that pestilence the Cholera Morbus.[9] We were not without apprehension of a visit from it here also, but thank God we have escaped so far, and as its course appears to be westward it has now past us so far that our apprehensions of danger are much on the

---

give considerable insights into the profits of the company. Galbraith, *Little Emperor*, 131.

9 An acute infectious disease of the intestines, resulting from water contaminated by the bacterium *Vibrio comma*. It first reached Canada in 1832, brought by immigrants from Britain.

wane. I am now indeed as well as ever I have been in my life, surrounded as ever with papers & digging my finger & thumb continually into a large snuff box ever planted at my elbow. You tell me of the single lives still led by my old friends Miss M. Dewey & Struthers & of their felonious designs on me when I return single among them. I dread they will find such a change in me, what with *Snuff*, & sun burning, not to mention the pestilent smell of the squaw and brush hut, that these fair damsels would turn up their noses at me when they perceive the change 14 years have produced. *Mais nous verrons*.[10] I like well to hear that Jaˢ Struthers & Martha are prospering, and that poor widow Struthers bears up so well in the lonely condition in which she is left. I trust my dear brother you will need no hint to remember the kindness of that family to you in past days, should she now have occasion at times for your services.

I can add little further regarding myself. I am happy as the day is long, and have hopes at some future year to be able to sit down with you in Canada, independent of the world, and with wherewith to provide for old age. I am sadly pressed for time, & write you when I should sleep, so growl not at the scanty measure I am obliged to give you in my letters this season. Tis possible I may not be able to write you all, however I will use every spare minute I have for that purpose, so pleasing it is to me, and trust you will be content with what I cannot make more lengthy. Let me hear next season, all about the same persons you mentioned this year, – Give a Kiss from me to each of the young lasses of my acquaintance who enquire after me, and tell me who they are. With warmest love for yourself
I am my Dear Andrew
Your affectionate Brother

JH

YF 11 July 1833

Mʳ John Hargrave
My Dear John

I have been greatly interested by the excellent account you give me of your farming operations, and rejoice to find that your labour has been rewarded with a comfortable home, and a well stocked farm. Industry my dear brother is the root of prosperity, and I have no doubt that with your

---

10   French for "But we shall see."

steady habits, and regular life both you and Andrew will yet be respectable & wealthy farmers, a situation in life more productive of happiness than most others. You appear now to have a sufficiency of land cleared, and you do well to improve that which you have under cultivation, preserving the timber on a portion of your lot, which will soon become valuable for firewood & buildings as the country gets bare around you. Your deferring purchasing lands till the question regarding their rents is settled is a very prudent measure. However this should not be too long delayed and as soon as practicable you should be doing something for yourselves also. I was quite delighted with the account you give me of our old fathers mode of spending the winter & the pleasure he takes in perusing the Newspapers. This taste I inherit greatly myself, and many are the long evenings they help me to beguile during our tedious winter. Were I to get down beside him during some of these political studies of his, I think I know so much of these matters now as would help me to puzzle him about Whig and Tory not a little. Tis a pleasing and innocent way of passing time, and consoling to me it is to think that the good old man has in these his evening years been so greatly favored by providence, with such a comfortable home, a happy family, ease and content. He seems also deep in the study of serious books, and contends with all his strength for the orthodox faith in opposition to the Sectaries around him. On these points he and I fully agree, but were we to meet I think I have still so much of the itch for argument left about me as would tempt me to dispute sturdily some of the dogmas issued by his favourite authors. God bless the good old man! I trust we shall yet be made happy by meeting again in this world.

I send my mother this season a Bill for £15 Stg – drawn out in your name which you will present at the office in Lachine & receive payment for her. You will require to write your name on the Back of the bill before presenting it as you may have seen mine on some formerly sent; – without this the Bill will not be paid, This, among merchants, is called endorsing it. I wish my mother to purchase with it good warm clothing, Tea, Sugar & Wine for herself, and the remainder she can dispose of as she may think best. It is all her own, a free gift to her from her absent son.

If you should see Mr Robertson give him my kind Compts, and tell him I long much to hear how he is prospering in Canada. I hope yet to pounce down upon him from this land in some future year, when we shall pass at least one happy day in recalling all the changes which have taken place, since we were old messmates at Norway Ho.

Excuse my Short letter I cannot make them longer & believe me ever Dear John Your Aff: Brother

JH

YF 13 July 1833

Miss Jane Hargrave
My Dear Jane

I have read several times with great pleasure your kind and well written letter of 17th March last, and have amid the crush of business which surrounds me at present got hold of a leisure minute to write you a few lines in reply. I regret to hear of the misfortune my poor cousin Mary[11] has met with last winter in the loss of her husband, and commiserate the helpless state she must now be in left as she is with 4 young children. These, my dear Sister, are some of the Miseries attendant on that state of life which neither you nor I have yet experienced, and which should make us contented with the station in life it is our fortune to occupy. Our own family has certainly been wonderfully preserved amid the mortality so general in Canada last season, and I trust we are all grateful to the Almighty for His keeping us a happy & undiminished family while so many around you have fallen under the Scourge.

I had a long letter from our uncle Ja^s Mitchel last year at which time they were all well. They mention having had one from our parents sometime before they wrote me and had written them again in return; they also add a great deal of news about Lindean &^{c} but in order to give you the whole information it contains I shall enclose it under Cover with my letters to you. What you say regarding Richardson I shall mention to them in my letter of this fall.

I am happy to hear that poor widow Struthers gets on so well deprived as she now is of such a portion of the numerous family I left her surrounded with. Remember me in the kindest manner to her & to Miss Marg^t, who I certainly expected to have changed her name long ago. I must say it shows little discernment in the young fellows around her to allow so spry a girl run so long the risk of leading apes. Should both she & you be not more expeditious than you have yet shown yourselves I may yet have an opportunity of dancing an indian Dance at both your weddings.

11 She was a daughter of James Hargrave's uncle, James Hargrave.

I have scarcely a word to say about myself. I am so exactly employed as formerly, that I am writing you in the same room & at the same desk, as where I have written you for these last Six years. My health is good, and I am as happy as a bluff batchelor without family or incumbrance can be. I can add little more my Dear Sister but that I am
Your Affectionate Brother

JH

YF 13 July 1833

Mʳ Joseph Hargrave
My Dear Father

I have perused several times with great delight your truly parental letter of 12 March last and amid the crowd of cares which surround me at this season have sat down with the greatest pleasure to write you in return though the hour is nearly midnight. Tis with a grateful heart to the Giver of all good that I learn you are all still preserved amid the desolation which has swept over Canada, preserved as if in the hollow of his hand while the pestilence walked abroad over the land choosing its victims. Oh how thankful ought we to be for this mercy! For some time before I received your letters I was in much anxiety regarding you, having heard last winter that the dreadful disease had reached Canada, and past several days very uncomfortably previous to receiving your letters. This season my letters from England contained good news to me, but none give me half the pleasure as the sight of all your letters amid the heap to me from Canada & Britain. Your fatherly advices I assure you meet in me with a ready & willing listener, and I can only say that our sentiments on religion coincide in every point you mention. In this land, we run little risk of being seduced from our fathers faith: – The preachers we have are of sound doctrine, and the country is too distant, & too thinly peopled to hold out encouragement to the wandering Sectaries you describe as abounding in Canada. On this point I want through Gods grace to incur little danger. I am not apt to allow others to think for me, and having examined and convinced my conscience of the truth of the faith in which I was bred I shall not, at every wind of doctrine, cast aside the convictions of much instruction reading & meditation, to embrace the hollow visions of the Sectary.

When I wrote you last year I mentioned the hopes I entertained of promotion in the service, which I know you will be happy to learn have not been disappointed. I have explained all this in my letter to my mother who will tell you of the prospects I now have of providing well for old age. What I have said however I earnestly desire may remain unknown to all but you two, for which desire I have material reasons.

I remain for ensuing winter at this place, as I have been for several years bypast, – and from whence there is little chance of my being sent for some time to come. As I must have already often mentioned in my journals & former letters the climate here is severe and the country waste swamps & barren, yet amid the marshes which surround us we contrive to pass our days both agreeably & I trust as innocently as we could do in more favored lands. You may guess at the severity of the climate here when I inform you that the earth is covered permanently with snow for 8 full months in the year, and only July, August & September are what may be called summer. Even during these 3 months tho the weather is frequently hot yet the swarms of Moschettoes are so thick that winter with all its storms, is more pleasant weather. In such a country of course nothing but the desire of improving ones fortune would detain a single European & when I can leave it with the means of independence, it shall no longer hold me. That this may be in time to allow me to see my venerable father once more in this life is the earnest prayer of
his Affectionate Son

JH

YF 13 July 1833

Mr James Ross
My Dear Brother

I was greatly rejoiced to find this spring on receipt of all your kind letters that you had thro' the mercy of God escaped from the effects of that dreadful pestilence which after visiting most parts of Europe had at last reached America, and in Canada had around you left such dreadful traces of its footsteps in the crowds of the widows & orphans who bewail the loss of their nearest & dearest. We have also not been without apprehensions in this secluded corner of the world of a visit from it but thus far have been mercifully spared; as among the poor natives, whose dirty habits & scanty fare render them most subject to infection, it would spread like fire in the forest. I have myself since I last wrote you enjoyed the best of health, indeed not knowing what a days sickness is, – and amid my usual occupations move round the circle of the year happy and contented. I again remain this ensuing winter in my present quarters which has now been a home to me for more than Six years and from whence I do not expect to be removed for some time yet to come. At this place we have many comforts and pleasures which those wintering inland are deprived of, it being the general Depot for the whole Northern Trade, where the European Supplies are landed & from whence the annual Shipment of Furs is made. By the Vessel we have also the advantage of obtaining large quantities of Newspapers Books &^{c} which after the pen has been thrown aside, aid well to while away the long winter Evenings in this Northern region.[12] In a Month hence at farthest we will be looking out for our annual Importation when the Factory, as quiet before as a solitary home in the Country becomes the scene of bustle & active labour night & day for about one month. The vessel then sails & the residents here allowed time to sit down & examine the various novelties which have been sent us.

I have read with much interest the account you give me of the advanced State of inland Navigation in Canada. The Canals made or yet in contemplation are of the greatest importance to the Upper province, and I hope yet before I visit Canada to hear that European Packages of a Ton Weight can be forwarded from London to Lake Superior without requiring bulk to be broken. You do well to look to farming as your main chance, and speculations foreign to such a pursuit can only with safety

---

12 James Hargrave to Geo. Copeland from York Factory, 1 September 1834. James Hargrave and family fonds, LAC. Hargrave wrote this Edinburgh gentleman thanking him for a case of clothes the latter had sent that year and that appeared to Hargrave to be "of good quality" and to fit him well. He attached a memo listing clothing, books, and papers he wished Copeland to procure and send to him at York Factory in 1835. "The Books and papers I am aware are not matters in your line of business, but having no other correspondent in the North your procuring of them for me would be very obliging." The articles listed included 1 Sfine Blue Cloth Frock Coat, 2 fancy Vests, 1 P^r strong Dble milled Kersey Trousers, 1 file "Chambers Edinburgh Journal" from 1 June 1834 @ 1 June 1835 ("The Nos between the date of your making up the Case for me & the 1st June '35 could be forw^d in a parcel P Steam Boat to Orkness – care of J. Rae Esq. Stromness."), 1 Copy Chambers Pictures of Scotland – half bound, 1 Taits Edin^r Magazine – latest no^s as above, 1 Copy Latest Edinburgh Almanach that is for 36 if to be got if not, that for 1835.

be prosecuted during the season when the farmer rests from his labours. I myself now see before me a certainty, if my life should be spared, of being able to procure an independence in this land, and will consequently remain in it till I attain that object, but my views are certainly a quiet seat in the evening of my days on the Snug farm in Canada or one of the Northern States. This I trust will be in such time as will allow me to hope for the happiness of seeing again those who are so dear to me in Canada, meantime I am
My Dear Brother   Affectionately Yours

JH

YF 13 July 1833
Mrs Mary Ross
My Dear Mary

All your kind letters reached me about 2 weeks ago, and amid my usual crowd of duties at this time I have got hold of a leisure minute or two to write you all a dozen lines in reply. I sincerely rejoice at your escape from that dreadful disease which has occasioned such Mortality in Canada, and consider our family highly favored by providence in its being preserved entire while so many were sinking around you. I am also happy to find that our poor old father bears the weight of years so well and that now fast approaching as he is to four Score he yet possesses all his faculties of mind & body. It is one [of] my purest sources of pleasure to hear that the old folks are so happy & comfortable, and whatever little help I may have given towards procuring them this I consider it the best spent money I ever laid out in my life. How different is now their condition from that which lay before them had they remained in Scotland till this day, and how little able might we have been to help them had we also never left our native land. Indeed had we remained in Scotland all our conditions in life would have been below what they now are: – I especially never could have hoped for any thing beyond a bare subsistence attained by much toil of both mind & body, being without friends to aid me forward or the advantages of birth to bring me into notice. In this land where man is measured with man & mind with mind, instead of obscure merit being kept down through the influence of birth & patronage I have had a field opened to me for putting to the test the value of the education & honest principles our worthy parents instructed us in, and my hopes have not been disappointed. I now look forward with confidence to the day when I shall return to those who are dear to me, with the means of providing for myself far beyond any thing that fortune promised me in my youth.

I have had a letter from our Uncle Ja^s Mitchel since I last wrote you at which time they were all well. Our cousin Effy is yet unmarried, nor indeed do I hear of any of them having yet changed their condition in life. This letter I send enclosed to our parents so should you be paying them a visit this winter you will be able to hear all the news of Galashiels & Lindean.

I have read with much interest the account you give me of your farm & Live Stock, and am really happy to find you are so comfortably situated. Your small family will soon grow up & be a help to you and a large family carefully instructed in upright & serious & industrious principles is the best riches a farmer can possess. You are certain should providence bless you with health to find yourselves ere long in easy & independent circumstances.

That I may have the pleasure of finding you so on my return is the sincere wish of your Affectionate Brother

JH

YF 13 July '33

Master Wm Ross
My Dear Nephew

I thank you kindly for your neat little letter of last Spring and am pleased to find that you have improved so much in your education. You write & spell very well, and if you continue to improve as you have so well begun you will find the advantages in mature years of the care which has been taken to instruct you in youth. We are as you say yet personally unacquainted, but I trust this will not be always, and I hope when I return to Canada, to have the happiness of being made acquainted with many who are near & dear to me yet to whom my face is still unknown. I again thank you for your well written token of attention to your far distant friend, and I hope will ever amid the busiest times I pass through, be able to find time to tell you how much I am
Your Affectionate Uncle

JH

YF 18 July 1833

J.G. McTavish Esq
My Dear Sir

I need not say with what delight I received your very kind favour of 25th Jany last, which both in bulk & spirit I esteem a full return with interest for the long file of paper pellets I have for these two last years been flying at you. As the Mont[real]' Canoe is getting ready I shall try amid the interruptions of my summer life to eke out a sheet for you in return, however knotty may be the fabric. I rejoice to hear that your health improves regarding which we had unpleasant rumors here last season, and I fondly hope that having gained the weather gage of an invalids easy chair, it will now continue prosperous.

I have this season got packed up & forwarded to you by the downward Canoes to Michipicoten the 3 maps I found in the Box here with the painting. These latter still remain here, that is an oil full figure of Lord Nelson and a sea piece also in oil.[13] They lie here in the Box as before: we are ignorant of their owner, but I think they might ornament our Mess Room as well as sleeping in a Case where they are more likely to meet with accident.

---

13 These two large oil paintings are by Bavarian-born Canadian artist William Berczy, also known as Johann Albrecht Ulrich Moll, 1744–1813. One of the paintings depicts a stately Lord Nelson looking out into the distance, and the other displays the Battle of Trafalgar. They were commissioned in 1805 by William McGillivray, a partner in the North West Company, and presented by him to the company to adorn the dining hall at Fort William, the company's inland headquarters. The fort was completed in 1804 at the western end of Lake Superior and named after McGillivray. After the merger in 1821 of the NWC and HBC, John George McTavish who commanded Fort William at the time moved to York Factory and took the two paintings with him. They remained in their packing case until 1834 when, following James Hargrave's suggestion, they were hung in the summer mess room. The artist, however, was unknown at that time. It was not until 1991 that a catalogue for the National Gallery of Canada exhibition on Berczy by Mary Allodi, Peter Moogk, and Beate Stock clarified how it is at last known that Berczy painted the pictures. The paintings are highlights of HBC's corporate art collection.

I have got the am^t f £5.12 s placed to your Credit, & the same placed to the debit of Fraser.[14] Mr Christie is uncertain whether this dress – was considered by the Govr in the light of a present to him from the Coy, but in the Govr's absence judged it most expedient to arrange it thus: He will however mention the circumstance to him this fall so that if intended otherwise it may be hereafter properly arranged. I have written young Kennedy[15] this summer enclosing him a Dft on your Acc^t for the sum you desired me say £1.2.6. The Telescope you describe had it appears been lent by the Govr to Mr Cameron,[16] believing it to be public property. It will now be settled, as Mr Simon has been writing to M^r [Robert] Miles regarding it, and the above explanation sets the matter to rest. Some Enquiries were also made regarding a Quarto Copy of an Encyclopedia which Mr Simon claims: no such article is however here.

I have written to Mr Harding[17] regarding the Musk [ox] Calf Skins you mention, and he promises every exertion to procure them. I find however that they will cost you something over 2s. Cash, that being the price they are credited the District as returns. This being so much beyond the Cost you mention & as they will not reach me to go by the Express Canoe I think I shall not purchase or send them via England till I hear from you again. Little Harding is still steady as ever, snugly roosted at Churchill, and expresses himself highly gratified by your remembrance of him. He adds "I beg you will convey my best respects to M^r McTavish & let him know that I have yet the liveliest recollection of his kindness to me while serving under his directions."

The news of the North this year are not momentous. M^r [Edward] Smith is now here from McK- R- on his way to Canada: – May his suc-

---

14 Colin Fraser (1807–1867), who was hired as piper to Governor George Simpson in 1827, became a trader in Rupert's Land, married Nancy Beaudry, a Red River Metis, and had 12 children. He died at Lac Ste Anne in present-day Alberta.

15 Perhaps John Frederick Kennedy (1805–1859), who was clerk and surgeon at Fort Simpson in Columbia Department from 1831 to 1839.

16 Perhaps John Dugald Cameron (c. 1777–1857), an experienced and respected fur trader from a Loyalist family, who was chief factor at Fort Alexander (Bas-de-la-Rivière) from 1832 to 1834. During this time he made several trips to the Red River settlement where he formally married his Indian wife in the Anglican church in 1833. Van Kirk, "Cameron, John Dugald."

17 Robert Harding (1801–), an Englishman who was clerk-in-charge at Churchill from 1826 to 1845.

cessor tread in the footsteps so judiciously traced for [illegible] affairs. M[r] Charles[18] manages carefully & prosperously the affairs of Athabasca, but next season a change will likely be in its superintendant as he I believe has either a rotation or leave of absence. [William] M[c]Kintosh[19] is growling & unhappy: talks also of a furlough next season. This man is most unhappy in his family, Wilson[20] this season turning off his daughter for misconduct and he (Wilson) himself having abandoned himself to Liquor.[21] The old Captain[22] has English R[r] in prime [illegible] but growls dreadfully at the prohibitory resolve anent killing Beaver. M[r] [John] Rowand [illegible] the plain Countries with credit & high profit. A great change has taken place in his ideas of economy of late & his demands for goods are now greatly lowered since 5 years ago. The Home Districts have also yielded respectable returns & they are now mostly here in good order waiting the vessel. In the Col[umbi][a] matters go on rather roughly, – and a great number of the gentlemen write they come out or leave the service there next season. I trust however that hearing of the absence of the Gov[r] a sentiment of duty will keep them at their posts. The American opposition on the Coast is dwindling away & it is hoped will soon be extinguished. The returns there are also respectable. The Colony will feel

18 John Charles (c. 1784–), an Englishman, entered the HBC in 1799. He was chief factor at Fort Chipewyan in the Athabasca District between 1830 and 1834. He then went on furlough for a year at the Red River settlement, and from 1836 to 1838 he was chief factor at York Factory. He retired in 1843 to Red River.
19 George Simpson described McKintosh in his Character Book of 1832 as follows: "A revengeful cold blooded black hearted Man whom I consider capable of anything that is bad: possessing no abilities beyond such as qualify him to cheat any unfortunate Indian and to be guilty of a mean dirty trick: Suspicious, Cruel & Tyrannical without honour or integrity, in short, I have never been able to discover one good trait in his character." Williams, "'Character Book' of Governor George Simpson," 181.
20 Andrew Wilson was postmaster at Nelson River in York district during the winter of 1832–33. Cowie, "Minutes," 689.
21 In 1825 one of McIntosh's colleagues reported to Simpson that "to indulge his ill nature, low cunning and the fancies of his Wife and Daughter (who in reality govern both him and the affairs under his Managemanet) would and does sacrifice his own and the Co[ys] interests." Merk, *Fur Trade and Empire*, 151.
22 Roderick McKenzie was known as "Captain of the Nipigon" among old Nor'Westers.

the absence of Govr Simpson & tho a better Factor for the peace could scarcely have been found than M^r C-[23] yet the diminished expenditure of the Coy will make his departure be sensibly felt. These changes none regret more than I from the alterations it brings round here; but in gratitude to Mr Simpson to whom I owe so much I shall be silent & look to another year for removing me from purgatory. This is not a moment when he expects every man to do his duty & to cripple the service, what ever I may personally suffer.

But what do you think of the Whigs now! For my part I feel proud of our country that she at length has set an example to the Nations of peacefully repairing the time worn edifice of her Government, & that with the most reverential regard for the old place & model of the Buildings instead of trying to cement a gaudy & untried theoretical pill with the blood of thousands of citizens. I trust they will have sufficient firmness to avoid on one hand the ravages of the radical as will they have combated the silly tho more respectable prejudices of the old Tories who believed devoutly in the faith "that whatever is is right." The selection of the new parliament shews the good sense of the nation an overwhelming part being those who will support such principles.[24]

I sincerely rejoice My dear Sir that you have been so fortunate in your alliance for life, & I honestly own I know none who more richly merit such good fortune both from the [illegible] which your mind is formed to enjoy domestic happiness, and the length of time I am well aware this feeling was a stranger to you at this place. You acted wisely & I am delighted the result has been so fortunate. I trust yet to see the day when I shall have the happiness to renew my [illegible] with yourself, and the honor of being made personally known to her who has so added to your enjoyment of life.

Meantime I am as ever My Dear Sir
Faithfully & firmly thine

JH

23 Alexander Christie was placed in charge of Red River in 1833 when Chief Factor Donald McKenzie was given leave of absence due to ill health.
24 The first election after the passage of the Reform Act of 1832 was held 31 December 1832.

[Letterbook]
N° 9.
Rough Copies Letters by
JHargrave
From 20th July 1833 @ 1st Septr 1834

YF 20th Septr 1833

Mr James Mitchell
Dear Uncle –

I had the pleasure of receiving your kind letter of 8th April last by the arrival of the Company Ship[1] a few days ago, and am rejoiced to find that you all still enjoy your usual health and are prospering in life. I had also letters from my dear parents & relations in Canada last Spring at which time they were all in good health, happy & prospering having been mercifully preserved amid the desolation occasioned by the Cholera Morbus, which had spread over Canada and proved fatal to multitudes in the summer & autumn of last year. We are in some dread of it here also in this sequestered corner of the world, but, thank God, we are so far without any symptoms of it. I think you mentioned in a former letter that my cousin Robert Elliot had gone to America: If so, I am greatly apprehensive that the following notice I met with in a Quebec paper of Septr 1832 refers to him: – "Died at Halifax on the 17th Augt. 1832 – Revd Robert Elliot, of Preston England, formerly pastor of the Independent Congregation of Pendlebury, – a Native of Roxburghshire"[2] I have nothing regarding any of the family except what you have told me.

I have read with much interest what you tell me of the Course of public affairs and the alterations brought round by the Reform Bill. I am also a bit of a Whig, and cordially wish success to every step which may improve the condition of my countrymen. I fully expect such results from that measure, should the nation & its representatives now do their duty. I regret however to perceive the ferment occasioned by the elections throughout the Country, and dread that the loss occasioned to the lower Classes by the waste of their time in attending to politics will more than

---

1 The *Prince Rupert*, under Capt. Bell, arrived 6 September at York Factory.
2 Rev. Robert Elliot started a Burgher group in 1831 in Musquodoboit, Nova Scotia, that was to become a Congregational Church. He was not ordained and died in 1832. Reid, *Musquodoboit Pioneers*, 2:799.

counterbalance the direct benefits they will for some time experience from it. The discussion of public Measures is also a thirsty duty, and the Ale House or Whisky Tavern is the natural House of Assembly to the Village Clubs. I have some fears that the Moral & religious Character of my countrymen will suffer by the experiment. I trust however that this will only be for a season, and that as the novelty of the thing wears off, they will leave the duties of public life to those who have time to spend in it, and consider more fully act their part by the weight of their vote when the periods arrive fixed by the law of the land for asking the opinions of the citizens at large. Political Clubs & Political Agitators have been the bane of all countrys subjected to their influence.

The alterations in your neighborhood which you mention have also been very interesting to me and when I visit Britain again Roxburgh and Selkirkshires will be the places where I will pass most of my time. I grieve to see that our respected Countryman Sir Walter Scott[3] has at length paid the debt of nature, an event I am certain hastened by his honourable anxiety to discharge his obligations to his Creditors. I should like much to hear how his affairs have been settled, whether Abbotsford still belongs to the family, and how his Son is liked in the neighborhood. Is Fyshe[4] still Schoolmaster in Galashiels, & I would like to know what is become of Rob.[r] Redpath who was a comrade of mine at his school. His father I believe was a Shepherd in the neighborhood. The Rev.[d] M.[r] Henderson[5] of Galashiels by whom he was much noticed, or any of my old school fellows about you, would be able to say.

My circumstances since I last wrote you are much improved and I have now a certainty that with health I will realise a competency for old age in this land. I trust in 5 or 6 years hence, should I be spared, to pay you a

---

3 Sir Walter Scott (1771–1832) was a prolific historical novelist and poet who was popular throughout Europe during his lifetime. When his publishing company nearly collapsed, rather than declare bankruptcy, he placed his home, Abbotsford House, and income into a trust belonging to his creditors and wrote his way out of debt.

4 Robert Fyshe was elected in 1810 schoolmaster at the parish school in Galashiels. He finally retired in 1849 and died in 1850 in his sixty-first year. Hall, *History of Galashiels*, 453, 457.

5 Rev. James Henderson, 1787–1858, was ordained in 1810 as the pastor of a Burgher congregation in Galashiels whose first meeting house and manse were completed in 1806. Rankin, "Congregational Reminiscences," 52–3.

visit, meantime with kind love to my dear Aunt & to all my cousins I am my Dear Uncle
Your affectionate Nephew

JH

YF 26 Septr 1833

J.G. McTavish Esq
My Dear Sir

As a packet will be leaving this in a day or two for the South I set about producing a few pages to give you a sort of Panoramic view of such matters in the north as I imagine may prove of interest & which may not reach you through other mediums. This vessel[6] this season was unnaturally late in arrival having only cast up on the 4th Inst. – since which time we have been up to the lugs in getting her emptied & refilled with the Home cargo. This has been accomplished, the packet was sent on board yesterday and she is now on the eve of crossing the Bar, – I trust yet in good time for the homeward voyage. Old Bill[7] still sails her, but is now so gouty & infirm that I believe this may be among the last of his fields. By her we had an import of several Gents – Messrs Hutchinson,[8] W. McTavish[9] & McKenzie[10] for the Service, with M^r McAllum & Mrs Lowman[11]

6 The *Prince Rupert*.
7 Captain Benjamin Bell.
8 John Hutchison, clerk, was to spend the winter at Severn in York district. He had returned home on leave of absence in September 1832 for a season for his health. Cowie, *Minutes*, 705.
9 William Mactavish (1815–1870) joined the HBC in 1833 and was posted as apprentice clerk at Norway House in 1833–34. He was Hargrave's future brother-in-law.
10 Hector McKenzie (1811–), a Scotsman who began as an apprentice clerk with the HBC from 1833 to 1835 in the Northern Department.
11 In 1832, David Jones, the Church of England missionary in Red River, proposed a boarding-school or seminary "for the moral improvement, religious instruction, and general education of Boys; the sons of Gentlemen belonging to the Fur Trade." The Red River Academy, the first English-speaking high school in the northwest, was privately financed by Jones but was dependent on Governor Simpson and the HBC's Northern Council for students and patronage. Construction of the academy's buildings was completed in 1833 and a female seminary was set up within the academy. Jones

together with a maid servant for the Messes Establishment, designed for the formation of the Boarding School at R.R. – under the management of the Clergy. Your young relative is a fine gentlemanly well informed fellow of hale constitution, smart & active – the proper metal for an intelligent & efficient Trader. The other, M{cKenzie, is also a strapping Youth, fresh from his native glens, with sufficient education for the country, possessed of much application to the desk – and is good humoured & agreeable. Both are in my estimation formed to rise in the Service. The latter is a nephew of our friend Finlayson, and resembles him greatly in person, mind & manners. Mr Christie left this for R.R. – on the 16th inst. – and had taken Mr M{c}T[avish] – with him to Nor. Ho – where he purposes placing him for the winter under the initiation of Mr Ross.[12] I should under other circumstances have liked to have seen him here, but as matters stand, believe his winter will pass as happy for himself elsewhere. Mr Christie was speaking to me on the subject, I gave this as my opinion, which entirely coincided with his own. I have no doubt Donald will do his utmost to make him intimate with the routine in theory, & the business now transacted at Nor. Ho- will bring his hand not a little into the practice. Hutchinson Started with the fall boat for the Saskatch[ewa]{n} which stayed remained here to take in a party of the new hands to that wintering Ground, & from Carlton will find his way to Athabasca to aid the upper Ranks in that District which this season is peculiarly weak. Mr Charles[13] is also, I understand, in hopes of a rotation next season preparatory to retirement which makes the sending in of Mr H. this season the more necessary to allow of his coming out conveniently in spring. [William] M{c}Kintosh is also growling & unhappy and is expected out in spring. His son in law [Andrew] Wilson[14] has left the Service & gone to R.R. He was here in summer – determined to get rid of his wife who it seems had with the aid of her Brother in law Master Ben Sinclair, been

---

asked the Church Missionary Society to find a "Governess ... of matured Christian experience" and a "Tutor ... practically acquainted with Land Surveying." Mrs Mary Lowman and John Macallum arrived in the fall of 1833 to fill these positions. Johnson and Bredin, "Jones, David Thomas."

12 Donald Ross was chief factor at Norway House at this time.
13 John Charles.
14 J.G. McTavish refers to him as "my poor simple Steersman." John George McTavish to James Hargrave from Moose Factory, 18 December 1833. James Hargrave and family fonds, LAC.

[illegible] his forehead. By persuasion of Mr C. he has gone to ruminate over the matter for a season in the Colony till he can set her father. The old Croche[15] seems almost in open rebellion, making ducks & drakes of public orders, upsetting attires & confusing in his own peculiarly happy style: His talk is full of breach of promises & what not, – closed with determination of leaving his District next spring. On the whole, the firm bridle hand of our worthy chief[16] is in many quarters much wanted; and indeed the signs of the times are such, that should he not next season be enabled to assume the reins, I fear anarchy & insubordination will mar the prospects of futurity not a little. We have however heard from him at Michipicoten, & have great hopes that the relaxation of this winter will set him firm on his feet again. R.R. is the worst wintering Ground for him in the country. What with Clergy, Churches, Schools, Farms, Cattle Companies, litigious Colonists & beggars, his days & nights are passed in labor & anxiety. 'Tis hard – 'tis too much for any one single frame to endure in continuance; and what makes it the more to be regretted is the greatest trouble & annoyance to him arise frequently from matters altogether unconnected with the trade, or of such trifling import as are best settled by an inferior officer: but while there, not a wife can sell her butter or a farmer his grain without requesting an audience of the Govr with a petition for higher prices strengthened by pleas of poverty &^{ccc}, to all which his door is ever open. Should he again remain in the country I trust he will be allowed to select a more quiet wintering Ground.

The Indent for this quarter next season was closed by M^r [Alexander] Christie before his departure, and tho' studied with great care, could not be squeezed within narrower limits than £20 M a great deviation from the Am^t fixed by the Minutes of Council. It is however all needed, not a shilling worth being asked for which prudence as I think would blot out.

15 John Stuart, chief factor at Fort Alexander, where Nancy McKenzie and her daughters had ended up, had joined with former Nor'Wester (and Nancy McKenzie's uncle) Donald McKenzie, chief factor at Fort Garry at Red River, to mount a vigorous campaign to discredit John George McTavish. The two of them did their utmost to make McTavish atone for his abandoning his country wife and marrying a Scottish woman in 1830.
16 Governor George Simpson had a mild stroke in Red River. Following the annual meeting, Simpson and his wife were then taken by express canoe to Lachine, from where they travelled to New York and England. While Simpson recuperated, Frances delivered a healthy girl in December 1833.

The Colony growing like an incubus on the shoulders of the Trade is loud & high in its demands: – The business connected with it is now such that to preserve regularity & escape waste I feel it will be necessary to fall back on the plan suggested by yourself 6 or 7 years ago – that is to have a complete line of separation drawn between Colony & Trade supplies, with separate Invoices & the packages for the Colony made up originally in such a shape & to such weight as would admit of their being sent on by the Winter Road the same fall as received. Without some such model we must have a Depot annually in the country equal to both the Northern Districts & the Colony Outfits which together with the necessary surplus for this Depot would almost reach to 100 pCent on our Outfit. This has been bro^t under the Gov^{rs} notice, and I trust he will this winter make such arrangements as will ensure it having a full examination & some settled plan adopted.

The Sloop from Ungava[17] reached us so late that it was found too great a risk to return her this season. Mr Duncan has accordingly been sent home by the Prince Rupert in order that such arrangements might be made in England for its supply next spring as may be deemed expedient.

We have heard little yet of the progress of Capt. Back[18] & party. An Indent for next season equal to about 45 P^s Goods reached us this fall from him at portage La Loche which has been completed & forwarded

---

17 The *Beaver* was commanded by sloop master Thomas Duncan. Badly battered on her only voyage from Chimo back into Hudson Bay, she was unable to return to the fort. Duncan then took a passage on the *Prince Rupert* which was also obliged to turn back and winter in Hudson Bay on account of the ice conditions. He transferred to the *Prince of Wales* which wintered at Charlton Island. Davies, *Northern Quebec*, 155.

18 Captain George Back (1796–1878) was a naval officer, Arctic explorer, and artist. His 1833–35 expedition was undertaken to search for John Ross, who had not been heard of since he had set out on an attempt at a northwest passage in 1829. In the summer of 1833 he searched for the Great Fish River which was supposed to flow north into the Arctic Ocean. After locating it at the end of August he returned to winter at Fort Reliance at the eastern end of Great Slave Lake. In the spring of 1834 he heard of Ross's safe return to England and explored the Great Fish River and its inlet that year before wintering again in Fort Reliance and returning to England in 1835. Holland, "Back, Sir George."

to Norway House. He there met with M^r McLeod[19] from McKenzies River, who I am happy to find volunteered at once to accompany him. With such aids as he and Annance,[20] tis hoped – if no lives be saved by them – at all events none will be lost.

I have yet had no time to look into papers tho files are around me, and therefore shall not this time sound my horn over the ruins of Toryism: I fear yet however that all is not right, and that both Whig & Tory will have to unite to keep under the Demon of Radicalism whose horns seem to have an ambition to usurp the mitre. This should never be – "The widest freedom, consistent with security" is my motto. Such could never be obtained under the rule of O'Connell,[21] Cobbett,[22] Hunt[23] & Co – I long much to have an opportunity to set these matters to rights during a bonny evening chat with you. God knows whether we ever shall see the day; but in fond expectation of it & with grateful remembrance of all your past kindness to me I remain
My Dear Sir
Ever faithfully & affectionately thine

JH.

19 Alexander Roderick McLeod, chief trader at McKenzie's River in 1832. He had been granted leave to withdraw from the district in 1833 owing to bad health but apparently decided to help out with the search. Cowie, *Minutes*, 680.
20 François Noel Annance (1789–), a Native of Abenaki background, was working as a clerk at Fort Simpson in the Mackenzie River district in 1833–1834.
21 Probably Daniel O'Connell (1775–1847), Ireland's predominant political leader in the first half of the nineteenth century, who campaigned for Catholic emancipation and repeal of the union between Ireland and Great Britain.
22 Probably William Cobbett (c. 1763–1835), a British journalist and reformer. He became a central figure in the agitation for parliamentary reform. After the Reform Bill was passed in 1832, he was elected to Parliament and became a member of the Radical minority.
23 Probably Henry Hunt (1773–1835), a British radical political reformer who advocated universal suffrage and annual parliaments. He opposed the 1832 Reform Act as it did not grant the vote to working-class males. He was defeated in the 1833 general election.

YF 8 Feby 1834

J.G. McTavish Esq
My Dear Sir

Scarcely any thing belonging to this land except the sight of your ever remembered hand yesterday could at present have roused me to this exertion. For these nine days I have been suffering horribly under a violent Bowel Complaint attending by Vomiting Costiveness [constipation] & the most excrutiating pains in the intestines & loins, which has reduced me to a perfect shadow; & rendered me incapable of the smallest exertion. In this however I am not alone[24] for it is a singular fact that at this moment the whole of our Mess is prostrated by the same disease except Miles[25] who was attacked about a month ago & is now recovered. Several of the people are likewise laid up from the same malady among the others poor George [Thorn] who is at this moment writhing in agony: – I trust however through the mercy of God we will all recover: – Nothing fatal as yet has happened. Under these circumstances it is with add^l pain that I am obliged to lay aside replying to your most excellent sheets for the present & content my self with noting such matters as may seem to require immediate attention. George says his fiddle cost him less than 20 s[hillings] so that whatever you get beyond that will be so much gain to him. I shall see the 10s paid to him next summer for his images – we send you on a Glazing Diamond. I find I have been premature in what I said about the transfer this season to your credit from Colin Fraser. It seems that foolish Lad has taken to himself a wife, bought guns Horses & Dogs &^c till he is plunged himself in Debt as deeply as to prevent

---

24 Known now as "The York Factory Complaint," an epidemic, sometimes fatal, disease ravaged the post on Hudson Bay during the winters of 1833–34, 1834–35, and 1835–36. Thirty-two people identified by name became ill and three died. Three medical practitioners suffered from the disorder, which was characterized by abdominal colic, weight loss, nervousness, a marked tendency to relapse, loss of function of the arms or legs and, in the most severe cases, convulsions, stupor, and death. No firm diagnosis was made at the time. Hargrave was stricken the first winter and suffered relapses each of the next two years. By June 1836 it was taken for granted that Hargrave would have to leave York Factory to recuperate. The epidemic seriously affected the running of the post at times. Roland, "Saturnism," 61, 65.

25 Robert Miles was chief trader in charge of York Factory from 1828 to 1833 before going on furlough to England the following year.

further transfers this season. M^r [Alexander] Christie writes me from RR last Dec^r – "This is also the reason (*Debt*) of my not ordering the transfer to M^r McTavishs credit as agreed upon, therefore if the Moose Express men have not departed from YF when this comes to hand, have the goodness to make offer of my best respects to M^r M^cT – & mention the circumstances – at the same time please say that the transfer will be observed in O^t 1834." It would seem to me that Mr Christie was ignorant of the Gov^rs promise about Mr William.[26] Mr Ross[27] had heard of his coming out & had petitioned M^r C to have him. This Mr Christie mentioned to me & asked my opinion as to the best plan for him. From the changes which had come round him, I believed conscientiously & still so believe that he would be better about this for the winter on a/c of several reasons, and on this subject my opinion happened to be in entire accordance with his, and he was sent to Nor. Ho. for the season. I hope however to see him at YF yet, in better times, when I shall be more at liberty to give information to my young countryman. What I said of him before is my sincere unvarnished opinion. He left his [illegible] trunk with me and I have been overhauling his vols. I find several among these indicative of a superior education & a thinking mind. His manners are diffident not bashful, & the remarks drawn from him in conversation are frequently urged with prudence & judgment beyond what is usually found in lads of his age. I may be mistaken but from what I can gather by looking at into & around him I think you will find him turn out what I have formerly written of him.

We have yet heard nothing further regarding Capt. Back & party. There certainly is a chance tho' almost one to a million of their finding the spark of life after 5 winters among the icebergs of the North. But as I see it in common parlance it appears a wild Goose Chase more calculated to procure Capt. B. a step [promotion] than to save the lives of British Subjects. The undertaking however is well & tho' ever so hopeless is due to the memory of a gallant man and his party, in the same light as funeral honors are paid is departed merit.

I thank you heartily for the 2 papers. They have wiled me through a night of pain. I with you forsee many changes yet to come round but have strong faith in the good sense & prudence of the *Middle* Classes of our Native Land.

26 William Mactavish.
27 Donald Ross was chief trader at Norway House in 1833–34.

I cannot enter into the painful subject of the Rupert:[28] you will have enough of it in the public documents. Suffice it to say that the insurance is the last anchor for security from immense loss to all concerned. The Cargo is pulp. Poor old Bell[29] is become quite imbecile & is only so much lumber amid the general wreck. Mannock[30] is no more, & the men are under no subordination. The whole is a burden of troubles & loss.

Excuse me I beg of you that I have made this sheet no longer or more interesting: Materials are around me, the spirit is willing but the head sinks over the page: – Should God spare me I will not forget what I owe you. I would also have written a few lines to our worthy chief but suspect that this will not reach you before your spring packet starts for Michipicoten. Should it however so happen will you have the goodness to make my apologies to him & tell him of my present condition. Please also add, that should I recover even a month hence, no deficiency or irregularity will be found in the store business next summer.

God bless you My Dear Sir & believe me ever firmly & faithfully thine

JH.

P.S. Feby 12th I now find myself much recovered since I wrote you a few days ago – and hope to be equal to Desk work again in a week hence.

YF 26th July 1834

My Dear Mother

I rejoice exceedingly that a kind providence has again mercifully preserved us all for another year to learn and rejoice at the great measure of happiness which he has continued to bestow on us during our journey through this life. Both you & my dear father as well as my sister Mary, you tell me, have been sick this last winter, but thanks to the Almighty we have all been preserved, and in my case I am now stout[31] & hearty as ever: may you all, my dearest Mother, have now the same reasons for

---

28 The *Prince Rupert* was forced by ice to winter at Churchill in 1833–34.
29 Capt. Benjamin Bell was master of the *Prince Rupert*.
30 John Mannock was master of the *Prince Rupert* and died 1 October 1833.
31 Hargrave appears to have been a large man, both in his portrait (perhaps commissioned after his rise to a chief factorship in 1844) and in the measurements he provided around 1833 regarding clothing. His chest size then

gratitude to our preserver. My disease has scarcely any name by which I could make you understand it. It began with violent vomiting, & after which I lost all appetite, my bowels became extremely *bound*, and for about a fortnight I could not, by every aid of medicine, get passage in my body. This I last obtained by means of a powerful purge aided by other medicines after which I gradually got better, and though greatly reduced recovered my appetite & strength, so that I have been able to go through my public duties actively & easily as ever.

I am very sorry to learn that my good old father has at length been deprived of his Sight so much as to disable him from reading, one of his greatest pleasures! Worthy old man! I feel for him as if it were myself – yet still have hopes that with return of better health he will also return again the power of seeing: – He has however the consolation under such a painful dispensation, to be able to occupy his mind pleasantly by looking back over the prospect of a Well Spent & blameless life filled with fewer things to regret & more good done to your fellow men than most who pass through nearly 80 years can in conscience say they have performed. I know he will say – those are all "filthy rags"[32] – I agree with Him they are so – but I trust he will also agree with me that they are a "Shewing of faith by Works"[33] – and are strong proofs that sound doctrine governs the heart from which such fruits proceed. In this light the recollection of them must ever be pleasing to the reflecting mind during the evening days of this pilgrimage. *
*This part inserted at O in my fathers letter

I again enclose you my Bill for the same Sum as I sent you last year, which I leave entirely to your own will, in laying it out, only requesting that you will look on it entirely as a present or rather a trifle I give towards paying the great debt of love & reverence I owe to such a mother as few Sons have been blessed with. May you live long my dearest mother to receive the same from your long absent & loving son.

---

    was 42", waist 38½", neck 16", head diameter 7 3/8", leg inseam 32½", and foot length 11½".

32 "But we are all as an unclean thing, and all our righteousnesses are as filthy rags; and we all do fade as a *leaf*; and our iniquities, like the wind, have taken us away." *King James Bible*, Isaiah 64:6.

33 "Yea, a man may say, Thou hast faith, and I have works: shew me thy faith without thy works, and I will shew thee my faith by my works." *King James Bible*, James 2:18.

I again remain here another season, and in the absence of the excellent Gentleman[34] under whom I have served so long, am placed in his room, to have the entire charge of York Factory & all the Coys Servants living here being one of the highest & most important situations in this Land. I have much anxiety on the Subject as the Situation is new to me, but if steadiness, & carefulness & a fine sense of what I felt from hard treatment when I was a poor Servant – will have any effect in aiding me to be a good Master I trust I will yet have some Chance of succeeding. Say nothing about this also to your neighbours: – I desire this very much. I fear I will not be able to write you all this season, but tell my dear brothers & sisters that my love to them is warm as ever & that good fortune makes no change in the affections of him who was once the poor Cow Herd – Jamie Hargrave. I will yet if I do not get too fat try a match at snow ball with both of them when I return among you on some future year. May you also my dearest Mother be then still preserved to welcome, to embrace and to ask a blessing on the head of your Most Affectionate Son

Jamie

YF 26 July 1834

My Dear Father

I regret extremely to learn by my mothers letter that your weak eye sight has deprived me of the pleasure of getting a letter from yourself this season. I was also very sorry to learn that both of you had been so sick last winter; but have great reason for thankfulness in hearing that you are now both much recovered ˣ I sincerely hope also that with returning strength your eyes will again recover so much as to allow of your being able to enjoy your especial source of pleasure the power of reading your Bible. – ᴼ In the mean time however you have the consolation under such a painful dispensation to be &ᶜ – – – – – – – – – –

I have also myself been sick last winter for about 3 weeks but am now thank God! stout and healthy as ever. We are surely a family favored by him above many, and ought to shew our sense of this by our especial regard to what he has informed us is our duty towards him. You have in almost every letter my dear father drawn my attention to this subject, and every one of these have been treasured up by me among my most valuable

---

34 Probably Alexander Christie.

papers so that they may ever throughout my life be a fathers advice to me: – May god grant me grace to follow the course pointed out to me by such a parent. Take particular care of your health my dear father & carefully avoid all chances by which it may be injured. Gather every pleasure which your position in life can now afford you & let those labor for you for whom you have labored so long. I hope through the Mercy of God to learn for many years yet of your welfare & to be able to assure you that I am as ever
Your Most Affectionate Son

JHargrave

YF – 26 July 1834

Miss Jane Hargrave
My Dear Jane

    I thank you kindly for your long and well written letter, which I am really sorry to say I can only repay this season by a few hasty lines, such is the crowd of business by which I am just now surrounded, & such the load of cares which at this season lay upon my shoulders. I was for some time very unwell last winter, but thank God! I am now again stout & healthy as ever. You seem to have passed a busy winter at your loom, & may make money by it should your payment be secure, but working for the poor around you who are more ready to pay with words than Dollars I think you act rightly in resolving to confine your labours to own family should they hereafter reward you no better. I observe what you hint about our brother Ruthers design of taking another Helpmate. He writes me also this season but says nothing on the subject: – I think however he does very right as a father must find himself in many difficulties surrounded by a small family without any to take proper care of them. When I write my uncle J. Mitchel in the fall I shall not omit telling him of your present condition & that his letter has been received. Remember me also to my worthy old friend Mr Barber. I rejoice to hear of his good Health at the Patriarchal age to which he has attained. He was the first Native of the United States I had met with in Canada, & the impression he made on my mind there in regard to the Character & morals of the New Eng[lan]{d} States left such a favourable opinion with me regarding them which has never been effaced, but which is, rather increased by every thing I have learned regarding them Since. God bless you my Dear Sister & believe me ever &{c} JH

YF 3 Aug' 1834

M' A. Hargrave
My Dear Andrew

I thank you kindly for your excellent letter of 16 March last, and have read with much pleasure the sketch you give me of my old acquaintances in your neighborhood. You will observe, by looking over them that tis only the sober & industrious who are prospering, and from the comfortable & happy state in which you yourselves are now, I draw strong proofs that both you and our brother John, are among the most Steady of the young fellows about Beechridge. I am happy to learn that Miss Dewey & M' Struthers are both well & have still a favorable recollection of me; – but am sorry to find that you still write of them by their Maiden Names. Tis now full 14 years since I bade them good bye, and you, or such as feel in want of a persuasive argument with them, should hint that time is no smoother of the brow, or painter of the cheek. Make my kindest remembrances to both of them, and tell them that both are in my debt a letter which I fully expect they will please to try and pay next Spring. Remember me also in the kindest manner to my friends J. & K. Stuart. I rejoice to hear that they are in such prosperous circumstances. Make also my kind Compts. to Jas Struthers, Martha, and to Philip. I am happy to learn they are pushing on so well in their voyage through life. I could run on much further, but what is the use – I must divide my news among you, and from my other letters to you all, you will learn every thing besides which think will interest you, about your
Very affectionate Brother

JH

YF 3 Aug' 1834

M' John Hargrave
My Dear John: I have read with great pleasure the very sensible letter you wrote me last March and I rejoice to find that tho' sickness had visited you last season, yet our dear old parents had been mercifully spared & were on the recovery when you wrote me. It is rather singular that during the very time of their sickness (the month of Feby) I was myself also in a very poor condition, which illness hung about me till the month of May when I gradually recovered & am now stout & healthy as ever. The accts you give me about your farm are very pleasing to me; – with your industry & the experience you are now independent of the world. I

do not hear whether you have yet got lots for yourselves which is a plan you should now be beginning to carry into execution: – that is, living still with our poor old parents whom I trust to your & Andrews care; – but still having a lot in your neighborhood, purchased at first a good bargain, and getting yearly into more value from the improvements you would even as you are, be still able to make upon it. I had the pleasure of seeing my old friend M^r [Duncan] Finlayson here this summer to whom I handed his relations letter which you enclosed me. Mr F. is now on his way to Canada through which he will pass on a voyage to Scotland; and I expect to see him here again in the course of next summer.

I have again this season sent a Bill to my Mother for which you will receive Cash in Lachine Office. It is as usual drawn in your name, and you will not omit writing your Name on its back before you present it for payment. Do see that our dear Mother get out of it every little comfort of which she stands in need. God bless you My Dear Brother – Yours ever Affectionately

JH

YF 5 Augt 1834

J.G. McTavish Esq. – Moose Factory
My Dear Sir

Your very kind sheet of 2nd Ult[im]^o has just been handed me, & that of 18 May reached me by our worthy chief about the end of June. [illegible] both these much prized favors I snatch up my pen, to make such reply as the spur of the moment & the cares of summer will allow to get utterance. First – as to my self: – I am again, thanks to God – well and hearty as ever; – tho I had certainly last May a hard tug for life. I could spin a yarn of some length about the scenes of last winter, but at present shall sum them up in the few words, that all combined to produce the most miserable winter I have yet spent in this land. Despite my collapsing in bed however I had the store work [illegible] as in former years, & by that means was enabled to get through the summer campaign sleekly as usual having cleared out the last inlander on the 17th ult^o. Poor [Robert] Miles got horrified at the idea of a hole & a shovel at the Old Factory, so to save his 14 Stones or thereabout of Bile steeped Beef, has got a certificate of ill health, to admit of his visiting England, and worthless I am stuck into the Hole he has evacuated, a nest I fear me I may not do great credit to, – but, courage! – I shall not sink without [illegible]. M^r [John] Ballenden is now Account^{nt}, a young fellow who came out the year you left this. He has a clear head & a good knowledge of the business so I have small fears about his success. He is besides a most amiable mess mate, and on the whole I look forward to quiet & happy winter this season. Your young Nephew[35] joins me from Nor. Ho – is one of my band, and you [may] rely on my taking some pains in enlightening him on Depot business.

Now for a glance at the world beyond our packets. In the North Countrie public matters, since I know this land never flowed in such an eccentric channel. All old things have become new; & from the true radical reason, because they were old. Of the two extremes commend me yet to Old Toryism: inasfar as over caution is superior to a blind & obstinate itch for change merely because such a system of things *is*. A cure however has come round, and that in a somewhat unexpected yet still very natural way. The doubtful issue of the old Croches[36] coming out is at last fixed by the circumstance of poor Mary having found herself unable to resist the manly attractions of Annance[37] who had been sent in there last summer. A discovery & a war in miniature was the result, attended by all the usual accompaniments of arms, personal violence, imprisonment, & guards. Both parties filed Bills of accusation before Council; – both most voluminous, minute in detail & [illegible] broadly expressed. It fell to my lot to entertain [illegible] & by reading them in Council, & I speak seriously when I say that I believe in consequence I never spoke so much *Barrody* [?] in all my life together, – composed of all topics from simple fornication up to the unheard of charge of a husband commiting a rape on his own wife. But to avoid this dirt, – let me hasten to the end. The Council declined interfering in what they justly considered a private charge, – not a hint being contained in the whole involving the Coys affairs with it. Both parties are hastening out, & both breathing threats of fire & revenge, the one, for the seducing of what was the owner says he considered "his legal wife before God & man," the other spouting about arranging imprisonment, personal violence including an

---

35 William Mactavish moved from Norway House to York Factory in 1834 at his uncle's insistence.
36 John Stuart went on furlough for health reasons from 1835 to 1839.
37 François Noel Annance was clerk at Fort Simpson in the Mackenzie River district in 1833–34. He was appointed but did not serve as clerk in 1834 at Oxford House in the Island Lake district and he retired to Montreal in 1834–35. In 1833 he became involved with John Stuart's wife, Mary Taylor.

assault for the purpose of castration, and bolstered up with charges of robbery (obtaining signatures to Bills in favour of the seduced) for the full amount of Annances means by threats & violence. The details would fill a volume – but the upshot is at present that both have full permission to leave the country & the result may be that our unfortunate character for Morals will yet receive a deeper dye by this exposure of the acts of two worthless & degraded fools. It may not however go so far, as I ever yet would not wonder to see Asop[?] & his Sposa come out lovingly as ever in the lap of the Portage Boats, if I may so judge from his language regarding her throughout all the wordy [illegible] where she is described as "contaminated in body but not in mind" – Annance is at present at Nor. Ho. Elsewhere all go prosperously & smoothly as regards the Trade. Our worthy Factor old [John] Charles, has done well in Athabasca. By the way he is here at present going on furlough to R.R. for the winter, & I did not omit classing him among those friends to whom you desired your respects & apologies for lack of manuscript. McKintosh rests this in R.R. but comes out next season. English R^r has also turned out well & Saskatchewan fairly as regards furs, though I dread their lack of pemmican will pinch us here this season. Further [illegible] the lines the returns are a fair average & the new Country districts yield their usual quarter, while the Beaver are fast increasing both here & on each side of us.

The Churchill wreck[38] is in process of cure as far as is practicable. M^r [John Lee] Lewes who is there with full powers over all has got the whole dried & at our last dates from thence, the end of last month, the most had been repacked. Nor ought Little [Robert] Harding to be forgotten. He has breathed nothing but steam all last winter, & had from 75–100 Bags dried previous to receiving aid in the beginning of April. The Rupert had been got off the Rock on which she has lain all winter, tho' not till it was shivered by gunpowder it having past so far through & being so firmly wedged into her timbers as to resist all other modes of ejection. The repairs will soon be through it is expected, as the requisite Oak plank was bro^t from R.R by Mr Christie & all naval stores (of which the vessel was totally naked in a way of sailing stock) has been furnished from this place. Tis a fact they had not a spare yard of canvas to repair a split sail. We are now daily expecting her here where her wants again will be innumerable. Poor old [Capt. Benjamin] Bell has become quite imbecile & will be superceded in his charge by the second mate for the

---

38 The *Prince Rupert* was forced to winter at Churchill.

homeward voyage. This last is however a determined Drunkard & our Sloop Master [Thomas] Duncan will I believe be sent also, in order to have somewhat of steadiness & sobriety on board.

I have been examining the Books of '29 & enclose you a note of such credits to your name as I find for that season. It is not explained for what consideration these sums were paid. I have been trying also to collect information as to who else might have rec[eive]^d copies of the pictures but can get hold of nothing definite on the subject. I have got transferred to Georges[39] credit & to Mr Faries[40] Acc^t the sum of 50s you mention. The poor fellow is now recovered, but leaves this place for Red River in the fall with Govr Simpson, he being now every season laid up with the Rheumatism a couple of months in the depths of winter. Gibeault[41] is his successor. This poor fellow has also broke loose again from his bonds anent Liquor, – and I must try & re-reform him. I fear me 'twill be as knitting ropes of sand.

I was greatly rejoiced to meet our Govr this spring so much improved, and am happier still to say that he now seems firmly set on his legs again. He is at this date stout, Ruddy & active, & from every thing I can perceive about him, I would say, barring accidents, he has a dozen good Campaigns in His belly yet. That is if he would but spare himself.

Have you seen that "Buzzing Letter" my old well wishing Colin [Robertson] has sent to the Northern Council this season? It [illegible] it has met with its answer – neatly & pointedly expressed, – all courtesy & all ice. Heavy lugs of cash however have been shoveled out by votes, much [illegible] – to my discontent who have been accustomed to think wages covered [illegible]. You may judge of my inherent spirit of obstinacy to all which does not accord with my own opinion & under all circumstances; when I add, that the first time our Chief did me the honor to ask my opinion in Council, I gave my voice in opposition to his motion. I fear that he will think he has caught a Radical. The alterations in the Deed [illegible] suggested by their Honors have been carried, I believe, without materially hurting such commissioned Gents as are capable of service. This is as it should be.

---

39 George Thorn.
40 Hugh Faries (1779–1852), a former North Wester, became a chief trader at the union and chief factor in 1838. He was in the Kenogamissie District from 1827 to 1837.
41 Belonie Gibeault (c. 1820–), who was from Montreal, was listed as butler at York Factory in 1829/30. HBCA, B. 239/a/141.

Mr Christie, who is still here, & to whom I mentioned your apologies for not addressing him at present, desires me to convey to you his kindest regards, & to mention that he will write you fully from R.R. – being as you, at present, perfectly worried with labor, & also, in his own native Doric, desired me to tell you that "we sometimes have aw'fu' work o'it this summer – but we aye manage to shouther thro" –

Now this you will own is passable as the work of 2 nights from 9 to 12 – after the worrying of the day is over – I shall still find somewhat to say when our winter packet gets under way – Meantime with respect & kindly regard I am
My Dear Sir
Every Yours mo: faithfully

JH

YF 8 Augt 1834

Mr Ruther Hargrave
Dear Brother

I have read with great pleasure your kind letter of 30th Jany last, and sympathize deeply with you in the afflictions you have endured in late years. A father with a young & helpless family around him with none to manage his indoor affairs must labour under the greatest difficulties & anxiety of mind; – and were I in your situation I should consider it one of my first duties to them to provide them with a careful & prudent second mother, which I am certain would add both to your prosperity & happiness.

I see you have last winter been paying a visit to our worthy old parents, a happiness I am, in this distant land, entirely deprived of; – They tell me they have been both sick last Spring, but at their years we have great reason to be thankful that the Almighty has mercifully preserved them. – I was myself also very sick during the Months of Feby & March last, and it was not till the Month of May that I was completely restored to health. I am now however healthy and strong as ever, but am again appointed to remain at this place, which is on the Coast of Hudsons Bay, and under a colder climate than any you have ever experienced. The snow lies on the ground above 8 months in the year & the summer is so short & soil bad that even a potato or Turnip cannot grow in it larger than a bean. We are however supplied with every thing from England, and through our long & gloomy winter, are both comfortable and happy. I cannot say when I will leave this country altogether, but hope to be able

at some no distant year to visit Canada for a winter when I will not fail to find you out. I would like to hear how you are prospering, of which you have said nothing in your letter. Write me again whenever you have an opportunity & believe me always
Your Affectionate Brother

JH

P.S. Give my kind love to Joseph & his family. Tho I have written them either once or twice I do not think I have had a letter from them since I came to this land.

YF 8 Augt 1834

Mr Ja^s Ross – ChateauGuay
My Dear Brother

Tho' I have not had a single line from either you or Mary this season, yet I cannot let the Canoe start for Montreal without writing you a few words. I heard from our parents that my Sister was sickly, but I sincerely trust that long ere this time she is again recovered. I was myself very unwell for most part of the Spring but thank God! am now again well & hearty as ever. I remain for the ensuing winter at this place where I have now been full Seven years, and for all the desolate appearance of the country and the little knowledge we gather of what is passing elsewhere, I am happy & contented with my lot in life. Do not omit another season in letting me hear of your welfare. One of my greatest pleasures every spring is to receive all your letters & to figure to myself the condition you are all in, and as far as I can make myself feel as if I were among you. Give my kind love to my dear Sister & to all your little family. I am personally a stranger to you all but her, but am sure when we meet we will feel as if we had been intimate from boyhood. Good by my Dear Ross – Yours Mo. Affectionately

JH

[Letterbook]
No. 10
Rough Copies Letters by
JHargrave
From 2nd September 1834 @ 13th July 1835

York Factory 7 Septr 1834

Mr Ja^s Mitchell   Galashiels Scotland
Dear Uncle

    I received your very kind letter of 7th April last about 2 weeks ago, and as our Ship[1] for England sails tomorrow, I have caught up my pen to make some answer such as the few leisure moments I can presently command will allow me. I had letters last spring from all my dear relations in Canada, and was indeed rejoiced to find that they were all at that time in good health: – My dear old father is however I fear me fast sinking into the vale of life; his hearing is nearly gone, and his eyesight so weak that he could not see to write me when the others sent off their letters: otherwise his health is said to be good. I had myself a narrow escape for life last winter, being stretched on a sick bed for upwards of two months by a severe bowel complaint which reduced me to a perfect skeleton. Thanks to God however I got over it and am now as healthy & nearly as stout as before. This place is again my wintering Ground for the ensuing year and the Coy has honored my length of services by placing me this season in the Command of the Factory, one of the most respectable & important situations they have to bestow in this land. I do not mention this to you out of vanity my dear uncle, but rather from a feeling of deep gratitude to my best of parents who out of the scantiest means which the poor in our native land possess contrived to bestow on me an education which none of my other brothers ever had a chance of. For myself, the remembrance of my lowly origin – the Poor Shepherd & *even poorer* Dominie[2] that I was, – shall ever preserve me from running riot into the vanities of the world. You will find me, should we ever be so happy as to meet again, – still Jamie Hargrave. I rejoice to hear that my dear aunt & all my cousins are yet in life & good health. Were I now at the lee side of my Aunts Marys tea Table or with you at a modest tumbler of punch, I could tell

---

1 The *Prince George* left York Factory 12 September.
2 Schoolmaster, from the Latin. DSL.

you in an hour more of myself, more of our Canada friends, and more of this country than a quire of letters could contain: – but this for some time cannot be thought of, so my utmost limits of news must still be circumscribed by a few words about myself still fewer about relations & the assurance that I am as ever, your unchanged & affectionate Nephew.

JH

P.S. Make no change in the address of your letters – simply as before. I will be much displeased at any alteration.

YF 1 Dec' 1834

J.G. McTavish Esq – Moose Factory
My Dear Sir

We will soon again be making up our Packet for you, and that part of it my previous sheet to you, & the pleasantest part of myself, must not be left to the last. My few public lines will inform you of the outs & ins of routine affairs which therefore require little further notice. Our worthy chief and our no less honest friend Mr Christie both left me for R.R- in Augt the latter on the 12th & the former on the 30th, – leaving poor me to get through the Shipping crush as I best might. With fortunate weather, willing hands, and incessant labour we however succeeded in clearing out the Prince George on the 9th Septr nearly two weeks within the period fixed by her Charter Party, and she left us with a favorable breeze on the 12th so that I trust there will this season be little chance of her revisiting us. The Cargo homewards consisted of some 200 Bales & those composed of Beaver Otters, Martins & mixed Furs, while mostly all the Mussquash of the Season were left here, and at Nor. House, the whole of McKenzie River, with most part of Athabasca, English River & Lac La Pluie Returns. Churchill skins also remain entered at that place for the winter. This scattered work will make '33 look miserable on paper next year, although the returns at our valuation are a good deal above an average.

Several inlanders left us all moving on here in wonted form, the servants are steady & industrious in their duties, & the Govr has favored me with unusual aid this season to get forward the bagging recounts of last year. I believe I mentioned before that your nephew has found me, and I [am] happy to say that I have no reason to consider I prejudged his character in what I formerly said to you of him. He is besides good humoured & yet holds his own among my youngsters, – a steady pen at the Desk & anxious to improve. You may depend on my putting him in the way to do so. His hand writing was but indifferent but in this he is fast mending. We have besides the Gov^{rs} little Esculapius Dr Whiffen,[3] a canty[4] Good Humoured John Bull – but of little use as a Clerk from weak eyes. He is however assiduous & apparently skilful in professional duties, & I will not have occasion to load him with much penmanship. We [illegible] together in the utmost harmony & time glides over, light as a feather. By the way the statement you sent us last summer of add^l wages to be credited our friend Barnston for 1826, 1827 & 1828 – £25 each year, I suspect has been drawn up upon imperfect information given you. The object, as I understand the Secys letter, was to raise his wages for these years to £100 P. Ann[um].; now for 1826 & 1827 he, by our Ledger, has been credited with only £60 P An: which for 1828 he has had the full amount of £100 already. I have therefore got a fresh statement made out with an add^l credit of £40 P ann: for each of the first 2 years, which with interest shows a further am^t in his favour of £7.10.2 in addition to the sum of your statement & which amount will be assumed by the Nor[thern]. Dept – in order that it may also be placed to his credit in your books. This I think will adjust the matter properly & give him £100 P ann. from the expiration of his apprenticeship till the date of his leaving the north. I had a very long letter from him by your summer Packet – written in Feby last from the wretched hole into whch he was stuck. It was sensible, steady tempered & worthy of himself in his best days. I cannot guess at the origin of his obliquity of mind on the single topic of Govr Simpson. It operates on my curiosity like an enigma I never can solve. On all other subjects his mind seems as clear as ever.

 Of northern news there is little to add to what I wrote you in August. As far as I have heard all got safe to their wintering Grounds and the voyaging season closed without accident. After all – Old [John] Stuart still sticks in the country. He came out to the portage, as I suspected, with Mary more loving than ever, and has thought proper to move back again with the boats to be a supernumerary in the north. What may be his future steps it woud defy dentation/dentition[?] to tell. Old Daddy

---

3 Dr Elzeard H. Whiffen, post surgeon, was recruited to look into the mysterious York Factory complaint of 1833–36. He became ill himself and was evacuated.

4 Lively, cheerful, pleasant. DSL.

Smith[5] is in charge of both the northern Districts and I fain hope will put all matters to rights as regards public affairs this winter. It is with much regret I see so many of our Seniors preparing to take flight. Yourself, Smith, Christie & Charles[6] seem all on the move, while the very dregs of the Factorship only stick the closer. I fear me we will feel the want of these best & clearest heads in the country which the next rank do not seem over well qualified to replace. I believe Mr Christie will take his furlough next year and I suspect this is only preparatory to a permanent movement. He has acted well in RR- last winter and indeed met with some trying incidents. Poor Cuth[ber]^t Grant at that place is going the way of most of his race. Ever plunged in liquor when he can come by it – he is just losing respect both among whites & natives.

I can scrape up little else worthy your notice: – so with kindest regards & grateful recollections of auld lang syne am with truth & sincerity,
Thine most faithfully

JH

I forgot to mention the unfortunate case of poor Poitras[7] who was drowned here this fall by the upsetting of his canoe while upon the River. I feel the want of him very dearly.

---

5   Edward Smith was chief factor from 1834 to 1837 at Fort Chipewyan for both the Mackenzie River and Athabasca districts.
6   John Charles (c. 1784–) was on furlough at the Red River settlement in 1834–35.
7   An entry in the York Factory Post Journal of 25 August 1834 is as follows: "I regret deeply having to add the account of a melancholy accident which occurred in course of yesterday evening but which remained unknown till about 10 a.m. this day. Medard Poitras a Servant of the Comp having a desire to see some of his Friends who were with the Hay party on the island opposite 10s Creek had borrowed a Canoe from an Indian and crossed the River yesterday morning. Towards evening he started on his return, although a Breeze was blowing up the River against the Ebbing Tide. He was observed last when about half across but nothing appearing unusual no apprehension was aroused for his safety and his absence was not reported here, his companions thinking that being a little indisposed and off duty he had remained on the other side for the night. The Indian who owned the Canoe however feeling anxious about it came in search of it about 10

a.m. and for the first time Poitras' absence was made known. Parties of Indians were immediately dispatched up the River in all directions, and the melancholy results were soon too certainly ascertained by their finding the Canoe drifted ashore at one place. The paddle at another, and the poor fellow's hat at a third. His body has not yet been discovered. He was a steady, trust-worthy servant, and his loss will be felt here where his services were of much value as a stirring active leader at the Sawing Tents." Another entry of 28 August 1834 noted: "A party of Indians kept in search of the poor man who has been missing since the 25th found his body today some distance above [?] Creek it having been drifted ashore by the Tide. A coffin is making for it and the interment will take place tomorrow." B.239/a/148.

[Letterbook]
N° II
Rough Copies Letters by
JHargrave
From 14th July 1835 @ 31st May 1836

YF 16th July 1835

M rs Jane Melrose[1]
My Dear Mother

    I was gladdened a few days ago by receiving all your very kind letters of last Spring, and thanked our God to find that you had, every one of you, been mercifully preserved, while disease was choosing its victims all around you. My dear Old father especially, though pressed down with the load of years and infirm of health I am delighted to find, still bears up wonderfully. The health of both you & him I am always particularly anxious about each Spring, and your letter is always the first one I open to be certain of this. Should the first lines contain no unfortunate news, I then lay it down and thank God for All his mercies, before I proceed further with the beloved pages.

    I have this season again been rather delicate in health, but nothing like to last season and am at present hearty as ever. I remain as usual here and have now the head charge of all the Company affairs at this Factory[2] and for 150 miles on each side of me. My good fortune and success in life have been great; should providence continue to preserve me in good health I have nothing further to desire in this land. One thing however it has deprived me of – that is the pleasure of writing each season to all my brothers and Sisters, which from the multitude I have now to perform, I find perfectly impossible. I have therefore come to the resolution of writing to you and to my old father alone, and in two letters for you all, tell you every thing which I could have done were I to have written you twenty. My brothers and Sisters may be disappointed at this but I trust they will believe that my affections are as warm as ever – and were they to know the crowded life I lead and the little time I have which I can

---

1 His mother's maiden name was Melrose.
2 Hargrave was promoted to be chief trader in 1833 when he assumed the management of York Factory but he was not officially given charge of the York Factory District until 1835.

call my own, they would rather wonder how I could have found leisure to write them so many as I have already done.

I this season again enclose you a Bill in 2 copies for £ 15 Stg – which like all I have hitherto sent you is designed for purchasing comforts for you and for my dear old father. This sum is the exact interest of what money I have yet laid aside in Banks for my old age, and the income from it shall be yours my dear Mother while providence blesses me with the happiness of so bestowing it. I notice what you say about lending money to my brothers to purchase lands in your neighborhood, but must say at once that I do not like the plan. My means in the first place are not yet large, and what I have is in England, placed at interest in such a manner as not to be easily touched: I am likewise averse to lending money to relations, also and am no yet so rich as to be capable of making a present of so much. I should much rather prefer seeing them taking new Lots at once, and by their own industry raising themselves to independence. Money or property so obtained is far more valued and is usually turned to better account than were it either borrowed or received as a present.

What you remark of Melinda Dewey has ever been my serious opinion of her. The mention I have ever made of her in my letters have always been only by way of jest to fill up a blank corner of my page. Think not my dear Mother that at 37 years I have so little prudence or so little respect for myself as to give my name to such a character. You may yet see me with a wife, but she will be one from the Old Country, & one which your own partiality will consider worthy of me; – or else I remain as I am.

I rejoice to find that your farm still prospers and that my brothers have grown up to be such steady and respectable men. I had a letter this spring from an old and worthy friend, Alex.^{r} Stewart, Esq.[3] – of Boucherville below Montreal wherein he mentioned having seen John & conversed with him about me. I was proud to find him speak highly of my dear Brother as a Manly independent and at the same time modest and unassuming young fellow. Both of them while they maintain such characters may rest assured of my kind love, and aid in life, however unfit I may be at present to shew much of the latter. To both my dear Sisters and to Marys family I can, as to the others, only send expressions of love and affection. In *three* years at furthest I am *now certain*, should providence bless us all with health, of being able to pay you a visit for a few weeks

---

3 Alexander Stewart had retired in 1833 from a chief factorship in the HBC.

or perhaps Months. That we may all be preserved till then is the earnest prayer of My Dear Mother
Your affectionate

Jamie

P.S. I send you as a little present a "Smoking Bag" as we call it in this land, given to me this spring by a young daughter of one of my friends; – who is a native of the Country. It is used on the voyage for holding our Tob° Box, pipe, Iron slate flint Tinder and such matters.

YF 17th July 1835

Mr Jno Hargrave
Dear John

I this year send to our mother a Bill of Exchange in duplicate / or in 2 copies/ made payable to you for £15 Stg – both copies of which you will take to the HBCoy Office at Lachine, and I have written to M^r [James] Keith, the Coys Agent at that place to put you in this way how to obtain money for it. I have drawn money this season in a form different from usual in the hope that you will obtain a little more for a Bill on England than for one on the Coys Agent in Canada.
I remain your affectionate brother

JH

YF 30th July 1835

J.G. McTavish Esq
Lachine
My Dear Sir

As the packet will soon be getting ready for Montreal I use a chink of time to reply to your very kind favor of Jany last, which reached me about the beginning of March. I regret to say that my news this season are again loaded with tales of sickness and loss of life, the health of all here having throughout the spring & summer been similarly affected to what we were in 1834. Added to this, the influenza got among our Brigades the Servants of YF & the natives: the freight business has been greatly deranged, for about a fortnight in the beginning of this month our Factory business was nearly at a stand, and about 13 of our Indians have perished in spite of every aid which could be afforded them. Thank God! Affairs are now somewhat clearing up. The Brigades are all cleared out, and disease here is on the wane, but the freight Brigades on which the Transport of about 2300 ps for the Colony and the Nor. Districts depend, are not making their appearance, in consequence of which I dread a large portion will rest in our Stores.

Our returns however are now nearly all here, and the furs of both 1833 & 1834 are in a shape ready for shipment. The summer crush is now over, & our worthy old Factor Mr Charles,[4] who superintends our Fur Store & will winter at Oxford, is still here with whom I am blowing a cloud now & then & taking over matters and things. Mr Christie

You will likely have seen the minutes of this season so I shall not touch on any – What think you of our old friend M^r [Edward] Smiths having taken a young wife, and what of the old Birds[5] having buried his calf, & in a few weeks after inveigled away Mr Jones school mistress to share his bed & a heavy lug of his purse? Truly age moves in a circle, and the days of youth are coming around again to old Waders.

I find something as I imagine in your last valued sheet which looks more seriously & gravely to the end than I had ever anticipated in regard to you. I trust in God that your state of health is yet such as to ensure you many happy years yet, and that better medical aid than what graces the boys which find their way to this land, will in a few months set you firmly on your legs again.[6]

With sincere & grateful regard I remain
My Dear Sir
Ever yours faithfully

JH

---

4 John Charles was chief factor at Oxford House in the Island Lake district 1835–36.
5 Retired Chief Factor James Bird married in January 1835 Mrs Mary Kelly Lowman who had come out to look after the Church Missionary Society's girls school at Red River. Bird's native wife, Elizabeth Montour, had just been buried in November 1834. Bird had retired in 1824.
6 John George McTavish was given a furlough in 1835–36 because of ill health. He then was appointed chief factor at Lake of the Two Mountains, Chats district, from 1836 to 1846.

YF H[udson]B[ay] 1ˢᵗ August 1835

The Revᵈ R. Redpath A.M.
Minister of the Scottish Secession Church
Wells Street/London
Revᵈ Sir

    I am about taking a liberty which to a Stranger must appear intrusive; yet when you cast your eyes on the Signature to these pages early recollections I feel satisfied will apologise for my thus introducing myself in this manner to an old School Comrade – one especially whose idea mingles with some of my fondest recollections of my Native Land. A similarity in name indeed may be entising me to address a Stranger, – but I think I am right in my conjecture, and if so, have no doubt that the words *James Hargrave*, *Fysche's School* and *Galashiels* Hill, will awaken corresponding feelings in the breast of Robert Redpath. My object in the present communications is simply this: – I have now few or no correspondents in Selkirkshire, my family having emigrated before myself in 1819, – and having a strong desire for information from Scotland of a more local nature than what can be gleaned from the public prints, I have for some time looked round me without success for an old friend who could tell me of what one likes best to hear regarding the Scenes & companions of youthful years. By chance I fell upon your name & address while examining a list of our Secession Church, and had I reviewed the whole of my young comrades I could not have found one who in every respect, I feel, can well realise my wishes. I remembered your early desire of entering into orders, and had learned from some source I do not now recollect of your having obtained a living in London: – this is all I have been able to trace of your path through life; – perhaps the course of mine may to you be as little known. When I left Galashiels Academy in 1817 I passed 2 or 3 years in some measure without an aim: – my education was worth something I fancied, but no opening to a friendless young man occurred in my native Country. I therefore resolved on following my relations to Canada, in 1819, with some fatherly introductions to some Gentlemen in that Province from our worthy Old friend Dʳ Douglass. In course of the following Winter I obtained a Clerkship in the service of the British Fur Trade, and since that period have spent the whole of my life in the Indian Country north of Lake Superior & to the East of the Rocky Mountains. Some years ago my Services were rewarded by the Coy in London with a Commission and the Charge of one of their Depots in this Country; – which has realised my hopes for independence in the decline of life should providence preserve me late. – my years sink into the sere & yellow leaf. I shall not now touch on any details regarding this land, many of which I fancy would be interesting to you, but leave these as materials for future Sheets should you please to favour me with the correspondence I so ardently desire. A Letter delivered at the "Hudsons Bay House 3 Fenchurch Street" in Feb[y] would be forwarded me by a packet which in the end of that Month is annually dispatched Via Canada for this land, and in the end of May another Chance offers by the Vessels which every season sail for this port. These are the only opportunities we have of hearing from *home*, in the course of the year.

Should I have all this time through Mistake been addressing a Stranger I trust *he* will please to allow my motives as an excuse and leave my letter unnoticed as one of those accidents in life which similarity in Names sometimes produces; – but should my conjecture be correct, I flatter myself I will yet hear from my early friend and in some no very distant year be also enabled to tell him personally how much I am
his Affectionate School-fellow

JHargrave

YF 6th Augt. 1835

M[r] Jos[h] Hargrave

My Dear Father – I thank God that we are both mercifully spared to write to each other once more, at a time when disease seems spreading over the earth: even these distant and frozen regions around me do not seem to be exempt, – as the influenza[7] has in many places been making its appearance, and in some proving very generally fatal to the poor indians. Among the whites, though many of them catch it, few or no deaths occur, and at this place especially, as I have a Surgeon[8] on the establishment, we run comparatively small risk. I am indeed at present as well as ever I have been in this land, but last spring my health was rather delicate from a return of the Sickness which affected me in 1834.

Were it not the risk of disease (and which indeed I might incur still more were I in Canada) I would find myself perfectly happy in this land. I have reached the rank in the country which I have long laboured for, and as my services now produce me something worth saving I shall by care-

7 An influenza epidemic occurred in 1835.
8 Elzeard Whiffen.

ful management & economy endeavour to lay up a sum sufficient for my wants, which are not extravagant, and then return to the civilized world. According to the rules of the Service likewise, every one in the rank I now fill have in their turn a year to themselves for visiting their friends while their income continues the same as if they were in this country; my time comes round in the summer of 1838 in which year should God spare me I assuredly will be in Canada, – perhaps for a few Weeks, perhaps for as many months. Indeed it may be sooner, as we can exchange our right with each other, and should I be able to do this with some of my friends I may see you in one or two instead of 3 years.

I have not heard from Scotland this season yet, but last fall had a letter from my uncle Ja^s Mitchell at which time his family were all well. This letter I enclose in order that you may have the whole News. I cannot find time to write all my brothers & Sisters now, for my duties are many and take up all my time but this they must not consider as a mark of neglect or forgetfulness on my part. I am the same Jamie as when I left them 15 years ago. That we may all be preserved, My Dear old father, to see each other again is the earnest prayer of
Your Affectionate Son

JH

YF 29th August 1835

Mr Alex[ande]^r Mitchell[9]
Galashiels
Dear Cousin, – I have read with great delight my uncles kind letter of 11th April last with your very interesting & intelligent addition to it; and before our Vessels sail for London which will be in a few days, I do myself the pleasure of filling a sheet in reply to all your kind inquiries & remembrances. I had letters dated in March last from my parents & relations in Canada which I am happy to say informed me of their continued welfare & prosperity. My dear father is now so old as to have his sight greatly impaired & my mother is also much failed, but thanks to God, they are still both in excellent health, and in such circumstances as raise them above all cares about want & the necessaries of life. My Brothers John & Andrew are grown up to be steady industrious lads, and yet reside with our parents being like myself still unmarried. The details

---

9 Alexander (1806–c. 1842–48) was a son of James Mitchell.

you give me as to the tone of politics in Scotland is peculiarly pleasing. I cannot help admiring the conduct of my countrymen in using the political power which the Reform Bill put into their hands [illegible], as it was entirely new to the great body of the Scottish Middle Classes, I own I had some natural fears about their first steps as *freemen*. The result has redounded greatly to their honor. The changes which have arisen last year among the Ministers of the Crown is to be regretted as retarding somewhat the advance of improvement, but one good result from such is the making manifest that none now can govern Britain who has not the full confidence of the great body of the Nation. The struggles among parties at General elections I regret however to perceive, as such must be productive of great waste of time to the Middle Ranks & of dissipation among many who otherwise are sober & steady. Riots, intoxication & turbulent Mobs are too frequently the produce of such colisions & when I read accounts of such I am inclined to think they might take a good lesson from the conduct of their Children on this side of the Atlantic. The Americans instead of such scenes meet on occasions of elections with much the same air & demeanour as for a religious ceremony; and after having given his vote the farmer returns to his plough the same day & leaves the single grain of political power which he has planted to shoot up & produce and under the fostering care of his countrys Constitution. But this topic is filling too much of my sheet.

I recollect well the Thorburns of Midlem Burn & remember with gratitude the extreme kindness of that family to me when I was a poor penniless Dominie in their neighborhood. Wish my kindest regards to them all please tell Mrs Thorburn that I trust in 2 or 3 years at the farthest to be able to assure them personally that I have not forgot them, and aim to return with interest my promise of a pound of Tobacco. Give my kindest remembrances likewise to my old friend Mr Lee of Hawick. I rejoice to hear of his prosperity. I have many schoolfellows and old playmates still around you, but when I look back through the mist of time, though I remember till this day many of their faces, yet their names have escaped me. To all such as inquire after me make my warmest regards & say that in this desert I am not forgetful Auld Lang Syne.

In writing me next year cull whatever topics you please from among your country mates & fireside subjects of conversation. To me the wild flowers of Scotland are all sweeter than the Roses of other lands. Nothing is so trivial as is uninteresting to me. Give my kindest love to my dear Cousin Effie, to my kind uncle & aunt, with all your Brothers & Sisters.

They are almost the only blood relations I now have in Scotland whom I personally know. By the way, what has become of Andrew Melrose a son of uncle John who when I was in Galashiels resided with his Grandfather Leach together with his sister Helen. He was a fine boy & tho' trained up to think ill of his father, sometimes with tears in his eyes told me how he loved him. Should he be near you give my kind Love to him likewise.

Again neglect not to write me fully next season, and with warm regard believe me my Dear Alick
Your Affectionate Cousin

JH

YF 20 Septr 1835

Mr John Hargrave
My Dear John

Your kind letter of 19th Ap^r last reached me only a fortnight ago by a packet which left Lachine during the summer, and as I had to leave your former one unanswered, I have tried to get hold of a little time to reply to your second token of affection tho' the crowded season is not yet over with me. Winter is now about setting in with us in this cold climate, and I am at present working night and day to get the Ships[10] laden, their papers finished, and themselves cleared out for their return voyage to London. One of them however will sail first for New Brunswick and to her Captain I entrust these few lines to be put into the post as soon as he reaches his Port.

My health still continues good, and as the business of the Company at this Depot, with which I am entrusted, goes on in a prosperous condition I have great reason to be contented with my lot. The style of Living, Lodging and Rank in life I enjoy is much beyond whatever in youth I had reason to expect; – but altho' I fully appreciate the value of such, I sincerely trust the smiles of fortune have not hardened my heart, or weakened my feeling towards those who I feel are at this moment as dear to me as they were 15 years ago when I was penniless and friendless.

The little picture you give of your comforts upon your farm is particularly interesting. You appear to have got well on with your new house and

---

10 The *Prince Rupert*, under Capt. John Grave, and the *Nonpareil*, a chartered brig, with Capt. W. Williams.

when I come to see you all 2 or 3 years hence I hope to find a snug room & bed for me under my fathers roof. The greatest privation we suffer here is the want of vegetables: how I long to get a brouzing in your garden among Carrots Cucumbers & Melons! These little matters may seem trifles to you and yet at this moment I would value the possession of them as much as you could do the possession of the sources of comfort & wealth which are presently mine. Such is man: indifferent about what he possesses, and longing for that which he has not. Fortunate is he who possessing a well regulated mind can hold his happiness independent of both.

The whole of our ships/ Three, 1 for Engd 1 for New Brunswick & 1 for Churchill/ will leave this in a week at furthest, and then till frost & Snow confines us within doors I determine to treat myself & my mess-mates to a regular Hunting Excursion among the Swans Geese Ducks and other fowl which presently swarm in the neighboring marshes & where they remain till winter sets in, – and drives them off to the Southward.

Whenever you have time be always writing me for when a letter is put in the Office at Lachine it always gets some chance or other of coming to me besides the regular packet in Spring.

I hope you received my last ones of July and that my dear Mother has got the Bill cashed, which I enclosed her.

I am Dear John

Your affectionate brother

JH[11]

---

11 The following month, Hargrave noted in the York Factory Post Journal of Saturday, 10 October 1835 that "It may be interesting to notice that the sky being clear this evening we were enabled to observe the return of Halley's Comet, which was first noticed about 8 p.m. among the principal stars in the Constellation of Ursa Major. In appearance it resembled a star of the first magnitude but less brilliant and surrounded by a pale halo, with a tail pointing in an easterly direction. This is stated by Astronomers to be its first appearance since 1759, as it requires 75 ½ years to perform its full circuit. It is to be regretted that there are no instruments at the factory by which its altitude could be ascertained." HBCA, B.239/a/149.

[Letterbook]
Nº 12
Rough Copies Letters by
JHargrave
From 2nd June 1836 @ 13 March 1838

YF 23 July 1836

Mr John Hargrave
My Dear John

    I have received all your kind letters about a month ago, but as usual find it impossible to answer them one by one as I used to do in former years when my labours were lighter and, my pen could be more easily turned to tell you all the little Outs & ins about myself. This however will be less necessary this year, as I trust to see you all next Spring and hope to find you all in good health and prosperity. I will this fall sail with one of our Ships for London from which I will visit Scotland, where I will spend the Holidays. After that I will return to London and settle such affairs, as may be necessary, and in the end of Jany – I hope to be able to sail from Liverpool for New York which place I may reach in the end of Feby – and hope to be able to get to Beech Ridge about the beginning of March. This will allow me to spend about 2 months with you before the Rivers Open & call me back to this country again. By this you will see that Traveler as I am at present, I will be much more so before this time next year.

    I again this year enclose you a Bill of Exchange in Duplicate for £15 Stg – as a present to our Mother for which I hope you will obtain the same Value as last year. I will write a few lines to my old & worthy friend Mr Severeight[1] who is now at the Head of our Estabᵗ at Lachine & should you find any difficulty in disposing of this Bill he will I am certain for my sake render you every assistance.

    I need at present say little more for I shall personally tell you enough about this land when I have the happiness of seeing you.
Your Aff. Brother

JH

---

1 John Siveright (1779–1856) served temporarily in the Lachine office as James Keith's replacement from 1835 to 1837.

YF 23 July 1836

J. Severeight

Dear Severeight – I thank you kindly for your very friendly Sheet of last Spring / and deeply regret that I am almost incapacitated from acknowledging it through severe sickness. In consequence of this I have leave of absence for ensuing winter & will visit England this fall by the Vessel of the Season and will return by way of Canada at an early date next spring to have some time to spend with my friends in your neighborhood when I trust to have also the pleasure of seeing you. I write to none also at present but Gov.r Simpson & yourself beyond a few lines to my relations and to whom I have said nothing about my state of health. I have sent a Bill such as last year to my brother John & tis possible he may be drawing on your kindness to help him in disposing of it. Should he be inquiring after me, please leave in ignorance about my present condition for I much fear my poor old parents would be in great anxiety about me should any rumour reach them about my sickness. I have really been in great danger, but the Doctors now consider me out of all hazard: – This letter is short but I will eke it out amazingly the first hour after I shall have the pleasure of taking you by the hand.
Ever yours most faithfully

JH

YF 23 July 1836

Mr.s Jane Hargrave

My Dear Mother – I duly received a few weeks ago the whole of your kind letters, and was delighted to learn that you all had been mercifully spared to tell me of your welfare. My letters of Latter years have decreased both in number and length; – This one will be no exception to the rule, but when I tell you that I have obtained leave of absence from the Country till next spring I trust you will wait with patience till I am by your own fireside, and will then tell you fifty stories about this Country that will be worth a hundred letters. I tried to get down directly to you by the Canoes now about to start for Canada; but this I could not obtain as when the Ship from London arrives here next month my acquaintance with the business was indispensable in order to aid the Gentleman[2] who takes my

---

2 Chief Factor John Charles was posted to York Factory from 1836 to 1838.

place in getting through successfully in Canadas and Shipping Goods. I will however sail for England in September then visit our old friends in Scotland, and will start again for Canada by New York in January, so that I hope to be with you at latest about the month of March.

I have again sent you this season a Bill for the same Amount as last year a continuance of which my dear mother you may depend on every year while you live. I have enclosed this in a letter to John who will obtain money for it for you. I am not altogether pleased with some matters you tell me of in your letter, but if those whose natural & bounden duty it is to support you, should leave you unprovided for except through the charity of your own children I shall consider it my duty to see whether the laws of Canada of which I know something, cannot preserve to those who have alone laboured and collected by industry the prosperity they now possess. I will however at present say no more on this subject for I am very unwilling to believe that such injustice will be attempted: – if it is so however the attempt may cost more than would purchase what these claim, and in the end will only have their labour & loss for their pains.

I hope of a happy meeting with you before many months are over. I remain my Dear Mother
Your affectionate Son

JHargrave

YF 24th July 1836

My Dear Andrew

I am so busied with the Coys business just now, that were it not the particular subject you wrote about to me I should not have answered your letter till next I see you in spring which I hope to have the pleasure of doing next March. In regard to your deeds for your farm should they be drawn to your wishes, I am strongly of opinion with our father that they should be taken out in the joint names of John & you. The whole of you have been joint labourers in collecting the property you possess, and the members of our family now living together have alone the only claims to it. At all events, the deeds being in your names will better secure it to you whatever questions may be raised on the subject. I shall strongly press on my father when I see him the propriety of making his will; and my opinion is that the farm, Stock, and all his property gathered since your coming to Canada should be divided into 3 equal portions, one to you, one to John and one to support our Mother & Sister Jane while the

latter continues single and during the whole of our Mothers life. John as the elder of you should remain on the Farm after such a division and our mother & Jane should live in his family. Your portion should be paid you agreeably to a valuation to be made by 2 honest & respectable Arbitrators of the Value of the whole property, and this third should be made good to you by John and our Mother as quickly as they possibly can. Your plan of getting married I approve of highly my dear Andrew, and if your intended wife be the daughter of honest & worthy people however so poor, & should her own conduct be modest, industrious and without stain, depend on it my dear brother, that I shall be proud of such a sister. Do not thrust our old father however on this subject but rather gain his consent if possible by humouring him and I shall lend you my best aid and when I shall have the pleasure of seeing you.
I remain your very affect^e Brother

JH

YF Septr 1836

Mr John Hargrave
Via London to Can[ad]^a

My Dear John   From what I said to you in my letter of last July by the Mont^l Canoe you will no doubt be expecting to see me in Spring but from the probably very late arrival of our Ship this Season I now fear that we shall all be disappointed. The usual date of her coming here is the 15th August about a month earlier than this day, and yet she has not made her appearance: this rending her departure home again so late, that there is great risk of our being stopt by ice in getting through Hudsons Straits into the Atlantic and there frozen up through the winter in which case our lives might not be over secure. I have therefore determined to go inland this Season should She not appear in a day or two, in which case my visit to Canada will not take place till next year at least.

I am still in as good health as when I wrote you last, but am seriously grieved that my expected pleasure of seeing you all has been so unfortunately disappointed. Tell my dear mother not to be grieved for I will yet see her, – and I have firm hopes that my dear father will find consolation to support him under the disappointment. The serious matters I wrote you and Andrew about in Summer I trust you have been able to get settled without much difficulty; to aid you in this way was one of my objects in wishing to see you all.

I will write you from Red River or elsewhere in Dec[r] if a chance offers. Meanwhile I am as ever your Affectionate Brother –

JH

YF 12th Septr 1836

M[r] W[illiam]: M[c]Tavish R.R.
My Dear Sir

I am favored with your interesting Letter of 17*th* August last, with its enclosures; and deeply regret to learn that your health instead of improving was daily getting worse. I trust sincerely that the comparatively salubrious climate of R.R. and the change of service which you will enjoy this winter in that quarter will long before spring set you firm on your feet again. I am myself gradually improving and indeed am nearly as healthy as usual, but such is far from being the general character of this Estab[t] at present. D[r] Todd[3] is down, as deeply tormented as we were last spring: – [John] Ballenden is confined to his room till today, [Robert] Harding is staggering about and will soon be in for it, – indeed it is difficult at present to keep 3 pens at work throughout the Factory. Added to this, the Ship is not yet arrived, so at this date my hope of a visit to Europe is now despaired of by me. Should this prove too true an Augury, I purpose to remain here till past the Holidays to help up our crippled Est- with the Materials for the winter packet after which I will start "in Cariole" and pass the spring at Norway Ho. The letter of introduction you favored me with to your friends, as it appears to be the only one from you to them I shall send notice by the packet by whatever route it goes, & mention in it my detention in this Country. I will enclose a copy of the few commissions you gave me, to M[r] Sec[y] [William] Smith, so that you may not be disappointed.

Please let me hear of your welfare by the earliest opportunity & believe me ever

3 Governor Simpson in the summer of 1836 temporarily posted William Todd to York Factory to deal with the York Factory complaint. Unfortunately, Todd himself succumbed to the dreaded "complaint" within a week of his arrival at the post and had four violent attacks in September which left him so weakened that everyone feared for his life. He was a sickly man for the rest of his life. Ray, "Todd, William."

faithfully & Truly Yours

JH

YF 4th Novr 1836

Mr Alex^r Mitchel
Dear Cousin

I duly received your very kind & interesting letter of last April, and fully expected ere this date to have seen you in Galashiels instead of again writing you from this place but unfortunately have been disappointed in my design. I had arranged all my affairs in this land for a years absence, and was waiting here till the Autumn for a passage home, but most unluckily our Ships[4] were detained so long in Hudsons Straits by the Ice Bergs which choaked up this whole passage that they only reached this port in sufficient time to be laid up for the winter. Even their Cargoes had to be left on board for want of time to unload them. I am however in hopes that I will secure a furlough for next season when I will return by way of Canada to see my parents, & will then sail from New York for England.

I am very happy to learn that the Old Country still holds on improving, and that the poorest find the means of procuring a comfortable livelihood. I fully calculate on finding many changes amid my old haunts at Lindean, but I suspect that in person you will find me as altered as I shall find them. A weather beaten North Wester suffers as severely from climate & years as ever can a Willow Bush, – though well do I remember some happy days I have spent under its shade, when it was simply a bundle of sapling twigs.

---

4 The *Prince Rupert*, *Esquimeaux*, and *Eagle*. The *Prince Rupert*, under Capt. John Grave, was beset in ice for a month before arriving at York Factory where passengers and a few items were landed before the ship returned to London with most of her cargo. The *Esquimeaux*, under Capt. Butterwick, was badly damaged by ice in the Bay but reached York Factory on 24 September. She was to winter at Churchill but was forced to turn back by ice and was driven ashore and the men wintered at Ten Shilling Creek near York Factory. The *Eagle*, under Capt. Charles Humphreys, arrived 7 October at York Factory, too late to return home and wintered in the Hayes River.

I had letters as usual from Canada last Spring and am happy to say that all my relations there were then in good health. My poor old father alone is heavy laden with years, his eye sight is nearly gone, and his course cannot I fear be long, – although his general health is said to be the same as usual.

I write this in much haste as the packet, by which it will reach you is on the eve of starting for Canada to which place it has to be carried all the way on Mens Shoulders together with their provisions, a change of Clothes & a blanket. These Packet Men walk the whole distance on Snow Shoes & sleep every night in the open air alongside of a large fire made of such dry timber as they may meet with in the forests they traverse.

On looking over your letter again I see several subjects inquired about which I have not time at present to touch on, but when I reach you in the Winter of 1837, I will then give you a long history about the wonders of this land, which will I warrant you make up for my present deficiency.

With my kind Love to My dear Uncle, Aunt, and Cousins – as also to the worthy family of the Thorburns
I remain, My Dear Cousin
Yours most affectionately –

JH

YF 4 Novr 1836

Mr John Hargrave
My Dear John   As a packet is just leaving this for Canada I send by it a few lines to say to you & to my relations that I at present am in good health, and that altho' disappointed this season, I trust to be with you in course of next summer. To be able to do this, I purpose leaving this place about 3 Months hence in a Dog Cariole and will remain at Norway House till I can see the Govr next Spring, when I have strong expectations of being able to obtain leave of absence for ensuing season in exchange for that in which I have this season been disappointed. This being obtained I will leave Nor. Ho. by the first downward bound Canoe for Canada, and may possibly reach you about the end of August. I will then remain with you for a few Weeks till the Govr also returns & will sail from New York to England with him in October.

We have this season been surrounded with many misfortunes in the detention of all our Ships in this bay for the winter, arising from the very great quantity of ice in Hudsons Straits, some of them being wrecked &

others driven out into the Bay through Stress of weather, in consequence of which I fear that our loss I fear will be a serious one. I will not however despond for I am still able to lay up a little money & when I am enabled to set up housekeeping in however small a scale I will "clear out" and settle down a *family Man*.

I had a letter last Month from Our Cousin Alex. Mitchel at Galashiels who informs me that his father, Mother, & all friends are well. Work is plentiful now in Scotland & wages far higher than in the days we left it. The change with us however need not be regretted, for however times may mend in the Old Country, people in general there can never improve their condition so well as in a thinly settled & improving Colony. Had we all remained there to this day, I would still have been a Starving Dominie & both you & Andrew plough Men or Shepherds, – and so from this view of things let us gather content with our present position in life.

I fondly hope that both our dear parents & and our other relations are well & thriving. I long much to see you all again & if not next year it will assuredly not be my fault. Meantime I remain
My Dear John
Your affectionate brother

JH

YF 1 Decr 1836

Mr W. McTavish
My Dear Sir

I add a few lines to our Packet now about starting to inquire about your health and whereabouts; as the latest news I had from you described your condition as still being somewhat precarious. At this place we are now in tolerable keeping considering the weakliest being myself, yet still I trust to be able to take a trip upwards to Norway Hou- a short time after the Holidays. You will have heard in this the dismal accounts of our fall shipping business, and the small supply of Goods which it was possible to land. It was certainly the wildest weather that I have ever witnessed on this coast for any continued space of time, but happily as far as we have yet heard no lives have been lost, – and as to "Worlds [illegible] why it is dross, – and the loss may hereafter be made up. Among the few MacK[illegible] landed, I saw a parcel of the Times Newspaper to your address, which I took the liberty to open for perusal, and found among these a number of letters which were forwarded to you in the beginning of last month. The papers I shall again parcel up & leave them here to your address. I have already mentioned to you that I forwarded in the fall the letter you entrusted me with to your father; and as I have a visit to Britain still in view next spring should you favor me with another I should feel much pleasure in making use of it.

With kind wishes for your health & happiness
I am D^r McTavish
Yours Most Faithfully

JH

Norway Ho- 8th March 1837

Mr W. McTavish – R.R.
My Dear Sir

Your kind letter of 14 Decr reached me before I left the coast, and I have great pleasure in being able to congratulate you on the recovery of your health & strength, – more especially as your imagination has proved too masculine to lend permanency to the supposed fated mortal character of the Factory climate. It certainly tries the stamina of a man more than an equable and temperate atmosphere; but with adequate aid in the performance of the duties there, no Scot, who has made a bed among heather with no cover but his plaid and no shelter but the lee-side of a hill, need fear a Coast fog more than a Scotch One. I am myself of opinion that you will be wished for at the Factory next summer were I to return to it I would certainly apply for you; – should therefore the same desire be expressed by others I would recommend a voluntary offer on your part as the handsomest step in the eyes of others, and one which will be of the greatest ultimate benefit to yourself. No inland Residence in this land places a man in the same chance for obtaining distinction & advancement.

I am still in very indifferent health & purpose a tour London-ward next summer. My trip hither was a short & pleasant one, which I would willingly extend to R.R. – could I find the means; – but these are not to be procured. Remember me kindly to my old messmate Hector,[5] I have not had a line from him, as to how he *hops* on the path to most perfect health.

5 Hector McKenzie was in charge at Lower Fort Garry in the Red River district from 1837 to 1840.

With kind wishes I am My Dear Sir
Most faithfully Yours

JH

Beechridge 12th Septr 1837

Captn F.H. Hebarde
N.Y. – Packet Ship Quebec[6]
Sir

I have to request that you will please reserve for me a Single Berth, as far forward as convenient, in the London Packet Ship Quebec – to sail from New York on the 10th Oct^r
I remain
Sir
Your Mo: Obed^t Servant
J.H.
HHB Coy Service

Beechridge – Friday Morning
15th Septr 1837

Mr Hargraves presents Comp^{ts} to Mrs Dewey – Has to regret that he will be deprived of the pleasure of drinking Tea & passing the evening in her family this afternoon, but will assuredly call upon her for that purpose on the afternoon of monday next.
Mrs Dewey
St Remis

Beechridge Friday Morning
15th Septr 1837

Mrs Struthers
St Remis
Dear Madam

I purposed doing myself the pleasure of calling on you this afternoon on my way to Mrs Deweys, according to my promise, but in consequence of Marys arrival last night & her design of spending this day with me I will have to delay my visit till monday afternoon when I assuredly call on

6 The Packet Ship *Quebec* made her first voyage from New York to London in 1836 under the command of Capt. Frederick H. Herbard.

you en passant. I expect the pleasure of seeing & accompanying you & Miss Struthers to church on Sunday next. With kind Comp[ts] to her and to the rest of your fine & amiable family – I am with high regard
My Dear Madam
Most Truly Yours

JH

         Beech Ridge – Wednesday Morning
              27 Sept[r] 1837

M[rs] Dewey
My Dear M[rs] Dewey –

As I find that my journey to town must be so expeditious as to deprive me of the pleasure of personally bidding farewell to my friends, I beg in thus apprising you of this circumstance, to express my best wishes for your welfare & to add my kind regards to M[r] James, his amiable wife & to the rest of your family
Yours Most truly

JH

                D° D°

Miss Melinda Dewey
Dear Miss Melinda

I will take tea this afternoon with M[r] McPherson[7] & will leave his house about 8 OClock in the evening: – Could you step out unperceived about that hour this evening & meet me near your Brother Alicks farm on the road you would make me most happy in thus being able to bid you personally farewell: – wrap yourself well up from the Cold & take care that none know you on the road. I will bring you the sample of indian work I promised you: – I will have a horse & caleche. Should we not meet at once, do not return for some time, and never leave the road for any distance.
Yours Most Truly,

JH

 7 Reverend Thomas McPherson was the recently installed Gaelic-speaking minister at Beechridge. He remained for seven years before moving on to Lancaster, Ontario, where he died in 1884.

B. Ridge Wednesday Morning
27th September

Mr Hargrave presents Comp^{ts} to M^r & Mrs Ainslie – regrets extremely that he cannot enjoy the pleasure of drinking tea with them this evening having previously promised to do so with M^r McPherson, – and that his time is already preoccupied for the few evenings he still will be able to remain in this Settlement.

Beechridge 28th Septr 1837

To The Revd D. Gordon
Annaquasscook
Washington County New York –

Revd Sir   I was this summer favored with your valued communication of 20 Feb last on my way hitherward from the indian Country and being now on the eve of my departure for England I do myself the pleasure of leaving a few lines to your address in reply to the scope of your inquiries.

My acquaintance with the North West Territory by having actually traveled through it extends from the frontiers of Canada up to the 57° of Nor[th]. Lat[itude]. and from the Shores of Hudsons Bay for about 1000 Miles in a direct Westerly direction. The whole of that country is in a state of nature, almost universally covered with timber, the soil sometimes capable of cultivation, but generally of a rugged mountainous or else flat swampy character, & from its natural secluded position & barren character not likely at any early date to attract civilized man thereto as a place of permanent residence. The Climate around the coast of HB is extremely moist & about the latitude of 57°: the cold much severer than in Canada. Winter prevails for 8 months, & the 4 of milder character sometimes in 24 hours vary in temperature from 90° to 40° of Fahr[enheit]: Thermo[meter]. In-land the seasons are more equal but still very severe. To health however these changes are not so prejudicial as might be imagined the early cold in the fall checking the effects of swamp evaporation. Both the whites & natives are now also extremely restrained in the use of spiritous liquors much more so than many civilized co: I know which no question aids materially towards this happy result. Little cultivation prevails among the natives nor indeed is the land filled for it. Potatoes, Turnips Barley & a few of the hardiest garden plants can be usually reared but not universally so, – the Natives & whites therefore depend on Natural & imported produce for their chief Support; – the former being principally the animals of the Chase now growing more rare, although the Whites use their utmost influence with the Indians to preserve the

Breed from extinction – and also in the peculiar richness in fish throughout almost all the Lakes & Rivers in the North. The population like that of all savage countries where the chase supplies the Natives with support is thinly scattered but I cannot venture on an estimate of their probable number. They have no fixed residence but live in units of one or two families at most which they remove to other places every week or fortnight as suits their purpose & the requisite supply of Game or fish. Their habits in general are of a pacific character through all the country I am acquainted with; – indolent & little inclined to exertion unless stimulated by pressing want & then they sit down to enjoy the result till returning necessity again arouse them. Their intellectual powers I have a high opinion of, & their shrewdness & sagacy relating to matters they comprehend are remarked by all who have had intercourse with them but their ideas are confined, & the success of Missionaries among them is still struggling with many difficulties arising from their general inaptitude to comprehend abstract truths of religion. The most effectual mode yet fallen on is the education of indian Boys by the Coys Chaplains.

 I had attempted a detailed answer to the several [illegible] you mention but the quantity of the matter which was the result was lately unfitted to be comprised within even a very bulky letter, yet still the picture was then so inadequate to the extended subject that I felt compelled to throw the whole aside & to say in general terms that on the most mature consideration I can hold out no hopes that missionaries labors alone can under present circumstances be productive of even limited good among the wandering Tribes which cover British North America. The labors of many zealous ministers have already been directed to this object under the patronage & authority of the HBC° & all that this has affected with adults is the assembling in the most favorable situations small colonies of these, but such is their disinclination to labor, their improvidence in using the fruits of it, and the small progress hitherto made in real christianity that the most sanguine among their many white friends almost despair of effecting real good among those arrived at maturity. Teaching the young in the rudiments of Truth & the arts of agriculture promise better & a school is accordingly taught under the auspices of the same beneficent Coy from which I expect better results, as such natives when grown up return to their tribes as missionaries or teachers and by a consequence of such I look forward to the eventual dawn of christianity among these simple & quiet but benighted tribes. Missionary labors alone in such a land unassisted by funds from the civilized world, must therefore of necessity be greatly circumscribed unproductive & surrounded with difficulties &c; to encounter which without such aid I could not feel myself authorised to hold out any encouragement.

I leave this on the 1st Octr & will sail from New York for London in the packet Ship Quebec. My return to the Indian Country will next summer be direct from London to Hudsons Bay –
With sincere respect & good wishes I remain
Revd Sir
Most Truly Yours

JH

Please consider this sheet as *private* & especially as undesigned for general perusal much less for the press.
JH

New York – Octr 9th 1837
Astor House }

Mr Josh Hargrave
My Dear parents – Before I leave this country I sit down with great pleasure to inform you all of my welfare, which I know you will be anxious about. I left Montreal on the 4th as my Brothers will have informed you, & after a pleasant & expeditious voyage of 3 days & 2 nights reached this place on the evening of the 6th without the slightest accident. Since then, I have been on board the Ship Quebec in which we sail tomorrow, and a better or safer conveyance I believe does not cross the Atlantic. I have likewise made the acquaintance of 3 of 4 of my countrymen military officers gentlemen of fortune &c who are going home by the same Ship in whose society I anticipate much pleasure during the voyage. One of them especially, a Mr White of Glasgow was some years ago intimate in the family of Mr Pringle formerly of Orchard, and was a warm friend of my old Play mate Antony, but who I lament to say he informs me is no more. His other brothers & Sisters are well & well settled at Cobourg in Upper Canada. This Town is extensive, & filled with splendid Houses Shops &c in walking thro which I have been much occupied since my arrival. The manners of the people are kind, & our own Scottish race especially are received among them as brothers, if their character & conduct deserve it. I had indeed imagined that I had completely rubbed off the Scottish twang from my speech & spoke English so purely as to escape detection

but find myself completely disappointed. Only yesterday when at table a gentleman & observer by my side claimed country relationship with me on that proof alone, & when I remarked with some surprise that all my efforts of polishing my tongue of the Lowland accent had been so fruitless he remarked with a smile "There are two things a Scotchman never forgets – His Mother Tongue & his Native Land." His own case is a proof of the latter attachment. By name of Grant, his relations have been settled in New Engl^d for more than 200 years, yet he himself in visiting England last year made a tour to Perthshire their original native place out of pure love & affection for Scotland alone. On the strength of this common feeling we contrived to empty a bottle of excellent wine between us. Several other introductions to American Gent^n has this connection procured me, all of them respectable, & all highly gratifying.

I will write you again my dear parents shortly after my arrival in England, & should any of you be in Montreal about the middle of January & call at the Lachine Office you will I trust find a letter from me. I am in excellent health & when I left you I have full confidence that the sea voyage will not diminish it. My parting injunction to you both my dear old parents, is that you take good care of your healths for my Sake. Remember me in the kindest manner to M^{rs} & Miss Mar. Struthers & to M^r & M^{rs} McPherson, to all the Ainslies, to James' 2 daughters & generally to every one by whom I was so kindly welcomed during the few happy weeks I spent among you.

With warmest love to both of you & to all the family I am
My Dearest Parents
Your Affectionate Son

JH

P.S. I had omitted to desire my kind Compts. to Mrs Hardesty your School Mistress. Tell her to rest assured I shall carefully attend to what she & Mr Hardesty said to me in regard to the tales they interested me with.

Now do get that abominable chimney of yours cured of smoke, and your Stove door Hinge repaired.

JH

New York
Astor House} Octr. 9th 1837

Mr Ja^s Ross – Chateauguay
Dear Brother – I use with great pleasure a few leisure minutes I have before embarking to inform you of my welfare and my success in traveling through this inquisitive nation. I left Montreal on the morning of the 4th much later than I had purposed – but by pushing the March in our Northern night & day style I reached this on the evening of the 6th – a little faded it is true but sound in wind & limb. As I had taken the precaution to write to the Captn when at my fathers, I found my berth secured for me on board the Quebec in one of the best places on board, my application being among the 1st that was made. Since then I have rambled about Town, seeing what was to be seen & losing for such gratification a few of my indian Dollars. I have indeed been much disappointed in the general aspect of the City. Fine Houses, Churches Shops &^{c} there are certainly a great number but at the sides of these in most instances little shabby hovels are stuck like swallow nests under shelter of their eaves. Good order is preserved by the Magistrates & I must say I have never witnessed in Europe so few scenes of disorder in the public streets.

We sail tomorrow at midday – the weather is fine & moderate but even in this southerly latitude beginning to feel a little sharp. I long for a sight of a Haze in Decr again, and am happy in leaving a settled frost behind for at least 12 months still ahead of me.

With kindest love to my dear Sister, to William & to all your little ones I am
My Dear Ross
Yours affectionately

JH

P.S. Please make my kind remembrances to your School Mistress – Mrs Ryan. I know the toils the anxieties, the privations of that path in life, & from my heart sympathise with every professional sister as well as brother who may be armed with that thorny sceptre the birch.

JH

George & Vulture Hotel[8]
Lombard St.   London
7th Novr 1837

Mr Joseph Hargrave

My Dear Parents – I arrived here in safety from New York four days ago, and I use the first opportunity to inform you of my welfare / in order that we may all rejoice in the favorable voyage which Divine Providence has blessed me with. I left New York on the morning of the 10th ult^o and after a happy voyage of 22 days we reached Portsmouth – a large Sea-Port on the South Side of England distant 69 Miles from this place and at which I arrived by coach on the following day. I found that Mr Duncan & Nicol Finlayson had both reached this about a week before me, and had taken lodgings at this Hotel: we accordingly met the first hour I was in London & I assure you we saw the bottom of some bottles wine on the happy occasion. You will tell their Cousin Matheson of their welfare & of their satisfaction in learning from me of their welfare. The next day Govr Simpson called on me & taking me to the Hudsons Bay House introduced me to the Secretary & some other Gentlemen by whom I was welcomed in the kindest manner.

You will expect that I should write you a long story about all that is wonderful to me here but my time has yet been too short to allow of my having seen much. I am in the very centre of the most crowded part & have not extended my walks yet beyond 5 or 6 streets but I hope soon to be through most of them between this & the west end as I desire that from having studied long the Map of London while in the North, I find my way easily among the principal Streets. This Quarter is filled with the most splendid & richest shops I believe in the World, the Houses are about 3 stories high – usually built of brick, and the Streets rather narrow but the best order and regularity is preserved. The Young Queen[9]

---

8   The George and Vulture was known from 1837 as the tavern that Dickens' Mr Pickwick and friends made their favorite city headquarters. It is still tucked away in the heart of old London, overshadowed by modern high-rise buildings. Because it was an easy walk from there to Hudson's Bay House, the company headquarters on Fenchurch Street, this venerable inn was commonly used by visiting officers from North America as their residence in London while attending to company business.

9   Queen Victoria (1819–1901) succeeded her uncle William IV in 1837, at the age of eighteen, and her reign dominated the rest of the century.

purposes coming into the City on the 9th 2 days hence – to dine with the city Magistrates and nothing is now talked of except about her reception. Illuminations, fireworks & processions are the universal topic. She is a "bonnie sweet sonsie[10] lassie" – to speak in our own tongue, & well deserving I believe all the attention they purpose paying her.

I have a letter waiting me from my cousin Alex. Mitchel from whom I rejoice to learn that all my uncles family were in good health last summer. I will write them in a day or two telling them of my arrival here and in a couple weeks at the farthest will be setting off for Scotland where I will remain till January or February.

You may expect to have a letter from me by the Spring packet from this place which will reach Lachine about the end of April as usual, and I will again write you before I leave England in June for Hudsons Bay. My health throughout has been excellent and I every day make a dinner on some of the best London Beef Steaks which are the finest I believe in the world.

Remember me in the kindest manner to all my old friends about you. I wish I had some of the lassies Jane Miss Struthers for instance, to take with me to the various places of amusement I have already visited. Such would give them subjects to talk about for the rest of their lives.
With kind love to you all I am
My Dear parents
Your Very Affect. Son

JH

P.S. I cannot omit adding that I have not met with one Smoky Chimney Since I left you.

Galashiels 30th Decr 1837

Geo. Simpson Esq
Dear Sir

I take the liberty of addressing a few lines to you, flattering myself that you will be pleased to hear how I am enjoying myself amid my native valleys. I arrived here about 10 days ago, after the usual incidents of a coast-

---

10 Esp. of women: comely, attractive, good-looking, very frequently in respect of the figure, buxom, plump. *DSL*.

ing voyage and a Stage Coach journey; improving in health, and greatly delighted with my tour. My present residence, this place where I received the best portion of my education, is filled with many of my School boy Mates, among whom I feel much of that happiness which reaches the heart. Our old Rector is also still alive, and his welcome was that of a father to a Son. I spend my holidays here and about a week hence will begin a tour along the border after which I will return to Edin^b about the 15th prox. – I then purpose visiting Glasgow where I expect to find my friend Mr Finlayson (Duncan) after which our route may tend to the North for a week or more.

I am at present residing within two miles of Abbotsford the seat of the late Sir Walter Scott, – which I purpose visiting two or three days hence, and it will go hard with me if I bear not away some relic or other that will be interesting to Mrs Simpson. I am indeed promised one of rare value & interest connected with that light of our Native Land, which, should I obtain, I trust she will allow me the honor of presenting it to her: – tis a lock of his hair, of undoubted authenticity.

My address will continue to be this place till the middle of ensuing month, after which letters addressed to The Waterloo Hotel Edin^h [11] will find me out in the course of my Northern Tour. I will, as I mentioned, ere my departure, remain in this Country till near the end of Feby, after which I purpose returning to Town to be there on the departure of the Spring packet via Canada. My time is presently spent most delightfully, and I must say that my return to my native Land instead of being gloomy and fruitful in disappointment as some of my Indian friends had foretold me would be the case, is on the contrary rich in enjoyment, & will leave long traces of favorable recollection on my mind both as regards the prosperity of the country & the kind, hospitable & warmhearted reception I have met from my countrymen. With warmest wishes for many happy returns of this season to Mrs S & to yourself –
I am Deepest regard & esteem I remain Dr Sir
Ever faithfully Yours

JH

11 The Waterloo Hotel on Waterloo Place opened in 1819, was the first hotel built in Edinburgh and contained a coffee-room and dining room 80 by 40 feet each. The inns that had provided accommodations before this time were unable to house more than fifty guests.

R[obert]. Fyshe Esq[r]
My Dear Sir
   Considering the value I attach on this subject I trust you will forgive me the annoyance I am occasioning. As the uncertainty which seemed to exist in your mind regarding the identity of "Sir Walters Hair" which you presented me with led also to some uncertainty in my own, I took the liberty of twice submitting it to professional Hair Dressers as to whether it was young or old – both of whom declared "that it had belonged to a young person & that the lock shown did not contain a single grey hair." Under these circumstances may I request that you will please make a rigid scrutiny for the other lock which being found & compared with that now believed to have belonged to Sir Walter – there will then be little difficulty as to which is the correct one. I like ill to [sentence left unfinished].
   I will see you again next month, when we will compare & decide on this matter.
Yours ever faithfully

JH
Tower Inn Hawick[12] 8 Jany 1838

Hawick Tower Inn
10th Jany 1838

The Rev[d] John Richmond[13]
Southdean Manse
Rev[d] Sir
   Being informed that a registry of my birth as the Son of Joseph Hargrave and Jane Melrose was entered in the records of Southdean Parish,[14] as I believe, between the dates 1797 and 1802, may I request the favor that

---

12 Drumlanrig's Tower was built as a stronghold in 1548 during the era of the Border Reivers by James Douglas. In 1773 it was converted into the Tower Inn, noted for its comfortable rooms, good dinner, and privacy. Today it serves as Hawick's visitor centre.
13 Minister, Southdean Established Church (listed in Pigot's 1825–26 Directory).
14 A parish in Roxburghshire, about 12 miles long by 7 broad, lying on the banks of the River Jed. Its population in 1801, around the time of James Hargrave's birth, was 697.

a regular Certificate of the Same, containing an exact Copy of such entry & date be forwarded to the address under Noted. As I am not certain as to whom I should apply I have to apologise for troubling you on this occasion and beg to enclose half a Sovereign to defray the requisite expenses connected with this matter. With much respect I remain Revd Sir
Your Obed^t Hble Servt,
James Hargrave
Hudsons Bay House
London

                                                                 Hawick Tower Inn

10th Jany 1838
The Revd James Clark[15]
Jedburgh
Revd Sir – Being informed that a registry of my Baptism as a Son of Joseph Hargrave & Jane Melrose was entered in the Records of the Antiburgher Congregation of Jedburgh as I believe, between the dates 1797 and 1802, by the Revd Robson, Robeson or Robertson one of your predecessors, may I request the favor that a regular Certificate of the Same, containing an exact copy of such entry and date be forwarded to the address under noted as early as perfectly convenient; and beg to enclose a Sovereign in order to defray the expenses connected with this matter.
With respect I remain Revd Sir –
Your Ob^t Hble Servt
"James Hargrave
Waterloo Hotel Edinburgh
To remain till
called for."

                                                        Edin^b Waterloo Hotel
                                                                   15th Jay 1838

The Revd Ja^s Clark
Jedburgh
Revd Sir,
   I am favored with yours of the 12th Ins^t and regret to learn that no registry of my baptism had been kept by your worthy predecessor. It is my belief that I was born in Novr 1798 – at or near Chesters in Southdean Parish & was baptised by the Revd Mr Robison then of Jedburgh during

---

15 Minister, Second United Secession (listed in Pigot's 1825–26 Directory).

the Same month on the occasion of an "Emanination"[16] which he then had held in that quarter of the country. A registry of my birth had been Made as I am informed in the Session books of Southdean & I have written to the rev^d Mr Richmond for a Certificate of the same but have not yet heard from him. Should you be able to obtain from any of your Congregation, contemporaries of that period a Document confirmatory of the above information you would greatly oblige me: – and whatever money of mine may eventually remain in your hands you will please bestow on any worthy person in needy circumstances in your congregation in such manner as you may consider most expedient. My address will continue during this month the same as at present –
With esteem I remain Revd Sir
Your very Obed^t Servt

JH

To such of my parents old friends as may yet be in your neighborhood, it possibly may be interesting to learn that they with all their family were last Octr still alive, & in very comfortable circumstances in the neighborhood of Montreal Lower Canada.

Edin^b Waterloo Hotel
15th Jany 1838

Mrs George Simpson
5. Trinity Square London
Dear Madam – I have been deeply gratified by the honor you have done me in answering my letter to Govr Simpson, and beg leave to add to my satisfaction by telling you personally of this. I arrived here last night after a tour a weeks duration through Teviotdale, the haunts of my Childhood and I need not add how delighted I have been in tracing scenes some of which I had not seen since I was 6 years of age, and of which I had still a perfect recollection. That wild & mountainous part of Scotland – "The South Highlands" – is altogether a pastoral Country into the Glens of which, the innovations of modern days & modish life have scarcely at all penetrated, in short the Country of the immortal "Dandie Dinmont"[17] a

---

16 Unknown word.
17 Originating from the border country of Scotland and England, the Dandie Dinmont terrier was first recorded as a distinct breed around 1700, long

representation of whom may be found in every solitary "Toun" throughout these Valleys. Indeed it is only three nights since I sat in the midst of a party of them, all Haliburtons, Kers Turnbulls, Elliots, Armstrongs & Laidlaws – genuine Borderers, as artless, hospitable, and *Bauld*[18] as of yore, changed in nothing since the days of Dandie, unless it might be, that Whisky Toddy though loved as much as ever, is consumed in quantities better suited than formerly to the calibre of such an effeminate descendant of them as myself. We had also next day a shot at a Black-Cock,[19] a rummaging out of a "Tod Lowrie"[20] – and in spite of Game Laws & "Closs Times"[21] speared a Salmon by Torch Light. As an indian who had been bred up in civilized life, is reported to have done, on witnessing the Simple habits of his fathers & of his childhood, – I could almost have felt it in my heart to have abandoned the world & its Cares, – resumed the Plaid, – & Sought for happiness amid the Cheviots[22] & the Carterfells.[23] But such imaginative dreams however, happily for myself, act little upon reason, and I am in consequence here again, with a full hope of having the pleasure of seeing you in London, in little more than a month hence.

---

before it had a name. In 1815, Sir Walter Scott, who proudly owned these engaging little dogs, wrote about them in his popular novel *Guy Mannering*. In it, a character named Dandie Dinmont kept a pack of mustard (tan) and pepper (grey) terriers. Renowned for its gameness and adaptability to almost any environment, the Dandie Dinmont became popular in nineteenth-century Britain.

18 Bold. DSL.
19 A bird of the grouse family.
20 aka "Mr. Fox."
21 "Close-times" referred to periods during which the catching of fish was forbidden. Annual close times for salmon were during the spawning season, while weekly close times were usually Sundays. At that time the Salmon Fisheries (Scotland) Act of 1828 was in force. The Game (Scotland) Act of 1832 prescribed penalties on summary conviction for any person who committed trespass by day in pursuit of game, otherwise known as poaching. Game included hares, pheasants, partridges, grouse, heath or moor game, black game, and bustards. Daytime was defined as from one hour before sunrise to one hour after sunset.
22 A range of hills on the border between Scotland and England that gives its name to a breed of sheep.
23 Carter Fell is a mountain ridge on the border between the Scottish Borders and Cumbria.

I am greatly delighted at learning that the relic I had expectations of obtaining will be of value to you. My Old Teacher had promised me, & when I last saw him, sought long for it without success; – but within these last Two days I have heard from him that he has recovered it & when I return by Galashiels on my way to England, that I shall have it. You can now depend on it. He describes it as being "white as snow." I leave this tomorrow for Glasgow & should I meet our friend M[r] Finlayson there he may entise me to a tour round by Inverness. If not, I return hither & will not leave this till I start for London by the Mail & Railway – about the 20th of next month.

With deepest regard & respect I remain

My Dear Madam

Ever Sincerely Yours

JH

Edin[h] 16th Feby 1838

D. Mactavish Esq[24]

My Dear Sir

I reached this on yesterday evening in safety and finding letters here for me from London contain parts of which will be interesting to you I take the liberty of addressing you at this early date lest through the medium of the public prints some loose exaggerated reports might reach you might occasion serious tho' groundless uneasiness. Govr Simpson writes under date the 19th ult[o] "The Grand Brulé Rebels rounded our friend Mactavish[25] out of bed one morning at the Lake (of the Two Mountains) asked him for the keys of the Stores, and without giving the poor Gentleman time to pull on his Breeches broke open the Doors and helped themselves to the Arms Ammunition & provisions; gave him a receipt for the Same in the name of the Provisional Government, and walked off with their plunder: – this is the head and front of the whole, – no violence appears to have been used, – and our friends were all in their wonted health;

---

24 Dugald Mactavish (1782–1855), eldest son and heir of the chief of Clan Tavish, became a Writer of the Signet and Sheriff Substitute of Kintyre, building Kilchrist House in Campbelton in 1824. His wife, Letitia Lockhart, bore him ten surviving children, including Letitia Mactavish, the future wife of James Hargrave.

25 John George McTavish was the younger brother of Dugald.

Kilchrist House, Campbelton, Argyllshire. Kilchrist House was built as Letitia Mactavish's family home in the 1820s, on an eight-acre property. Courtesy of University of Manitoba Archives and Special Collections, Margaret Arnett MacLeod fonds (PC 13) folder 1, photograph 11, July 1949.

– tho' no doubt John George was foaming at the robbery & insult to which he had been subjected." Govr S. adds – "We have little to fear as regards our interests, and from the measures Government is now taking I am in hopes we have heard the worst." All this, confidentially to yourself & family.

I have had great pleasure in delivering your letters to Mesdames Worsley & Ellis & feel deeply flattered by your friendly attention in thus introducing me to such respectable and accomplished Ladies. The former especially with whom I dine this evening is evidently of an energy and style of character rarely to be met with, (and the gratification I enjoy in her conversation I am rejoiced to find I can in some measure return by telling her of my friend William,[26] – in whose prosperity her heart is deeply interested. I will spend tomorrow evening with Mrs Ellis & will leave this at the latest early on Monday as my time is now nearly up. I expect also to see legredale[?] on whom I have called, but was not so fortunate as to find him at home. Mr^s Ellis has furnished me with the addresses of the Miss Tairns [?] & and as I learn they were enquiring after me, shall do myself the pleasure of waiting on them but will touch on nothing of the above details, – beyond an assurance of the perfect health & safety of their friends at the latest date which has reached this country.

I leave the North at present much against my will & will if possible return before I bid farewell to Britain in June. Affectionate regards to Mrs M: and the Young Ladies with high esteem & regards for yourself from
My Dear Sir
Yours ever faithfully

JH

Warmest regards to our excellent friend Capt. Tom. I long for a [illegible] his [illegible] & [illegible] with Miss Charlotte

London 23^d Feby 1838

Dugald Mactavish Esq.
Kilchrist House Campbelton[27]

My Dear Sir: – Since writing you on the 16th from Edinburgh I proceeded on my journey to the South, and arrived here yesterday by the Mail in perfect safety. This early and sudden departure from Scotland arose from having received from Govr Simpson a communication acquainting me with the necessity from unforeseen causes of my proceeding to the Indian country this spring and thus depriving me of the happiness which I expected, could I have been permitted to remain in this Country till June. Much of this anticipated happiness & indeed that on which the enjoyment of my future life I feel will greatly depend, allow me to say my dear Sir is connected with your approbation of what I am now to state to

---

26 William Mactavish was the eldest son of Dugald Mactavish.
27 Dugald Mactavish had moved his family in 1821 to Kilchrist House, a property of about eight acres near Campbelton, Argyllshire. He was a lawyer and was appointed sheriff or chief judge of the country, with Campbelton as the seat of his court.

you. My residence in your family during the few delightful days I spent at Kilchrist, made known to me the amiable mind, superior character & sweet disposition of your daughter Miss Mactavish. With me to witness such merit was to admire and to admire was to love. My firm resolution on departure was to return to Scotland this spring as soon as my duty would allow me & with your approbation to endeavour to make my hand & fortunes if possible acceptable to that young Lady. I feel all the boldness & perceive many of the difficulties, much augmented by my present position, which present [illegible] in thus aspiring to the honor of an elected son in your family; but still hope, tho' faint & distant, bids me with your favorable consideration to look forward to success. I will not speak in praise of myself, further than that my name & character I am proud to think is esteemed by all those to whom I am fully known & whose good opinion would be honorable to me. Govr Simpson has been acquainted with my public & private conduct for nearly 20 years, – an intimate & tried friend in the person of Mr Duncan Finlayson one of our most valued Officers – has thoroughly known me for nearly the same period; the latter purposes a tour this spring round the west coast of Scotland & will probably oblige me by calling on you – to both these gentlemen I will with confidence refer you for such inquiries regarding both my character & prospects in Life as a father will no doubt consider it his duty to make. I will also by the present opportunity address Miss Mactavish, & however my feelings may be wrung by the fears of hurting the cause nearest my heart, will fairly as I can, state what hardships may have to be borne & what sacrifices made in listening to my suit, – in return for which I can only offer her an honest hand & a heart devoted to her honor & happiness. Should this meet with her approbation, as also the sanction of yourself & Mrs Mactavish, I have already made arrangements that I shall again please God visit Britain Two years hence, that is in the autumn of 1840 – for the sole purpose of suing for the hand to the possession of which I now aspire.

I have now said what my agitated feelings have scarcely permitted me to explain in intelligible language: – your & her answer may possibly reach me before I sail from hence in the beginning of next month, at all events it will find me next summer at York Factory; – and finally rest assured that whatever may be your decision I can never otherwise consider myself than as, Yours most sincerely & affectionately

JHargrave

P.S. I enclose the letter above mentioned which will better point out the lamented necessity by which I am thus early forced away from Britain & happiness. I also enclose a couple trifling presents to Miss Mactavish & to Miss Mary[28] & of which I beg their acceptance.

JH

London 23^d Feby 1838

Miss Mactavish
My Dear Madam

 The unforeseen circumstance of being called on to leave my native land again at this early period is the occasion of my addressing you by letter on a subject regarding which I have now such cause to regret I had not personally explained myself to you before I bade farewell to the happy family at Kilchrist. My residence among you for a much shorter time than has been my good fortune, must have made me well aware of your merit and your amiable character. As it was, every day deepened the impression, and I now beg to say, even under all the difficulties before me, that with you and on the encouragement you may condescend to afford to my suit, will certainly depend the happiness of my future life. When I reflect on the weak effect these words may produce in comparison with what I might have urged had I trusted nothing to futurity and to this imperfect mode of pressing on your favorable notice a topic so near to my heart I doubly condemn my weak procrastination, more especially, as should you please to listen to me, fortune will for several years lead us both to a land far distant from that of our nativity. Honorable dealing to yourself compels this candid confession from me; – as also, that altho' my present income, position in life, & future prospects are such as to fully warrant my hopes of supporting a family in respectability & easy circumstances, yet a considerable number of years must be spent in a solitary land before we can attain to perfect independence of fortune & can return to civilization & those pleasures of life from which it derives so many of its charms. Weigh this duly, – but along with it, – oh allow me to add also permit yourself to estimate the value of that heart which will not permit, tho' wrung with anguish while tracing these words, the slightest chance to arise whereby you might be drawn into a position to be afterwards repented of. Should your favorable sentiments & firmness of mind overcome these obstacles,

---

28 A younger sister of Letitia.

rest assured that two years hence I revisit Scotland, to sue for that hand, the possession of which will ever be esteemed by me the dearest object this world can award me. I enclose this open to your father, who, should he approve of my proposals will hand it to you: – May I beg the honor of a reply in return, & however you may decide, rest assured I shall ever remain, – My dear Madam,
Most devotedly Yours

JH

London 23^d Feby 1838

D^o D^o

Dearest Letitia, – My open Letter, tho warm from the heart, contains not half what I would wish to say – nor, as, being designed for the perusal of your parents as well as yourself, could I pour out my feelings so unreservedly as I could wish and I mean to do in this solely designed for yourself. Little did I think when my hand last clasped yours, futurity had such trials in store for me – And I can ill describe the state of mind with which I received the enclosed letter, which postpones to such a distant day, what I had so lately stored in my mind as my chief wealth – the possession of your hand & of your society. My word, my honor is already pledged to you, – and I glory in the pledge. To have accepted of yours, *then*, would I still think have been unworthy of me, as drawing you into a snare without the consent of those so dear to you, & who as well deserve to be consulted. Now however should my present advances be approved, your assurance would be the day star which would guide my hopes forward to the time I have mentioned, when I have secured my return to your society, – I hope never again to be separated wherever fortune may chance to lead us. On reflecting upon my attachment to you, reason & feeling alike commend my passion to my self. The amiable mind, the candour, the sense & judgment which your conversation so lavishly exhibits sank deep & indelible the impressions your personal charms & accomplishments first impressed on my soul. You thought me little likely to be governed by Mauvaise Honte,[29] – I tell you these confessions lingered many days on my lips while in your company – & tho' struggling for utterance found none, till chance & the despair of losing you finally led to a few

---

29 French for bashfulness, sheepishness

incoherent expressions when time was almost no more which I will ever bless as being the Seeds from whence I trust my earthly happiness will eventually take its rise. Bear with me my gentle friend in my uncourtly & unpolished language: Believe me this subject either in words or still less in writing is a new one to me: I left Britain very young, & unlike many of my friends, found little to admire in women – they of the land where I have spent so many of my years uneducated as they are & uninformed. The elevated passion of Love has been till now, a novelty to me, and tho' shy in its expression I still Glory in owning myself a willing votary at its shrine. Rash you thought me. Ah little did you know, how beat my heart as I willingly yielded my affections an offering to love – or how reason applauded & still applauds the offering. Excepting this delay – our prospects otherwise are cheering. My path in life is smooth before me, & my position in it such as to afford us a certain prospect (as certain as any thing in this life can be), if not of overflowing wealth, at least of respectability and independence.

When thinking of you, & when do I not? – a thousand subjects present themselves that I would talk of were I by your side, but to repeat them by this mode of conversation defies my pen. I will hope to hear from you before I leave Britain which will not be till the 10th of March long ere which I trust you will have received this: – should this be otherwise, my address will be what I left with you "York Fy HBay House London." I have long wavered whether I should not have returned to Scotland & pressed for your accompanying me on this occasion, for which time might have served; – but when I looked to the long spring voyage thro' sleet & rain for many thousand miles and to the shock of feeling at being called on to leave all on such an alternative & at such short notice, I own I dared not risk my final hopes on such a chance. Time will soon fly past, & my faith shall be found only the purer from the trial to which it will be put. God bless You Dearest, – My warmest my purest aspirations are yours & yours only. Ever yours Most affectionately

JH

Please accept of the accomp[an]y[in]g trifle – as a Token that in spirit you are ever present with me. The medical Gents here give me every encouragement regarding my health in future. Kind regards to my worthy friend Captn Ivan: – & to the Young Ladies –

London 3rd March 1838

Mr Alexr Mitchell

My Dear Cousin – I am so busied with my preparations to be off for the Indian Country by way of Canada, that I can neither write you so fully as I wish nor recollect all that I should say – however imperfectly that may be.[30] I reached this in safety of the [illegible] of the 21st ulto – after a rather hard journey outside of coach most of the way – as all inside seats had been taken to Birmingham. I found my worst fears confirmed about my leaving England, my friends here from the north being in very precarious health[31] & I the only partner in this country the Direction had to depend on. I have however secured the main chance and will in the fall of 1840 be again in this country to take with me the following spring her whom it pains me so much to leave on this occasion. I have also written to her parents for their consent & am every day expecting an answer confirmatory of my most Sanguine hopes. Hers as I told you before I had secured. So much for a Fur Traders knowing how to employ a fortnight properly. All this to yourself especially her *Name* and *residence*.

I have made arrangements to get up the famous Mustd & Pepper[32] from Leith hither, which I most anxiously trust you will procure for me *without fail*, as the Gentn for whom they are intended, is the surest hope I have for returning again to Scotland, and as his heart is set on obtaining these animals – such a matter will be of the highest personal importance to myself. Little attentions like these are often of the greatest consequence in life. You will send them in to Edinb by a *Carrier* or any safer conveyance you may devise – & direct them to be delivered to Mr Thomas of No 12 Miss Rutherfords Union place near Gayfield place head of Leith Walk. I have written him to deliver them to Captn Mill of the

---

30   One of the things that busied Hargrave that day was a memo for Governor Simpson asking the latter to arrange that twelve volumes of books which Hargrave had laid aside at Longmans be paid for and forwarded to the ships. They included five vols. Standard Novels, four vols. Edinburgh Cat. Library, one vol. Diary of a Physician, one vol. Pickwick papers, one vol. Meg Dods Cooking. The latter book was undoubtedly bought in the expectation that Letitia Mactavish would accept his marriage proposal.

31   Duncan and Nicol Finlayson.

32   The Dandie Dinmont terriers that he wished to procure for Governor George Simpson.

Royal Victoria Steam Vessel & have spoken to that Gent^n to bring them hither giving him the direction of the Gent^n here for whom they are. Make my kindest regards to Mr Wilson & say that in no matter could he oblige me more than by this – should such be within his power

I expect to hear from You in May. Make my kind Love to my Uncle & Aunt – to Cousin Effie & to all the family. My best regards to Mr Fyshe & to your worthy [illegible] Bailie. His eternity[?] of Whisky & Salmon I shall not soon forget. To Miss Sym & to her father I also beg to be remembered in the kindest manner, – and to your Chere Amie,[33] – whether wife or still mistress, I present a hundred kisses, you being my proxy. Excuse my hurried Lines & believe me ever
My Dear Cousin
Ever yours affectionately

JH

Compts to D^r McDougall & to Mr Barclay.

London 3 March 1838

Mr Thomas
12 Union place [Edinburgh]
My Dear Sir – I have made arrangements for getting from Abbotsford a pair of Mustard & Pepper Terriers for Govr & at his request have directed my Agents to deliver them to your care to be sent up to London. I have likewise spoken to Capt Mill of the Steam Boat Royal Victoria to bring them up, you will consequently please deliver them to him on his next trip hither after you may receive them & he will take them in charge till they reach 5 Trinity Square. In attending to this Matter you will much oblige Govr Simpson as well as My Dear Sir
Yours ever Sincerely

JH

I am on the eve of Starting for the Indian Country.

---

33 French for Dear Friend

London 4th March 1838

Captn Mill
Royal Victoria Steamer

My Dear Sir – I had expected the pleasure of a second Trip to Scotland with you again this season, but find that I must leave Britain within a few days for my former residence in the Indian Territories of North America. While on the Borders last Decr I made arrangements for procuring a Pair of the far famed "Mustard & Pepper" Terriers for a highly Valued friend here and have lately written to my Agents there to forward them to you in order that they may be brot hither on board your vessel. I expect they will be procured in course of the Spring & will be delivered to you by Mr Thomas a young Medical Student – presently boarding with Miss Rutherford – 12 Union place Edin^b. They are designed for "Geo Simpson Esq – 5 Trinity Square London," to whom you will forward them on arrival, & who will pay all expenses connected with this matter. I am very anxious about the success of this, – and from the kindness and attention I experienced from you while on board with you in Decr I have been induced to confide them to your Care as a gentleman whom I have found ever ready to oblige.
With much Esteem I Am
My Dear Sir
Most Sincerely Yours

JH

London 6th March 1838

Mr Wm Lockie

My Dear Lockie – I regret having to inform you that I am at this Moment busied with preparations for my departure to the Indian Country again, via Canada. – instead of the hope I had of spending a pleasant Spring in my Native Land. The Sickness of two of my friends here has occasioned this Call upon me, and there is no avoiding of it. The voyage itself is nothing, – for such is my profession, – and I care not tho' it were to cast a loop round the Globe but the letter calling for my presence here found me engaged in a matter near my heart and like Sir Walters fiery Cross[34]

---

34 In Scotland the "fiery cross," known as the *Crann Tara*, was used as a declaration of war, which required all clan members to rally to the defence of the area. The practice is described in the novels and poetry of Sir Walter Scott.

— carried me off if not from "The Bride at the Altar,"[35] – at least from within a few weeks prospect of such an event. I am past my days of poetry – look at this disappointment with the sober eyes of real life – & bear it with what philosophy I may. The matter is only postponed for a Short time, – & another visit to Britain will be the Result. I cannot now say more – and to none other of my friends in Scotland have I said so much. Keep it to yourself. I part Hawick in a Storm of Snow as fast as 4 pack horses could carry me, – & while changing our Reeking Steeds thought of my promise of leaving a pound of Snuff for my friend Mrs Lockie, but the haste and the hour and the lack of time & opportunity have also postponed the performance of this. I trust hereafter to be remembered.

My residence will be as heretofore at YF, – and could honors make amends for other disappointments, – I must say our Board of Direction here has liberally gratified me. My route thither will be that I came last year, and in the Spring is a most trying & inclement one. No lady could endure or survive it – else I know one who would have dared its dangers. I will hereafter say when I will be back again, but whether I may reach your hospitable fireside on that Occasion is an event on which I shall not prophesy. My motions being so meteor like.

Write me in May & With kind love to all the fireside believe me ever My Dear Lockie, ever truly yours –

JH

London 11th March 1838

My Dear Miss Mactavish

Your highly prized [letter] written the day after Mr Mactavish had returned to Kilchrist reached me here only five days ago and has since been at least fifty times perused, with what delight I shall not attempt to

---

  A small burning cross would be carried from town to town and was noted in 1745 during the Jacobite Rising.
35 A line in the following verse taken from the *Gathering Song of Donald the Black* by Sir Walter Scott:
  Leave untended the herd,
  The flock without shelter;
  Leave the corpse uninterr'd,
  The bride at the altar;
  Leave the deer, leave the steer,

tell you. I had for some time previous been under much anxiety of mind, – arising from not hearing from you, – in answer to letters which I had addressed both to your father & to yourself explaining candidly to him the state of my feelings towards yourself expected some reply before I should leave England which will now be two days hence. I acquainted you also with the painful necessity for this, – and in the event of a favorable answer to my proposal [illegible] my determination to return to this country two years hence – solely to fulfil my pledged word to you. This uncertainty of my fate agitates my mind much, – and till I hear from you – I shall not be able to control my apprehensions. –

This will be handed you by my old and intimate friend Mr D^n Finlayson to whom I have confided my sentiments regarding you, and who can give you or your relations more information regarding me than any one now in Britain. He is a man of honor, and you may implicitly rely upon all that he may tell you. He is making a tour such as I had projected for myself this spring round the west Coast of Scotland, & was desirous of a few lines from me introductory to your fathers Hospitable circle with which I have used the liberty of furnishing him.

Whenever I become oppressed with anxiety I return to your beloved pages, and they operate as a spell on my troubled fancy. Tis my fault alone, that our correspondence in any shape has been private, – and my present fearful State is my merited punishment. I feel in my heart that I have no worthy of you; and the bright hope of a happy termination to my timid suit is like the wretched hope of heaven, – this love alone and not deserts – My mind recoils from the supposition that you eventually may never be mine with the same pain that it would view the prospect of its own dissolution. How often have I bitterly repented my silence & loss of [illegible] when with you: – these were my fortunate moments – I have neglected them, – and the same may never return to me. I thank you from my soul for having had such confidence in me as to write at all; and if my letters have reached their address our after correspondence if to be continued, will be so in the open face of day.

I sail from Portsmouth on the 13th by the Gladiator[36] for New York, will be in Canada in April & leave it for the North on the 1st May – My

---

    Leave nets and barges:
    Come with your fighting gear,
    Broadswords and targes.

36 The packet ship *Gladiator* was one of a line of twelve such ships plying the route between London and New York in these years just prior to the era of

appointment is again for York Factory with two partners and 4 Clerks as my Assistants, among whom is my friend Willie [Mactavish].[37] I think I have that influence with him as to steer him clear of any risk of taking a *semi* squaw in tow. Your picture of Mrs MacLary is delightful. The vulgar old Woman in her night Cap whimpering and feigning a feeling her heart was never capable of deserves richly to be hung up to ridicule. How [illegible] Miss Charlotte under the deferred hope of Six Winters and cherishes she as much as ever her love for the "breezes among *the tresses*"? I trust my friend Miss Mary has at length finished the everlasting Mit. I have fairly lost my Wager, – the packet above referred to contained a trifling keepsake in discharge of this as also something for yourself and should it have miscarried, the loss would if possible add to the distress I feel on an infinitely more important point. These hasty pages, my sweet friend, are confided to the partial inspection of an eye which I flatter myself will not overlook their incoherency. I write amid a babel of noises and among the interruptions & distraction of getting ready for my departure. God prosper you, [illegible], I claim a remembrance in your secret thought, and believe me that I am ever, Dearest Letitia Thine Most Devotedly

JH

My friend F[inlayson] may return to the North next June, & perhaps not till 1839. Would that Miss Mary could find in her heart to accompany him. He is a noble minded fellow, – with whom she might well be happy. Her being in that country and Willie also – might render the prospect not so dreary to *Some one* else. Call you this Selfishness?

JH

London 11th March 1838

Dugald Mactavish Esq –
My Dear Sir – Permit me to introduce to your acquaintance, my valued friend Duncan Finlayson Esq – of the Hudsons Bay Coy – who purposes making a tour this summer round the West Coast of Scotland.

---

the steamships that superseded them. A line of Liverpool packets had been established in 1815, to be followed by the London packets about 1823.
37 William Mactavish.

Any attentions you may be pleased to show him I shall consider as added to the deep obligations I am already under to you. He has long been in habits of intimacy with my more than friend John George, and is also more widely acquainted than myself with the habits & Manners of the Indian Country.

I wrote you on the 23rd Feby last enclosing 2 packets for the young Ladies. From not having heard from you since, I am greatly apprehensive that some misfortune has befallen my parcel which was forwarded to your address by the Mail. Should this be so, M^r F who has long been to me as a brother and who is aware of the Nature of that communication, has kindly undertaken to explain the purport of it to you. The letters for my friends W^m & Dugald[38] reached me only on the 6th Ins^t – I shall have great pleasure in putting both into their hands. I thank you for your continued attention in favoring me with introductions to such respectable names in Scotland. My bad fortune has deprived me of much of the pleasure you had so liberally provided for me but I hope some future year may yet repay me for this. Kindest regards to all your happy family – and with high esteem – believe me ever

My Dear Sir

Most faithfully Yours

JH

London 12th March 1838
6 OClock Evg

Miss Mactavish

My Dear Letitia. Two hours hence and I will be far distant from this place on my way to Portsmouth, from which place I embark in the Gladiator which left this port yesterday at noon, and will touch there to take up such Passengers as did not go on board in the Thames. I have yet heard nothing from you in answer to both mine of the 23^d ult^a, – and had I not implicit confidence in the constancy of your mind, I would be miserable: As it is, fears will arise not of your affection but of the chances that life is subject to and where my whole heart is centred and at stake hope can never be so firmly fixed as not to be crossed by clouds of despondency. It would be unmanly to whine and accuse Fortune for the temporary

---

38 Letitia's brother.

separation which has been made between us. I know your superiority to that effeminate Spirit which would sit down with folded hands and affect a sentimental lament about the trials of life. Could I but know that my affection for you would meet the approbation of those we are both bound to consult, I would glory in wrestling with such disappointments as I have yet met with: – I have the warm support of our Govr in my proposed arrangement: your name is frequently mentioned by him with highest regard as a niece of my good friend John George – and nothing he assures me (and I have firm faith in his words) nothing would please him more than seeing me form such an alliance. I need not mention his power – as he has the will – to greatly contribute to our future comfort especially as to the situation where we should pass the years I would yet have to spend in the North. My dread lies elsewhere: you may remember I hinted to you my apprehensions about whether your father could bring himself to part with a being in whom I observed the strongest proof that such a large portion of his happiness was centred. I judge of his love by my own & tremble for the result.

What I hinted at in the postscript of my yesterdays letter I would delight in finding realised. I know that my friend purposes settling in life; – and should our pretty Miss Polly[39] [illegible] make a conquest I know not one more deserving of her. My hopes are constantly entwining my own desires with whatever may forward them, – and should this dream of mine prove as propitious a road *might* be opened to us to meet sooner than I have yet dared to look for. Whatever he may say to you in my name believe. Our conversations have been frequent about you, he is a friend of twenty years tried & entrusted a hundred times, – in what has hitherto been of the deepest interest to me, – and you may rest assured honor and integrity will be found in whatever he may say or suggest.

This is now the fourth sheet I have devoted to you: – My mind is never and my chief pleasure is to cover pages which I figure to myself will eventually be where the heart which dictates them is. Say not that you fear I will not long to hear again from you, or that your letters are uninteresting. Do more justice to your own elegant taste, and more to my affection. Believe me that every thing I have which you have ever touched is treasured up as a relic not to be parted with and in my esteem without price. Time however compels me to close. The latest dates for letters this spring

---

[39] Letitia's sister, Mary.

to HBay – is about the 20th May, and the HBHouse here the address. I will anxiously look forward to the Ships arrival and I trust she will both bring & carry back cheering news to both of us. May our God preserve us both till we meet again in happiness! Ever believe me – Dearest Letitia. Your most affectionately

JH

[Letterbook]
N°. 13
Rough Copies Letters by
JHargrave
from 15th March 1838 @ 15th September 1838

Lachine May 1st 1838

Dugald McTavish Esqr

My Dear Sir – Your highly valued sheet of 12 March enclosed in one from our Worthy Govr followed me within one days Voyage from Portsmouth to this country where it reached me on the 29th Ulta – and I cannot sufficiently express my sentiments of gratitude for the frank & candid manner in which both Mrs McTavish & yourself have so promptly & favorably met my application: – it shall be my part to prove to you, I now fondly trust during many future happy years, that the noble confidence you repose in my feelings of honor & principle is fully appreciated in the same spirit it has been bestowed. This letter found me out whilst with my old parents in Beauharnois & I accordingly used the opportunity to make them acquainted with its contents & my wishes. I need not add with what feelings of pride and gratification they yielded their willing consent to my prosecuting of a suit so honorable to me and to them. I left them both this day bearing with me their ardent prayers for happiness in my anticipated new position in life. I believe I mentioned that I had made Govr Simpson acquainted with the tenor of my last communication to you. This was due to him, both from his uniform fatherly kindness to me individually, – & politically necessary as his influence on our future fortunes & local residence in the country will be of weighty importance in many respects. His sentiments were those of warmest approbation in congratulating me in having aspired to a choice in a family than whom, from his respect for it & friendship for such branches of the name as he has met with, – he considers I could not in Britain have found another so appropriate nor so desirable in every point of view. 'Twas he who then pledged himself, should my application to you be met favorably – that in the fall of 1840 – I should have another furlough to allow me to return to sue for success & fulfil my engagements. On reaching the North, I shall gladly take an opportunity to explain to William what views and sentiments my visit to his happy home had awakened in me, – and invite him to consider me hereafter in the light of a brother, as he has hitherto ever done me that of a friend.

Dugald is at this moment in the house with me, – well and hearty. His application to business is most regular, – and his improvement in the knowledge of the Coys affairs I understand highly satisfactory to M^r [James] Keith, – a gentleman by the way most rigid and exact in his judgment of others' talents & whose approbation is therefore the truer test of merit. I hear that my old friend John George with his family is well: – I trust in 2 or 3 days to drop in on him & spend one night among them in passing. As I was not expected by any in the North through this route in spring, – no letters from thence have reached this to my address. The latest dates however, up to the beginning of winter, speak of health and tranquility among all the Residents at YF where William now is.

You will hear again from me in the Autumn by our return Ships – Meanwhile with kind love to all – believe me ever
My Dear Sir
Most faithfully thine

JH

Lachine 1st May 1838
Miss Mactavish
My Dear Letitia – Your fathers very flattering answer to my letter of Feby last followed me hither; and on being put into my hands two days ago removed a weight from my heart which had pressed on my spirits ever since I had lost sight of the British Shores. Let me assure you that the honorable confidence both your parents have been pleased to repose in me it shall be my unceasing study in after life to show myself not unworthy of. To you especially my sweet friend whom my heart now with confidence welcomes to itself, as its chief solace, confidant and counsellor amid the vicissitudes of future years, permit me to say that my unceasing purpose shall be to prove myself deserving of the devotion and entire reliance on my character which activated you when we in anticipation of this consent pledged ourselves to each other in private on the day which closed my happy residence at Kilchrist. Your looks, tones and words have never since been absent from me: – They haunt me by night, and are the hoarded subject of sweetest reflection in my waking hours. Time will hang heavy upon me till I can again rejoin you to claim you as my own, and my sincerest aspirations are for your safety and prosperity till that desired day shall come round. My heart can never admit of another affection, – and should the Almighty see meet to blast my future life with a loss never to be repaired, – I shall never seek for happiness in another. I

love you with that unity of feeling, with that singleness of heart, which I had never hitherto experienced, and by which I never expect to be again activated. But I will not indulge in such views: – I hail with confidence as a favorable omen, – the good fortune which has hitherto been mine since the hour we first met, – & which I will consider as the first rays of that felicity which is to attend us in after years.

I am just parted from both my aged parents to whom I have made known my sentiments towards that amiable being whom I aspire to unite to their name. Considering their years I fear I may never have the happiness of seeing them both again, but I leave them with their warmest approbation of my purpose, – and sincerest prayers for both our happiness. That worthy pair has the most sacred claims on my duty as a Son, – and it is one of my sweetest subjects of reflections, – that providence has by the position in which it has placed me, – enabled me to smooth their descent into the vale of years. Their memory and their blameless life, well can be held in honor by me. While with them I had the pleasure of a visit from M^r & M^{rs} McPherson the worthy clergyman of their parish. The lady especially was inquisitive about my travels in Scotland and on my mentioning my visit to Kintyre,[1] inquired with much interest whether I had also visited Kilchrist. On being answered in the affirmative, she with much feeling claimed connection with your family, and particularly spoke in the warmest terms of both your parents & of yourself. In course of our continued conversation, she laughingly expressed her wonder that such merit could have proved of such little apparent effect upon me. Little did she know how musically every word she uttered sounded in my ears! I fancied a resemblance between you & herself: – her eyes especially recalled forcibly your own sweet & mild glances which I have so often worshiped in my secret soul.

I had a pleasant & considering the season an expeditious passage of 33 days from Portsmouth to New York. I leave this two days hence & will be at York Factory about the end of June. All your relatives in this country are well. Depend on hearing again from me in Nov^r, and – with warmest feelings of attachment believe me ever, my own Letitia
Yours most Devotedly

JH

1 Kintyre is a long peninsula in Argyllshire pushing out toward Northern Ireland.

Hudsons Bay House, Lachine L:C: –
1 May 1838

Mr Alex Mitchel –
My Dear Cousin – This is the second time I have commenced a letter to you since I left England &^{c}
Sent –

JH

Lake of the Thousand Islands
On the Route from Lake Superior to Lake Winipeg
27th May 1838

Miss Mactavish
Dearest Letitia, – I am at present prevented by stormy weather & contrary winds from continuing my voyage towards *home* and I turn with delight from the gloomy and Savage Scenes around me to that home, from which my heart has never been absent since you taught me to know its value. I last wrote you from our House at Lachine, which place I left on the 3rd Ins^t in a Bark Canoe, manned by 14 Canadian Voyageurs, with a Catholic Clergyman,[2] going on a Mission to the Shores of the Pacific, as my traveling Companion. The same day I left, I reached the Lake of the Two Mountains where I had the pleasure of finding my old friend your uncle with the whole of his family in good health, and the country around which so lately had been the Scene of warfare restored to its former tranquil state. I spent one happy evening with him & M^{rs} McTavish, – and the following day started on my voyage up the Ottawa River. In 12 days I reached Lake Superior, spent 6 more in coasting the British Shores of that fresh water Sea and am now on my way from it through the Lake of the Woods & Winipeg to my Indian home at York Factory. The weather has been very inclement throughout, fresh Snow, Sleet & rain, varied by occasional days of burning heat, have tried us on all tacks, and altho' I can still maintain my name as an Indian Traveller, I feel about me some lingering remains of that Sickness which caused my

---

2 François Norbert Blanchet (1795–1883), the son of a Canadian farmer, was a missionary who became the first archbishop of Oregon City. In 1837 he was appointed vicar-general for the Oregon mission, a vast region never before visited by a Catholic priest, and he set out in May 1838 with the annual express of the Hudson's Bay Company.

visit to Scotland. I am however much improved since we parted and I merely mention this from a flattering belief that you will be interested in knowing how I am. We are presently encamped on the lee Shore of a thickly wooded Island, one of the many contained in this Lake/ as its name betokens;/ – an immense fire of dry logs sends its Smoke curling up through the Matted Canopy of pines overhead, the gigantic Stems of which rise around us like the pillars of a Gothic Cathedral; – the *Snow* is falling thick & fast, the wind roars on the lake, & the white curly waves dash up on the Sandy beach. A canvas tent opens its door to the crackling blaze, and Monsr Blanchette[3] & I are within reclining on our Traveling beds with our feet to the fire, he occupied with his Breviary – I with this page to my Lady love. He addresses me now & then to make some commonplace observation, little knowing what he is interrupting on a belle Ecossaise[4] and I answer at random which causes the old man to smile & turn to his prayers again. The voyageurs are stretched around another fire, wrapped up in blankets & asleep. The snow gradually covers them over & all is white but their bronzed features on which the flakes melt as they fall, – yet they sleep sound and healthy and vigorous. A single house or White Man besides the party, is not within a hundred miles of us; a timid & shy Deer is sometimes seen fleeing through the trees; the Beaver may be found busy in a Solitary Creek forming its dam, and the drumming partridge is at intervals heard among the branches courting the notice of its little mate. I paint miserably, but these are a few rough outlines which your livelier fancy can better dispose & fill up than my own. The Scene is Solitary & savage yet custom renders it dear to me: – Am I too selfish in my ardent wish to have your company even amid such, – and would its gratification cause my lovely Letitia a too painful Sacrifice?

I long greatly to hear from you. Write me, my love, as often and on all such matters, as you would wish to talk to me personally. Your letters will be my chief delight till I again can return to you. My promise to do so, Dearest, my name & fortune as dear to me if possible as yourself my pledge, – and my hand & heart, I consider now as entirely yours as if I had already exchanged vows with you before the Altar. Could I find language still stronger & more expressive I would gladly use it, to allay whatever anxiety may happen arise in your mind about the future. My

3 François Norbert Blanchet.
4 French for a pretty Scottish woman.

Mind is little apt to be swayed from its purpose naturally as deeply & as surely as man can engage himself – I am, Letitia, for life, thine & thine only. One favor I have at this time to beg of you, – which in my present position I trust you will not refuse me: – a Miniature portrait of your own lovely features to be the inseparable companion of my person in this land. Perhaps you could get such without allowing the purpose of it to be known & forward it in a parcel to London to my address by the end of next February; – by which means it would reach me about this time next year. Listen favorably to this Dearest, your own heart will tell you how mine would welcome it. As I expect to hear of or from William after I get 6 or 800 miles further into the interior I shall leave this unclosed till I can tell you of his welfare. Meanwhile Health & sweet dreams to you my darling little radical: the storm is over & I must on the water again.

How expressive – how true this chorus of our simple Voyageur Songs
    Elle a les doux yeux et la bouche vermeille:
    Ah! Quel sera doux d'avoir un baiser d'elle!–[5]

Norway House – N. End Lake Winipeg – 14th June 1838

I am now dearest Letitia within 500 miles of my home after a pleasant & fortunate voyage of 18 days since I began this sheet. As William does not expect me till the fall I have not opened a letter from him at this place; – but the news from York are not above a month old, and tell me of his good health & prosperity. It is particularly pleasing also to find, that in consequence of almost all the Officers at York being lately appointed to that place & little acquainted with the duties of Head Quarters, your brothers efficiency & experience in them have been of the highest importance in retaining in the requisite order the rather complicated business of the General Depot of the Trade. Every one speaks highly of his services, as also of his amiable & gentlemanly manners in private life. In a weeks time, please God, I shall be with him.

    I must at last close these pages. They convey to you My love the warmest truest feelings of a heart entirely yours. The crowd of this country and the cares of public life again surround me: arduous & often delicate duties apparently engross my whole mind: but beyond & within these is found a sentiment which sweetens & softens the asperities of every day

> 5 "She has gentle eyes and bright red lips: Ah, how sweet it would be to have a kiss from her!" The song's title is "Voici le printemps" and it originated in the Liège region in present-day Belgium.

Voici le printemps

Unknown

"Voici le printemps" was the song of the voyageurs that Hargrave refers to in his letter of 27 May 1838 to Letitia Mactavish. Its origins lie in Wallonia, the French-speaking part of Belgium.

life with all its cares. This is the full confidence that you are mine & that when a few more seasons shall roll round we shall meet again to part no more. May our God bless you, & preserve us both till that thrice happy day!
Yours ever most affectionately

JH
☐ See 2nd page from this (16th)

Norway House 14th June 1838

Mr Dugald McTavish
Lachine
My Dear Sir – I enclose to your address a letter for your father (double) which you will oblige me much by getting forwarded to address as early as possible, paying postage as far as will be received in Canada and charging

the same to my Acct at Lachine. I am thus far on my way to the Coast having performed our voyage in as short a time I believe as it has almost ever heretofore been done 30 days from the Lake of the 2 Mountains to Lake Winipeg. On passing Lac La Pluie I made inquiry about some wild Rice but fear that the Indians had purch[ase]^d the whole of last years crop, as far as yet known, but should I obtain any, I will forward it to Kilchrist by the Ship. At all events, I shall have some next year. I have not heard from William as he does not expect me this spring, but learn that he is in good health, as well as all those at York this season.

Let me hear from you next year my dear fellow. I am getting drawn into the whirlpool of the Depot again and can scarcely command a minute for letter writing, but shall always feel happy to hear from you, as well as to tell you at least by a couple lines, how much with sincerity I am
My Dear Sir
Most faithfully Yours

JH

YF 23^d July 1838

Mr Dugald Mactavish – Lachine
My Dear Sir

The packet is getting ready for Canada – and all are busy in the composition of some part or other of it – yet with my share must be a few lines for yourself – by which you see I am determined to allow you no apology for letting dropout of mind your promised sheet to me of next spring. I wrote you a few lines from Norway House, enclosing a letter to your fathers address – both of which I trust will have reached you long before this can. I reached this place about a month ago in safety – where I had the pleasure of finding my friend William in good health, and of handing him a budget of lines from *home*. He will of course be writing you by this occasion. He still remains the steady, honorable and manly young fellow I have ever found him, – indeed of all the youth in the North, – there candidly is not *one* that can bear a comparison with him, – an opinion confirmed to me by every additional month I spend in his society. When I can retain him with me in the Service we never separate. I have him at present in charge of the Gen[era]l Store, – one of the most important departments in the duties [illegible], – and he already shows an extended knowledge of the Trade, and an expertness in business, – which it is frequently not acquired by some – during a whole life of plodding labor.

Of general incident here not one single circumstance rises above the usual inanity of a Fur Trading life. All our Brigades of Boats were off two weeks ago for the inland Districts, – and we expect nothing of novelty till the Ship[6] makes her appearance from England. We had a few lines from Mr T. Simpson of the Arctic Exp^n this spring but these cont^d nothing of importance. The party was passing a quiet winter had plenty of food, & were waiting impatiently the time for to set out on their travels to the eastward. They purpose devoting a third year to complete this discovery – and whether successful or not will not return till the fall of 1839 – or spring of 1840. Keep this little piece of news to yourself.

I enjoy now the best health, and all fears attendant on a residence upon this coast have disappeared from the Inmates of the Factory. That I have the like good news from you next spring is the hope
My Dear Dugald –
Yours Most faithfully

JH

YF 24th July 1838

Miss Mactavish
My Dear Letitia – The last opportunity of the season for sending letters to England via Canada lies now at hand, – I use it as I will do all to tell my love of my welfare – and to repeat to her my vows of unchangeable affection. There is a fascination in this which for the time shuts out all matters that occupy my daily attentions, and which carries me back to Kilchrist, its happy family, and your delicious society. Well was I aware on parting from you that I was leaving behind me what on earth could alone render me happy, – but had no belief tho' some fears that our separation would exceed a few weeks at most. Even when these fears became a certainty I still imagined that I could bear up under the anguish of hope deferred with more firmness than I seem likely to do, – time as it flies past, adds daily to my impatience, and the dreary length of time which may yet separate us appears to my fancy never ending. This impatience has increased with me the more painfully since I have reached my home at this place – I find myself alone: – the crowd, the press of business and the anxieties attending it wear through the day, – but the evening of retirement comes, and my harassed mind, seeks shelter in my solitary apartments to dream over the happy days of last February, – and

---

6 The *Prince Rupert* would arrive at York Factory 28 August.

to waste the hours in fruitless wishes for the Society of her the sunshine of my life who only can complete my happiness. Fears for your safety, and dread of the accidents to which life is exposed – will also sometimes intrude. Guard yourself, my only love, as far as providence can, from the chances of these. The infectious disease so prevalent around you when I left Kintyre has cost me many sleepless hours: – May God preserve you from the dreadful scourge. Think not less of me my sweet love for all this: – weakness I myself would once have called it; – what little did I then know the bliss of loving, – or of feeling the persuasion that I could [illegible] anything in the estimation of one so amiable, so good, so perfect.

I arrived here about a month ago, and was welcomed back as I set my foot ashore by my friend Willie. He is as well as your own kind heart could desire, – and being a character, both publicly and as a gentleman, of which his friends may well be proud. I have him placed as my second in the Genl Depot, one of the most important charges among the various duties of the Factory, – and he already shows a splendid knowledge of the Trade & an expertness in business which is frequently not acquired by many during a whole life of plodding study. Was it from no other consideration than – as a public man, he is of the highest value to all and while I may have influence so far with our Board at Home as to retain him with me, – we never separate. This place besides, is one of the most prominent positions in the service, and is justly considered by all as among the Shortest roads to promotion in it.

The whole of the Furs traded last season are now here, and while they are about being packed, for sending to London, – I have directed the Clerk who attends to that duty to select for me a few of the finest Sables &^{c} – which in my own mind are intended for you. He is among the best judges of furs in the Country & I feel confirmed that better will not reach England this season. They will go home by our Ships in Sept^r – and I shall take measures that they reach you in safety. Please accept of them my loveliest, my sweetest, as a trifling token that your dear idea is never absent from me, – and honor me by wearing them for my Sake. I regret that I cannot obtain a Sea-Otter to accompany them, but these, the most esteemed of all our articles of Trade, are only found on the West Coast of this Continent, near Vancouver Island, and are sent to England direct from thence. I have however an intimate friend in the Officer who commands the Factory[7] there, – and have already written him to select me

---

7 James Douglas (1803–1877) was chief trader in 1839 at Fort Vancouver. During John McLoughlin's absence in England in 1838–39, Douglas had charge

one of the very finest, which I confidently expect will be sent to me next summer & which will reach you in the fall of 1839. Now my love, do not feel vexed at my taking the liberty of sending you these trifles. Their cost I value not, – all I possess I consider as truly yours as it is mine; and besides by the bald request I presumed to make in my letter to you written during the Voyage hither, you will perceive that I literally adhere to our professional Motto: "Pro Pelle Cutem."[8] A miniature portrait of your lovely features to be sent the next fall with – so I will not admit the profane idea of talking of our exchange here. Your indulging me in this will impose on me a debt of gratitude which even a life of love can only prove, – not repay.

This is my third letter since I landed on this continent, – on the former occasions I wrote your father & enclosed them: Willie will do me this favor on the present occasion. I do not write the Sheriff just now, as I expect our fall letters will reach you as soon as this, – but to pass any opportunity for telling you how much I love you is impossible. Please make my affectionate remembrances to both him & to your excellent Mother; – and tell her what I say of Willie. I assure both you & her I have *under* rather than *over* stated his true merits. Say likewise that I have not forgotten my promise about sending her a Specimen of our cranberries – in a week or two they will be ready for gathering, & then I shall have a band of *Squaws* into the Woods to collect them.*

In about three weeks I confidently hope to hear from you. May these news be *such* as I hope and pray for. I will write you again in course of this Autumn – Meanwhile farewell, my own love – farewell!
Yours ever Most affectionately

JH

* Her anxiety about Willies taking a fancy to any of the Brown Faces I think quite groundless. I have observed him closely and can perceive no traces of any penchant in that direction. In fact the days for such esca-

---

    of Fort Vancouver, the coastal posts, the trapping expeditions, and the shipping. In 1839 he was promoted to chief factor. Ormsby, "Douglas, Sir James."

8 Latin: translates roughly as "a skin for a skin." The HBC motto may have a clever double meaning. One interpretation is that it means that the skin, *cutem*, was wanted for the sake of the fleece, *pro pelle*. The other is that it means "for the pelts which we collect, we risk our skins."

pades are past: – a different tone of feeling on these matters have gradually come round, – & a young Gent[n] from Britain would as soon think of matching himself with the contemporary of his grandmother as now a [illegible] with a pure Squaw. True it is some tempted by money now & then give their hand to the daughter of an Officer & some few from kinder Motives. But William I feel convinced is too noble minded for the first – & has too good a taste to be attracted by the latter feeling.

YF 24th/28 July 1838

J.G. M[c]Tavish Esq
My Dear Sir

The Canoe with the fall packet is now about starting, and altho' we have in the North little except parish news to catch up, this season, yet to write any thing to you always gives me pleasure. After a pleasant & considering all things an expeditious voyage up of 31 days to Red River, I reached this after several delays about a month ago, and found all well. M[r] [John] Charles both professed to be and I believe the worthy old man really was delighted to see me back, in order to get rid of a situation that two years of which had [illegible] him more than 6 spent any where else would have done. The business of Outfitting has been got over, and every brigade cleared out for their winter Quarters – more than 10 days ago, – the time gained from not holding a Council having enabled us to get through the routine earlier than usual. All has gone over quite smoothly – not a single feud or misunderstanding has arisen to furnish a topic for a letter. My own situation is rather a delicate one, and with some I have to walk gingerly as if on weak ice. Young in the service, deficient in rank, and of a party whose superior efficiency & services have more frequently been repaid by envy & back-biting rather than by praise, – I have not resumed my old station, being [illegible] without sundry obliging hints about favoritism. God help them, – the situation was open, offered to them, & actually refused by such as they themselves considered qualified to fill it. This Janus like treatment however discourages not a jot. I feel myself equal to the charge, – have now assistants on whom I can rely, am in good health, – and am proud in having my friends among the reasonable & public spirited of both sides, – so with good fortune to spend, I move on without appearing to notice the gnawing of rats and doubt not that I shall keep the wheel rolling.

I have now considerable labor in getting the Am[t] Req[n] into shape, but have at length produced such a one as will serve for the Can[a] packet. The Am[t] is not quite 19 .m. My worthy friend M[r] C[harles]: – had labored long at the task, but his ideas appear to have been confused a little among the various Outfits to be considered, – I have therefore to begin at the beginning. Out of paper however his management does him high credit, – and his only oversight is in not being aware of his own capacity, – and a diffidence in himself which left him open to be swayed by every breeze. The General Depot is now completed on a plan which I believe I formerly mentioned to you, and we have ample room with every convenience for the Transaction of business. My friend William[9] is with me, and with Gladman[10] and him I have no anxiety about the issue. I have him placed in the Genl Store where he occupies the same position I so long filled. It is only bare justice to him to say that I have never had one at the Factory in whom I can more confidently repose trust. His clear head, careful habits and steady interested conduct, are every thing I could desire; – and I believe I really am rather not over easily pleased when I see indifference, or careless indolence about me. Gladman goes to Oxford, as I have found it prudent to bring Grant[11] hither. The silly fellow got engoué[12] last winter of an Indian wench, took her to his bed, to his table, and the world called her his wife. I stood unmoved against his struggles to get back, and now hope that a separation has been made, which will prevent the matter from getting more blazoned.

I fully expect to hear from you next spring, and to learn that your health goes on steadily improving. Please make my kindest regards to M^{rs} McTavish whose kindness to me in passing I shall not soon forget, – & with warmest feelings of auld lang syne believe me ever My kind old Bourgeois
Most faithfully & truly Yours

JH

YF 10 Septr 1838
For Miss Mactavish
My Dear Letitia. You can better imagine than I express the exulting delight with which I welcomed both your invaluable favors of the 15th &

9 William Mactavish was a clerk at York Factory from 1834 to 1841.
10 George Gladman (1800–1863), born at an HBC post in Upper Canada, was chief trader at York Factory from 1839–41.
11 Richard Grant, 1793–1862, a Canadian, was chief trader in 1838 at York Factory. He had a son at Oxford House by a local woman.
12 *S'engouer* is French for to be infatuated with.

16th May. – which reached me 6 days ago. To attempt to put into words the slightest shadow of my emotions would be to make me appear foolish even to myself – stark mad as I am. Your kindness, your dear confidence in me I have never had a moments doubt of since that notable time which you so archly recall to my recollection. – famed for my most judicious advice: – "to hear all and say nothing." Do you know that on that occasion I was so full of my own emotions – and so *bothered* how to find expressions to convey to you all which then possessed me, – that I felt I wad better interpret silence then and you to clothe it in language – You have made me the happiest fellow this country contains, – yet as this condition is never without alloy – you have only added to my impatience for that time when I shall be again blessed by catching you in my arms & telling you in broken language how much I love you. Bear up however with my awkward fortune I must: – the day *will* come I feel confident it will, when by your side & reading your minds emotions through your sweet glances I shall yet have a reward for the bitter years of absence which it has been my fortune to experience. Even these are not of unmixed pain & regret. They have already awarded proof to me (could proof have been required to increase the confidence I have ever entertained), how greatly you surpass all others in intellect, taste & good humour – as well as in feminine charms – and bewitching attractions. Your pages possess a spell over my spirit, and I could have fallen in love with you, had I only seen you through the magic which shows in every word you say – any idea you express. Let me not draw a blush to your cheek however by expressions your Modesty will be saying are the rose colored feelings of absent love: – I will therefore check my pen – too apt to run riot over such a theme & such merit will spare you – & enjoy these feelings in my own day dreams.

You will have learned ere this that your fathers letter of March did not reach me till I was in Canada, and the kind & honorable promptitude with which he met my advances dispelled all the clouds which had hovered over me since I left Britain. From the unfortunate delay of my packet & in the immediate improvement of time which such had produced, I saw a sufficient reason for your silence then: – I *knew* our fall packet would repay me – and I have been more than repaid. I wrote both you & him from Lachine: – which letters I believe will have reached you a few days after you last wrote me. I addressed Gov. S. under the same date, made him aware of my good fortune, & added an expression of confidence in his promise to be permitted to revisit *home* in 1840. This he received the same month & 10 days after the date of yours says in answer. "I am rejoiced to find you have accomplished so much of your voyage in safety & that you have such pleasing & satisfactory advices from our friends in Argyle Shire. Rest assured my Dear Fellow that it will afford me sincere pleasure to meet your views in regard to leave of absence – and in every other respect in which it may be in my power to consult your interests & comforts." Again he adds – "My wife desires to be most kindly remembered to you – and often says how happy she will be to see Mr & Mrs Hargrave under our humble roof." Were he but to know of your *rebellious* wrath – how he would tease you, after we reach London in the winter of 1840/41.

Your picture of the amiables about you the ludicracy, the laughable, the vixen the Sentimental is so lively so racy – that I would spend my life in listening to your narrations. Such however only tempts me to press on you with still more earnestness my burning desire to have you to write constantly to me whenever your fancy wanders so far as these solitary deserts. Send me sheet on Sheets & packet on packet. Could you but witness how they relieve my wearied mind in the quiet hours of retirement when in the depths of night I can shut out the world, & turn my mind entirely to you you would out of sheer compassion indulge my *unreasonable* wishes. *Above all*, permit me again to solicit your favorable attention to my former request of your portrait. Till the substance shall be mine – how I should worship the Shadow! William is still with me, and amidst the crush & turmoil of our most busy season, is my most trusty and trusted aid. I go to Red River Colony ensuing spring to attend the Meeting of Council when I will meet Gov. Simpson. Willie will remain to manage the Depot duty till my return. My mode of traveling will be yet described to you, in a carreau/or cariole/ drawn by Dogs. I am getting a beautiful one made, which one day may be honored by your using it for our excursions into the surrounding forest to see a Beaver House. I now send home by the Ship[13] a Box to your fathers address containing a Dozen Sables, and Beaver, an Otter, and a Lynx. As the Beaver possesses too shaggy a fur for a Lady it will make a splendid winter cap for the Sheriff if you please to present it to him for that purpose: – In this country our Squaws extract all the Coarse Hair which makes the fur look much richer. The furrier should be able to do the same. The rest are for

13 The *Prince Rupert* left York Factory 17 September and arrived in London 21 October.

you alone: – I need not add they are the finest this continent can produce. I feel Convinced no lady in Scotland will be able to produce any to excel them, any more than she can ever equal you in all that is amiable, and attractive. I have full confidence in being able to add a Sea Otter to them next Season. I also send a Keg of Cranberries to the same address for Mama. Her kindness to me during the happy time I spent in the family was that of a mother: – she shall soon be honored by me with all the affection of a Son. I would also thank Polly personally for her very kind though *extremely* short letter, but fear my sheet would not be worth the tax of postage. I hope Miss Charlotte is now quite recovered. She is an amiable Girl of whom I saw too little while with you. Do Hector & Alex[r] prove Guid Gullie[14] Scholars, & is Lockhart as anxious as ever to shoot a Buffalo?[15] You make me shiver at the mistake of Willie about a *Lady*! Believe me my Love, it is a mistake – I cannot imagine how originating & I do not like to ask him. No woman in this country or any where else till I met you had ever the slightest claim on me. I pledge you my honor for the assertion. It is a land however short of *News* & lots are fabricated to supply the scarcity. Various rumors are afloat just now: – some changes I have been making in my lodgings, pantry Rooms & enlarging my accommodations look very suspicious, & a Lady was fully expected by the ship. This theory has for the present exploded & the [illegible] at so far quite at a nonplus. M[rs] Worsleys good opinion I desire much, as the little I saw of her led me to esteem her very highly.

^Poor Willie had been sad to believe the most fatal ruminations to Johns sickness & was in great distress, You can imagine how rejoiced we were to learn his recovery. I only wonder how a lady of her superior talents & mind ever in the [illegible] of hymen could have been matched with such *Bodie*. Love on the occasion must have not only [illegible] but gone blind.

    I write this Dearest while all who can are asleep. Our duties while the Ship[16] is here are through night & day. Mine are now of the highest, but to think & speak to you refreshes me more than the state of unconsciousness. Your trust will gain a week to our Directing in the Dispatch

---

14 Pleasant, agreeable. DSL.
15 Hector, Lockhart, and Alexander Mactavish were three more younger brothers of Letitia.
16 The *Prince Rupert* had arrived 28 August at York Factory and departed again 17 September.

of the Ship: – and if my wishes have virtue to bear her in safety home, – you will have this 3 weeks after its date Health & happiness to you my love: – would to God indeed that your wishes could place me beside you. What intoxicating delight in the supposition! The time however will come – May I have patience to endure the interim. The Middle of February will be the latest date you can safely trust to for dispatching your spring *packet*. The boat will bring it out to me from London. Your last address was perfectly correct. With kindest love to all esteem me my dearest sweetest friend – Yours ever Most affectionately

JH

I am sorry to find that my excellent friend Mr Finlayson has been so indisposed all spring as to have been detained since my departure till the sailing of the Ship in London under the control of the Medical faculty. I fear his health is irrecoverably damaged. I notice your praises of my favorite Ed. Brougham.[17] I have had his treatise on Nat[ural] History sent me this season – with his edition of Paley[18] – but have not yet perused them. The gloomy days of winter will [illegible] with such grave studies. I regret to learn the retirement of Mr Murray:[19] – I had a high esteem for him & have just been reading his manly defence of his conduct in answer to Sir Ja^s Graham[20] on the occasion of a debate regarding election riots in that nest of Radicals, – my almost native town Hawick. They are a band of polissons[21] after all – stark moss-troopers every one of them till this day – & require a rod of iron to keep them within bounds in these days of carpet consideration. I have been looking round for some novelties from this land to diversify a page from such a distance, but find none. Our days evaporate as barren of interesting features as all pine forests are of fruit. A poor indian Widow has just breathed her last – & left me a family of small copper imps dependent on my charity. I have as many in the Tents which fringe the plantation as would replenish a respect-

---

17 Henry Brougham (1778–1868), Lord High Chancellor of Great Britain.
18 Brougham edited William Paley's *Natural Theology*.
19 John Murray (1778–1843), publisher of the *Quarterly Review*, the recognized organ of the Tory party.
20 Sir James Robert George Graham (1792–1861), British statesman and strong advocate of the Reform Bill.
21 French for mischief makers.

able parish Workhouse. The fatherless & the widow however have sacred claims upon us whatever color may tinge their skin. The poor creature died from the effects of starvation last spring – she proved too debilitated for recovery. The husband perished from the same curse & his last breath entreated his partner to leave him & attempt to save their little ones by trying to reach the Factory. Fortunately she met others, too late to save her husband, but by this aid, the family reached us – she [illegible] to sink, tho' I trust the sons will live to become good hunters & the daughters industrious Squaws.

15th – My Dear Love – The ship is on the point of sailing & our packet will be on board of her this evening. It pains me now to close this sheet, as if it were in a manner parting with yourself. It will in a few weeks be in your own hands, and I in imagination picture to myself your reception of it – Would to God that I could accompany it – but I will not touch on this theme. Farewell – my own – my only love, farewell!

JH

YF 8th Septr 1838

Mr William Lockie
Stouslea

My Dear Lockie – I was favored with your very kind Sheet of the 2nd June last, a few days ago by the safe arrival of our Ship the Prince Rupert from London and although I am the centre of the turmoil consequent on her presence in this port, I am nevertheless sit down about the witching hour of night to acknowledge the receipt of it, and to answer in return as much as the spirit can find time to give utterance to.

My voyage to New York & from thence to Canada was expeditious, safe and as pleasant as a floating palace, Splendid Hotels, and Magnificent Steam Vessels could make it. A striking contrast by the way to the lowly style & anxious mind with which I first crossed the Atlantic about 20 years ago. The last feature however, was nearer in resemblance to those days than in contrast – but of that hereafter – meanwhile – en avant. I dropt down among my parents and my friends at Beech Ridge – on the 26th Apr – as if from the Clouds, – first roused my brother Andrew from the side of a new Married bride about 6 in the Morning, – then reached my fathers house, and found the Old patriarch himself seated at the head of his breakfast Table, a Noble dish of porritch & Milk before him, while the rest of the family with a visitor or two following the effeminate taste of the modern world – by preferring to our national dish – a smoky breakfast of eggs Coffee & Tea. The old Boy himself was at the moment deep in explanation to a neighbor of the mysterious line which separates free will & necessity, – & almost blind as he was he imagined me another next door friend & accordingly invited me most hospitably to a Share in his breakfast & in his dissertation. You may guess how I bothered the latter, when he saw my old Mother catch me in her arms, – & when I grasped his own hand. The worthy old soul was quite overcome for some time & did not recover his self possession till he had vented his feelings in mental devotion. As I hinted my brother Andrew had lately married a pretty gay Scotch Girl named Lawson[22] & has now a farm within a few miles of my father: John is also on the eve of tying the knot with another young country woman,[23] – but is still in my fathers house. I could only remain with them a day or two & then started on the 1st May for this place in a Bark canoe, – whence after a Voyage full of incidents but of which I can cram none into this Sheet I arrived in Safety on the 26th of June.

I have read with great sympathy & emotion the interest all your worthy family feel in the fortunes of the Wanderer my friend. To Miss Jane I owe my warmest thanks & *almost* one of my warmest embraces the next time we meet. Should William & I ever forgather in Canada he may depend on my best interest & countenance & protection. To the affections of the worthy heads of the same family I have long had pretensions & long have been persuaded that I possess them.

On the one particular subject which interested you in my last I cannot just now be so open as I could wish, tho by & bye you shall know all. You already know more than any in Scotland; barring the family in which I trust soon to become a son. For the present – & what I say keep to yourself & to your own family – as you value my friendship – I can only inform you that the young Lady to whose hand I have now the most cordial sanction of both her parents – as well as her own blushing consent, – belongs to a hand & a rank in society far superior to the original lowly option of the border Shepherd. I had long known branches of it in this land & have ranked them among my warmest friends and benefactors. My name to her was also not unknown; – her conduct as a daughter & as sister has ever been of the first order, her education carefully finished, & to crown the whole – I *feel* that deeply as the same emotion pervades

---

22 Margaret Lawson married Andrew Hargrave in 1838 and died in 1845.
23 John Hargrave married Jemima Moffat (1818–1869) in 1839.

myself – she loves me. Should I live – I as certainly visit Scotland in 1840 – as I now breathe, and till then we are pledged by the most sacred engagement that human hearts can twine around them. She resides so far from Hawick that you never could have seen her, tho the name could I utter it – is not unknown to you nor to History. In short I felt (tho' not till I saw her) that *here* I wanted a partner to place at the head of my estab' & of my table: – I have every season many gentlemen & sometimes Ladies to entertain & a bachelor is not quite the character to fill the position I hold. I also feel myself alone, & [illegible] these wilds require a companion of taste whose talents for reading, conversation, Music &' will raise a paradise within my own home. I have found all these in the Lady I have fixed my mind on, & so close is our mutual feeling, that in a letter of last May now at my elbow – overflowing a Couple of Sheets – she tells me – that to leave the world & all the blandishments which now surround her, in order to accompany me to these wilds "would be little or *no* sacrifice on her part." One of her brothers besides is a Clerk within my estab'. Her uncle is a brother Officer, so that in this land we will be surrounded with friends & allies.

Should my impatience to reach the North – allow of a Night at Stouslea in the Winter of that year you shall again see me: – At all events you shall certainly know the whole, which you now can only guess at. My watch points one and I dream & *can* dream only of my present subject: – Have patience with my hurried letter & with affectionate regards to all the fireside believe me always my antient friend
Yours ever Most faithfully

JH

[Letterbook]
N°. 14
Rough Copies Letters by
JHargrave
From 15th September 1838 @ 25th July 1839[1]

Nor. Ho— 4th March 1839

Wrote under the above date to – W. McTavish – enclosing Mr Butchers[2] Letter & requesting him to get the Com[missio]^{ns} executed.

R.R— 20th March 1839

Mr W. McTavish
My Dear Mactavish
  News – Kintyre – Canada &^{c} Remarks on pack^g Iron Kettles &^{ccc}

Red River 20th May 1839

Mr W. McTavish
My Dear friend
  The boats are about starting &^{c}&^{c} mentioned Mr Mc Dermots Essence spruce[?]

---

1 James described in the York Factory Post Journal, 1 January 1839, the last New Year's Day he would spend at this post before returning with his new bride the following year: "This day, which concludes the festive season in this country was like each of the past holidays, spent by the people in good order and with propriety. The usual visits and gratulations occupied the morning, a warmly contested match at foot ball upon the ice, joined in by all the laboring servants on the establishment consumed most part of the day; and a dance to "all hands," given in the public hall by the Officers of the Factory wound up the festivities of the season. All was closed by midnight, and it is peculiarly pleasing to add that not the slightest accident has occurred to interrupt the general enjoyment." On 18 February 1839 he departed for the Red River Settlement to attend the Council meeting in June at the request of Governor Simpson, leaving Chief Trader George Gladman (1800–63) in charge in his place. HBCA, B.239/a/151.
2 Francis Butcher, 1810–, was clerk in charge at Great Slave Lake in Athabasca district from 1837 to 1841.

Red River 6th June 1839

Miss Mactavish

Dearest Letitia – A few hours ago I received your delightful letters of 12th Dec‍r and 7th Feb‍y – both of them in our Express Packet from London but the parcel you allude to which contains your so much desired portrait has not come to hand, tho' I still have a chance yet, as it may be in some cases of parcels which are in Canoes not yet arrived. Finlayson did not see it in London, but has some confused recollection of noticing some such for me on the voyage to New York. Let not this however annoy you my love for I shall at all events receive it by the ship and I have more cheering news to tell. My last winter proved so extremely lonely to me, and my mind was so harassed with anxiety about your happiness that I ultimately came to the resolution of trying my strength on the bonds which confine me to this land, and to snap them in the struggle, should more gentle means not avail. The result has been extremely favorable. Within this hour I have settled with the Gov‍r that I go home by our Ship[3] from York in the fall, and should providence protect us both, the period of our probation shall be shortened by one twelvemonth. Finlayson has in this, as in all other occasions stood my staunch friend. His vote is mine and mine his whenever our affairs are in question: its effect in the present instance turned the Scale of perhaps my destiny. You shall thank him for this as I have already done for the consolation his visit of last summer had given to your feelings. His brother in the winter & himself next summer will have charge of York till our arrival in the fall, – which will allow us till June to enjoy together our last taste of civilization for some time. One part of this arrangement is strictly a secret. It is publicly understood that I return in spring as before, but privately it will be arranged otherwise, – and M‍r F's lady still in England will accompany us on our voyage to York Factory where he will be to receive her. His permanent residence will be in this Colony, – almost our next door neighbor, tho 700 miles asunder. This lady has long been sickly and tho' anxious to accompany him was considered too delicate to bear the rude voyage from Canada into the interior, so she remains with her parents in London for the present.

I had felt somewhat annoyed at not having received a single line this spring from the Sheriff, – but on second thoughts believe that I still shall find a sheet in the missing parcel. I wrote him on the 20th ult. by way of

---

3 The *Prince Rupert* left York Factory that year 11 September and arrived in London 16 October.

the States and mentioned to him my determination to get home; – but begged he would conceal such from you till this should reach you, – for fear of ultimate disappointments. William is well, and prospering, I now send on a couple letters from him for Mrs Mactavish & Mrs Worsley and dared not trust them by the States as my conveyance was as likely to turn out a War party as a caravan of peaceful Travellers. The same reason prevented my also writing you but I knew you would do my feelings justice should your fathers letter reach him before that this can find you.

I feel I write gloomily altho' I have such deep cause for happiness in your affection and our preservation thro' the weary months since we parted; – how little did we think it was to be for such a time! You will not be surprised however at my gravity when I add that the same packet that gladdened me with your precious letters also conveyed to here the melancholy information that my poor mother was no more. I little expected such a blow but God's will be done! My venerable father is arrived at the utmost limits of human life & his period was also apprehended as near at hand. All these things quite unman me. Last spring when they gave me their blessing – it was joined with one for her who was to be added to their name. My poor mothers last words conveyed the same idea. This subject is too painful for me to continue to dwell upon it.

I do not wonder at M^{rs} M's reluctance, after my letters reached you the spring of my departure. Your future happiness was not only at stake but to be held in suspense for a period of which she had already experienced all the heaviness. Few mothers could have done otherwise, and allow me to add my sweet love – that few daughters I believe are to be found who with equal firmness of mind, could have trusted with such unswerving devotion the vows of one – almost a personal stranger – unless through his own account of himself and the too flattering introductions of others. It shall be the principal object of my life to attempt a reward for such affection.

I rejoice at my friend Capt. Toms good prospects for his [illegible] life. His son Donald must be a most worthy fellow. I find I have in my blundering way of misapplying names led you to think I spoke of his daughter Charlotte while I meant your younger Sister Miss Flora. The latter I have a high regard for the former is too wrapt up in mystic sentimental dreams, to allow of any other sentiment in me than that of pity. When you write next Mrs Worsley please to mention my name in connection with the highest regard for her. I am glad to find that our cranberries met with such favor at Kilchrist. I shall bring another keg home this season. I have

a few Gallons Wild Rice for the Sheriff, – and a sea otter skin has crossed the Rocky Mountains this spring for yourself. You speak too flatteringly of the Trifles of last Season. I will write you again by way of Canada in course of the summer, but should such not travel *faster* than the one of last season I'll wager a gold ring that I shall reach you first. With kind Love to both your parents, to Polly, Flora & your brothers I am
Dearest dearest Letitia
Most affectionately Yours   JH

x We are just now all in a bustle with some wandering strangers – two Cols of Her Majestys Guards[4] who have dragged their way hither in the Govrs suite and who are determined to depopulate the plains – of Buffalo. Two such scarecrows I could never have imagined as holding such a rank. One takes in both sides of the Horizon with his eyes – and weighs somewhat above 20 s[tone].[5] The other is a mere shadow – well fitted in one respect to be a soldier as an enemy might as well attempt to hit the edge of a penknife. They are yet not out of the horrors into which they were thrown by our Style of Marching in Express Canoes. To be regularly raised from bed at 1 in the morning, and have to finish their nap in the canoe lulled by the Song of the voyageur with the dash of their paddles & washed by the spray nearly washed away the little wits the gay life of London had left them. One of them, an old Peninsular Campaigner declared that had he drilled his soldiers so severely as the Govr had them on the march – they would have shot him in five days.[6] If these are a sample of poor Victorias Guards – she has more reason than one to trust for her protection to the affection of her subjects.

I owe a scolding to Dugald for not having written me in answer to two letters of mine of last summer, but must pardon him I think as he I

---

4 Colonels Wigram and Fowler of the Coldstream Guards, 2nd Regiment. The regiment was stationed in Quebec City from 1838 to 1842. Col Fowler was nearly sixty at the time. Raffan, *Emperor*, 332–3. Also Nevins, *Narrative*, 93.

5 A stone was 14 lbs. weight.

6 Colonel Wigram. A slightly different version of his statement was provided by J. Birkbeck Nevins in 1847: "Col. Wigram, after travelling through this country, remarked, 'If we were to work our soldiers in an equal degree, we should receive a shot from behind, in the very first engagement into which we entered.'" Nevins, *Narrative*, 93.

Sir George Simpson passing the Chats Falls in an HBC canoe, 1841. Painted by Henry James Warre. The HBC governor was famed for his speedy journeys via canoe across the wilds of North America. Courtesy of the Royal Ontario Museum © ROM, 2006_7613_1.

am told is bringing himself up in the loaded canoes to answer personally for all matters. I understand he is designed to cross the Rocky Mountains to the Col[a] the only field now for a young Gent to distinguish who does not rise by the pen. From Lat. 43° our right of Trade now extends there as well as on the east coast to the Frozen Ocean. The Russians occupy a corner of the continent about Bherrings Straits, but instead of being rivals to us, depend rather upon our assistance both for provisions & merchandise to trade with the Indians. A new Colony[7] has lately been

7 The Puget Sound Agricultural Company (PSAC) was formed as a joint-stock enterprise headquartered at Fort Nisqually at the southern end of Puget Sound. This "Colony" was jointly owned by the HBC and PSAC. Technically at arm's length from HBC, PSAC restricted ownership in its shares to members and officers of HBC. Fort Nisqually, due to its superior grazing lands, proved that its primary value lay in the raising of livestock. PSAC was intended to supply foodstuffs to HBC posts along the Pacific coast as well as to Alaska and Hawaii. Despite clauses in the Oregon Treaty

established by us on the north shores of the Col[a] River near its mouth. The climate is very mild the soil excellent, and the finest grazing pastures extend through unmeasured distances. This last circumstance has encouraged the formation of a joint stock Coy – connected with our present business for the exportation of wool which I have no doubt will in a few Years rival that from Australia. Your Uncle John George has taken shares to the extent of £1000 and I have been tempted to follow for as much in the same *beau chemin*.[8] But what care you about stock & shares? – a pretty subject indeed for a letter to you from me! Willie winters again at YF. His assistance has been of the greatest value to me, and in my absence he will be the principal conductor of the Depot, and the only one there who is capable of performing its Duties.[9] I fully expect that we will be able to keep him with us after our return, in which case you will only have to leave one part of your family to join another. I fondly trust you have recovered from the serious cold which you mention: – I call myself in good health, yet the effects of that horrible York Sickness have not yet quite left me. I am however considerably stouter, and on the whole improved within the last year. My voyage hither from York was unusually heavy and disagreeable owing to a thaw in Feby a month when mercury even usually freezes. The whole distance was got over in 19 days, traveling about 40 miles a day. Fresh relays of men & dogs were obtained at the end of each 150 miles, and the whole was completed without the slightest accident. I will leave this for YF from the 12 to the 15th and my successor will join me there in course of next month. Depend on hearing from me on my very first approach to the shores of Britain.

P.S. A few minutes after closing this letter I was called to assist in giving audience to the principal Indian Chief[10] in this quarter with about 100 of his followers. On such occasions a good deal of form and ceremony is

---

of 1846 which guaranteed HBC and PSAC's lands to them, the establishment of the border at the 49th parallel spelled the end to both companies' operations in Washington and Oregon.

8 French for beautiful road.
9 While Hargrave may have been correct in his assessment of Willie's abilities and importance to the depot, as a clerk William was outranked at York Factory by chief traders George Gladman and Nicol Finlayson during the 1839–40 outfit year.
10 Probably Peguis (c. 1774–1864), the Saulteaux Indian chief, one of five chiefs who signed a treaty in 1817 with Lord Selkirk to provide an area for settle-

observed. Speeches are made, Interpreters intervene tho each party may and often do understand the other, and the audience closes with presents of Clothing, Tobacco, Gunpowder & Ball. The use of liquor is entirely prohibited among all our indians, but the chief burden of the harangue was for all that a repetition of their earnest request for the beloved Kootie Wâbuai – or fire water,[11] – a petition as hopeless as those of our poor radicals will be when Tories come into power. The principal speaker on this occasion was a venerable Indian upwards of 90 years old, tall, gaunt, and emaciated. Naked from the loins upwards, his long floating hair is white as snow and bearing on his head the valued emblems of the number of scalps he had carried off during his long life – (upwards of 15 I believe) – he stood leaning on a staff, and poured out his oration with a fire and energy quite astonishing but which sounded from his ample & attenuated[?] chest hollow unearthlike. The attentions of his younger followers to him were most tender and careful. Two assisted him to rise, watched on each side of him during his speech lest his strength had failed him, and when he had finished carefully replaced him on his seat. The whole party shone with paint & vermilion, Furs, feathers & Scarlet Cloth, and left the room on their departure redolent of Tobacco smoke and Sturgeon oil. There is a sketch of your new subjects for you! – to complete which know that when they may chance to see you, you will be regarded as of a superior order of being throughout the Kingdom of York – more than equal to twice the size of Great Britain –

F^t Garry – R.R. 6th June 1839

M^r & Mrs Ja^s Ross
My Dear Brother & Sister

I yesterday received here both your valued letters, and I need not and cannot disemble the effect on my feelings that your melancholy news occasioned. The Death of my poor old and most kind Mother was the

---

ment purposes. He supported missionary work among his followers who lived in the Netley Creek Indian Settlement near Lake Winnipeg. In 1836 St Peter's mission was built to serve the Christian Indians, and in October 1840 he gave up three of his four wives in order to be baptized. Peguis was recognized and honoured by the HBC throughout his life. In 1835 Governor Simpson gave him an annuity of £5 a year in recognition of his contributions. Dempsey, "Peguis."

11   Fire water = iskotewâpoy. *Online Cree Dictionary.*

last thing that I had expected to hear – But Gods will be done: I shall become a child should I dwell longer on this most painful subject.

Your very kind and considerate aid to my brother while borne down by affliction so deep I shall not soon forget nor will he. My poor father appears to be fast following her who is now no more, – and nothing but the consolations of Religion bears up his mind so far under the loss we have all sustained.

I am here this season attending the meeting of Council a duty at present which I am very unfit for, and have neither time nor spirits to write you each a separate letter, or even one at any length. I observe the distracted state of the country around you, and feel for your precarious situation, as well as for your poor deluded neighbors the Canadians who are being led on to their own destruction by men who are trying to make their countrymens blood a cement for their own miserable fortunes.[12] Such will meet their rewards and are doing so. I trust however that the Regular forces will be able to keep down all insurrections and that the fire will eventually die out of itself.

As a matter in which I am deeply interested leads me this season again to Scotland, I have just obtained leave of absence and will sail for London from York Factory in Septr on board the Companys Ship. I am not certain that I shall return by way of Canada. I will however in course of the winter write to my brother John and you will hear through him of my motions.

I can really write no more at present. My mind is so confused. I scarcely know what I have been saying. May God bless you both is the earnest prayer of your Affectionate friend & brother

JH.

F^t Garry R.R. – 6th June 1839

Mr Jos^b Hargrave

My Dear father. Your last letters to me have overwhelmed me with grief, and altho' I have begun to write you a few lines in reply I cannot collect sufficient composure of mind for the purpose. My loss is irremediable, –

---

12 After the Patriot insurrection of 1838 in Lower Canada, villages south of Montreal were pillaged and burned by British troops. About 850 people were arrested; of these, 108 were courtmartialled, about 60 were deported to Australia, and 12 were hanged in the Pied-au-Courant prison in Montreal between December 1838 and February 1839.

but the Lord gave and the Lord has taken away – blessed be the name of the Lord! Join your prayers to mine my dear parent – now my only parent – that I may be enabled to say this with my whole heart and that I may be enabled to resign myself in all trials to his holy will. I rejoice to find that you yourself my dear old father have been supported through this severe dispensation of providence with a fortitude of which I lament to say I feel myself utterly incapable. Your firm reliance and entire confidence on the promises of the holy Scriptures have strengthened you beyond what I can experience. I mourn, but yet trust that I shall be able to say – Gods will be done!

I have read many times all that you have last said to me, and own that you are right in the whole. You have done your duty to me, would I could feel that I have always rendered the same duty, and affection to you in return. The passions, the headstrongness and heedlessness of youth have often led me astray & made me disobedient, – where I have offended you my father – oh grant me your pardon for such while this world holds us both.

I really cannot write you at present at any length, and our God only knows whether we shall be spared to write to each other again. The remembrance of you however is ever present with me, and your instructions and example shall through life and in all my actions never be forgotten.

I am this summer going again to Scotland, and will return to this country next season. I do not think I shall on either occasion be able to pass through Canada. How it would have delighted me to have seen you again and to have asked for your blessing on the head of a new and affectionate daughter which my voyage may add to your name. I fear I will not succeed in so arranging my journey, but still trust such will be conferred with the same readiness that you yielded your consent to my union with her before my departure last spring.

I pray that I may hear from you again – and that our God may bless and preserve you long to your Dutiful & affectionate Son.

J.H.

YF 6 July 1839

J.G. McTavish
My Dear Sir
The first Canoes for Montreal are about pushing off from shore, & I have merely a moment to say that I forward by these to your address

a Couple Doz Buffalo Tongues in a Cask which Mr Rowand[13] informs me you had requested him to send. Mr Dugald[14] arrived safe & is on the eve of starting again for the Colo. I can no more at present but will again try and write you at more length by the Express Canoe. Meantime with kindest regard to Mrs M{c}Tavish I am My Dear Sir
Most faithfully Yours

JH

YF 16th July 1839

My Sweet Letitia –

The Express for England via Canada is in process of being made up,[15] and when all pens are busy with the dry pages of business mine seeks apart from the crowd a subject infinitely more delightful to my feelings. In my last from Red River of the 6 June I mentioned that your portrait had not come to hand: – I now have the happiness to say that it reached me by the loaded Canoes at Norway House – while on my return to this place; – and I need not add how it was welcomed, – or what *caresses* have been bestowed on it as your proxy. – It is evidently of high merit as a painting but wants the sweet & animating charm that dwells only with the original. William says it has an expression of sadness: – I do not trace this, altho' I peruse it more frequently & closely than any page in possession. It however tells me to shorten my absence as much as I have

---

13 John Rowand was clerk in charge at Fort Assiniboine in the Saskatchewan district from 1836 to 1841.
14 Dugald Mactavish was ordered in 1839 to the Columbia Department as clerk at Fort Vancouver.
15 James wrote up a list of books to be procured and forwarded to York Factory in the fall of 1839. The list included George Crabbe's *The Life & Poetical Works of the Rev. George Crabbe*, 8 vols., Thomas Hope's *Anastatius*, James Morier's *Hajji Baba*, James Fenimore Cooper's *The Last of the Mohicans*, *The Pioneers*, and *The Prairie*, William Hamilton Maxwell's *Stories of Waterloo*, William Harrison Ainsworth's *Rookwood*, Horace Smith's *Brambletye House*, Robert Jameson's *Narrative Of Discovery & Adventure in Africa, from the earliest ages to the present*, Rev. Michael Russell's *View of Antient & modern Egypt*, Tytler and Wilson's *Historical View of the Progress of Discovery on the more Northern Coasts of America: from the Earliest Period to the Present Time*, *History of China*, D.M. Moir's *The Life of Mansie Waugh*.

the power of doing; – and its persuasive eloquence shall be a law to me. I mark the token which encircles the lovely neck & when I see you next will replace it by another still more worthy of it. You made me tremble for your safety as I read the narrow escape you had had from fever while in Edin^b. For my sake, dearest, let me implore you to preserve yourself from a similar risk again. You do not know how distressed I have been: my heart has lately been much wrung by the loss of one once nearest to me, judge what a second – I will say still *more* touching to my feelings would weigh me down. Dugald with his party of young recruits reached this place on the 1st Inst. a few days after me and started on the 8th for the Shores of the Pacific in company with the officer in charge of the west side of the Mountains. He will be entrusted with the General Accounts of that quarter of the Trade, – a situation of respectability[?] & confidential Trust – one which he is every way competent to fill. Willie was rejoiced to meet him & no less sorry to part: – it is however expected that he will visit this again a year or two hence. He looked thinner than usual, owing to the roughness of the Spring voyage/ but full of health and spirits.

I have [been] greatly interested by the little notices you have given me of the [illegible] young or antiquated around you. Poor Charlotte Tom's affaire de coeur has evaporated as such slender liens usually do. I am happy to find that her spirits have suffered so little on the occasion & that this has shown more firmness of mind than I had imagined could be possessed of such a devoted admirer of Sentiment. The marriage of Miss Isabel Campbell I am rejoiced at. I distinctly remember meeting Mr Duncan in his fathers Country House while there on business – evidently a fine young fellow – while she appeared to me from what I saw of her the most amiable of all the young ladies of your acquaintance & most worthy of your friendship. Capt. Toms coolness was quite characteristic. You made me smile at your allusion to the fable of the fox & crow. Your precious sheets now covering my desk – full of their valued gifts of last spring are no more to be compared to the poor crows tribute than your beauty to the same[illegible] of the [illegible] from my soul. I thank you for them & for the sweet Shadows which accompanied them. Never did I pray so sincerely for the safe & early arrival of our ship; – as when I look forward to the next expected packet and to the time when I shall step on board to return to you. I need not say, Love, that few hours will be needlessly spent here after that the Prince Rupert has reached our Roads. The present packet is sent off at least 10 days earlier this season – the secret reason that you may receive this so much earlier than last year; – altho by this I ensure the loss of the wager I pledged. Such loss however shall always be esteemed my richest and most cherished gain.

When writing you last I alluded to my voyage upwards last spring but dwelt little I believe on the incidents attending it. I kept however a few rough notes during the journey, and when I am at length by your side they shall serve as hints towards a more detailed narrative of indian adventures – should such prove musical in your ears. I mentioned that our remaining scraps of white mens politeness were wofully tasked to do honor to two stray Cols of her Majestys Guards. They had then left us under an escort of 30 or 40 armed & mounted Brulés to make war on the poor inoffensive Buffalos which are to be found a few days march from that Colony. Little was certainly expected from them, but still less did we hope to learn as I the other day have done that both these Gallant Colonels were fairly put to flight by a few old curly headed bulls and that men of war – though they be – they literally returned without drawing blood. I regret all this – for the sake of our country: – because these are the first specimens of a british militaire that most of our Natives have seen; – and neither in person, equipage or acts have they served to increase or win support [for] the idea formed here of the appearance or prowess of a British Soldier.

In order that this may reach you as soon as possible I enclose it to a friend in Canada who will put it into the safest & most expeditious channel for crossing the Atlantic. It leaves me in health much improved by my spring Travels. I sincerely pray it may find you in as flourishing a condition as your sweet portrait bespeaks you. Please make mention of my affectionate regards to the Sheriff and to Mrs Mactavish. I rejoice to find that our Cranberries are such favorites: it will encourage me to repeat the same & to add to them another delicacy or what we esteem such in this land – a few cured Buffalo Tongues. I have also for the Sheriff – a quantity of Wild Rice for seed – together with every information I could obtain regarding its natural history – to enable him to fulfil his promise to his friend Mr Campbell your County representative. I may be detained some time – a week or two not more – in London should the Govr not have arrived from Canada before me – but will write you the first moment I touch land. Should this reach you first – favor me to my address at the House with a sheet as to your prosperity. I will likely come by Railway & the Mail Train to Edin^b & from thence thro Glasgow to you. I shall hasten hither, Love, by the way. I promised to call on Mr^s Worsley the first time I should again find myself in Town & will do so. Mr^s M: had again the [missing word] in the same terms: do you remember the occasion when I made it? JH

Since I began the letter I have received a packet from Severn – a Trading Estab.' within my District at the mouth of a River of the same name about 160 miles to the South along the Shores of the Bay. Among a harvest of letters containing information about fur hunts [illegible] news &.' &.' I have received one from our fisherman there on rather a Novel subject. The period of his contract of Service having expired, he coolly tells me that he is perfectly willing to re-engage for three years longer at his previous wages on condition that I will permit to take to wife a young half Caste or whole Caste Squaw in that neighborhood. Now this would be all very fine, and soft hearted as I am while the success of the tender passion in any of its Shades depends on me, I felt much inclination to listen favorably to the application, – tho by so doing I encumbered the Trade with the maintenance of another [illegible] & a whole Kill Rail [?] of Dependants, but to [missing word] in the next letter I opened [illegible] I am informed that the villain has a wife & family at home in the Orkneys. Now, love, what would be your decision in the case. Mine I am seriously tempted to make banishment from this back to his Native Islands, and inform also his poor wife of his infidelity. I guess & [illegible] as the Yankees say, – that she would complete the sum of punishment in the most exemplary manner.

While I write the sun looks in on me with one of the pleasantest Smiles it ever wears in this dismal climate. The sky is azure & cloudless, – in this open air the Thermo. stands in the Shade at 87° and every person, animal & object feeling the genial influence. Unfortunately these are angel births here, transient and strange. Before evening, such is the mutability of the Climate, a change of wind to seaward, may sink the therm.° to 40° and wrap the gloomy pine forests around us in chilling fog – or drenching rain. Till the middle of August such is only too true a description of our Climate. For a month and a half afterwards – the weather is usually more settled; and the clouds of Moschettos having been laid by the increasing sharpness of the air, we enjoy more of the genial influences of the open air than in any other portion of the year. Winter sets in, – in October with rain, sleet, hail & Snow. Nov.' is gloom personified; – but after the holidays – the open water being all frozen over & the hoar frost in consequence diminished, – we enjoy many days even more pleasant than the Summer, – the weather then is generally calm with light snows – and altho so cold, as during the nights to freeze mercury – in the day time wrapped up dressing proper to the Climate we take long excursions out of doors either on snow Shoes or dashing along in a Cariole as fast as 4 dogs can carry us. Altho' at this time the weather be so warm, the ice full

6 feet thick which covered the whole Bay through the Winter is still in sight northward off the mouth of this River, and two Schooners[16] which I had dispatched 3 days ago to Churchill on the coast northward from this – are this morning only attempting to leave the mouth of the River about 6 Miles to the North East – to try & find a passage along between the ice and the Shore. I have been led into this long harangue unawares, but I do not regret it. I never concealed the gloomy character of the clime to which my selfish love is attempting to lure you yet I believe never dwelt on much detail upon it before. Familiarize your mind to it, sweetest, and altho society be none, and the adventitious helps which civilization furnishes for consuming time be unknown, – our mutual affection shall supply all deficiencies during the time our fortunes may render a residence here necessary to us.

JH

---

16 The schooners *Jane* and *Frances*.

[Letterbook]
N°. 15
Rough Copies Letters by
JHargrave
From 26th July 1839 @ 18th May 1840

On board the Prince Rupert – in the
English Channel off Portsmouth
15 Octr – 1839

Dearest Letitia –

After a passage of [blank] days[1] from YF I am once more in sight of the British Shores and I seize the very first chance for sending a few lines ashore to acquaint you of my arrival. I received in August the whole of your precious letters forwarded by this ship, and am at a loss for language to tell you what I felt on perusing your narrative of what you have had to endure from the gossips in your neighbourhood. Should that Ass McEachern not have ceased his annoyance – I shall find a means to clap a stopper upon him. Still less can I express to you my feelings of pride & exultation on receiving from you such repeated proofs of affection especially at a time when you could only look to my return to you as an event still at a considerable distance. I had ever confidently believed my noble hearted Love capable of such sacrifices, and called up coming from half way to the Antipodes to rejoin you – would have as cheerfully made the circuit of this Globe to shew myself worthy of such devoted faith to obtain such a unsullied prize. I sympathise I assure you most deeply as to your being the subject of gossip to the Slippered pantaloons & the antique spinsters around you. My return I trust will end this exultation – as whatever may be their opinion of me – few of the latter I believe will ever be found possessed of such attraction as to conjure a lover whatever may be his merit to their feet from a distance of 4000 miles & as full of the former, it may be permitted me to add, – would for any of them have so much chivalry as to dare the adventure.

I wrote you this last summer from Red River in June and from YF in July – when this reaches you write me to the HB House – as soon as practicable to assure me of your welfare. I will be ashore this evening, and will

1 The *Prince Rupert* left York Factory 11 September 1839 and arrived in London 16 October.

reach Town tomorrow travelling express, as I have in my possession the Genl Dispatches & packet from the North to the Govr & Committee. I do not expect that Govr Simpson will yet have arrived from Canada: – and if not – will have to wait that event in London – much against my will – to review many points with him, both in matters of business – and in reference to my own affairs. I will however write you frequently – and so soon as I can will acquaint you when you may expect to see me. I take this ashore with me by the pilot boat – I trust in 3 or 4 days it will be in your possession. In a week hence I hope to be made happy by receiving a sheet from you. We have had a tedious passage partly beaten about by contrary winds and at other times the Sport of storms – than which I have never hitherto experienced any so severe. We are all, in consequence, in rather a dripping and battered condition; but a walk on shore will wash off all stains – and recover our exhausted spirits.

William is well – all news from him are forwarded along with this. I have many things to say to you – but a crowded cabin & stiff wind[?] preclude all chance of writing this at present. I will write to you again & to the Sheriff very shortly after I reach town. Meanwhile with much[?] kind love to him, to M^{rs} McTavish – and to all dear to you – I am as ever – my sweet beloved –
Most faithfully most affectionately Yours

JH

London – George & Vulture Hotel
19th October 1839

Miss Mactavish
My Sweet Love –

Within this hour I have received your most prized Sheet of the 14th Ins^t which, from the anxiety I expressed in my last to hear from you – you may well imagine made my heart bound with delight as I noticed the address in your neat style of manuscript. (Mine which should have been dated off Brighton where I landed) was by mistake dated a day in advance – so that it appears we had almost in the same hour been addressing each other – My friend Mr Christie[2] (a brother Officer & I –) reached town about 6 a.m. on the 15th and ever since I have been worried with the many

---

2 Alexander Christie, then chief factor and governor of Assiniboia, came to England on furlough in 1839.

calls I have to make and to endure – in so much that however my mind is filled with your dear idea – I have not from the dissipated life I lived so far as late hours go, been able till now to devote another page to you. Govr Simpson has not yet arrived but by the British Queen[3] we heard from him that he may be expected home about a week hence. Last evening I dined & spent in the family of Mr Geddes Simpson his father in law – about a mile out of town to where I had the great pleasure of meeting both Mrs George Simpson & Mrs Finlayson. With the latter I had a long conversation perfectly unreserved regarding her and our intended arrangements for next summers voyage. Through her husband she of course knew all, and your name consequently mingled largely in our talk. She is an amiable accomplished lady whom I think you will like: her health however is not yet quite re-established – but her purpose is most firm to [illegible] the voyage with us to Hudsons Bay next year. She is delighted with the hope of having your company – and expresses the strongest desire that arrangements could be made to allow us also to proceed to Red River. This last idea however is of course a hopeless one. By the bye while looking forward to those happy days – it occurs to me to mention that it would be well for you to look quietly around for a suitable maid Servant to accompany you. One bred in your own family, if possible – and of mature years rather than a young lassie – would likely be of most value to you. Our Staunch old Ship[4] the Prince Rupert has her faults – yet with all these – is one of the stoutest Ships that sail out of London Docks. She has however at present very unladylike accommodations – and will require considerable amendment in that respect before next June. Two days hence her homeward Cargo will be discharged – after which a few packages which I have to the Sheriffs address will be passed through the Customs Ho: & forward by Steamer via Leith & Glasgow to him. In one of the Cases will be found your Sea Otter Skin[5] accompanied by two

3 The *British Queen*, the largest steamship in the world and renamed from the *Royal Victoria*, sailed on her maiden voyage to New York on 10 July 1839 with Governor Simpson on board. The ship was owned by the British and American Steam Navigation Company.
4 The *Prince Rupert* was to leave London 3 June 1840 with the newly married Hargraves and arrive at York Factory 9 August.
5 A list of the contents of the packages for Dugald Mactavish and James Hargrave, probably written by JH 31 August or 1 September 1839 was as follows:

Black Fox Skins – which last summer had appeared so beautiful in my eyes and so worthy of you that I could not resist the temptation of adding them to the former. For Muffs these are the most valuable and the most ladylike furs that are procured throughout the North; – and are extremely rare. Should you fall deeply in love with these, there is no [illegible] they would [illegible] so beautifully as your own: – but if your passion be more moderate, – perhaps Mama would feel gratified by such a present from us: – Act however, my love, in the disposal of them – entirely according to your usual excellent judgment. I have still something besides for you – but I will not say what till I see you; – which I hope will be soon after

Packing Acc^t of Packages forwarded to London P The HHBCoy Ship Prince Rupert, fall 1839, to the Care of Wm Smith Esq.

D^d. Mactavish Esq — 1 Cask Containing
        50 Cured Buffalo Tongues

        1 Box #2 – Containing
         1 Sea Otter Skin
         1 Silver Fox D^o
         1 Cross " D^o
         1 Bag Wild Rice Seed
         1 Parcel – Soil producing Wild Rice

        1 D^o #3 Containing
         1 Jar prepared Cranberries

Ja^s Hargrave Esq.
        1 Hair Trunk Containing
         6 Pairs Indian Shoes
         1 " R: Mountain Sheep horns
         1 Indian Womans Dress
         0 Musk Ox Robe
         3 Buffalo Robes
         1 flat-head Indian Skull
         50 Weasel Skins
         1 Esquimaux Dress Consisting of
          1 Capot
          1 P Boots
          1 " Shoes
          2 " Gloves

your return from your Glasgow Tour. I will assuredly call on Mrs Loudoun[6] en passant lest I pass you there – & will address this to Woodside Crescent so it will reach [illegible] I hope before you set out for Campbelton. Till about the 27th this will continue to be my address: after that – the Waterloo Hotel Edin{b} & the Black Bull Hotel – Argyle St Glasgow will be my marching stations.

I have left merely a corner on this page to renew the expression of my love to your excellent parents & all your relations – (soon I hope to have a claim to the same names from me) and to repeat that I am & ever shall be most affectionately Yours

JH

PS I am sincerely grieved by what you say of the low state of poor Capt. Tom. His original Character interested me much, and I had fondly imagined that many happy days were still before him – rendered so by the liberal & dutiful conduct of his very worthy son Donald, – whom I long much to be acquainted with.

The result of Captn MacEacherns matrimonial spec is in my opinion a righteous judgement – upon his unpardoned attempt to cross my path. I owe him a certain sum of thanks therefore – which should his wife not fully liquidate I will. Her conduct however as you most justly observe is very hearty in marrying a man whom she cannot love.

         1 " Trousers
     1 " Doll
     1 " " Boot
     2 " Combs
     1 " Small Kettle
    1 pot preserved Soup – part of what
    Captn Franklin brought to Ruperts Land
    on his first Expedition in 1819. – 20 Years
    old. To be opened and its state of
    preservation ascertained.
    1 Deal Box Long –
    3 Cree Indian Bows & 3 quiver arrows

 6 John Loudoun, agent for the Phoenix Fire & Pelican Life Insurances Offices in Glasgow, and his wife were friends of the Mactavishes and lived at 13 Woodside Crescent at this time.

London – 19th Octr 1839

Mr Wm Lockie
My Dear Lockie – I was favored with your very kind yet extremely mournful sheet of 27 May last – and as I had again obtained liberty to spend the ensuing Winter in Britain I delayed answering it till I should have reached our native land. It is most painful to perceive the straits to which your parental affection has reduced you, – and the only consolation under your afflictions must be the integrity & uprightness which you have observed towards your creditors. As to the risk of a jail I sincerely hope there can be no danger, as every man of sense must see that such a step would be the first to deprive both you & them of any chance of ever coming to a favorable settlement. I should rather imagine that they will come to an equitable composition with you on the matter to do which could never leave any stain on your name, as it is the fate of the most honest of men every day.

My own News on this occasion my dear friend, are also of the most melancholy description. I have lost – what my worldly wealth or fortune can ever again purchase for me – I have been deprived by Death of a fond and doting Mother whose whole happiness was bound up in my prosperity, and whose Dearest wish for many years had been to have the happiness of once seeing me again. This wish in gods providence was gratified once & again – and within half a year of the latter occasion – the Amighty was pleased to remove her from this scene of earthly hopes & fears. I mourn, yet still have comfort: – the weary round of this state of things will at the long last come to a close – & I fervently hope we will all meet again: – would to god that I may be equally prepared for the great & momentous change. My poor old father, in a state of second childhood – bears up with great fortitude – & by my last letters from the family was in his usual state of health.

I will be down to Scotland in a fortnight or 3 weeks hence. I really am not sure whether my affairs will allow me to get to the Borders – but if I can catch hold of a weeks leisure – for that purpose – you shall assuredly have one day out of the same. I am greatly occupied with business & have written this with a mind much occupied and agitated about things affecting me very closely. I would most heartily have made it much longer – but for the present must crowd all I have to say into the assurance that I am as ever – my worthy old friend
Most cordially & sincerely Yours

JH

Kind Comps to Geo. Arthur & Etty & to all inquiring after me.

JH

London – George & Vulture, Lomb^d S^t
27 Octr – 1839

My Dearest Letitia –

I owe many thanks to your kind friend Mrs Loudoun for having come so successfully between you & the threatened arrest of the sheriff: – I am convinced that the change from Kilchrist to Glasgow must both be advantageous to Mama's health, and for the time exhilarating to your Spirits: – it besides enables us both to hear from each other one day earlier than otherwise we should do. I am myself chafing in no gentle humour just now upon the chain which still binds me to this. Our Govr arrived safe & well – two days ago; – and a Genl Meeting of the Committee is ordered on the 30th to attend on which I have so long been confined here: – After that I shall nominally be at liberty – yet still have no chance of being practically so till about this day week; – or the 3^d prox°. I have not yet made up my mind whether to choose the route by rail way or Steamers to the North, – but most likely may decide on the latter. A few old friends on the Border are clamorous that I should give them even a few hours en passant – and if I have not self-denial enough to do this previously to reaching you – their chance of seeing me after that I feel is hopeless indeed. My time my existence is yours so soon as my feet are free from the present fetters, – say, Love, are not these thieving Moss Troops[7] deserving of a right turn "Jeddart Justice"[8] for thus attempting to delay our meeting.

The public mind here has for some days been much agitated by the rumoured death of Lord Brougham, which happily turns out – (and deeply to the shame of the inventor) a most wretched Hoax. [illegible]

---

7 In 1650, the Moss Troops based at Dirleton castle near North Berwick caused so much damage to Cromwell's line of communication that in 1651 he sent an army out. The Roundheads under the command of General Monk bombarded the castle for twelve days and devastated the building to such an extent that the garrison surrendered.

8 The town of Jedburgh also has been called Jeddart. Scotland's style of hanging them first and trying them afterwards is known as "Jeddart Justice," a term which originated when Sir George Home summarily strung up a gang of so-called rogues during the reign of James VI.

to the honor of the provincial press – almost every one of his political Enemies – lamented the supposed accident as a great public calamity. The deaths of the Dukes of Argyle & of Bedford[9] – are unhappily better authenticated – both of them highly estimable in private life – and both a heavy loss to the public Cause which they had [illegible]. The ferment is still great here on the subject of the poor Lady Flora Hastings;[10] and the strongest language is applied to Majesty herself – in public placards & pamphlets. If woman was ever done to death by scandalous tongues – such was her most miserable fate. The month so fatal to English lineage is close at hand, – and fearful accidents are daily giving note of its effects. A Mania had set in for blazoning their exit by a leap from the dizzy height of the Monument. A young Lady[11] & again since my arrival a young lad of seventeen[12] have pass^d thro that gate to another world; – & the magistrates fearing that such would become a common practice have prohibited all permissions to ascend it. I have since I landed seen little of town beyond these wearisome rounds of [illegible] parties – and have only been one evening to any place of public amusement. On this day week I made a tour through the Hide,[13] Green & St James Parks – which still retain so much of their summer features as yet to be pleasant promenades. The Scene I believe is deeply valued by a Cockney – but for my part I would prefer the Shaggy wood, roaring falls & the grey scalps of Lake Superiors rocks – to all the [illegible] finery that [illegible] meets the eye of a London cab[?] while whirled along in his gig. Some of the Royal Parks however deserve more praise: – the Gigantic Trees – the long green vistas that penetrate deeply their recesses – & the unbroken

---

9 George William Campbell, 6th Duke of Argyll (1768–1839) and John Russell, 6th Duke of Bedford (1766–1839).
10 Lady Flora Elizabeth Rawdon Hastings (1806–1839), an unmarried lady-in-waiting to Queen Victoria's mother, was suspected of becoming pregnant when liver disease caused an enlarged liver. Defamed by the Queen, she died in her sleep at Buckingham Palace at the age of thirty-three.
11 In September 1838, Margaret Moyes, aged twenty-three, leaped to her death from the London Monument. This case achieved great notoriety at the time.
12 In October 1839, Richard Hawes, a fifteen-year-old servant in the home of a surgeon, dismissed from his job for lethargy and threatening to jump out of a window, on the day of his dismissal re-enacted the suicidal plunge of Margaret Moyes.
13 Hyde Park.

solitude & silence which pervade such haunts – better accord with my taste of forest Scenery. But above all I long for a view again of that pretty valley which stretches away towards the sea in front of Kilchrist – & to enjoy the prospect hand in hand with you – in a quiet and private walk – unseen & unnoticed by the World.

I heard a few days ago from uncle John George who writes in good health and spirits: – a few letters for Mama and the Miss [illegible] likewise fell into my hands which I forwarded immediately by post. I am happy that you have been able to select from among the Retainers of your family a female Servant whom you think you may depend on. When the time shall arrive that such will be wanted – you can offer her whatever wages you please in order to secure her services.

I have deeper reason to be ashamed than you, in leading you astray as to when I leave this: – your apology is also mine – that I am under authority, and altho with miserably bad grace – and compelled to do as others wish. Trust not so confidently even to the dates above noticed, for they are only the calculations of my fond wishes not those of a secure understanding with such as guide my motions. This will reach you still in Glasgow, & as there will still be time to hear from you before I leave, even at the earliest date, – I cannot deny myself the luxury of another letter from you: – Write again love & tell me that you are not offended by my wearisome sauntering. You know not how leaden footed time is to me else you would deeply pity me.

JH

Campbelton – 5th Decr 1839

Messrs Simpson & Starky
29 Halton Garden [London]
Gentlemen –

I would feel obliged by your making and forwarding on my a/ & to my address at the "Waterloo Hotel Edinburgh" the following articles viz.

1 Gold cable chain – such as I received in Oct^r – the best that can be made for £———————————————————— £8.8.–

2 Pair Gold Ear Rings similar to a pair I purchased in
    Oct – ea about 40/   4.–.–

1 fashionable Gold Brooch for a Young Lady containing
    a Cairngorm Stone of the finest Color in the centre to be made to such a price as will raise the whole Bill after the usual discount is allowed to –   £15.–.–

If possible, I should wish these to be forwarded as above so as to arrive there on or before the 17th – when I expect to be at that place. They are designed for holiday presents, & a late arrival would not answer so well. I remain
Gentlemen
Most Truly Yours

JH

18 Woodside Crescent[14] [Glasgow]
Sunday Evening [15 December 1839]

My Sweet Love –

I am just on the eve of starting upon a night journey to Edin^b by Mail and have a few lines with the Sheriff to tell you how our Trip has prospered so far. The Voyage from Kintyre to Glasgow proved most propitious – forerunner in all respects to us – as the Small Boat was so sunk in the water by heavy Cargo that the slightest Sea would have washed us from stem to stern. We reached this at half past 5 – and found the worthy couple in the highest State of preservation: – "Johnny my man" – was in his Most cheerful humour – and his better half thus chirruped in consequence like a Grasshopper. Wine added its rosy hue to the hour and the pair to the music of their own sons waltzed arm in arm round the Table for closing the amusements of the evening.

I have just been laying the Time & Placement to the extent of my journey & now perceive, that to meet all the sheriff expects me to do, as well as making up for the waste of Time already spent – I will not be able to reach Kintyre till the evening of the 21st when I think you may expect me. Depend on it Sweet that I will not remain one hour from you that I see is possible for me to preserve for such a delicious use. When I look back now at this distance over all my life & actions since I last joined you I feel oppressed with the sense of my [illegible]. I love you deeply – intensely – I have truly felt bound[?] to you as my passion in life – and it is only in this light – that I could ever expect to retain in your mind that position I am so ambitious of possessing. Love me – Darling with all my frailties – extravagance is blindness – and believe me that my heart must be cold indeed when such a passion shall no longer be returned by me. I have

---

14 This was the home of Mr and Mrs John Loudoun in Glasgow.

only a few minutes to pack up & prepare for the coach – so with a thousand kisses – *my* kisses – Good night & God bless You!
Ever yours most devotedly

JH

9 OClock [16 December 1839, Edinburgh]
My Sweet Letitia – I reached this four hours ago, and snatch a single minute to tell you that so much more of my journey has been finished without inconvenience or accident. I leave this at half past one for Melrose – and having a few calls to make & commission to execute here I shall this morning be busily employed. Last night was fair and unusually mild so that my outside Seat on the Mail Coach was very pleasant – and my cold is positively improving. I will be in Galashiels this evening. I long much to hear from you and expect a few lines in a day or two. Do not oppress yourself by long letters. A Dozen words will suffice to inform me of your welfare. I will be here again on the 19th & leave for Glasgow on the 20th. Take care of your health Darling, and have full confidence in the unchanging affection of Your most affectionate

JH

Galashiels – 16th Dec^r
Monday Evening

Dearest Letitia,
I arrived here, the haunts of my boyhood, an hour ago and am already surrounded by several of my old School fellows upon whom I have dropt as if from the Clouds. I am now quite recovered of my late Kintyre sickness – but find that what I had considered [illegible] years ago is in no degree allayed by distance from it and from you. I will spend the day in town and tomorrow will visit Selkirk where my young protegé is at an Academy. The following day Thursday I return to Edin^b & am still determined to be with your pere [illegible] on the evening of the 21st. I sincerely trust that your throat is now so far recovered as that you can venture [illegible] the opera [illegible] & fully expect to [illegible] in a short time – With kind love to Mama, Polly Flora & to all I am as ever My own Sweet little Wife
Most Affectionately Yours

JH

Galashiels – 19th Dec[r] 1839
9 OC a.m.

Dearest Love – I am just about starting for Edin[b] on my return to you & drop this into the post Office – to try a race with it which shall reach you first. I have not yet received any lines from you and am in some anxiety in consequence lest worse health is the cause of your silence. This may however be occasioned by the slow pace of the post when compared with my imagination & trust to find all well when I reach Edin[b]. My Sickness is now totally gone – but as colds always do with me – the effects of the last have settled on my lip – and when I reach you there will I fear be a truce to my amusements for some days. I last evening attended a dinner given me by some [of] my old school fellows – and spent a few hours very happily. My head however is not quite the better of it this morning.

The porter waits for my luggage so I must close so with kind love to all – I am ever Darling
Very very affectionately Yours

JH

Edin[h] 27th Jany 1840

George Simpson Esq.
My Dear Sir

I have only within this hour been favored with your & M[rs] Simpsons most kind and valued congratulations. In my new position in life and, in my own & my Letitias words beg to return you both our heartfelt thanks for your warm and hearty good wishes. In the Honey Moon future prospects are, I am aware, as always apt to wear a Rosy hue; – but in all my steps in Life I have been accustomed to take reason as my polar Star – and in this last most important one, I am firmly persuaded that I could nowhere have hoped to be so perfectly happy as I now find myself. We are here for a week or two – visiting some friends of the Sheriffs and in the beginning of next month will return again to Kilchrist.

While in the Borders in Dec[r] I at length succeeded in procuring you a Sleek Terrier of the True Pepper & Mustard Breed – obtained directly from M[r] Davison – the Son of the far famed Dandie Dinmont. She is not yet Broke in – or in Dandies Language "her education has not been properly seen to – a great fault whether in beast or bodie". My old School fellow M[r] R. Gill will be in London in May or June – and has kindly taken her in charge for the present & will bring her with him for you – as well as a Dog Pup which we expect to secure for you.

A couple days ago I forwarded to the House a parcel for Mr Ja^s Keith containing the Books he requested, & now enclose a Copy of their Bill parcels. Another is contained in the parcel along with the volumes. Please cover the amt to be transferred to my credit at the House.

I have read with much interest the information you favor me with on the subject of the Shipping for the Nor. Dept. – & highly approve of the substitution of two moderate sized vessels for the cumberous & expensive Prince Rupert. I am also of opinion that if two of these vessels in any season with a single one in another – will for some time to come – be perfectly competent to bring us out all our wants – and the only thing in drawback that occurs to me is that should each of the new ships not stow so much as the Rupert it might happen in the years of the single ship that we would not be able to ship in her the whole Returns of an average years trade. I am however apprised of the Tonnage of the Col^a & Vancouver & have no doubt that the above consideration has already received full consideration. With regard to curtailment in next shipment – the Goods asked for are to complete Outfit 1841 – & to keep up a reserve of at least one quarter of an Outfit. In [illegible] I think not more than one fifth could be reduced – In Luxuries one third – In provisions not above one fifth – In Grains nothing – In Gunpowder about 50 Kegs – and generally in other Goods that might be bulky – about 25 per cent throughout.

I write in haste for the nights post – but as the time for the Spring express is fairly nigh, I purpose adding a few words on the Te[?] affairs for ensuing season & will again have this pleasure in a few days –
Meantime with deep & grateful regard
I am
My Dear Sir
Ever Most Sincerely Yours

JH

You have gladdened my heart by the few kind words you favored me with on my poor friend Barnstons future prospects. This noble act of yours will give more pleasure hereafter than – but what am I saying – tis only of a piece with the whole Tenor of your Conduct since ever I have had the honor of knowing You.

Kilchrist House – 1st March 1840

J.G. McTavish Esq

My Dear Sir – I have much pleasure in using the present occasion of the Spring Packet to acknowledge your very kind letter of the 26th Septr which reached me in London in Octr. My voyage home was a tolerably fair one – and after being detained in Town waiting for Govr Simpson till the 4th Nov. I at length got loose and reached this place on the 7th of that month. I found all well with the exception of my Letitia who had been confined from sore throat during some weeks and from which she did not recover for two months. In Jany however all apprehensions were at an end and we were united at this place on the 8th of that month. Soon afterwards we made a Tour round by Inverary to Glasgow and Edinburgh and have only a week ago returned to this place again where the Sheriff wishes us to remain till we leave for Town in April. I need not dilate on that subject so dear to young husbands – my present happiness – you yourself have known how much pleasure is added to existence by the society of a devout[?] innocent and loving young Creature – of a carefully cultivated mind. This happiness has also been yours – my imperfect description is therefore unnecessary. We return to YF for the present altho' I hope to prevail on Govr Simpson eventually to get to a more agreeable charge.

While with him in Town last fall – I drew from him that my chance of [illegible] to succeed Mr Faries[15] was pretty certain – & that I might depend on his interest – support in the matter. I know the great value of such an assurance – but yet votes are very essential also. I believe I never yet worried you for support during all the years you have known me. In this last lift [promotion] however your voice & interest with some of those who are so likely to listen to your opinions should you really consider me ever highly as well almost certainly turn the Scale. I understand for written[?] support & [illegible] friend Rowand is the only one likely to compete it with me. I had a letter from our chief the other day and he informs me that with some management he has succeeded in Barnstons[16]

---

15 Hugh Faries was promoted to the rank of chief factor in 1838. He retired from the fur trade in 1840. James Hargrave apparently hoped to obtain the vacancy created by his retirement. He did not obtain his wish for a chief factorship until 1844.
16 George Barnston was transferred to the charge of Fort Albany in 1840 and was promoted chief trader.

elevation to a Tradership. I was as rejoiced at this as when received my own.

M[r] Christie[17] has spent all winter in the North – in rather delicate health. When in town we agreed after much reflection, to make Gov[r] Pelly[18] acquainted with the intentions of the Gent[n] of the Trade in reference to the Testimonial for Gov. Simpson in order to have the benefit of his advice and assistance in the choice of the same. He was delighted to learn of these intentions – and was entirely of your sentiments about making additions to the last Service by the present vote. A Note of it was therefore obtained by our [illegible] – to which Gov Pelly made such additions as will render it really a superb one indeed. Of these an estimate, a [illegible] of the [illegible] were to be obtained by M[r] Christie after I left in order that they might be here until this spring to the country for the examination and approval of the Gentlemen named in a commission.

I have scarcely left room to squeeze in a word more. I will therefore only add that with kindest regards to M[rs] Mactavish in which I am cordially joined by my Letitia – I am
My respected & dear Bourgeois
Most faithfully & affectionately Yours

JH

---

17 Alexander Christie.
18 HBC governor John Henry Pelly, 1802–64.

Journal of 1828–1829

August 15th 1828

The summer business at this place[1] has for these two last months so completely occupied my time, that hitherto I have not been able to commence my journal; this pressure is however drawing to a close, and from the few leisure moments now at my disposal, I gladly deduct a part, to commit to paper a few notes of what is passing around me.

Early this morning the alarm was given that a Vessel was discovered approaching the mouth of the River,[2] and at 9 OClock A.M. on the clearing away of a partial haze we could plainly discover her with our glasses from the top of the Factory. A Boat[3] was immediately got under way to meet her, and should she prove the Coys Ship from London, we may expect the packet ashore in the course of the evening.

16th Yesternight the Boat returned, bringing the wished for Packet Box & Bags of Letters. The people inform us that the Ship is a new Vessel of the Coys called the "Prince Rupert" Ben: Bell Commr, being only the second voyage she has made to the country, having gone down the Bay to Moose Factory last season. In a Short time our letters were opened & distributed among us, four of which proved to my address from friends in Scotland, exclusive of some others on business from London. One of these was from the Revd Mr Rattray, one from Mr Lockie, one from my uncle Jas Mitchel, and one from My Cousin Effy. As the news contained

---

1 York Factory.
2 The Hayes River.
3 At York Factory, the transatlantic ships anchored at "Five Fathom Hole," some seven miles from the factory, where they were met by the factory sloop and several York boats to ferry cargo back and forth. Johnson, *York Boats*, 93.

in the whole of them will be more or less interesting to my dear parents, I shall extract from each of them a few passages.

Mr Rattray writes me from the Orkney Islands under date the 23rd of June last. I had not heard from him for these 3 years last past, and had given up almost all hopes of again being favored with a letter from him. He informs me that since he left Selkirk in 1825, he has not yet been established in charge of any particular Congregation, but has been constantly employed in traveling through the Secession Church in the north of Scotland, and employing his services as occasion offered in preaching. His tone in writing is melancholy and desponding, mainly occasioned I believe by the severe trials which he has undergone lately. Since I last heard from him he has had the painful misfortune of being deprived by Death of both his amiable Wife & three small children, being now left alone in the world with 2 helpless Orphans and with apparently but scanty means of subsistence. He is a truly worthy man, a pious christian, and a zealous minister of the Gospel. Where Clergymen are so few & so greatly required, how usefully could such a man be employed in some of the Scottish Settlements of Canada! He desires his kindest regards to my worthy parents.

From Lockie I had also my annual Letter. He is still a Teacher in Stouslee, and his school appears to be much enlarged since I was one of its inmates. He no longer talks of coming to Canada, but now seems to have made up his mind on remaining where he is: – his circumstances appear improving, and as he now evinces little inclination to venture on a transatlantic speculation I have avoided pressing him on the subject. He says that the prospects among the lower orders have much improved within last year; – work is plentiful, and wages pretty fair. He gives me a long account of my old schoolfellows, & how they are pushing their way through life. I shall mention some of them, as they were mostly all known either to my parents or my brothers. Walter Cavers of Leehead, studied Medicine, and about the time I left Scotland he likewise sailed for the West Indies as a Surgeon. He was prospering well in Jamaica but had not resided there 3 years till he fell victim to that unwholesome climate. Walter Scott of Boonraw prosecuted his studies with much success and is now a respectable Teacher in Edinburgh – is married, & doing well in the world. His elder brother Robert is also married, – a farmer along with his father "the Elder" – and bears a decent and respectable character in life. "Little Johnnie Reid" of Baghall is now a shepherd at Deloraine on Etterick, is married, & prospering in the world. Willie Grey follows his fathers occupation of a Barnman, a hopeless life of drudgery. "Laird Luddle" enlisted as a Soldier and was several years with his Regiment in Ireland, till some years ago on some reductions in the Army he received his discharge. Some time after his return he became possessed of the property of Dykenook[4] & Stinty Knowes as by the death of his mother, – he then married, dashed away in style till his means & credit would no longer keep him afloat, – the whole was sold to pay his debts, & he is now a pedlar. George & Etty Aitken are still in Stouslee, likewise George Reid, all of whom are anxious to be remembered in the kindest manner to my parents & myself. R. Ormiston of Drinkston is dead some years ago, and that farm is now let to another. His Son Andrew, my Comrade & School fellow is yet a shepherd on the same farm, is married & has a large family. "Nell & the eye" is yet alive, & *stumping*[5] about quite lively, tho' now much bowed down by age. Her daughter Mary is yet unmarried, *tho' with a daughter nearly as tall as herself*. The remainder of Lockies Letter touches on subjects less interesting to my friends, I shall therefore conclude my extracts from it with the following. "When did you hear from your worthy parents? How are they? Let an answer to these last questions be in all your future epistles to me. I shall never forget their friendly offers to me which I *do* sincerely regret I was & still am prevented from accepting. Remember me kindly to them in your next letter after the receipt of this."

The letter from my uncle is dated Galashiels 7th April last. At that time the whole of his family were in good health, and tho' he complains of hard times, for all that he seems to be prospering well in the world. He mentions having written to my father last summer, that is, the summer of 1827, by John Curry, son of John Curry that was Shepherd in Faldonside. He is a blacksmith, and was going to Montreal; which letter my uncle supposes they would receive, "as Curry spoke of going to see them, as he knew them all." Hector Elliot & family are still in Edinburgh, and he says they are doing well: in what capacity or occupation he does not mention. Two of the Sons are Merchants & Two of them Masons. One of them has gone to America. Robert is now a licensed Minister, in

---

4 Stinty Knowes was a small farmstead beyond Stirches, near Dykenook or Dykeneuk loch. Hargrave's schoolmaster William Lockie was born at Stinty Knowes.
5 The manuscript includes underlines of some of the words. The underlines are shown in this transcription as italics.

England, but he does not mention where. The principal country News he gives me are regarding Lindean, a place he knows I have many recollections of. Young Wilson was lately married to Miss Milne of Faldonside, and has of late become a regular church going person, – quite a reformed character. Old And^w Grey is dead some time ago, also George Greys wife. My Old "Chere Amie" Maggie, is yet single, a sure prize for me, my uncle says, *should I yet retain the sentiment of 12 years ago*. I however consider it a *merit* to have thoroughly *changed* them. George last season left Lindean, out of favor. Ja^s Leitch was still in the Mill.

The letter from my Cousin Euphie, it would not be quite fair in me, to shew, or repeat what she says in it; – a rule which I observe in all my *feminine* correspondence. I may however remark that she is yet unmarried, and is presently living as nursery-maid in the family of Mr Fyshe my old Teacher in Galashiels. Her letters are written with much correctness, and she expresses herself with great propriety of language, – indeed much better than I should have expected, from her education under Dominie Chapperton. She seems to be a steady, acute and lively young girl, – greatly improved since I left Scotland. She desires her kind love to her Uncle & aunt, also to all her Cousins at Beechridge.

The perusal of all these letters has been a great treat to me, and yet the pleasure is attended with some painful feelings. What these are I need not expatiate on, – those who have been so long separated as I have been from the face of a Relation, can well divine the yearnings of the heart to which I allude. These however must be borne; – and it is only on such occasions as reading their correspondence that I feel myself lonely in the world. It is however consoling to think, that though far asunder, there are those to whom my name is musick, – & whose image is scarcely ever absent from my recollection.

Sept. 10th – Our busy time, consequent on the vessel for England being here, is now drawing to a close. The Goods have all been landed amounting to upwards of Two Thousand Bales, Casks, and Cases; and the remainder of the Homeward Cargo of furs was this day sent on board. The Vessel now only waits the arrival of some Boats from the Interior with the Furs from McKenzies River, and which we expect every day. The passengers this season for England are not numerous. These are The Revd Mr Jones, Mr Jos^h McGillivray C.T. and Mr Rae, Clerk; – all of them to return hither again next season. To Mr Jones I have given a commission to purchase for me in Britain a collection of Books to the value of about Thirty Pounds, and from his good taste and sound judgment I expect a choice Assortment. I have hitherto had no opportunity of procuring a proper Collection. My Correspondent in London furnishes me with all my necessaries in the articles of Clothing &c but from the small commissions I have formerly given him I found that he was no judge of Books. The Copies he sent me were very inferior, and the prices extremely high. This great want I am happy in now being able to remedy, – which will add greatly to my pleasures during our long and solitary winters here.

Sept 16th Today the last Boat for the Interior, that is for Red River, took their departure, much to my satisfaction, as for these two weeks last past I have had my hands so full that by this time I am greatly in need of some relaxation. The Ship will also sail in a few days, and then we will be at length left again to ourselves. The Boats from Portage La Loche with McKenzies River furs arrived here on the 13th Inst with their Cargoes in good order. These furs are now about packing for England & will be shipped in a day or two which will conclude the European department of business for the Season.

20th The packet for England was finished Yesternight and sealed up this morning, when it was delivered to Capt. Bell. About Noon that Gentleman embarked for the Vessel, accompanied by all the passengers, also Mr Miles and myself who went on board to spend the day with them. After dining with them and demolishing nearly a dozen of The Old Boys Wine, we bade them farewell and returned ashore with about half a dozen more bottles for amusement on the way. These, to tell the *whole* truth, were also near a close before we reached the Launch end; and having had a pretty strong breeze ahead on coming up the River, either that notion or the wine must still have been in our noddles when we got ashore, from the zig-zag course we made on steering up from the Shore to the gate of the Fort. We however found that the Gentlemen who had remained ashore were also improving the occasion as comfortably as we had been doing: – so to it we went again; and at this moment I have just made my retreat good, – with just as much sober sense left me as to be able to set down and add a few lines to my journal. The Ship got under way with a fair breeze about an hour after we left her, and if she makes a favorable voyage will be in London in 4 or 5 weeks hence.

Octr 10th Since the ship sailed, little duty has been done, and we of York Factory have had our time entirely at our own disposal. This leisure season, between the closing of our summer avocations & the commencement of those of the winter, is employed either in hunting, fishing, or reading the piles of Newspapers, Magazines & Books left with us by the Ship. Many of these are Scotch papers, and my evenings are now chiefly spent in perusing them. With such amusement this period is indeed the pleasantest season of the year with me. Not above two weeks ago, and my days from peep of day till near witching time of night, was one unceasing round of hard & undivided application to my public duties. One day found me buried in papers, Invoices, letters from all quarters of the Interior on business; and with peering eye & anxious brow there I sat arranging the first in order, summing up or copying the second, and from time to time seizing hold on my rough Letter Book, and addressing answers to the last, to be copied out as occasion offered for forwarding them. Another day saw me with two or three Store assistants immersed in piles of Cloths, hills of Blankets, or whole housefulls of Clothes, issuing them out to the gentlemen from the interior for the use of the ensuing winters trade, – while on a third morning I might have been seen with Bills Lading & pencil in hand, turning out from the Stores & dividing Cargoes among the Boats ready to set out on their inland voyage. These and a hundred other matters filled up the chasm of time from morn till eve, while the *chinks* or spare moments, which occurred but rarely, served me with a chance of running over a private letter to my Dear relations, *eeked* out from time to time, as a moment for thought or reflection turned up. A few weeks spent in this way got all the Inlanders off from the Factory, cleared out the Ship from our Port, and left us with our hands across, sauntering through the solitary squares of York Factory, which but a few days, nay, hours ago were crowded with active hands and busy faces. This sudden change has a saddening effect on the spirits. The *beginning* of one week found every moment of our time crammed with even double allowance of active business; while the *end* saw us lounging listlessly on the launch pacing backwards forwards for hours, talking over the affairs of this land, or canvassing the changes which had taken place in our native country since the former autumn had shut the door of the civilized world upon us for the season. Various indeed are the amusements to which we have recourse in order to dispel the *ennui* consequent upon this sudden change, but to me none is so effectual as a pile of our Scottish Newspapers. With an armfull of them by my side on a chair, I tumble myself down on a sopha or across my bed, and in a short time, transported in spirit to the Calton Hill of "Auld Reekie," or imagining myself *daundering* about the Blae-berry covered Hill of Galashiels I soon lose all thought of the Land of forest and flood through which my present pilgrimage runs. On other occasions I draw from my private drawer the precious bundle of letters, containing *every one* of those my Dear parents & relations have written me since I left Canada. Their kind & affectionate pages are perused & reperused; – till totally engrossed by the subject I imagine myself in the middle of them, hear all their little stories, listen to the laugh of gladness, and see all their happy & smiling faces! What a treasure is a letter from a parent to the Wanderer of a distant land. Old times are brought back to the mind, – parental advices and parental tenderness, – too little noticed, or I fear me, valued, when first bestowed, – return on the soul with power and efficacy; – and the revered Guardians of my youthful days, appear as it were in person before me, – their precepts a safe & true guide to me in all my actions; their parental love, a cordial to the wearied mind & drooping spirits, – like the fresh dews of evening to the scorched up fields of Summer. May our God, who is gracious & merciful, preserve us all, if such be his holy will, till we meet again to part no more!

Oct[r] 20th The weather this season is unusually mild, and as yet no snow has fallen to allow us to take exercise on snow shoes. The fall & spring are indeed the most disagreeable periods of the year in this quarter of the world. The whole country around us is flat and marshy, – in which should one step off the small spot of cleared ground which surrounds the Factory one inevitably sinks to mid-leg in the mire. This is a great privation to us poor fellows who are confined to the house and the Desk, as without exercise we soon lose our appetite for food, and our health suffers in proportion.

Nov[r] 6th Made my first round on Snow Shoes this morning but the partridges were very scanty, and I only succeeded in knocking down one. The weather is now getting colder, tho' the River is not yet frozen over. What a long view it is to look forward to next June before we again hear from the civilized world. Shut up in this solitary corner, time of necessity hangs heavy on our hands, and I must own that nothing but the want of a sufficiency to support me in Canada prevents me from leaving this desert and again joining my dear relations.

Nov[r] 19th This, according to my calculation is my Birth Day, which completes my 30th year. A memorable period such a date must always be in every persons life, and in mine no less, when I think on the number of years that have rolled over my head, and of the little good I have done to sweeten the recollection of them. The freshest years of my course are spent, life has reached its meridian with me, and soon the path will tend downward to the house of forgetfulness. Many are the false steps, which on looking back, I perceive I had made since my course was alone guided by my own judgment; – many are the errors which I ought to have avoided, and many are the duties which I have in the heedlessness of youth neglected. Were half of the years that are gone, again before me, my heart tells me that so much precious time should be better improved; – but on this subject regret is useless. Whatever is yet before me I have in my power to amend, and let me hope that with the Almightys aid, I will not neglect the lessons which have been taught me by reflecting on the past. Enough of time has been given by the vain pursuits of this life, may I be strengthened in my resolution to devote to the great concerns of the soul, a greater portion of my future existence!

Decr 10th A month has nearly elapsed since I made the last addition to my journal, yet since that period not one circumstance has cast up worth mentioning in the quiet round of our life here. This day the packet for inland was closed, (which contains accounts of our summer business, letters which came by the Ship &^{c},) and will set out tomorrows morning. By It I wrote to most of my acquaintances in the country, – a matter of mere form, as country letters usually are, news from the frozen Shores of Hudsons Bay being out of the question.

Decr 17th This Day our packet for Moose Factory & the South^n Dept^{mt} was made up, ready for being dispatched. Last season I wrote by it to my parents, but this year unfortunately it will not go so far as last, and no chance offers by it of sending letters to Canada, so that I am obliged to wait till next summer before I can again inform them of my welfare.

1829

March 1st Winter is now nearly over, yet so few occasions has it furnished one for making remarks, that my journal is yet little more than begun. Since last December our days have slipped past us one after another, so like in employment, and so dull throughout, as far as regards what is called amusement in the civilized World, that out of Two months on looking back I cannot pick out ideas to fill a single page. My Days are

Snowshoes from York Factory. These snowshoes, donated by James Hargrave in 1858 to the Industrial Museum of Scotland in Edinburgh, are 171 cm. long, 40 cm. wide, and approximately 30 cm. high. They were made with a network of skins of reindeer and moose or red deer. Courtesy of The Trustees of the National Museums of Scotland, Acc. no. A 282, PF.8173.

past at the Desk, from 9 in the morning till 8 in the evening; – tho' this may be considered long hours, yet they pass over lightly, – I take a turn on snowshoes for a few miles with my gun, whenever I feel inclined for a walk, besides Saturday is always a holiday, so that out of the week no more than 5 days are devoted to business.

March 8th Saturday. This day I have had a walk of about a dozen miles with my gun, but have been very unlucky, as not a single head of Game did I procure. The weather is now even in this hard climate, beginning to have intervals of mildness, and in consequence, snow-shoe walking becomes very heavy and fatiguing. My friends in Canada must be as well acquainted with these articles & their use as myself, but I believe they never saw such large ones as we make use of here. The snow is deep & loose, so that a small shoe would sink even below a boy, we are therefore obliged to make them nearly 7 feet long & about 2 feet broad in the middle, and with such machines tyed to the feet it requires a good deal of practice before one can walk on them with ease, or even without the risk of tumbling. Accustomed as I am now to them, I must own that when in the eager pursuit of partridges I sometimes upset, and as on such occasions one goes head foremost into the snow, it would [make] any one laugh to see me floundering and struggling to get my feet out of the snow shoes, without doing which one cannot succeed in recovering ones legs. Many is the good flock of partridges which I have lost by a stumble when just in the act of pointing my Gun at the Covey. Gun hunting is now however nearly over for the winter, and indeed I have only killed 4 in the course of the byepast week.

May 3rd My journal has for these Two months back been nearly neglected. This has arisen, partly from a more than ordinary pressure of business on my hands, partly from want of any matter worthy notice, and in fact I fear I must add, partly from my own indolence, – a vice which when indulged, only grows more craving by every additional indulgence. The near approach of summer however has at length induced me to take up my pen in order to fill this book with something or other before the time for writing my letters comes round. With this view, instead of adding from day to day the few trifles of nothingness which occur in this quiet corner, I shall give my pen wider scope, and collect both from other parts of the country, and from a wider period of time such little subjects as I conceive would form topics of inquiry were I personally sitting and chatting among my dear relations for whose perusal I design these lines.

The first and greatest subject of interest to them will be, I am well aware, in what manner we pass our Sabbath days; how we maintain our claims to the name of Christians, in a Land where the light of the gospel has never yet even dawned on the minds of the greater part of its inhabitants; and of the state of white Society in general, as regards the great end of our being as rational and accountable Creatures. This subject is a delicate one, difficult to give a fair & just opinion on, and indeed I humbly conceive should be viewed in a different manner & judged of by other rules than would guide the mind when reflecting on the state of society in a country distinguished as civilized. That is, I mean to say, when the real state of things is laid open to view of a stranger, the circumstances we are placed in, and the wants and experience should also be fairly weighed before a judgment be formed of how far society here comes short of the grand rules of a christian life as laid down by our holy religion. The Companys Servants are either Europeans Canadians or Halfbreeds. The former consist principally of men from the Orkney Islands, a few English, and a number of Scotch. These people are in general, men of good character, decent in their conduct and are esteemed with very few exceptions as worthy of confidence as honest & trustworthy men. They nearly to a man can read, most can write, and the greater part have bibles and other books. Indeed as regards this class, the lives they lead are fully as free from vice as could be expected from their conduct were they residing in a country where more opportunities for the improvement of piety were to be found. The Canadians, tho' a more volatile and less reflecting people than Europeans, are however, taken as a body not to be classed below them in a moral scale of comparison, when their great want, the want of education is allowed its proper weight in the balance. They all come young into the country, the greater part of them modest young lads, with minds deeply impressed with the duties of religion as taught by the Catholic Church. Many times when on the voyage I have caught poor Jean Baptiste on his knees at his morning prayers before embarking and tho' this regularity of devotion in many fall into partial disuse during a long series of years in the "pays Sauvage," yet I can well say from my own experience, that Grey hairs & a deep sense of Religion often meet together among this light hearted lively, yet, I will add, innocent Race of ˣpeople; – innocent, when their ignorance & the temptations they experience are allowed to be considered in palliation of what they fall short in, as civilized men and as Christians. ˣof Half-breeds, the Offspring of white men and natives of the country, [end of journal].

Bibliography

MANUSCRIPT SOURCES

Archives Nationales de Québec à Montréal, Montreal
Henry Griffin notarial records. CN601,S187, number 3114.

British Columbia Archives (BCA), Victoria
Schofield family papers 1829–1950, MS-1144. "The Hargrave Family 1749–1923. Information obtained by James Hargrave (1846–1935) of Medicine Hat, the son of James Hargrave's younger brother, John. Compiled by Luetta Ross Williams (1882–1924) and typed by Jean Ross Williams (1905–?), granddaughter and great-granddaughter, respectively, of James Hargrave's sister, Mary. Title-page, 1 leaf unnumbered, 39 leaves. Loose-leaf notebook, 10 ¼ x 8 ¼." Box 3, file 4, item 2. Hargrave Family, data concerning. Compiled by Annie Laurie Ross Marshall (1871–?), a sister of Luetta Ross Williams. 5 leaves. Typescript. Box 3, file 4, item 3

Hudson's Bay Company Archives (HBCA), Archives of Manitoba, Winnipeg
Section B: Post Records
B. 235/a/7–8, microfilm 1M153
B. 239/a/136–151, microfilm 1M164. York Factory Post Journals, 1826–39
B. 239/b/89b, microfilm 1M259
B. 239/d/287–304, microfilm 1M692. York Factory Account Books, 1823–28
B. 239/f/10–12, microfilm 1M785. York Factory Lists of Servants, 1821–22
B. 239/f/13–15, microfilm 1M786. York Factory Lists of Servants, 1821–23
B. 239/g/5–8, microfilm 1M800. York Factory Abstracts of Servants' Accounts, 1825–29
B. 239/g/9–12, microfilm 1M801. York Factory Abstracts of Servants Accounts, 1829–33
B. 239/g/17–20, microfilm 1M803. York Factory Abstracts of Servants Account, 1837–41

B. 239/u/1, microfilm 1M853. York Factory Servants' Engagement Registers, 1823–51

Library and Archives Canada, Ottawa
James Hargrave and family fonds, Hargrave family papers. R7784-0-9-E. Letterbooks of James Hargrave, 1826–58, vols 21–6, microfilm reels C80–C82
Robert Sellar fonds. R1935-0-3-E. Manuscript oral history "Notes and Conversation with First Settlers of the District of Beauharnois" preserved by Robert Sellar, vols 1–4

McGill University, Rare Books and Special Collections, McGill University Library, Montreal
James Hargrave, CH17.S53, MSS. "Journal 1828–9"

PUBLISHED AND ON-LINE SOURCES

Arthur, Elizabeth. "Cumming, Cuthbert." In *Dictionary of Canadian Biography* edited by Francess G. Halpenny and Jean Hamelin, 9:169–70. Toronto: University of Toronto Press 1976
– "McKenzie, Roderick." In *Dictionary of Canadian Biography*, 8:562–3. Toronto: University of Toronto Press 1985
Ballantyne, Robert M. *Hudson's Bay; or Every-Day Life in the Wilds of North America, during six years' residence in the territories of the honourable Hudson's Bay Company.* Edinburgh: William Blackwood & Sons 1848
Barr, William, ed. *From Barrow to Boothia: The Arctic Journal of Chief Factor Peter Warren Dease, 1836–1839.* Montreal & Kingston: McGill-Queen's University Press 2002
Beardy, Flora and Robert Coutts, eds. *Voices from Hudson Bay: Cree Stories from York Factory.* Montreal & Kingston: McGill-Queen's University Press 1996
Beaver Staff. "Contents of the library at York Factory." *The Beaver* 37, no. 3 (1957): 60–1
Beechridge Presbyterian Cemetery. *Monument Inscription Names Index.* http://www.rootsweb.ancestry.com/~qcchatea/cemeteries/beechridge/namindex.htm (last accessed 3 February 2009)
Bell, Charles N. *Some Historical Names and Places of the Canadian Northwest.* Manitoba Historical Society Transaction Series 1, no. 17. The paper was read 22 January 1885. Winnipeg: Manitoba Free Press. http://www.mhs.mb.ca/docs/transactions/1/names.shtml (last accessed 3 February 2009)
Booth, Abraham. *The Reign of Grace, from its Rise, to its Consummation.* Leeds 1768
Boston, Thomas. *Human Nature in its Four-Fold State ... in Several Practical Discourses: by a Minister of the Gospel in the Church of Scotland.* Edinburgh 1720

Bowsfield, Hartwell. "Christie, Alexander." In *Dictionary of Canadian Biography* 10:167–8. Toronto: University of Toronto Press 1972

Brisson, Jacques and André Bouchard. "The Haut-Saint-Laurent wilderness at the time of settlement based on Sellar's history. Part II: Forests and wetlands." *Chateauguay Valley Historical Society Annual Journal* 39 (2006): 29–45

Brown, Callum. "Religion." In *Modern Scottish History: 1707 to the Present; Volume I: The Transformation of Scotland 1707–1850*, edited by Anthony Cooke, Ian Donnachie, Ann MacSween, and Christopher A. Whatley. East Linton: Tuckwell Press 1998

Brown, Jennifer S.H. "Clarke, John." In *Dictionary of Canadian Biography* 8:158–9

– "McDonald, John." In *Dictionary of Canadian Biography* 6:436–7. Toronto: University of Toronto Press 1987

– *Strangers in Blood: Fur Trade Company Families in Indian Country*. Norman: University of Oklahoma Press 1996

Brown, Jennifer S.H. and Elizabeth Vibert. *Reading Beyond Words: Contexts for Native History*, 2nd ed. Peterborough, ON: Broadview Press 2003

Brown, Jennifer S.H. and Sylvia M. Van Kirk. "Barnston, George." In *Dictionary of Canadian Biography* 11:52–3. Toronto: University of Toronto Press 1982

Bryce, George. *The Remarkable History of The Hudson's Bay Company*. London: Sampson Low, Marston 1900

Buchanan, Alexander Carlisle, Sr. *Official Information for Emigrants, Arriving at New York, and Who Are Desirous of Settling in the Canadas*. Montreal: Printed at the Gazette Office 1834

Bumsted, Jack M. "The Scottish Diaspora: Emigration to British North America, 1763–1815." In *Nation and Province in the First British Empire: Scotland and the Americas, 1600–1800*, edited by Ned C. Landsman, 127–50. Lewisberg, PA: Bucknell University Press 2001

Cameron, Agnes Deans. *The New North: Being Some Account of a Woman's Journey through Canada to the Arctic*. New York: D. Appleton and Co. 1909

Campey, Lucille H. *Les Écossais: The Pioneer Scots of Lower Canada, 1763–1855*. Toronto: Natural Heritage Books 2006

Catchpole, A.J.W. and D.W. Moodie. "Archives and the Environmental Scientist." *Archivaria* no. 6 (Summer 1978): 113–36

Combined Pigot's Directory of Scotland 1825/6. CD-ROM. Archive CD Books 2004

Cowie, Isaac. "The Minutes of the Council of the Northern Department of Rupert's Land, 1830 to 1843." Bismarck, ND: State Historical Society of North Dakota 1915

Croil, James, John Jenkins, and Alex Mathieson. *Life of the Rev. Alex. Mathieson: with a funeral sermon; and three discourses*. Montreal: Dawson Brothers 1870

Cunningham, Allan, ed. *The Works of Robert Burns: With His Life, vol. 3*. London: Cochrane and McCrone, 1834

Daniells, Laurenda. "Ross, Sally." In *Dictionary of Canadian Biography* 11:775–6

Davies, K.G., ed. *Northern Quebec and Labrador Journals and Correspondence 1819–35: With an introduction by Glyndwr Williams*. London: Hudsons Bay Record Society 1963

Decker, Jody F. "The York Factory Medical Journals, 1846–52." *Canadian Bulletin of Medical History* 14 (1997): 107–31

Dempsey, Hugh A. "Peguis." In *Dictionary of Canadian Biography* 9:626–7

Devine, Thomas Martin. *Scotland's Empire: 1600–1815*. London: Penguin 2004

Dickson, David. *Truth's Victory over Error. Or, an Abridgement of the Chief Controversies in Religion, which since the Apostles days to this Time, have been, and are in Agitation, between those of the Orthodox Faith, and all Adversaries whatsoever*. Glasgow 1725

Dictionary of the Scots Language (DSL). http://www.dsl.ac.uk/dsl/ (last accessed 3 February 2009)

Ermatinger, C.O. "The Columbia River under Hudson's Bay Company Rule." *Washington Historical Quarterly* 5 (1914): 192–206

Evans, Francis A. *The Emigrant's Directory and Guide to obtain lands and effect a settlement in the Canadas*. Dublin: William Curry 1833

Fisher, Edward. *The Marrow of Modern Divinity: touching both the covenant of works, and the covenant of grace: with their use and end, both in the time of the Old Testament, and in the time of the New. Wherein every one may clearly see how far forth he bringeth the law into the case of justification, and so deserveth the name of legalist; and how far forth he rejecteth the law in the case of sanctification, and so deserveth the name of antinomist. With the middle path betwixt them both, which by Jesus Christ leadeth to eternal life. In a dialogue betwixt Evangelista, a minister of the Gospel. Nomista, a legalist. Antinomista, an antinomian. And Neophytus, a young Christian. By E.F.* London 1645

– *The Marrow of Modern Divinity*. With notes by Philalethes Irenaeus (Thomas Boston). 12th ed. Edinburgh 1726

Fleming, R. Harvey, ed. *Minutes of Council Northern Department of Rupert Land, 1821–31*. Toronto: Champlain Society 1940

Foster, John E. "Cockran, William." In *Dictionary of Canadian Biography* 9:134–7

– "Pemmican." In *The Canadian Encyclopedia*, 1639. Edmonton: Hurtig Publishers 1988

Friesen, Gerald. "Finlayson, Duncan." In *Dictionary of Canadian Biography* 9:260–1

Galbraith, John S. *The Little Emperor: Governor Simpson of the Hudson's Bay Company*. Toronto: Macmillan of Canada 1976

Garry, Nicholas. "Diary of Nicholas Garry," *Proceedings and Transactions of the Royal Society of Canada*, Second Series, vol. 6, 73–204. Ottawa: James Hope & Son 1900

Gibbon, Edward. *The Autobiographies of Edward Gibbon*. Elibron Classics, Adamant Media Corporation 2005

Glazebrook, G.P. de T., ed. *The Hargrave Correspondence: 1821–1843*. Toronto: Champlain Society 1938; New York: Greenwood Press 1968

Gluek, Alvin C. "The fading glory." *The Beaver* (Winter 1957): 50–5

Goldring, Philip. "Keith, James." In *Dictionary of Canadian Biography* 8:454–5

– "MacKintosh, William." In *Dictionary of Canadian Biography* 7:567–8. Toronto: University of Toronto Press 1988

Gregg, William. *History of the Presbyterian Church in the Dominion of Canada*. Toronto: Presbyterian Printing Publishing 1885

Hall, Robert. *The History of Galashiels*. Galashiels: Alexander Walker & Son 1898

Hargrave, Joseph James. *Red River*. 1871. Rpt, Altona, MB 1977

Harper, J. Russell. "Rindisbacher, Peter." In *Dictionary of Canadian Biography* 6:648–50

Holland, Clive A. "Back, Sir George." In *Dictionary of Canadian Biography* 10:26–9

– "Franklin, Sir John." In *Dictionary of Canadian Biography* 7:323–8

Houston, Stuart, Tim Ball, and Mary Houston. *Eighteenth-Century Naturalists of Hudson Bay*. Montreal & Kingston: McGill-Queen's University Press 2003

Hudson's Bay Company Archives. *Biographical Sheets*. http://www.gov.mb.ca/chc/archives/hbca/biographical/index.html (last accessed 3 February 2009)

Hyam, Ronald. *Empire and Sexuality: The British Experience*. Manchester: Manchester University Press 1990

Hyman, Barry E. "McDermot, Andrew." In the *Dictionary of Canadian Biography* 11:545–6

Johnson, Dennis F. *York Boats of the Hudson's Bay Company: Canada's Inland Armada*. Calgary: Fifth House 2006

Johnson, Stephen M., and Thomas F. Bredin. "Jones, David Thomas." In *Dictionary of Canadian Biography* 7:454–5

Lemieux, Lucien. "Provencher, Joseph-Norbert." In *Dictionary of Canadian Biography* 8:718–24

Lower Canada Legislature House of Assembly. *Appendix to the XLIInd volume of the Journals of the House of Assembly of the province of Lower Canada, session 1832–3*. Quebec: Neilson and Cowan 1833

Macleod, Margaret Arnett, ed. *The Letters of Letitia Hargrave*. Toronto: Champlain Society 1947; New York: Greenwood Press 1969

Marshall, Walter. *The Gospel-Mystery of Sanctification opened in Sundry Practical Directions, suited especially to the case of those who labour under the guilt and power of indwelling sin. To which is added a sermon of justification. By Mr. Walter Marshal, later preacher of the gospel*. London 1692

May, Ruth. "The cycle of commerce: York Factory records of Hudson's Bay Company supplies for the Northern Department, 1843–1845." In *Archivaria* 24 (Summer 1987): 47–68

M'Crie, Thomas. *Life of John Knox*. Edinburgh 1812

McGoogan, Ken. *Fatal Passage: The Untold Story of John Rae, the Arctic Adventurer Who Discovered the Fate of Franklin*. Toronto: Harper Perennial Canada 2002

McLoughlin, John. *The Letters of John McLoughlin, from Fort Vancouver to the Governor and Committee: second series, 1839–44*, edited by E.E. Rich. Toronto: Champlain Society 1943

Merk, Frederick, ed. *Fur Trade and Empire: George Simpson's Journal 1824–25*. Rev. ed. Cambridge: Belknap Press 1968

Munro, Alice. *The View from Castle Rock*. Toronto: McClelland & Stewart 2006

Nelson, Jay. "'A Strange Revolution in the Manners of the Country': Aboriginal-Settler Intermarriage in Nineteenth-Century British Columbia." In *Regulating Lives: Historical Essays on the State, Society, the Individual, and the Law*, edited by John McLaren, Robert Menzies, and Dorothy E. Chunn. Vancouver: University of British Columbia Press 2002

Nevins, J. Birkbeck. *A Narrative of Two Voyages to Hudson's Bay with Traditions of the North American Indians*. London: Printed for the Society for Promoting Christian Knowledge 1847

Nute, Grace Lee. *The Voyageur*. St Paul: Minnesota Historical Society 1955

Officer, Lawrence H., and Samuel H. Williamson. "Purchasing power of British pounds from 1264 to 2005." MeasuringWorth.Com. http://www.measuringworth.com/calculators/ppoweruk/ (last accessed 3 February 2009)

Online Cree Dictionary. www.creedictionary.com

Ormsby, Margaret A. "Douglas, Sir James." In *Dictionary of Canadian Biography* 10:238–49

Pannekoek, Frits. "A probe into the demographic structure of nineteenth century Red River." In *Essays on Western History*, edited by Lewis H. Thomas, 83–97. Edmonton: University of Alberta Press 1976

– "Ross, Alexander." In *Dictionary of Canadian Biography* 8:765–8

Pedrick Genealogy Notebooks, Ripon Public Library, Ripon, WI. Extract: "Hargrave, Walter, 1st" from *Portrait and Biographical Album of Fond du Lac County, Wisconsin*. Chicago: Acme Publishing 1889. http://www.riponlibrary.org/Pedrick/Gen_Notebooks/Hargrave_Walter_O_I.pdf (last accessed 3 February 2009)

Raffan, James. *Emperor of the North: Sir George Simpson & the Remarkable Story of the Hudson's Bay Company*. Toronto: HarperCollins Publishers 2007

Rankin, James. "Congregational Reminiscences, 1805–1890." In *Memorials of the Centenary of the East United Free Congregation, Galashiels*. A. Walker & Son 1905

Ray, Arthur. "Todd, William." In *Dictionary of Canadian Biography* 8:888–90
Rea, J.E. "Logan, Robert." In *Dictionary of Canadian Biography* 9:472–3
Reid, Jennie. *Musquodoboit Pioneers: A Record of Seventy Families, their Homesteads and Genealogies, 1780–1980*. 2 vols. Nova Scotia: Musquodoboit Enterprisers Historical Committee 1980. Available online at: http://www.rootsweb.com/~canns/musq2.txt (last accessed 3 February 2009)
Rich, E.E., ed. *Colin Robertson's Correspondence Book, September 1817 to 1822*. Toronto: Champlain Society 1939. Available online at: http://link.library.utoronto.ca/champlain/search.cfm?lang=eng (last accessed 3 February 2009)
Roland, Charles G. "Saturnism at Hudson's Bay: The York Factory Complaint of 1833–1836." *Canadian Bulletin of Medical History* 1, no. 1: 59–78
Scott, Douglas. *A Hawick Word Book*. Draft version of 25 January 2009. http://www.astro.ubc.ca/people/scott/book.pdf (last accessed 3 February 2009)
Sellar, Robert. *The History of the County of Huntingdon and of the Seigniories of Chateaugay and Beauharnois from their First Settlement to the Year 1838*. Huntingdon: The *Canadian Gleaner* 1888
Simpson, Alexander. *The Life and Travels of Thomas Simpson The Arctic Discoverer*. London: Richard Bentley 1845
Smith, Shirlee Anne. "Stuart, John." In *Dictionary of Canadian Biography* 7:837–9
Southwestern Quebec Genealogical Resources: http://www.swquebec.ca/ (last accessed 3 February 2009)
Tranter, Neil. "Demography." In Cooke et al., *Modern Scottish History: 1707 to the Present*
Van Kirk, Sylvia. "Ballenden, John." In *Dictionary of Canadian Biography* 8:59–60
– "Cameron, John Dugald." In *Dictionary of Canadian Biography* 8:121–2
– "'The Custom of the Country,' An Examination of Fur Trade Marriage Practices." In *Canadian Family History*, edited by Bettina Bradbury, 67–92. Toronto: Copp Clark Pitman 1992
– "Hargrave, James." In *Dictionary of Canadian Biography* 9:364–6
– *Many Tender Ties: Women in Fur Trade Society in Western Canada, 1670–1870*. Winnipeg: Watson and Dwyer Publishing 1980
– "McKenzie, Donald." In *Dictionary of Canadian Biography* 8:557–8
– "McKenzie, Nancy." In *Dictionary of Canadian Biography* 8:561
– "McLeod, John." In *Dictionary of Canadian Biography* 7:570–1
– "McTavish, John George." In *Dictionary of Canadian Biography* 7:577–8
– "Rowand, John." In *Dictionary of Canadian Biography* 8:779–81
Venema, Kathleen. "'As we are both deceived': Strategies of Status Repair in 19th C Hudson's Bay Company Correspondence." RHETOR, vol. 1, 2004.

http://uregina.ca/~rheaults/rhetor/2004/venema.pdf (last accessed 3 February 2009)

Warkentin, John. "The Western Interior: 1800–1870." In *Canada Before Confederation: A Study on Historical Geography*, chapter 6, edited by R. Cole Harris and John Warkentin. Montreal & Kingston: McGill-Queen's University Press 1991

Williams, Glyndwr, ed. "The 'Character Book' of Governor George Simpson 1832." In *Hudson's Bay Miscellany, 1670–1870*, 30:151–236. Winnipeg: Hudson's Bay Record Society 1975

Wilson, Clifford. "Forts on the twin rivers." *The Beaver* (Winter 1957): 4–11

Withrington, Donald. "Education." In Cooke et al., *Modern Scottish History: 1707 to the Present*

Woodcock, George. "Grant, Cuthbert." In *Dictionary of Canadian Biography* 8:341–4

– "Robertson, Colin." In *Dictionary of Canadian Biography* 7:748–50

Index

Aboriginal people: described by JH, 18–19, 95, 99–100, 125, 241, 295–7; hunting methods of, 131–3; religion of, 61, 107, 190; rituals of at trading posts, 348–9; war among in Northwest, 85
Acts (of legislatures), 164n20; Acts of Union (1707), 156n2; Anatomy Act (1832), 164n20; Catholic Relief Act (1829), 171n39; Game Act of Scotland (1832), 306n21; Reform Act (1832), 231, 248n24, 249–50, 281; Salmon Fisheries Act of Scotland (1828), 306n21; Acts of Union (1707), 156n2
Adams, Miss M., 157
Addison, Joseph, 199n5
Aitken, George and Esther, 136, 157, 375
Alcock, Margaret. *See* Hargrave, Margaret Alcock
alcohol: banned by HBC, 107, 349; usage among: Aboriginal people, 62; fur traders, 52–3
Anatomy Act (1832), 164n20
Ancrum Moor, Battle of (1545), 222n25
Anderson, Alexander Caulfield, 227
Anderson, James, 128n36
animals and birds of Rupert's Land, 169–70; beaver; hunting of, 131–2; birds of prey, 169–70; buffalo (bison): disappearance of (1825–27), 57–9, 79; deer, 211; fox hunting methods, 132–3; fur-bearers, 29, 110; game animals, 169; goose hunt at York, 211; owls, white, 169–70; ptarmigan, 169–70, 211; seal hunting methods, 133
Annance, François Noel, 255, 264–5

Back, George, 254, 257
Ballenden, John, 161, 263; ill with York Factory Complaint, 288
Barber, Mr (Beechridge neighbour), 191, 216, 261
Barnston, George, 188–9, 194, 196, 229, 234, 369, 370–1; wages owed to, 271
Beaudry, Nancy, 246n14
beaver. *See* animals and birds of Rupert's Land
Beaver (HBC sloop), 186n9, 254
beaver pelts as standard of trade, 54
Beechridge, Lower Canada, 8, 120n21, 128n36
Bell, Benjamin (HBC ship's captain), 136n52, 186n11, 249n1, 373; infirmity of, 251, 258, 265
Benoit, André, 228
Berczy, William, 245n13
Berens, Henry Hulse, 232

Berens, Joseph, 232
Bird, James, 72, 277n5
Bird, Joe, 72–3, 80
birds of Rupert's Land. *See* animals and birds of Rupert's Land
bison. *See* buffalo
Blair, James, 199n1
Blair, Robert, 165n24
Blanchet, François Norbert, 326n2, 327
Bourke, John Palmer, 74, 148
Bouvet, François, 228
Brainerd, David, 62
Brandon House, 79n86
British Queen (steamship), 359
Brougham, Henry, 339
Brown, John, 199n3
buffalo (bison): disappearance of herds (1825–27), 57–9, 79
Bulger, Andrew H., 195n34
Burke, William, 162–3
Butcher, Francis, 343
Butterwick, William Taylor (HBC ship captain), 289n4
By, Colonel John, 125n28
Byron, George Gordon, 165n27

Cadotte, Laurent, 81
Camden (ship), 208n9
Cameron, John Dugald, 246
Campbell, "Capt." Tom, 345, 353, 361
Campbell, Charlotte, 345, 353
Campbell, Donald, 345, 361
Canadian Gleaner (Lower Canada newspaper), 5n7
canoes, 46–7, 60
Catholic Question in Britain, 171–2
Catholic Relief Act (1829), 171n39
cattle at Fort Garry, 81
Cavers, Walter, 51, 374
Charles, John, 247, 252, 265, 277, 285n2; difficulty with yearly requisitions, 334–5

cholera (1831–32), 239; in: Canada, 249; England, 227; Lower Canada, 234, 236; Scotland, 230, 231
Christie, Alexander Sr, 39, 184, 185, 225n29, 234, 371; in charge at Red River, 248n23, 252, 272, 358
Clarke, John, 183
clothing, fur trade, 53; JH's order for, 242n12
Cobbett, William, 255
Cobourg, Upper Canada, 297
Cockran, William, 22, 58, 131n45, 171n38
Coldstream Guards, 2nd Regiment, 346n4; and buffalo hunt, 354
Colen, Joseph, 27
Cook, William Hemmings, 27, 75n69, 148n18
Corrigal, Peter, 75
Cowie, Robert, 227
Cree, Swampy, 29
Cumming, Cuthbert, 124
Cunningham, Patrick, 212
currency: equivalents; Sterling and Canadian, 150; Sterling and Halifax, 114n8; purchasing power of, 112n3, 115n11, 120
Curry, John Jr, 375
Curry, John Sr, 375

Dandie Dinmont terriers, 305–6, 314–16, 368–9
Davison, John, 56n12
de May, Captain, 71n55
De Meurons (regiment), 71n55
Dewey, Martha, 24–5, 89n3. *See also* Struthers, Martha Dewey
Dewey, Melinda, 32, 89n3, 123–4, 220, 237, 262, 275; trysts with JH, 294
disease. *See* cholera; influenza; York Factory Complaint
Dobson, Nancy (Annie). *See* Hargrave, Nancy (Annie) Dobson

Douglas, James, 332n7
Douglas, Robert, 13–14, 209, 231, 278
Drever, William, 228
Drumlanrig's Tower, Scotland, 303
Drummond, Robert, 125n29
Dumoulin, Joseph Nicholas, 131n46
Duncan, Thomas (HBC sloop master), 254n17, 266

Eagle (HBC brig), 289n4
education. *See* schools and education
Ellice, George, 84n97
Elliot, Hector, 209, 214, 375
Elliot, Robert, 214, 249, 375–6
Ermatinger, Edward, 95n9
Erskine, Ebenezer, 117n13
Esquimaux (HBC brigantine), 289n4

Faries, Hugh, 266, 370
Fenton, Andrew, 127
Ferguson, Archibald, 117n12
Finlayson, Duncan, 39, 69–70, 76, 87n1, 155, 219–20, 236, 263; in Britain, 300, 302, 318; ill health of, 82n95; supports JH's promotion, 339, 344
Finlayson, Isobel Simpson, 69n52, 344, 359
Finlayson, Nicol, 69n52, 300, 348n9
Flett, George, 196
flood(s) and flooding (1826), 59–61
food and diet in fur trade country, 53, 168n33, 169
Forrest, Grant, 34
Fort Frances. *See* Lac la Pluie House
Fort Garry, 52n5, 67n43
Fort Nisqually, 347n7
Fort Severn, 212
Fort Vancouver, 332n7
Fowler (Colonel, Coldstream Guards), 346n4
fox: hunting methods, 132–3

Frances (HBC coasting schooner), 356
Franklin, John, 62, 85
Fraser, Colin, 246n14, 256
Fyshe, Robert, 12–13, 250

Game Act of Scotland (1832), 306n21
gardens and gardening, 295; at Fort Garry, 81; at York Factory, 267
Garrioch, William, 75
Garry, Nicholas, 19n47; describes York Factory, 26–7; views on de Meurons, 71n55
George and Vulture Hotel, London, 300n8
Gibeault, Belonie, 266
Gladiator (Atlantic packet ship), 318, 320
Gladman, George, 335, 343n1, 348n9
Glazebrook, G.P. de T.: describes JH, 41
Goldie, Agnes. *See* Hargrave, Agnes Goldie
Graham, James Robert George, 339
Grand Brulé Rebels: rob J.G. McTavish's post, 307
Grant, Cuthbert, 74, 79, 80, 272
Grant, Richard, 335
Grave, John (HBC ship's captain), 282n10, 289n4
grave-robbing (resurrectionism), 162–5
Gray, James: emigrates to Canada, 189
Gray, Thomas, 157
Grey, Andrew, 376
Grey, Peggy, 100
Grey, Willie, 374–5
Grey family (Scotland), 100n14
Grierson, Lady Mary Jane, 4n3
Guiboche, Louis, 81

Halley's Comet, 283n11
Hamlyn, Richard Julian, 77

Harding, Robert, 246, 265; ill with York Factory Complaint, 288
Hare, William, 162–3
Hargrave, Agnes Goldie, 224
Hargrave, Andrew (brother of JH), 12, 66, 94, 105; JH's advice to on property ownership, 286–7; marries Margaret Lawson, 341
Hargrave, Andrew (cousin of JH), 106
Hargrave, James
  birth date of, 379–80; search for birth and baptism certificates, 303–5
  childhood and education, 12–15
  described: character of, 22, 40–1; physical stature of, 258n31
  financial affairs of: investments, 215; salary, 20, 23n56, 45, 115, 151–2, 182
  furlough: plans for, 290
  fur trade career of, 19–25; promoted to: Chief Trader, 235, 269, 274n2; takes charge of York Factory, 260
  health problems of, 22, 285, 292; York Factory complaint, 256, 260, 267, 269, 274, 276, 348
  letterbooks and journals of, 3–5, 6–8
  life plan of, 55, 83, 98–9, 115, 122, 123, 142–3; for retirement, 175, 176
  marriage of, 24–5, 31
  parents and siblings of, 11, 63, 65; advises: brothers to buy property, 202, 286–7; John on new house, 119–20; against move to New York, 88–9
  financial assistance to, 166; annuity for his mother, 104, 111–14 passim, 153–4, 200, 216, 236, 238, 275, 286; for farm expenses, 93–4, 106, 117; for Jane's "dowry," 150, 172–3, 177–8; for Mary's "dowry," 177–8
  pastimes of, 99; exercise, 52, 168, 379; fishing, 65; hunting, 110, 180, 283, 382; reading, 129, 199, 378–9; personal library, 165–6, 242n12, 314n30, 352n15, 376–7; studies: bookkeeping, 81–2; Italian, 86n99, 166
  relationships with women, 30–40; Miss Wilson, 138–9; proposes to Letitia, 309–13; rumours about, 37–9, 338
  religion and: Christian beliefs of, 15, 17–18; church adherence, 102–3, 104–5; church politics, 117–18
  retirement and death of, 25
  views on: alcohol use, 106; bachelorhood, 64, 123; British politics, 255, 281; country marriage, 32–4, 36, 82–3, 335; emigration, 93–4, 98, 121–2, 291; seigneurial land holding system, 118; women's place, 40, 112, 114
  visits family in Beechridge, 293–7, 340–1
Hargrave, James Sr (uncle of JH), 19, 84n97; leaves his Beechridge farm, 157–8, 216, 222
Hargrave, Jane, 11, 66, 100, 140, 204; and farm labour, 112, 114; mishandles dowry money from JH, 172–3, 177–8; romantic hopes of, 150, 204; disappointment in, 173
Hargrave, Jane Melrose (mother of JH), 65n37; death of, 345, 349–50, 362; purchases made with money from JH, 127–8

Hargrave, John, 66, 94, 105; JH warns against debt, 174; marries Jemima Moffatt, 341

Hargrave, Joseph Jr, 11, 19, 65, 182–3, 209; lack of generosity of, 89, 91; prosperity of, 175, 178–9; settles in New York, 65, 88n2

Hargrave, Joseph Sr (father of JH), 11, 217; accident on New York trip, 174, 175, 178, 179, 198, 209; health of failing, 259, 269, 290; JH tells him to repay Jane's dowry, 180; prosperity of, 93–4, 98; purchase of land in Beechridge, 84n97; religious views of, 16, 117, 128, 145, 158–9; second marriage of, 65n37

Hargrave, Letitia Mactavish, 4, 23, 307n24; death of, 25; described by JH, 31; gossip about in Scotland, 357; JH orders jewelry for, 365–6; JH's gifts to, 359n5; letters of published, 6; marriage of, 24–5

Hargrave, Margaret Alcock, 25

Hargrave, Mary. *See* Ross, Mary Hargrave

Hargrave, Mary (cousin of JH): widowed, 239

Hargrave, Mary Russell, 158n8

Hargrave, Nancy (Annie) Dobson, 175, 179, 182–3

Hargrave, Ruther, 11, 19, 65, 182–3, 209; death of his wife Agnes, 216, 224; emigrates, 88; prosperity of, 175, 178–9; second marriage of, 261; settles in New York, 65, 88n2; takes money from parents, 89; visits Beechridge family, 267

Hargrave, Walter: JH's low opinion of, 158

Hargrave family, ix, 10–11
Beechridge property of, 84n97, 119–20, 127, 166; new dwelling on, 89, 93–4, 117, 122, 151–2, 173; Jane's dowry misused for, 173; purchase of, 84n97
daily life of in Beechridge, 142, 144–5
emigration of, 19
religious adherence of, 15–19

Hastings, Lady Flora, 364

Hawes, Richard, 364

Helmcken, John Sebastian: describes JH, 40–1

Henderson, James, 250

Herbard, Frederick H. (ship's captain), 293n6

Heron, Francis, 70n54

Hudson's Bay Company: employee and wage reductions after 1821, 23n56; organization and operations of, 53–5; territory of, 3n2

Hume, David, 75

Humphreys, Charles (HBC ship captain), 289n4

Hunt, Henry, 255

Hutchison, John, 232, 251–2, 252

influenza, 276, 279

Ingles, James, 156; JH's low opinion of, 159

Inuit seal hunting methods, 133

Isabella (brig), 193

Isbister, Thomas, 228

Jamieson, John, 166

Jane (HBC coasting schooner), 356

Johnson, Samuel, 165n28

Jones, David Thomas, 58, 69n51, 82n95, 131n45, 171n38, 251n11, 376

Keith, James, 114n10, 276, 324, 369

Kennedy, John Frederick, 246

King Comcomly (Chinook chief), 95n9

Knox, Robert, 162n17, 164

Lachine Canal. *See* travel and transportation
Lac la Pluie House, 78n79
Laidlaw, Adam, 171
La Loche Brigade, 167n31
Lane, William Fletcher, 227
Larante, Jacco, 73
Lawson, Margaret: marries Andrew Hargrave, 341
Leask, Charles, 212n15
Leblanc, Louis, 228–9
Leblanc, Pierre, 229
le Borgne. *See* McDonald le Borgne, John
Lee, Mr (of Hawick, Scotland), 281
Lees, James, 100
Leitch, James, 376
Lewes, John Lee, 212, 265
Lockie, William, 12, 51n2, 86n99, 156–7, 191, 209, 374; JH's advice to on emigrating, 93–4
Logan, Robert, 39, 68
London, England, in 1837; described by JH, 300, 364
Loudoun, John, 361, 363, 366n14
Lower Fort Garry, 67n43
Lowman, Mary Kelly, 251–2, 277n5

Macallum, John, 251–2
MacEachern, Captain, 361
Mactavish, Dugald John, 31, 320, 324
Mactavish, Dugald Jr, 352, 353
Mactavish, Dugald Sr, 307n24, 309n27; JH's gifts to, 359n5
Mactavish, Lachlan, 185
Mactavish, Letitia. *See* Hargrave, Letitia Mactavish
Mactavish, Letitia Lockhart, 307n24
Mactavish, Mary: JH hopes to match her with D. Finlayson, 319, 320

Mactavish, William, 25, 33, 251–2, 257, 309, 323; his mother's fears of a country marriage, 319, 333; his work and character approved by JH, 270–1, 335, 348
made beaver, 79n89
mail service: HBC system of, 90, 99, 100; packets, 56n13, 63, 76, 120; in Lower Canada, 213, 226; uncertainty of, 63, 65, 86, 88, 90–1, 114, 120–1, 156
Mandan villages: and 1826 flood, 61
Mannock, John, 258
Marion, Narcisse, 228
Mary (Mith-coo-coo-man E'Squaw), 148n18
Massan (Cree courier), 194
Matthy, Frederick, 195
McCrie, Thomas, 118, 165–6
McDermot, Andrew, 37, 73–4, 148
McDonald, Angus, 38
McDonald le Borgne, John, 75
McGillivray, Joseph, 376
McGillivray, William, 245n13
McGregor, Magnus, 228
McIntosh, William, 227–8, 247, 252, 265
McKenzie, Donald, 58, 75n71
McKenzie, Hector, 251–2, 292
McKenzie, Nancy, 161, 195, 253n15; marriage to Pierre Leblanc, 212n17
McKenzie, Roderick, 195, 228, 247n22
McKintosh, William. *See* McIntosh, William
McLeod, Alexander Roderick, 255
McLeod, Angus, 38
McLeod, John, 35–6, 72, 186
McLoughlin, John, 332n7
McPherson, Thomas, 128n36, 294
McRae brothers (Alexander and Duncan): JH warns father against, 158

McTaggart, John, 125n30
McTavish, Catherine Turner, 161n13
McTavish, John George, 23, 27, 67n44, 212n17, 245n13, 348; belongings forwarded by JH, 187, 192, 195, 210; criticized for deserting his native family, 184–5, 184n4; and campaign to discredit, 253n15; health problems of, 277n6; mentors JH, 21, 48, 155–6; robbed at Lake of the Two Mountains post, 307–8
McTavish, Simon, 67n44
Melrose, Andrew, 282
Melrose, James, 103
Melrose, Jane. *See* Hargrave, Jane Melrose
Metis: subsistence activities of, 79
Miles, Robert Seaborn, 146n10, 147n15, 160–1, 193n27, 256, 263
Milnes, James, 84n97
Milton, John, 165n26
missionaries, 61–2, 131, 145n9, 296–7; need for in fur trade country, 190
Mitchell, Alexander, 66, 280n9
Mitchell, Euphemia (Cousin Effy), 31, 66, 99, 141, 244, 376; JH's advice to on marriage, 138
Mitchell, James (uncle of JH), 63n29, 189
Mitchell, Mary, 141
Mitchell, Mary Melrose, 208
Moffat, Jemima: marries John Hargrave, 341n23
Moll, Johann Albrecht Ulrich. *See* Berczy, William
Montour, Elizabeth, 277n5
Montreal Herald, 125n31, 219
Montreal in 1821: described by N. Garry, 19
Moyes, Margaret, 364n11
Murray, John (Scottish publisher), 166n30, 339

Native people. *See* Aboriginal people
Newhouse, Sewell, 131n47
New Year's Day: celebrations at York Factory, 343n1
New York in 1837, 299
Nolin, Augustin, 67, 68, 72, 73, 80, 148
Nolin, Jean Baptiste, 67n49
Nolin, Louis, 67n49
Nonpareil (chartered brig), 282n10
North West Company: 1821–22 Lists of Servants, 21n50
Norway House, 217

O'Connell, Daniel, 255
Oregon Treaty (1846), 347n7
Ormiston, Andrew, 93n7, 375
Ormiston, Miss J., 93
Ormiston, R., 93n7, 375
Osterlag, L., 76–7
Ostervald, Jean-Frédéric, 192
Outitawas, 37
owls, white, 169–70

Patriot Wars (1838), 350
Peguis (Saulteaux chief), 348
Pelly, John Henry, 371
Pelly, Robert Parker, 195n34
Phelp, Lachlan, 212
Plessis, Joseph-Octave, 58n23
Poitras, Medard, 228; drowning of, 272
Pope, Alexander, 165n25
Porteous, John, 163–4
Presbyterian Church in Lower Canada, 145–6
Prince, Jane, 35
Prince George (supply ship), 269n1, 270
Prince of Wales (HBC supply ship), 56n12; winters in Hudson Bay, 254n17

Prince Rupert (HBC supply ship), 282n10, 289n4; ice bound in Hudson Bay, 254n17, 258, 289n4, 359, 373; repairs to, 265
"The Professor." *See* Ross, Alexander
Provencher, Joseph-Norbert, 58, 131n46, 193n26
ptarmigan, 169–70, 211
Puget Sound Agricultural Company, 347n7

Quebec (packet ship), 293n6, 297

Rae, John Jr (HBC doctor), 147n12; describes JH, 40–1
Rae, John Sr (HBC agent in Orkney), 147
Rae, Richard, 187, 376
Rae, William Glen, 186
Rattray, William, 56n11, 156, 159, 374; and his family in Orkney, 143n5
Rebellion of 1837–38, 350
recreation in fur trade country, 97, 108, 377–8. *See also* Hargrave, James, pastimes of
Redpath, Robert, 250, 278
Red River Academy, 251n11
Red River settlement, 52, 254; flood of 1826, 59–60; recovery from flood, 70–2
Reform Bill (1832), 231, 248n24, 249–50, 281
Reid, George, 375
Reid, Johnnie, 136, 374
religion: and Hargrave family, 15–19; observances of at HBC posts, 131, 140; sects and sectarian politics, 117–18, 145n6–8, 159n10
Rendall, John, 228
Richardson, John, 84n97
Rideau Canal. *See* travel and transportation
Rindisbacher, Peter, 195n34

Roach, Walter, 128n36, 145n9
Robertson, Colin, 188n20, 226, 266
Robertson, James, 217, 220, 221–2, 223–4, 238
Robertson, William, 165n23
Ross, Alexander, 74, 81, 148–9
Ross, Donald, 37, 252, 257
Ross, James, 66n39, 85n98; farm woodlot sales, 225n30; settles in Beechridge, 175, 176
Ross, Jane, 109n18
Ross, John, 254n18
Ross, Mary Hargrave, ix, 85n98, 100, 140–1; dowry from JH, 177–8; marriage of to James Ross, 66; settles in Beechridge, 175, 176
Ross, Sarah (Sally), 73
Ross, William, 109n18, 124
Rowand, John, 227, 247, 352
Royal, Robert (ship's captain), 208n9
Royal Victoria. *See British Queen* (steamship)
Rupert's Land, 3n2, 94–7, 99–100, 135, 295–7
Russell, Mary, 158n8
Rutherford, Janet, 11, 65n37
Rutherford, Margaret, 224n28

salaries of fur traders, 21n50, 23n56
Salmon Fisheries Act of Scotland (1828), 306n21
schools and education: in Galashiels, Scotland, 12–13; in Red River, 61, 251n11; Scottish rural school system, 14–15, 134
Scots in Canada, 5–6, 145n9
Scott, George, 170
Scott, Robert, 136, 374
Scott, Robert (Rob the Elder), 92n6, 374
Scott, Sir Walter, 165n21–2, 209n11, 250; lock of his hair for Frances Simpson, 302

Scott, Walter (of Boonraw), 92n6, 374
seal: hunting methods, 133
Selkirk, Lord: and de Meurons, 71n55; 1817 treaty of, 348n10
Sellar, Robert, 5n7, 84n97
Severeight, John, 284
ships, HBC, 56n12; ice closes Hudson Strait, 290–1
Simpson, Frances, 78n79, 232n3, 253n16
Simpson, Geddes, 359
Simpson, George, 8, 69n52, 75–6, 77n78, 91, 232; career of, 23; has a stroke in Red River, 253n16
Simpson, Isobel. *See* Finlayson, Isobel Simpson
Simpson, Thomas, 187, 193–4; Arctic Expedition of, 331; describes JH, 41; on JH's unmarried state, 30–1
Sinclair, Ben, 252
Smith, Edward, 35, 187, 196, 227, 228, 246–7, 272, 277
Smith, William, 288
snowshoes, 381
standard of trade, 54
starvation on prairies 1825-26, 57–9
St Denis, Jacques, 76–7
Stewart, Alexander, 72, 194, 275
St Peter's mission, 348n10
Struthers, Alex, 104, 216, 221
Struthers, Hannah Derick, 201, 216, 221, 237, 239
Struthers, James, 221, 237, 262
Struthers, Margaret (Peggy), 216; makes mitts for JH, 90, 104, 113; unmarried state of, 220, 222, 237, 239, 262
Struthers, Martha Dewey, 221, 237, 262. *See also* Dewey, Martha
Struthers, Philip, 262
Struthers, William: death of, 201, 204

Struthers (family in Beechridge), 89
Stuart, John, 36n82, 184n4, 227, 253n15, 271; and wife's adultery, 264–5
Stuart, Norman, 201, 204, 205; suicide attempt of, 91–2
Sword, James, 100, 130, 136

Taylor, George, 35
Taylor, Margaret, 36n82
Taylor, Mary, 35–6, 271; and François Annance, 264–5
Thomas, Thomas, 72
Thorburn family, 281
Thorn, George, 185, 194, 196, 210, 229, 256, 266
Tillotson, John, 199n2
Todd, William, 77n78, 227; ill with York Factory Complaint, 288
trade goods, 53
traders, American: cut into HBC trade, 79–80
traders, petty, 74, 79–80
travel and transportation
  brigades, 167n31
  canals: Lower and Upper Canada, 109n18, 242; Rideau, 125, 140n3, 226
  canoes, 46–7, 60
  in fur trade country, 46–8
  routes inland from: Montreal, 47–8; York Factory, 29–30, 96n10, 167n31
  winter road, 233; Red River to York Factory, 233; Winter Road Bubble, 187–8
  York boats, 60n24, 167n31
Turner, Catherine. *See* McTavish, Catherine Turner

Union Bridge, 125
Upper Fort Garry, 67n43

Valois, Alexis, 194
Victoria, Queen, 300–1

Waterloo Hotel, Edinburgh, 302
Waverley novels of Sir Walter Scott, 165
weights and measures: standardization of, 135n51
West, John, 61n25
Whiffen, Elzeard H., 271, 279n8
Wigram (Colonel, Coldstream Guards), 346n4
Williams, W. (ship's captain), 282n10
Wilson, Andrew, 247, 252–3
Wilson, Miss A., 31–2, 136; JH's relationship with, 138–9

Wilson, William, 148, 149, 228
Winnipeg, 52n5
women: seminary for in Red River, 251n11
women, Aboriginal: and fur trade marriages, 32–4

York Factory, 25–8, 211, 373n3; climate and weather at, 96, 99–100, 230, 291, 292, 355–6; daily life at, 167–9, 180, 206; New Year's celebrations at, 343n1; population of in 1829, 146n10; Swampy Cree at, 29
York Factory Complaint, 256n24, 276, 279, 288
Young, Edward, 199n4